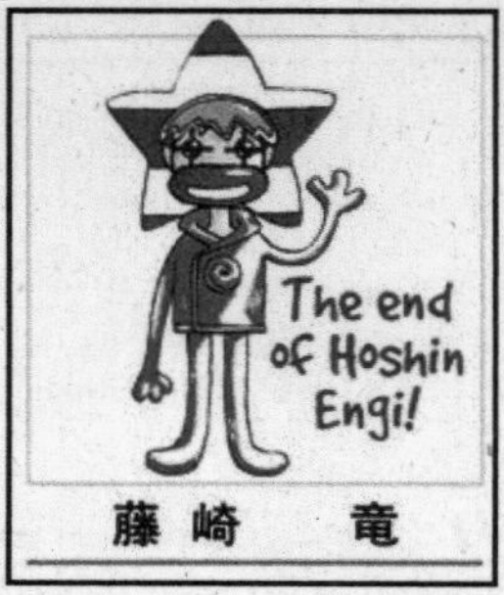
The end of Hoshin Engi!
藤崎　竜

It's been a little over four years since I recklessly started to draw a history manga in *Weekly Shonen Jump*.

Now, thanks to my readers, my assistants, Mr. Shima and various other people, I was somehow able to finish it.

Feeling a mixture of gratitude, regret, pride and humility, I will now enter a long period of vacation.

Let us meet again somewhere someday.

Ryu Fujisaki

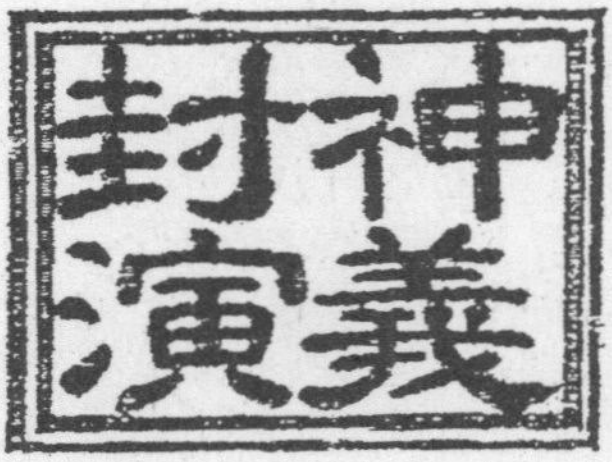
封神演義

Ryu Fujisaki's *Worlds* came in second place for the prestigious 40th Tezuka Award. His *Psycho +, Wāqwāq* and *Hoshin Engi* have all run in *Weekly Shonen Jump* magazine, and the *Hoshin Engi* anime is available on DVD in Japan and North America. A lover of science fiction, literature and history, Fujisaki has made *Hoshin Engi* a mix of genres that truly showcases his amazing art and imagination.

HOSHIN ENGI VOL. 23
SHONEN JUMP Manga Edition

STORY AND ART BY RYU FUJISAKI
Based on the novel *Hoshin Engi*, translated by Tsutomu Ano,
published by Kodansha Bunko

Translation & Adaptation/Tomo Kimura
Touch-up Art & Lettering/HudsonYards
Design/Matt Hinrichs
Editor/Jonathan Tarbox

HOSHIN ENGI © 1996 by Ryu Fujisaki, Tsutomu Ano
All rights reserved. First published in Japan in 1996 by SHUEISHA
Inc., Tokyo. English translation rights arranged by SHUEISHA Inc.

The stories, characters and incidents mentioned in this publication are
entirely fictional.

No portion of this book may be reproduced or transmitted in any form or
by any means without written permission from the copyright holders.

Printed in Canada

Published by VIZ Media, LLC
P.O. Box 77010
San Francisco, CA 94107

10 9 8 7 6 5 4 3 2 1
First printing, June 2011

www.viz.com

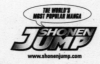
www.shonenjump.com

PARENTAL ADVISORY
HOSHIN ENGI is rated T for Teen and is
recommended for ages 13 and up. This volume
contains realistic and fantasy violence.
ratings.viz.com

HOSHIN ENGI

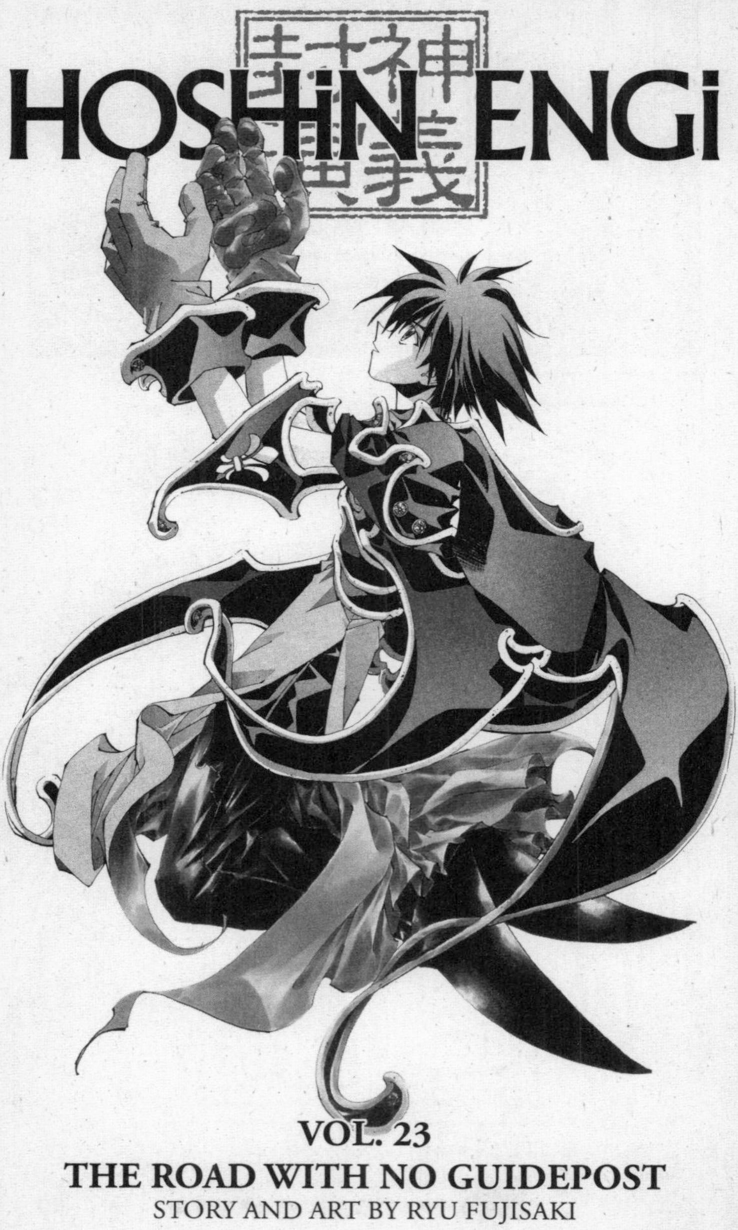

VOL. 23

THE ROAD WITH NO GUIDEPOST

STORY AND ART BY RYU FUJISAKI

THE CHARACTERS

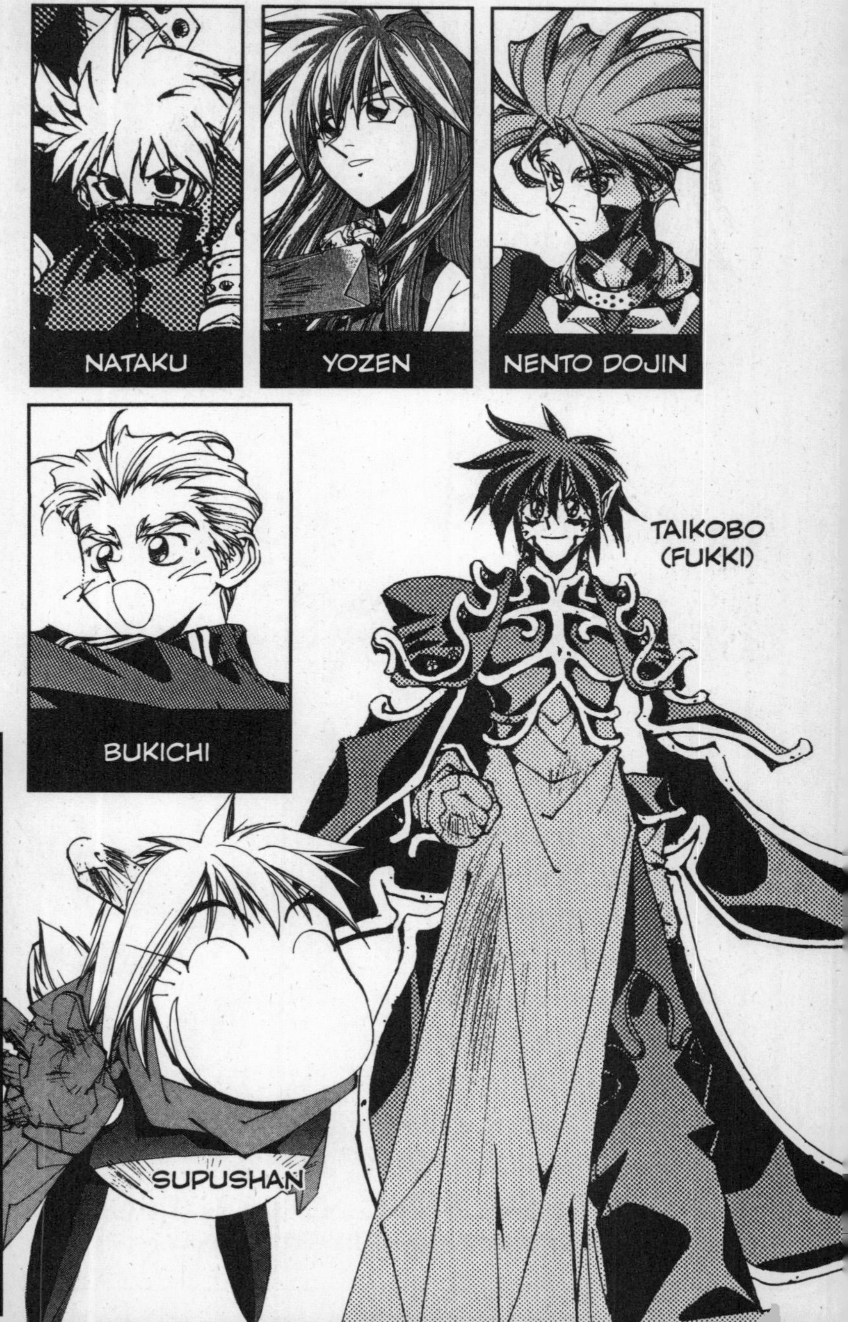
NENTO DOJIN
YOZEN
NATAKU
TAIKOBO (FUKKI)
BUKICHI
SUPUSHAN

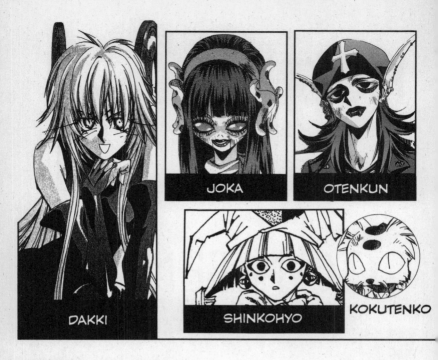

JOKA

OTENKUN

DAKKI

SHINKOHYO

KOKUTENKO

The Story Thus Far

Ancient China, over 3,000 years ago. It is the era of the Yin Dynasty.

After King Chu, the emperor, married the beautiful Dakki, the good king was no longer himself, and became an unmanly and foolish ruler. Dakki, a *Sennyo* with a wicked heart, took control of Yin and the country fell into chaos.

To save the human world, the Hoshin Project was put into action. The project will seal evil Sennin and Doshi into the Shinkai, and cause Seihakuko Sho Ki to set up a new dynasty to replace Yin. Taikobo, who was chosen to execute this project, acts to install a new dynasty.

The "Hoshin Project" changes as they go, though. It is revealed that true objective of the project is to defeat Joka, who appears at turning points in history and manipulates them with her incredible powers. Taikobo and his comrades go to Horai Island, where Joka resides. Taikobo is unexpectedly sealed and finds out that he and Otenkun are the same person. The two merge in order to survive, and Taikobo is resurrected as the "first human" and regains his memories. Taikobo and his comrades fight Joka's soul with their super paope while she tries to free her body...

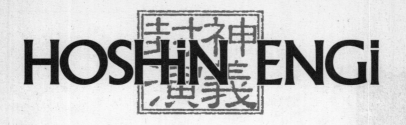

VOL. 23
THE ROAD WITH NO GUIDEPOST

CONTENTS

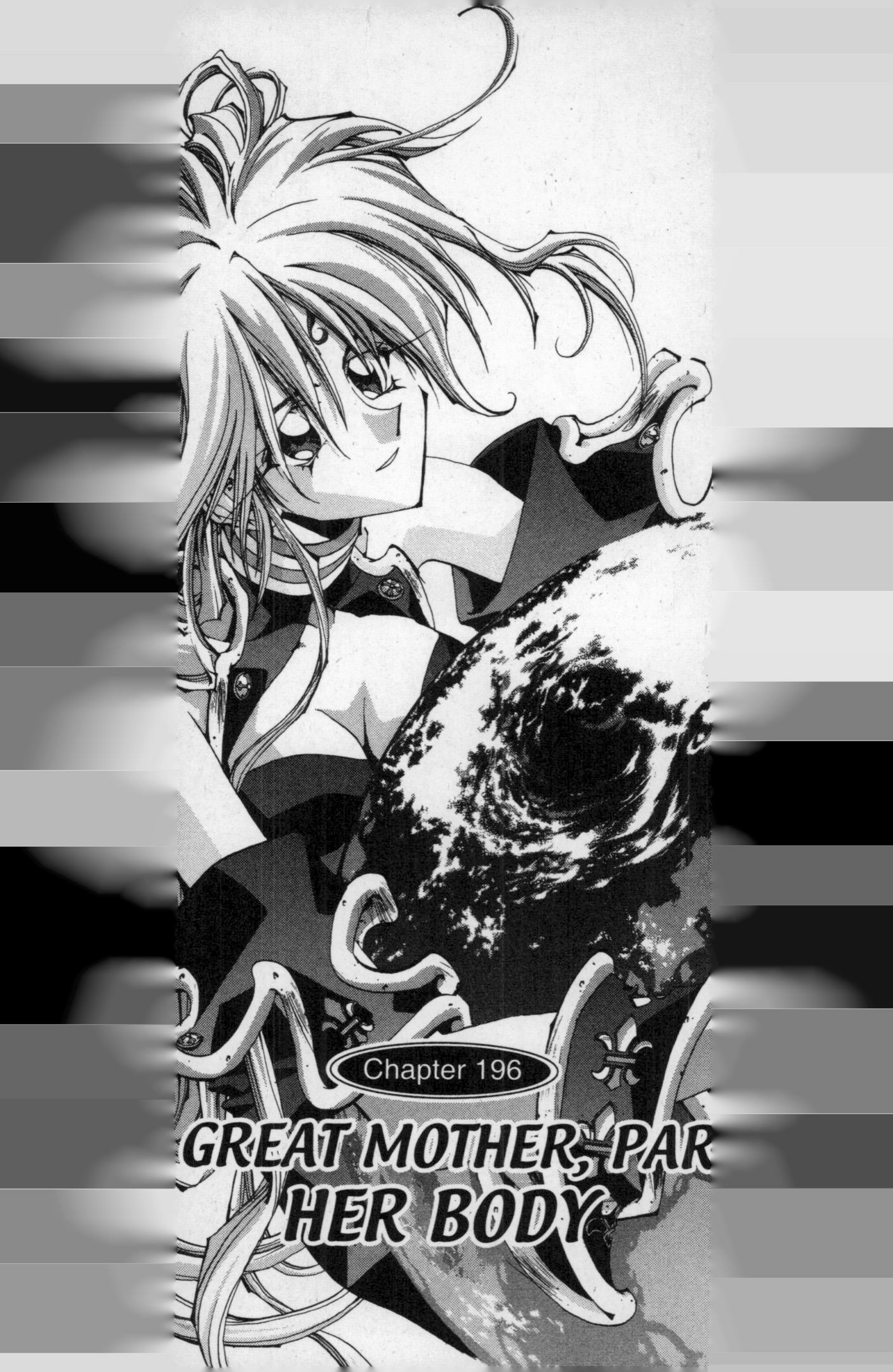
Chapter 196
GREAT MOTHER, PAR
HER BODY

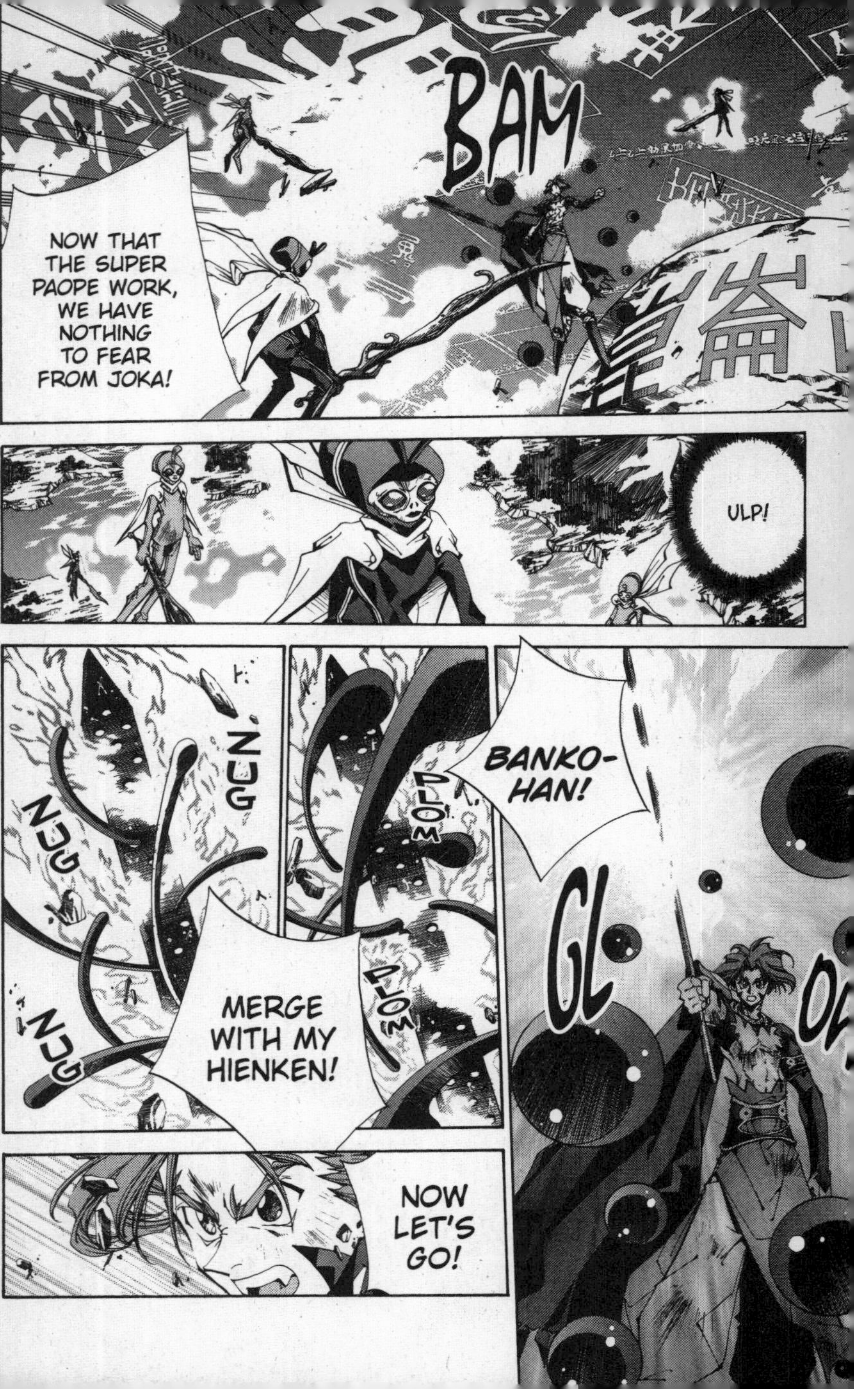
BAM
NOW THAT THE SUPER PAOPE WORK, WE HAVE NOTHING TO FEAR FROM JOKA!
ULP!
BANKO-HAN!
GL
OW
PLOM
MERGE WITH MY HIENKEN!
PLOM
ZUG
NUG
NUG
NOW LET'S GO!

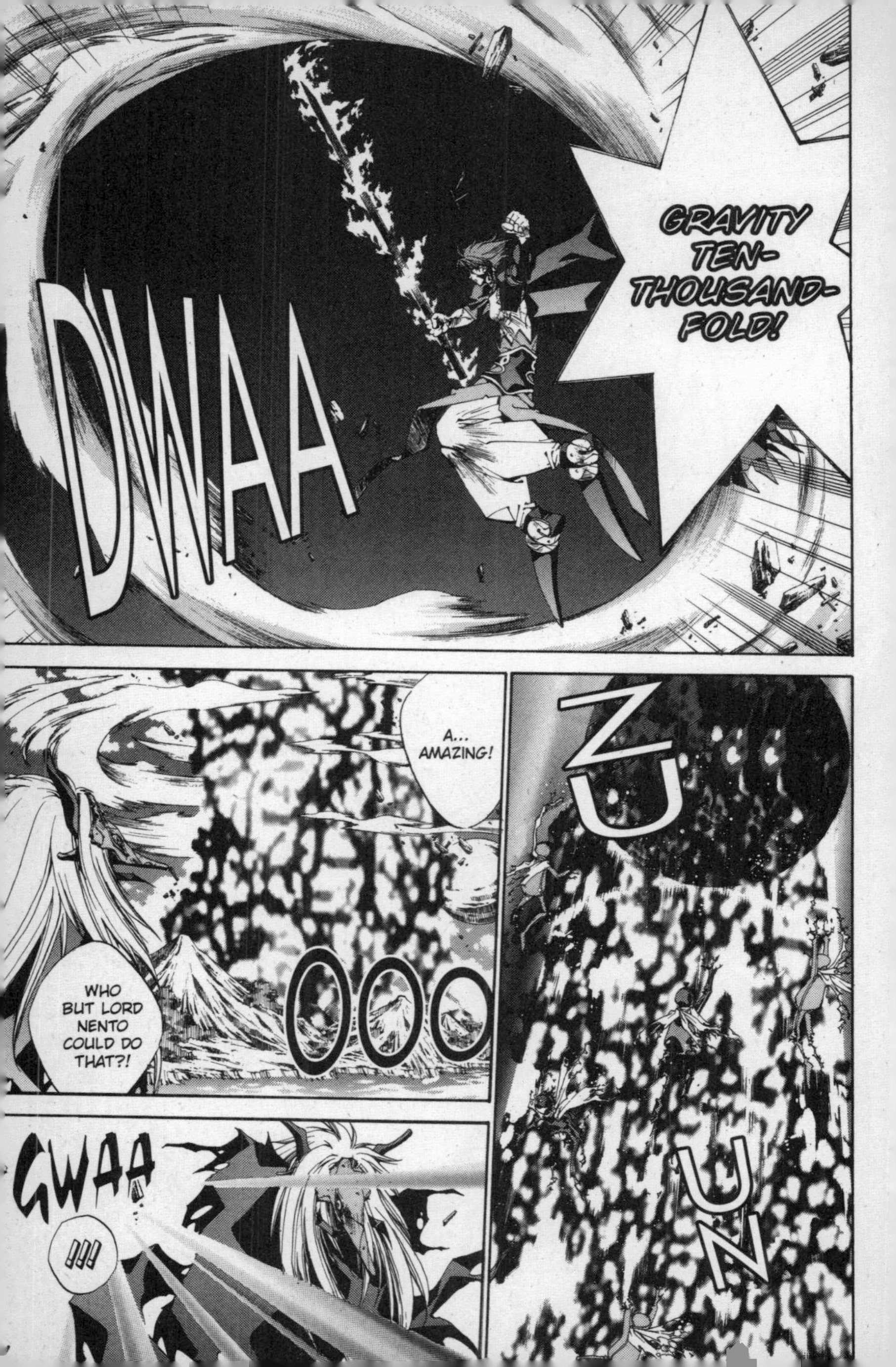
GRAVITY TEN-THOUSAND-FOLD!
DWAA
ZU
UN
A... AMAZING!
OOO
WHO BUT LORD NENTO COULD DO THAT?!
GWAA
!!!

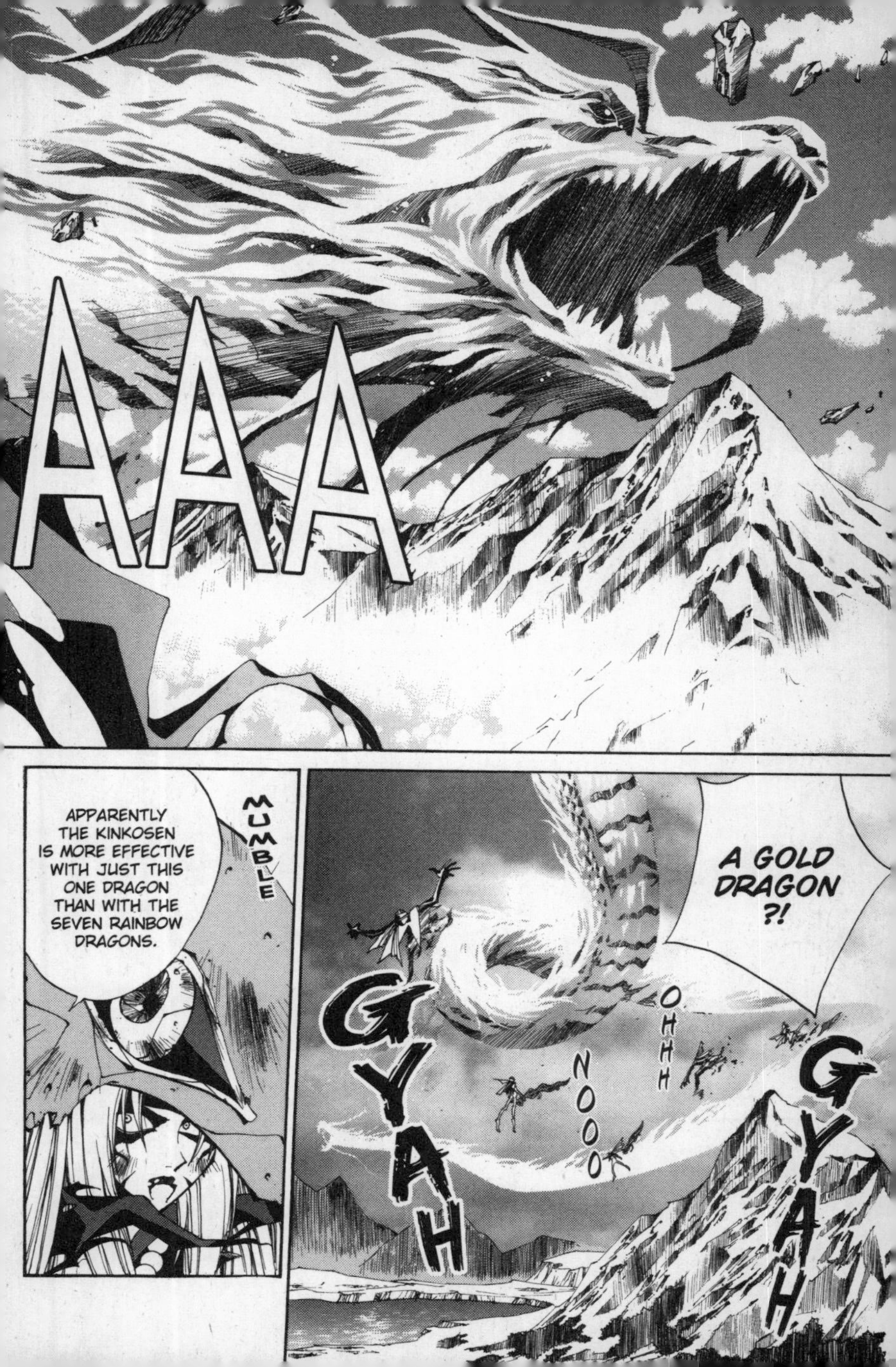
AAA
A GOLD DRAGON ?!
GYAH!
OHHH
NOOO
GYAH
APPARENTLY THE KINKOSEN IS MORE EFFECTIVE WITH JUST THIS ONE DRAGON THAN WITH THE SEVEN RAINBOW DRAGONS.
MUMBLE

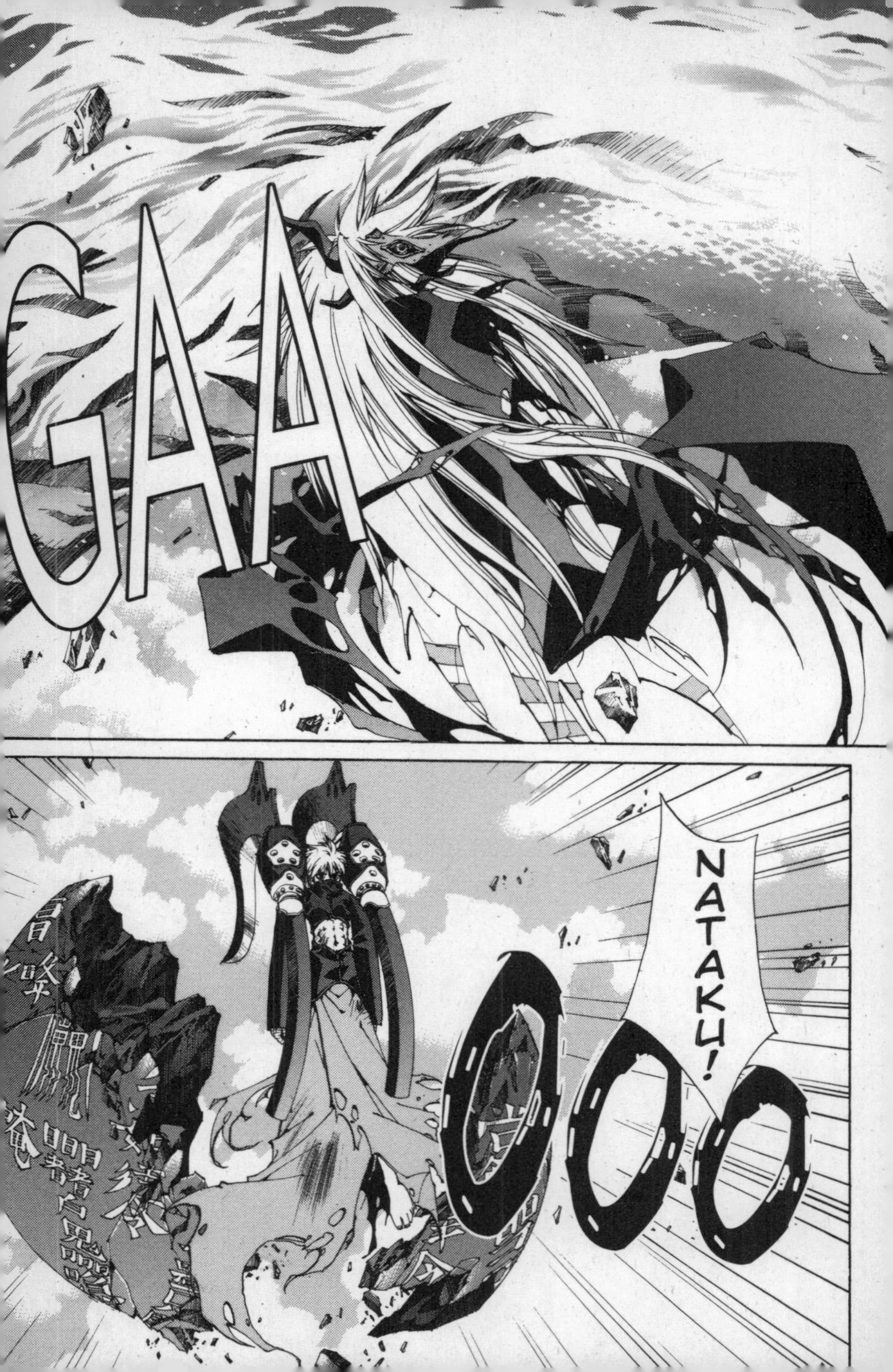
GAA
NATAKU!
OOO

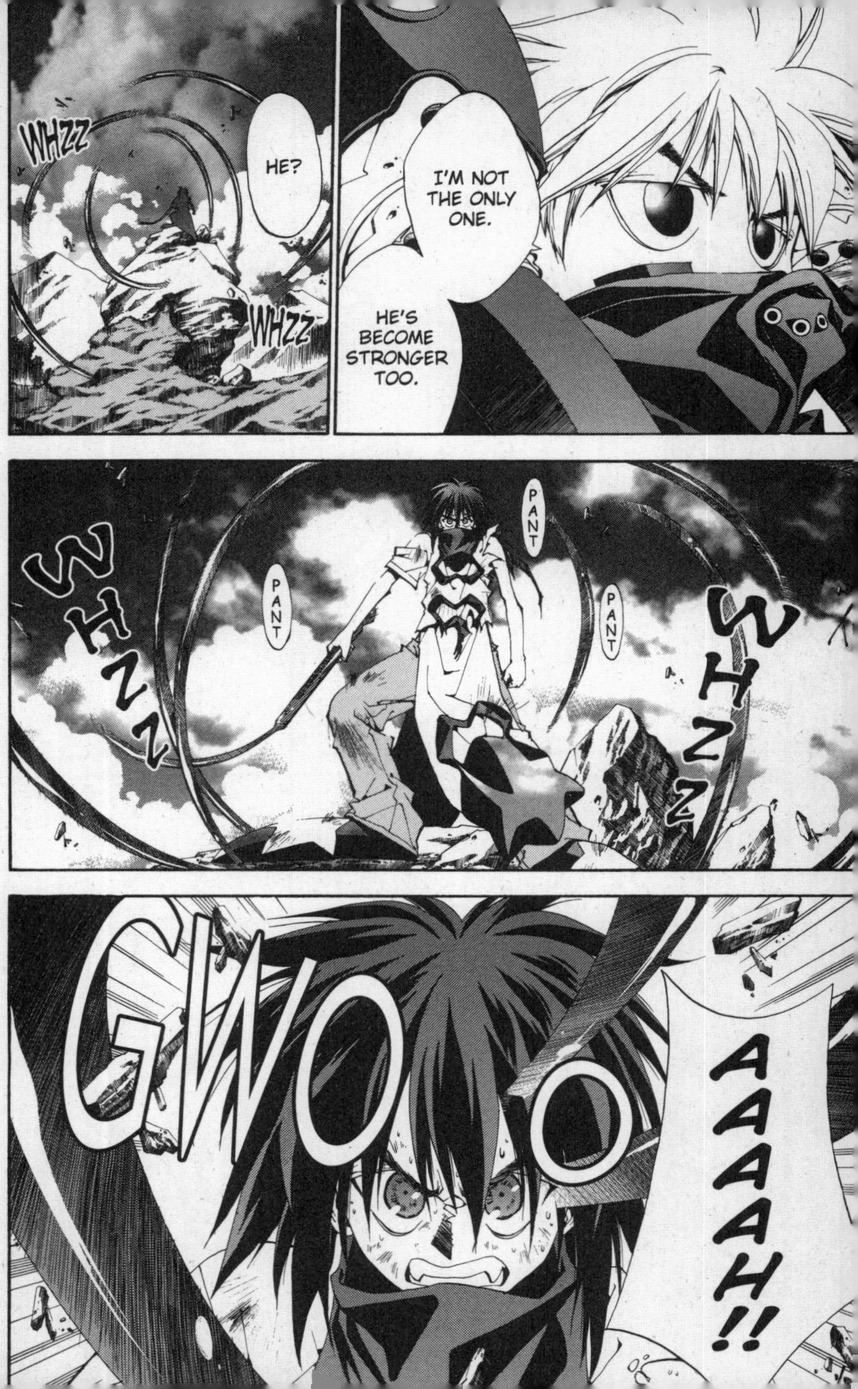
I'M NOT THE ONLY ONE.
HE'S BECOME STRONGER TOO.
HE?
WHZZ
WHZZ
WHZZ
PANT
PANT
PANT
WHNN
GWOO
AAAAH!!

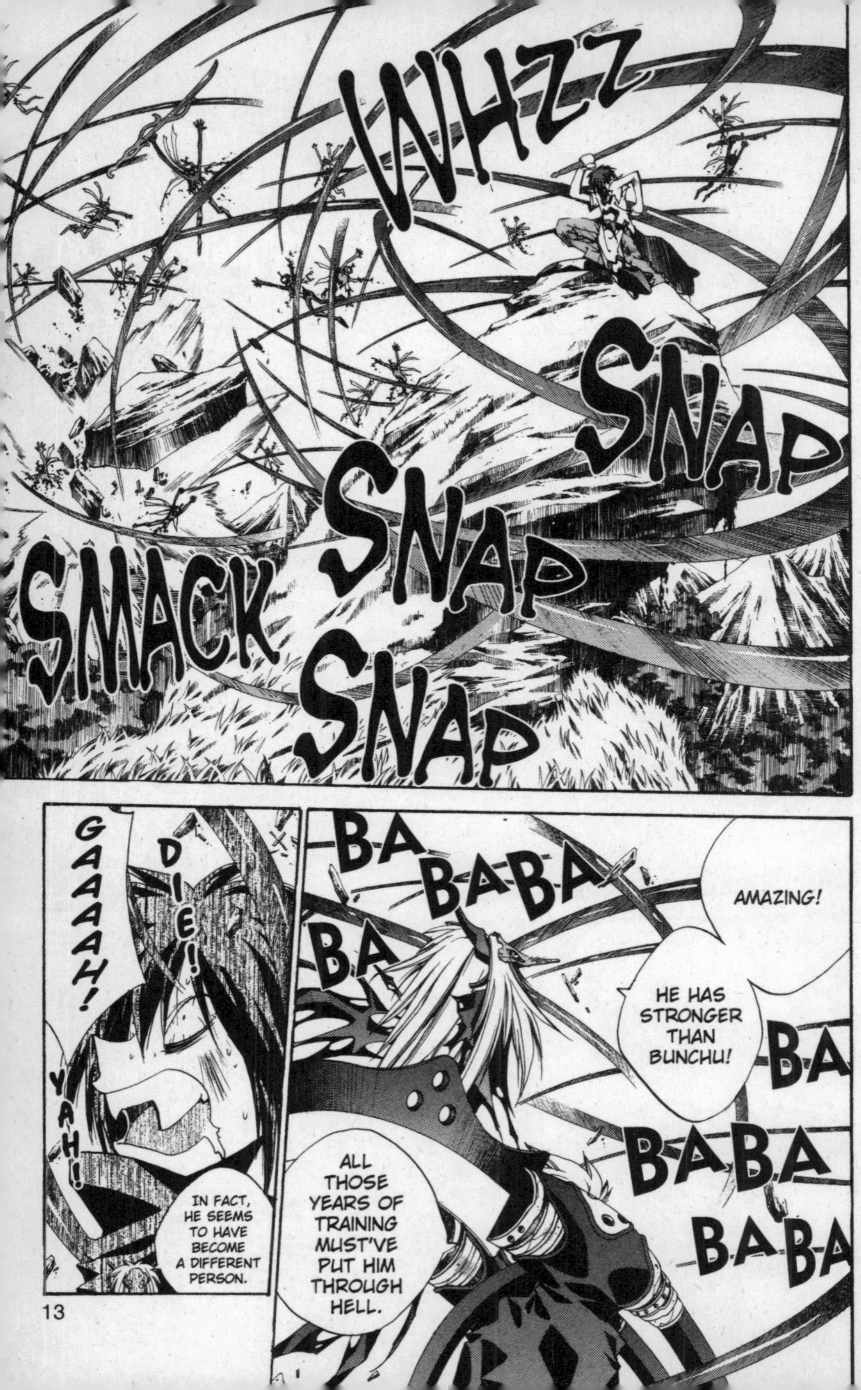
WHZZ
SNAP
SNAP
SMACK
SNAP
BA
BA BA BA
BA
AMAZING!
HE HAS STRONGER THAN BUNCHU!
BA
BA BA BA
BA BA BA
ALL THOSE YEARS OF TRAINING MUST'VE PUT HIM THROUGH HELL.
GAAAAAH!
DIE!
YAH!
IN FACT, HE SEEMS TO HAVE BECOME A DIFFERENT PERSON.

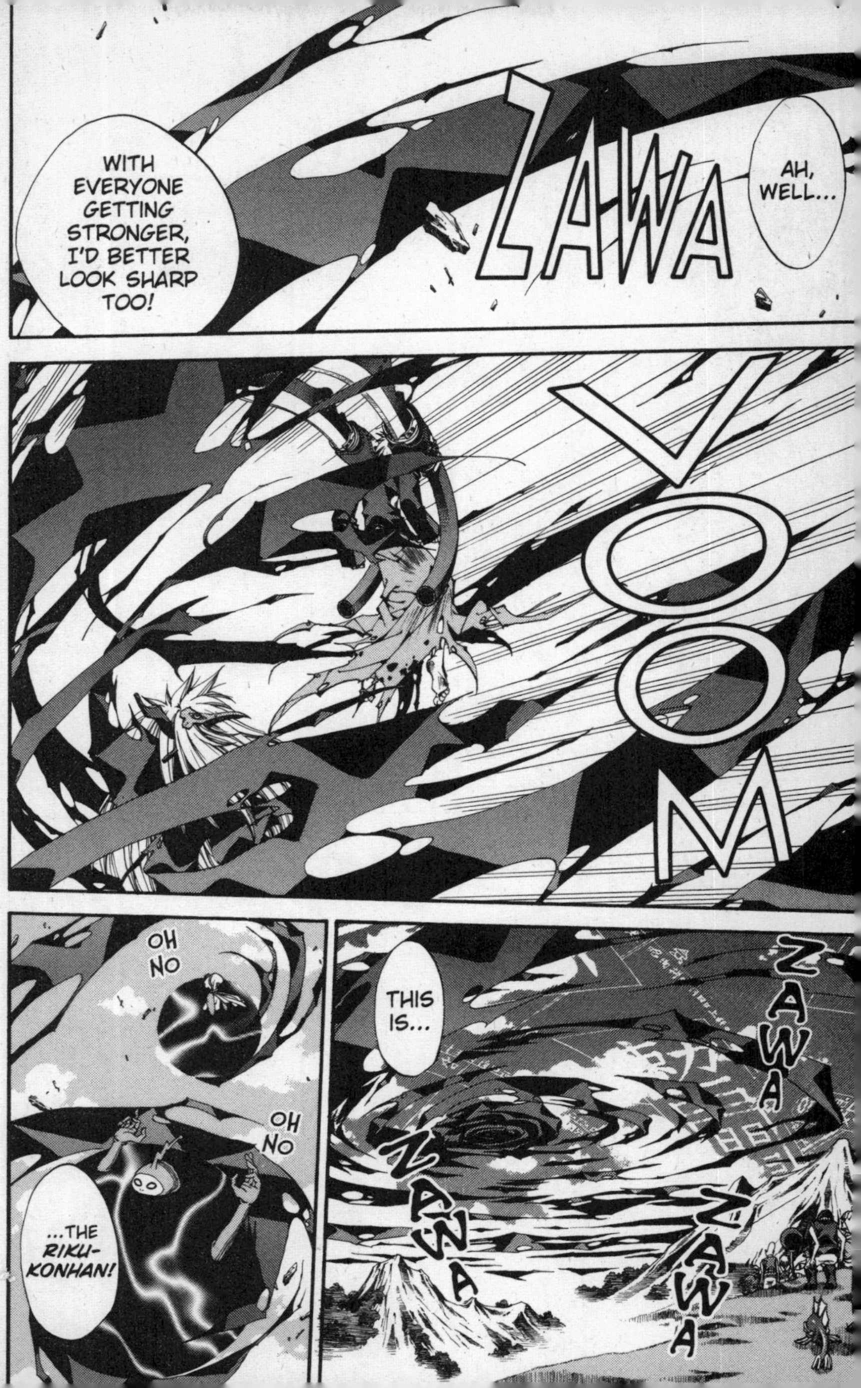
AH, WELL...
ZAWA
WITH EVERYONE GETTING STRONGER, I'D BETTER LOOK SHARP TOO!
VOOOM
THIS IS...
ZAWA
ZAWA
ZAWA
ZAWA
OH NO
OH NO
...THE *RIKU-KONHAN!*

READ THIS WAY

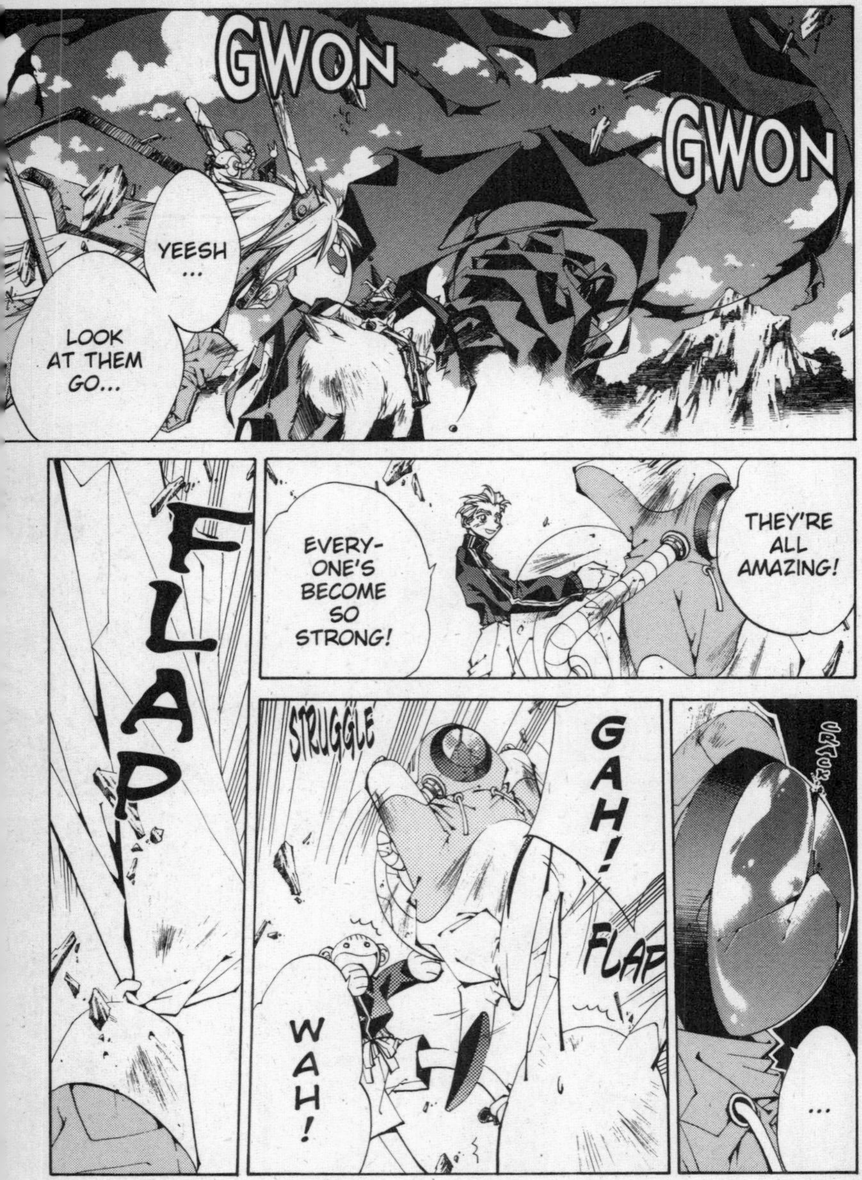
GWON
GWON
YEESH ...
LOOK AT THEM GO...
THEY'RE ALL AMAZING!
EVERY-ONE'S BECOME SO STRONG!
...
GAH!
FLAP
STRUGGLE
WAH!
FLAP

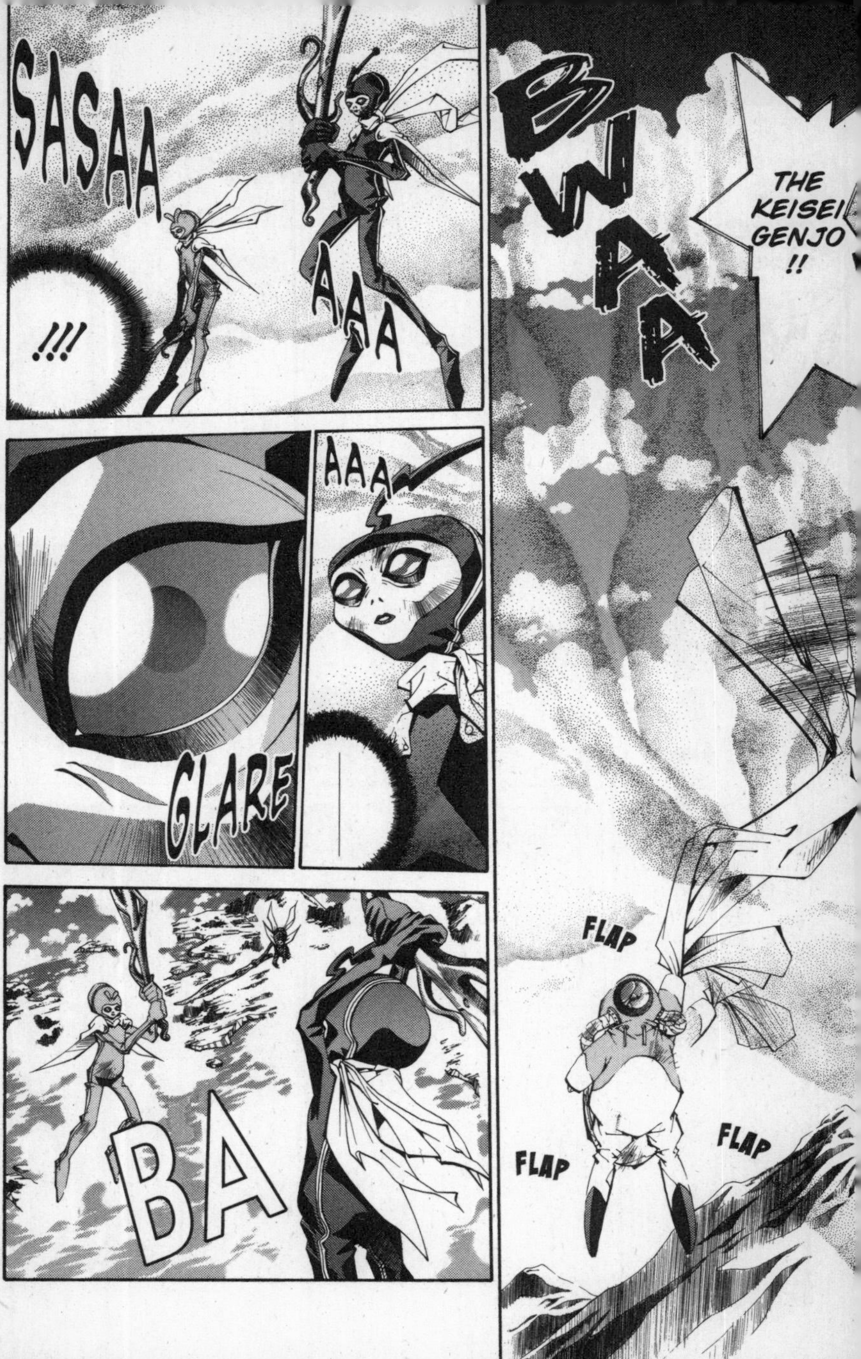
BWAA
THE KEISEI GENJO !!
FLAP
FLAP
FLAP
SASAA
AAA
!!!
AAA
GLARE
BA

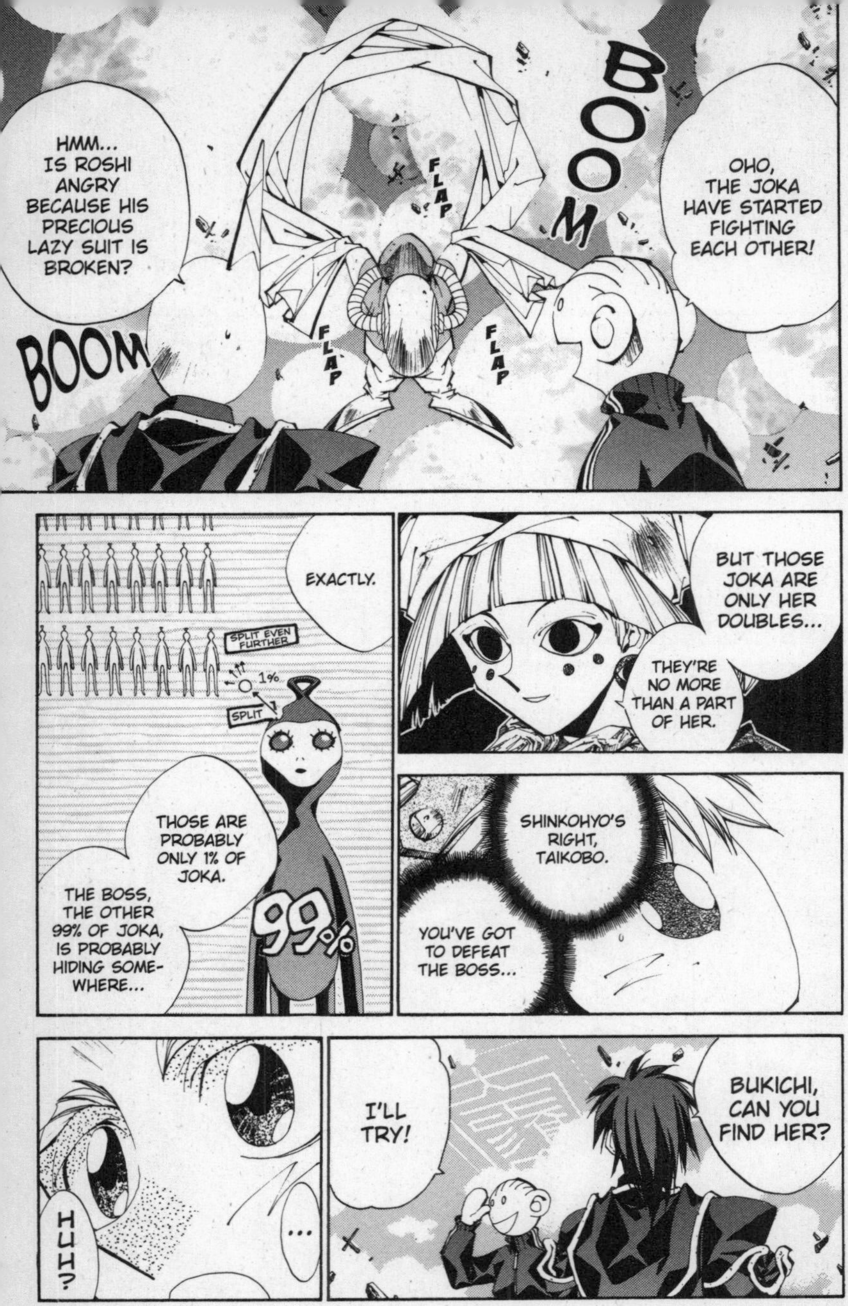
BOOM
OHO, THE JOKA HAVE STARTED FIGHTING EACH OTHER!
FLAP
FLAP
FLAP
HMM... IS ROSHI ANGRY BECAUSE HIS PRECIOUS LAZY SUIT IS BROKEN?
BOOM
BUT THOSE JOKA ARE ONLY HER DOUBLES...
THEY'RE NO MORE THAN A PART OF HER.
SHINKOHYO'S RIGHT, TAIKOBO.
YOU'VE GOT TO DEFEAT THE BOSS...
EXACTLY.
SPLIT EVEN FURTHER
1%
SPLIT
THOSE ARE PROBABLY ONLY 1% OF JOKA.
99%
THE BOSS, THE OTHER 99% OF JOKA, IS PROBABLY HIDING SOME-WHERE...
BUKICHI, CAN YOU FIND HER?
I'LL TRY!
...
HUH?

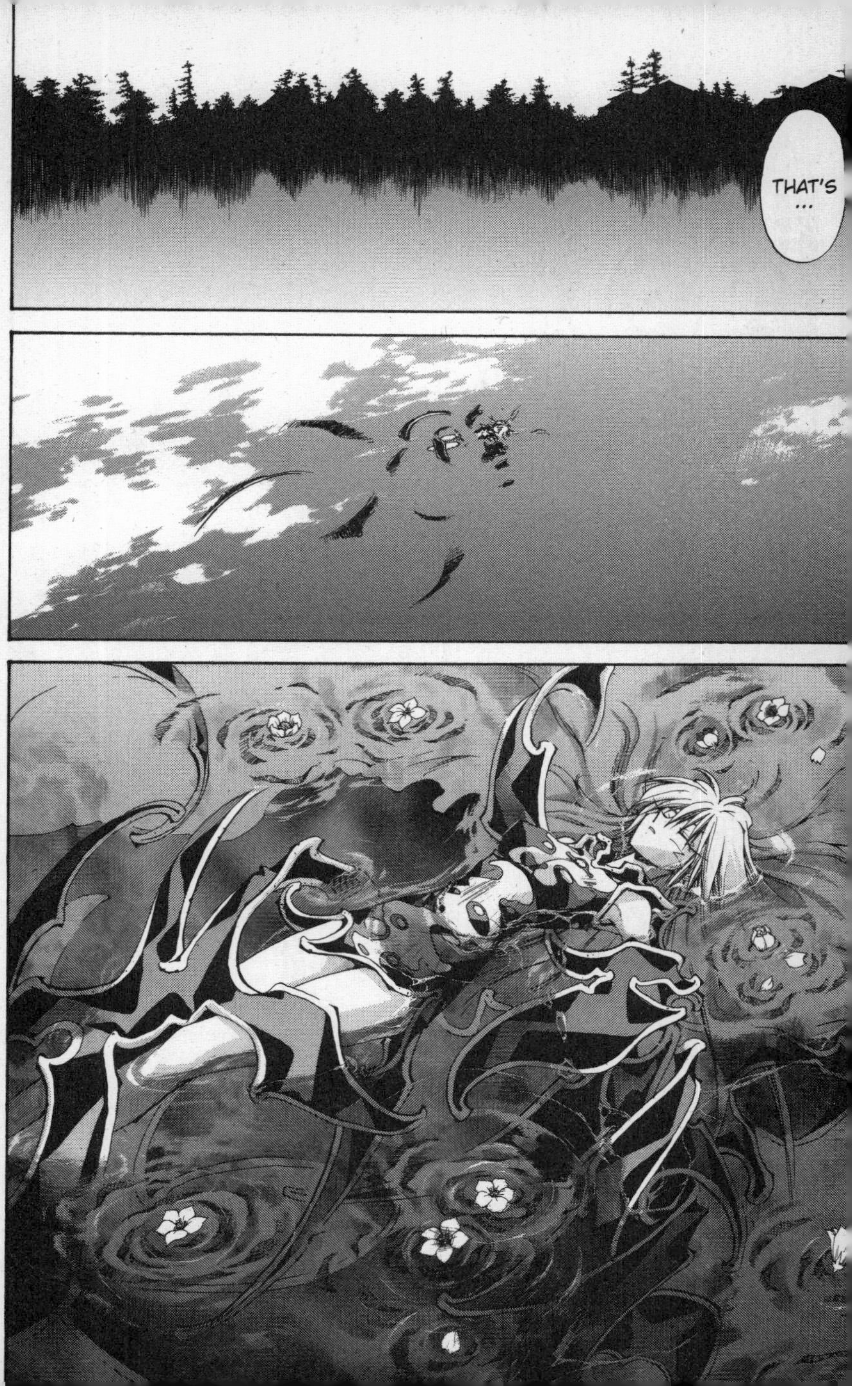
THAT'S ...

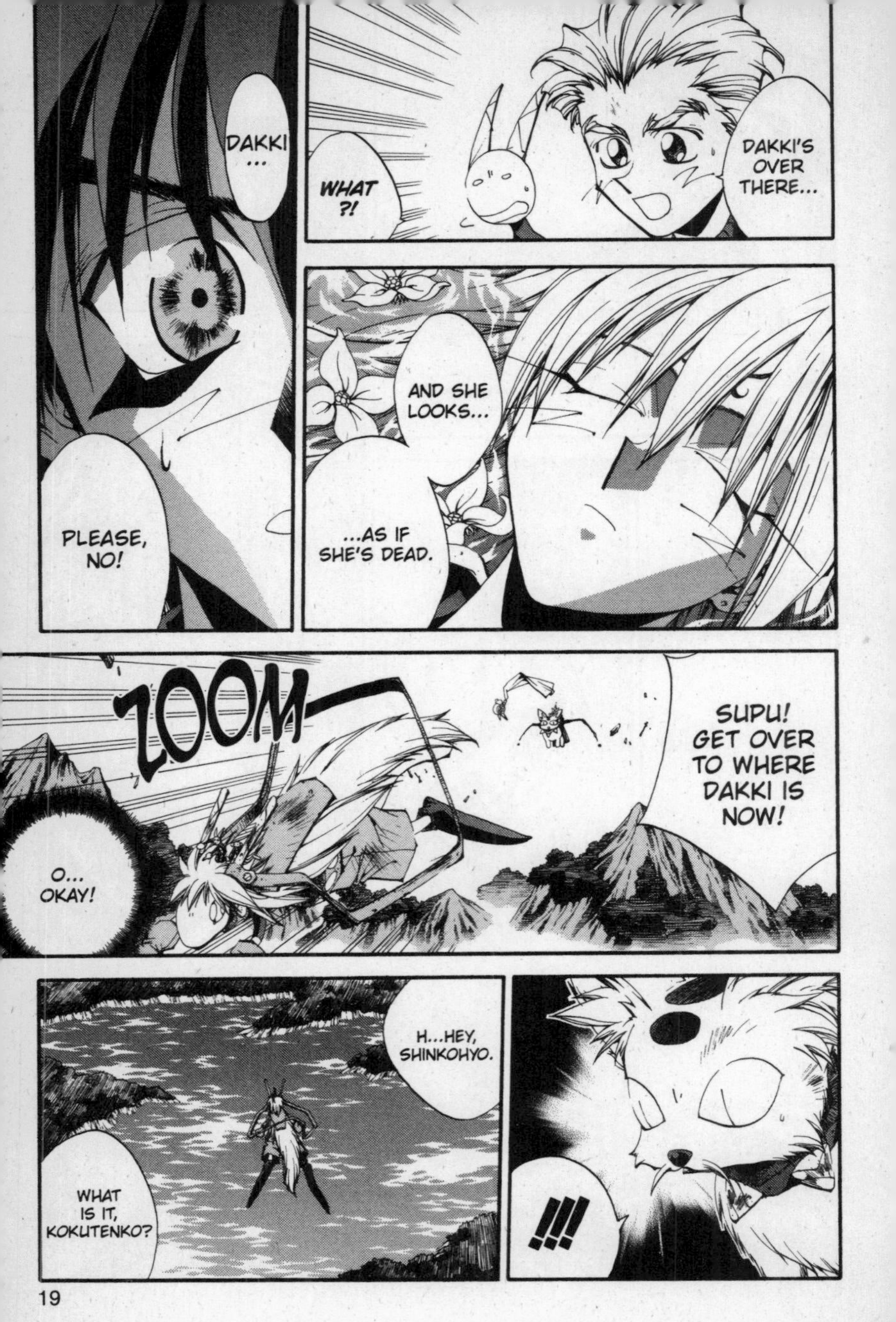
DAKKI'S OVER THERE...
WHAT?!
AND SHE LOOKS...
...AS IF SHE'S DEAD.
DAKKI...
PLEASE, NO!
SUPU! GET OVER TO WHERE DAKKI IS NOW!
ZOOM
O... OKAY!
!!!
H...HEY, SHINKOHYO.
WHAT IS IT, KOKUTENKO?

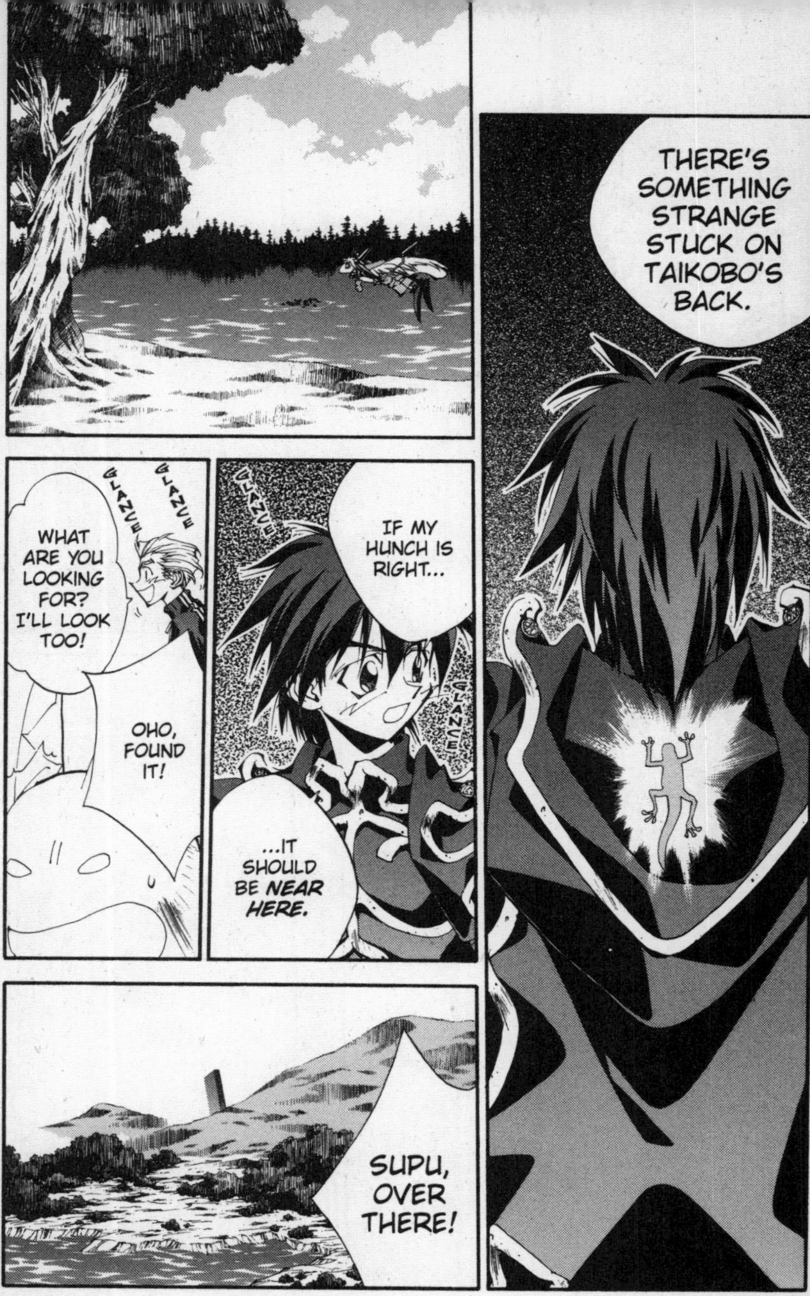
THERE'S SOMETHING STRANGE STUCK ON TAIKOBO'S BACK.
GLANCE
IF MY HUNCH IS RIGHT...
GLANCE
...IT SHOULD BE *NEAR HERE.*
GLANCE GLANCE
WHAT ARE YOU LOOKING FOR? I'LL LOOK TOO!
OHO, FOUND IT!
SUPU, OVER THERE!

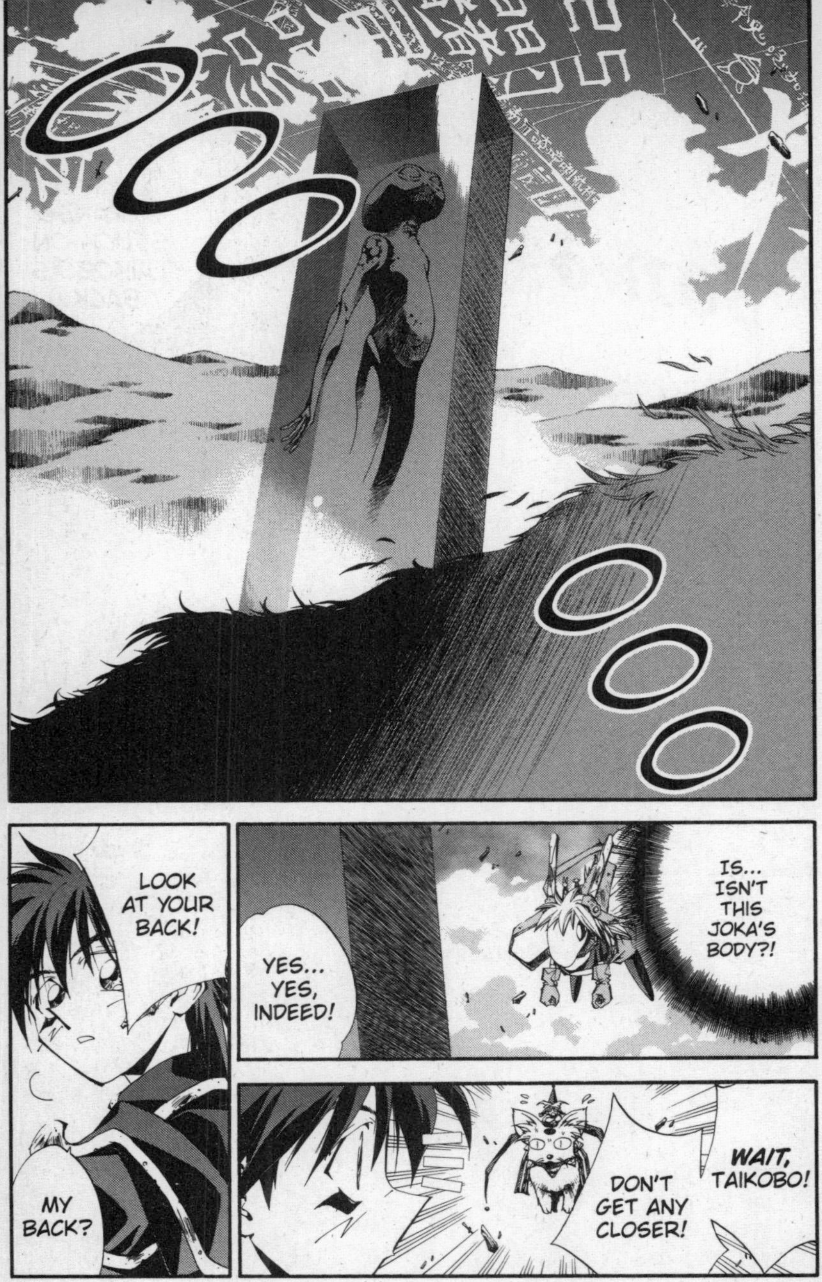
IS... ISN'T THIS JOKA'S BODY?!
YES... YES, INDEED!
WAIT, TAIKOBO!
DON'T GET ANY CLOSER!
LOOK AT YOUR BACK!
MY BACK?

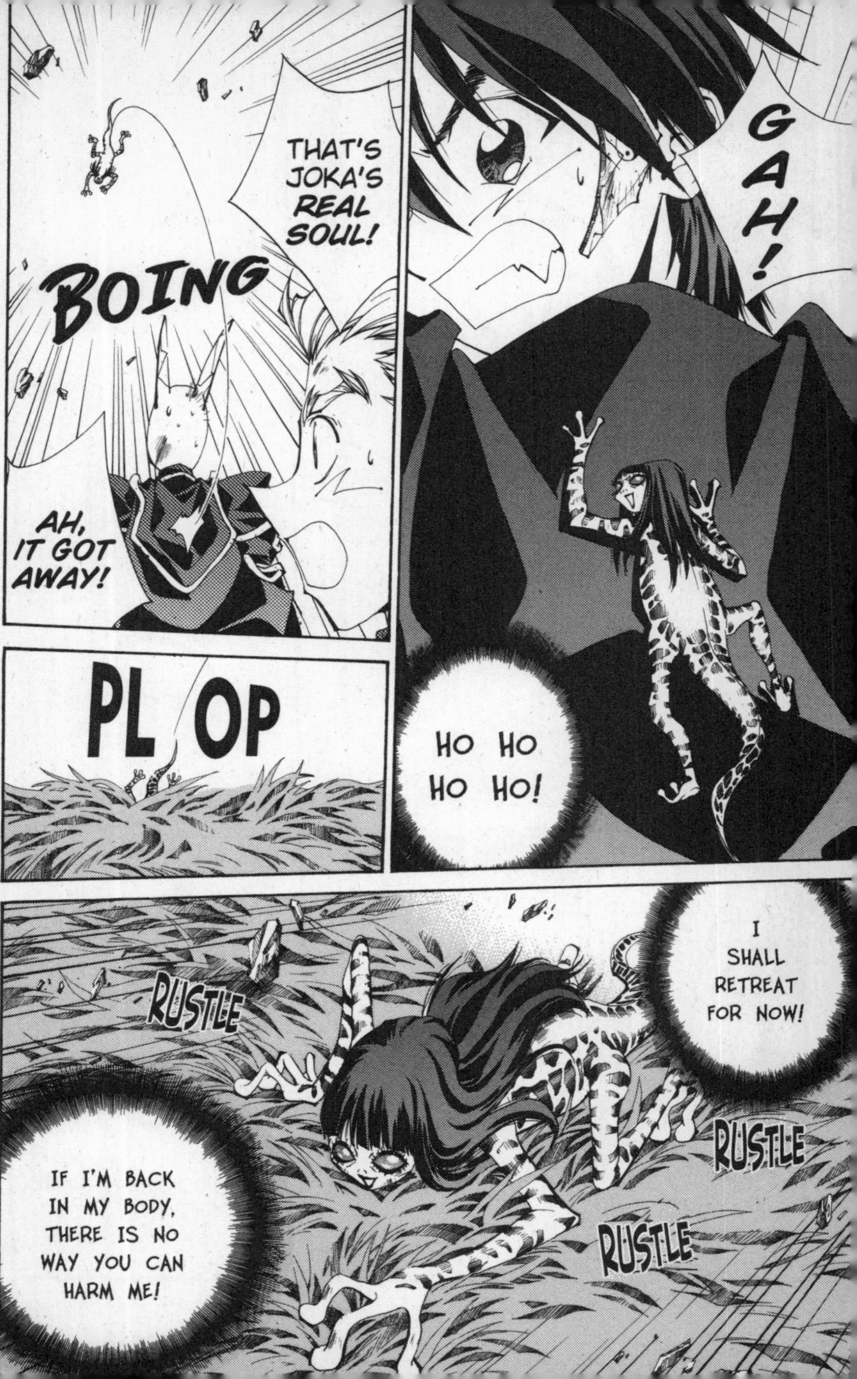
GAH!
HO HO HO HO!
THAT'S JOKA'S REAL SOUL!
BOING
AH, IT GOT AWAY!
PL OP
I SHALL RETREAT FOR NOW!
RUSTLE
RUSTLE
RUSTLE
IF I'M BACK IN MY BODY, THERE IS NO WAY YOU CAN HARM ME!

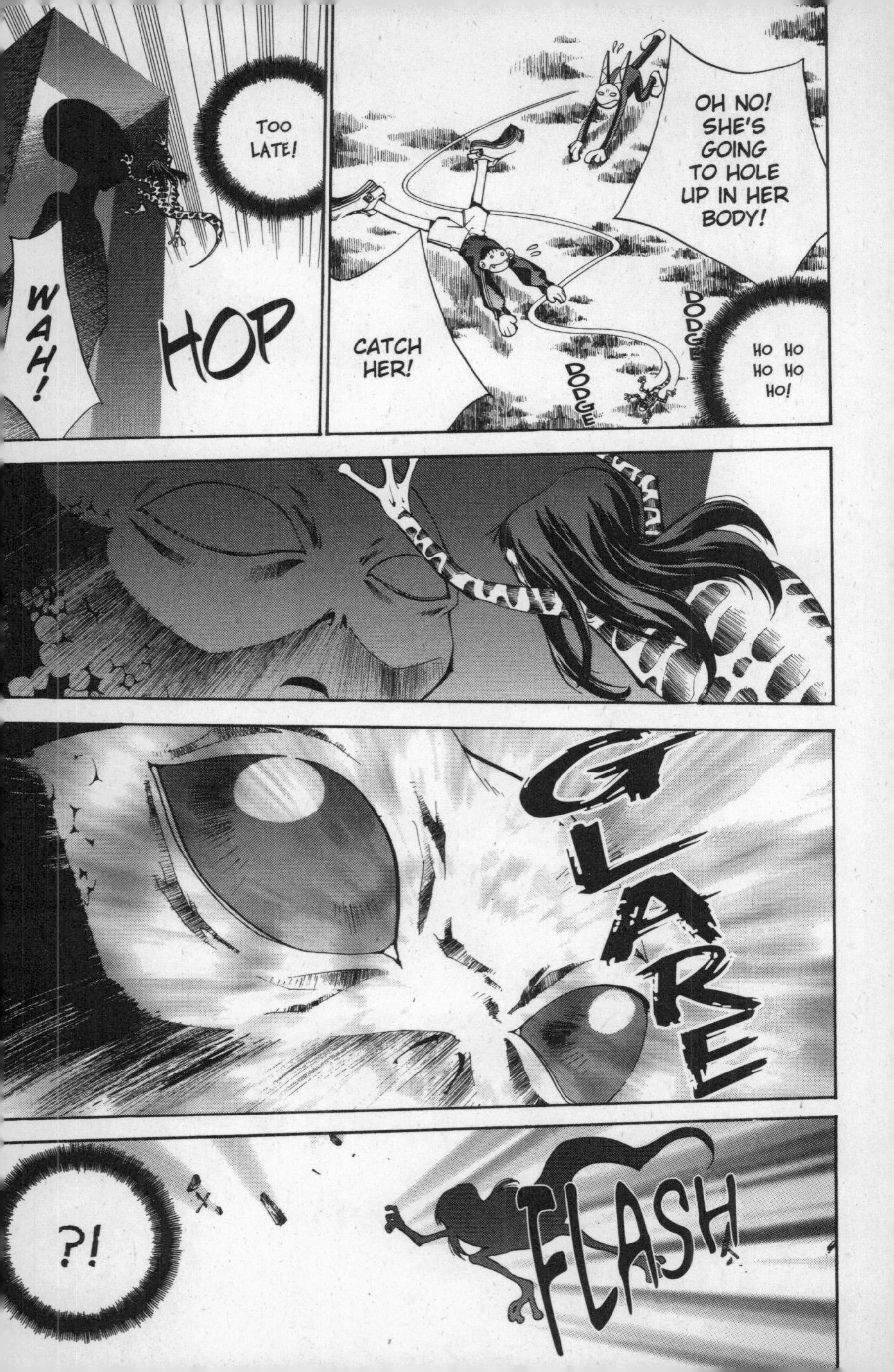
OH NO! SHE'S GOING TO HOLE UP IN HER BODY!
HO HO HO HO HO!
DODGE
DODGE
CATCH HER!
TOO LATE!
HOP
WAH!
GLARE
FLASH
?!

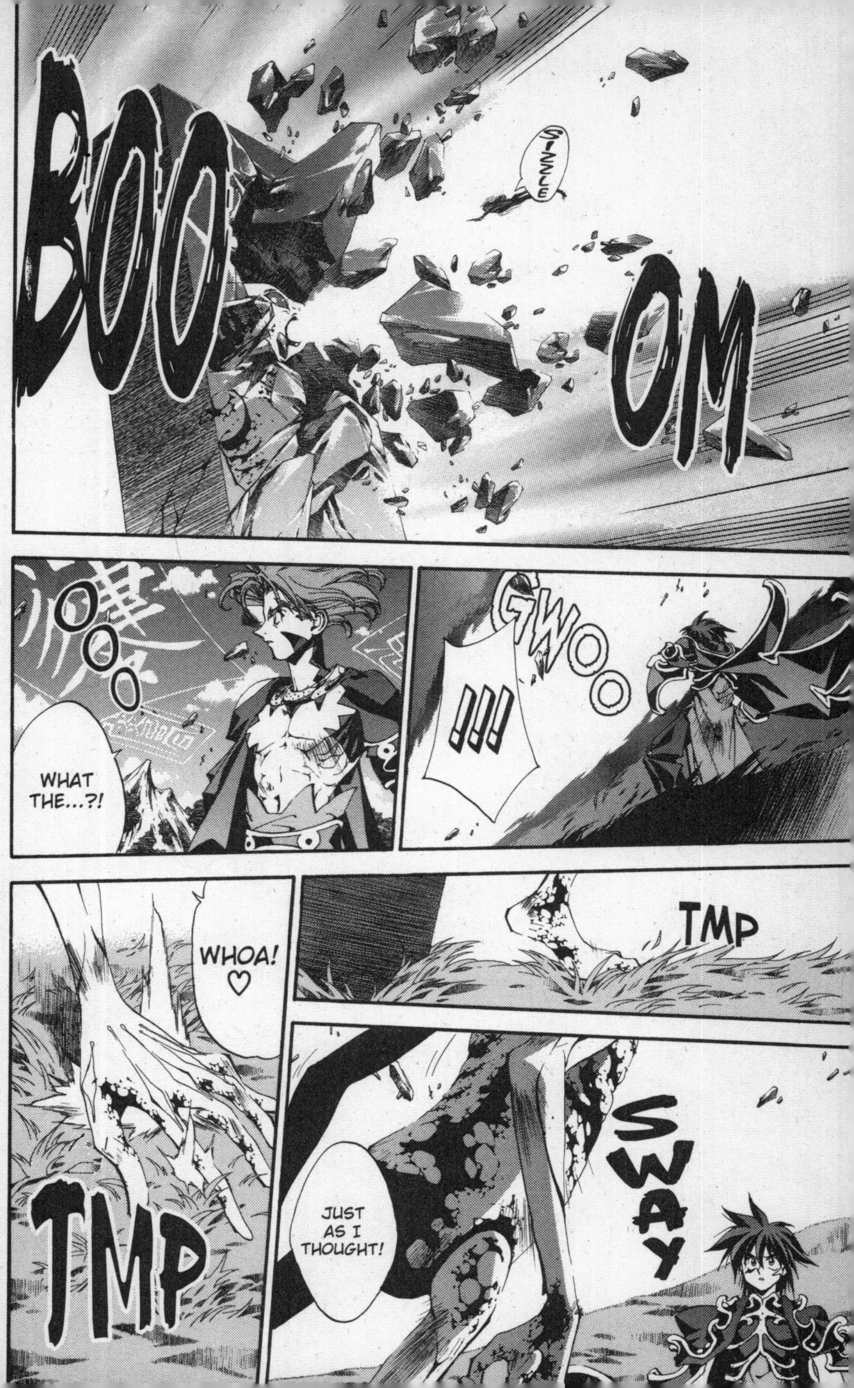
BOOOM
SIZZLE
GWOOO
RR!!!
WHAT THE...?!
TMP
WHOA! ♡
TMP
SWAY
JUST AS I THOUGHT!

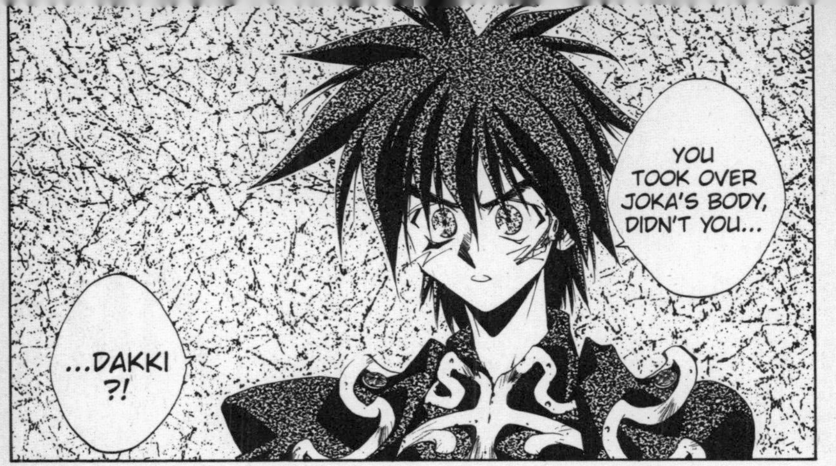
YOU TOOK OVER JOKA'S BODY, DIDN'T YOU...
...DAKKI ?!

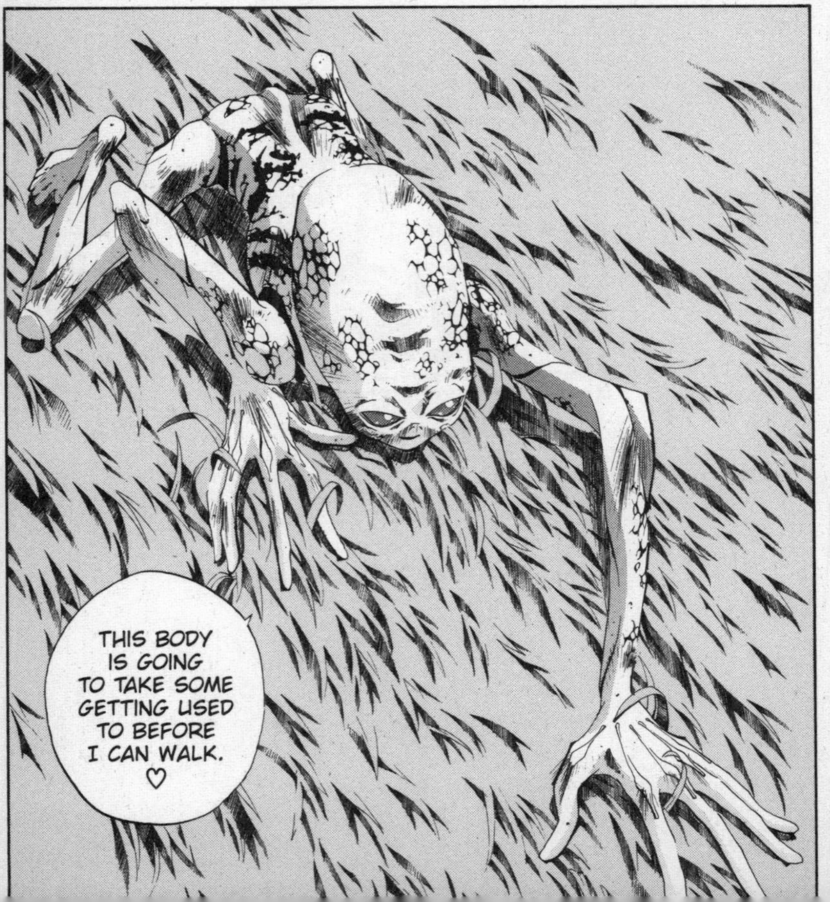
THIS BODY IS GOING TO TAKE SOME GETTING USED TO BEFORE I CAN WALK. ♡

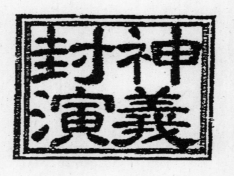

封神演義

Chapter 197

THE GREAT MOTHER, PART 3
DAKKI'S SECRET

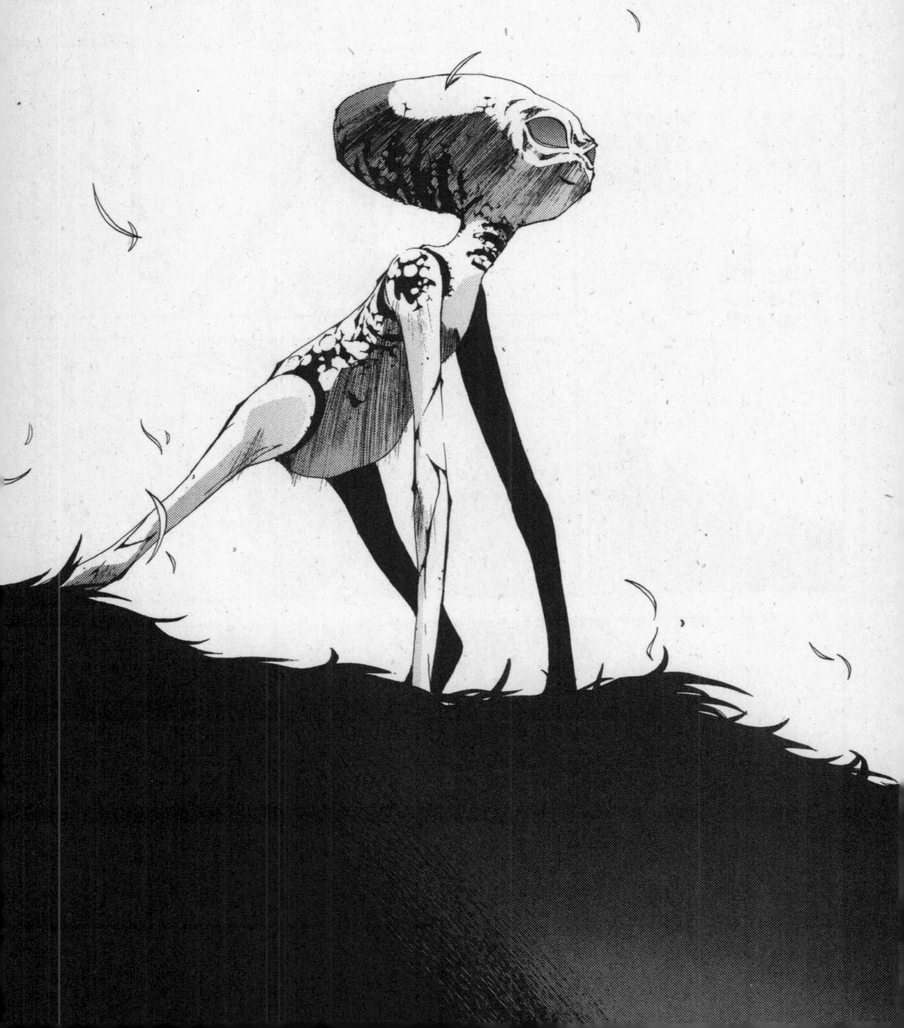

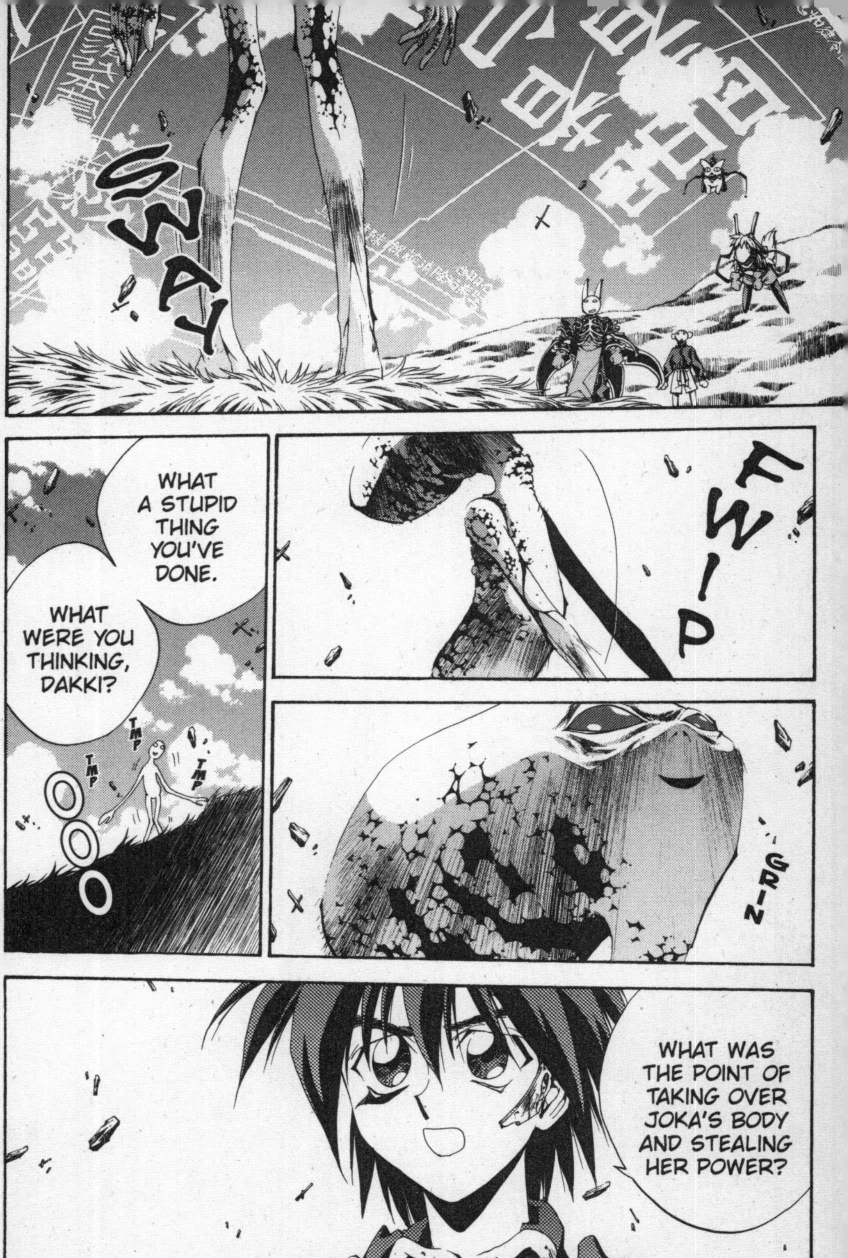
SWAY
FWIP
GRIN
WHAT A STUPID THING YOU'VE DONE.
WHAT WERE YOU THINKING, DAKKI?
TMP
TMP
TMP
OOO
WHAT WAS THE POINT OF TAKING OVER JOKA'S BODY AND STEALING HER POWER?

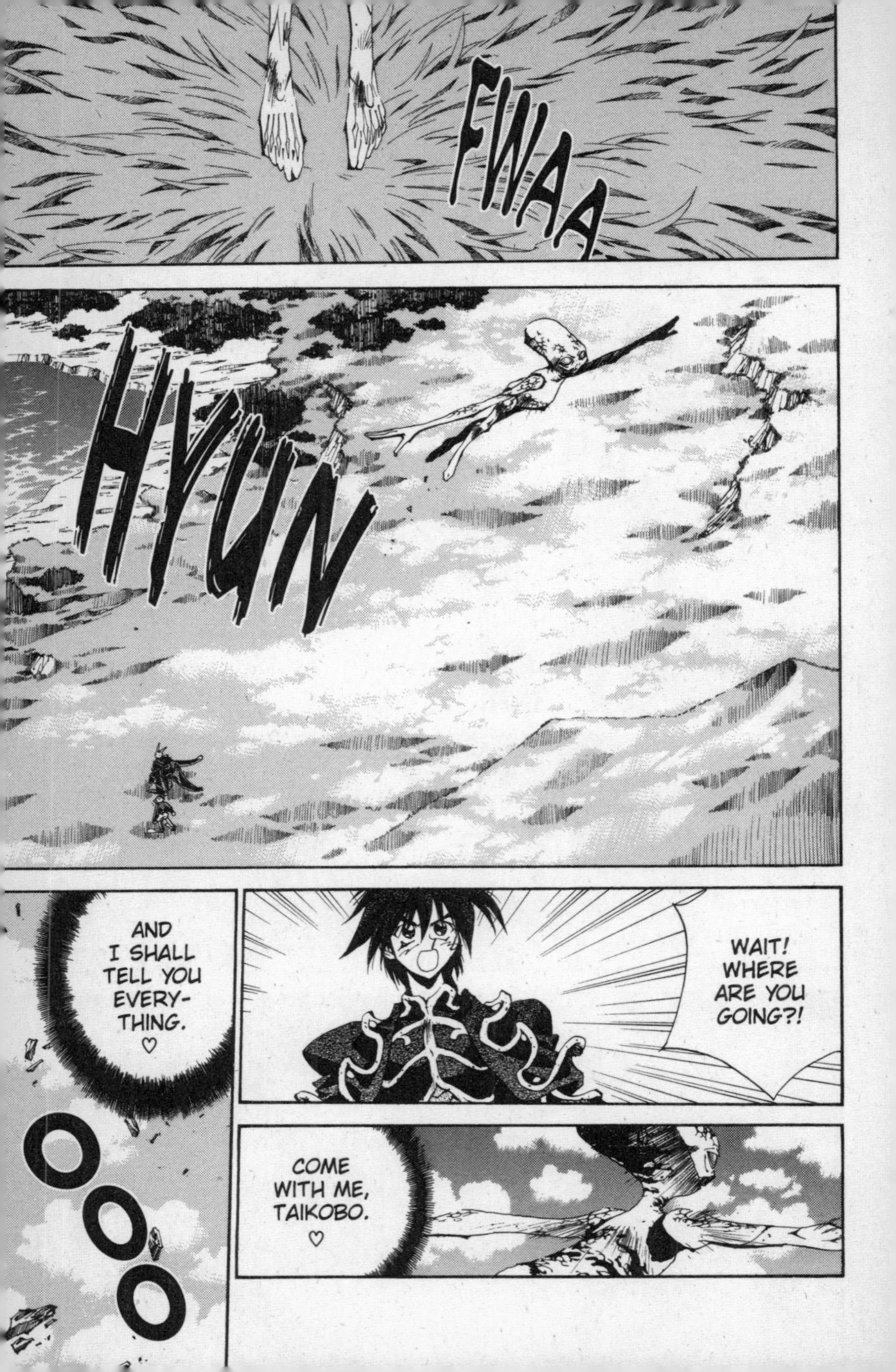
FWAA
HYUN
WAIT! WHERE ARE YOU GOING?!
COME WITH ME, TAIKOBO. ♡
AND I SHALL TELL YOU EVERY-THING. ♡
OOO

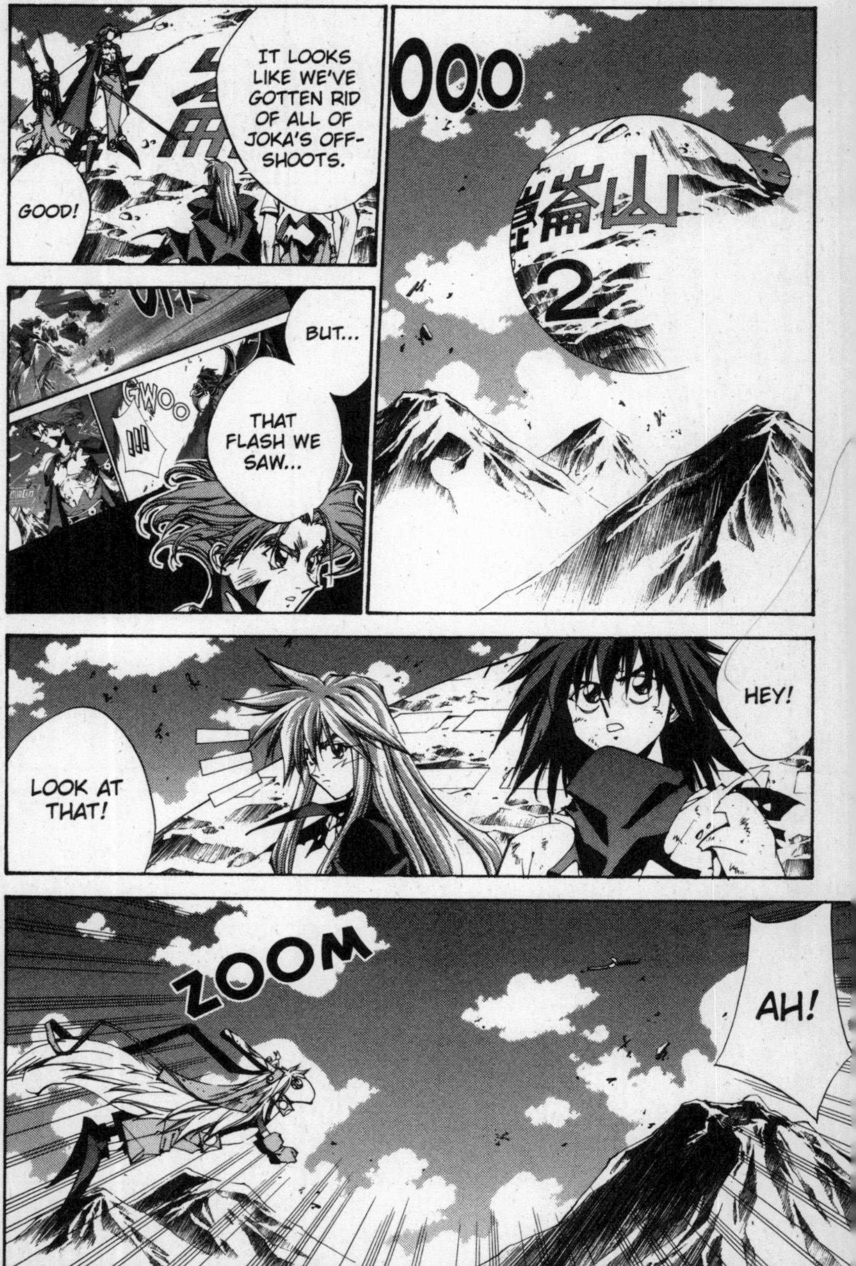
OOO
2
IT LOOKS LIKE WE'VE GOTTEN RID OF ALL OF JOKA'S OFF-SHOOTS.
GOOD!
BUT...
THAT FLASH WE SAW...
GWOO
HEY!
LOOK AT THAT!
AH!
ZOOM

READ THIS WAY

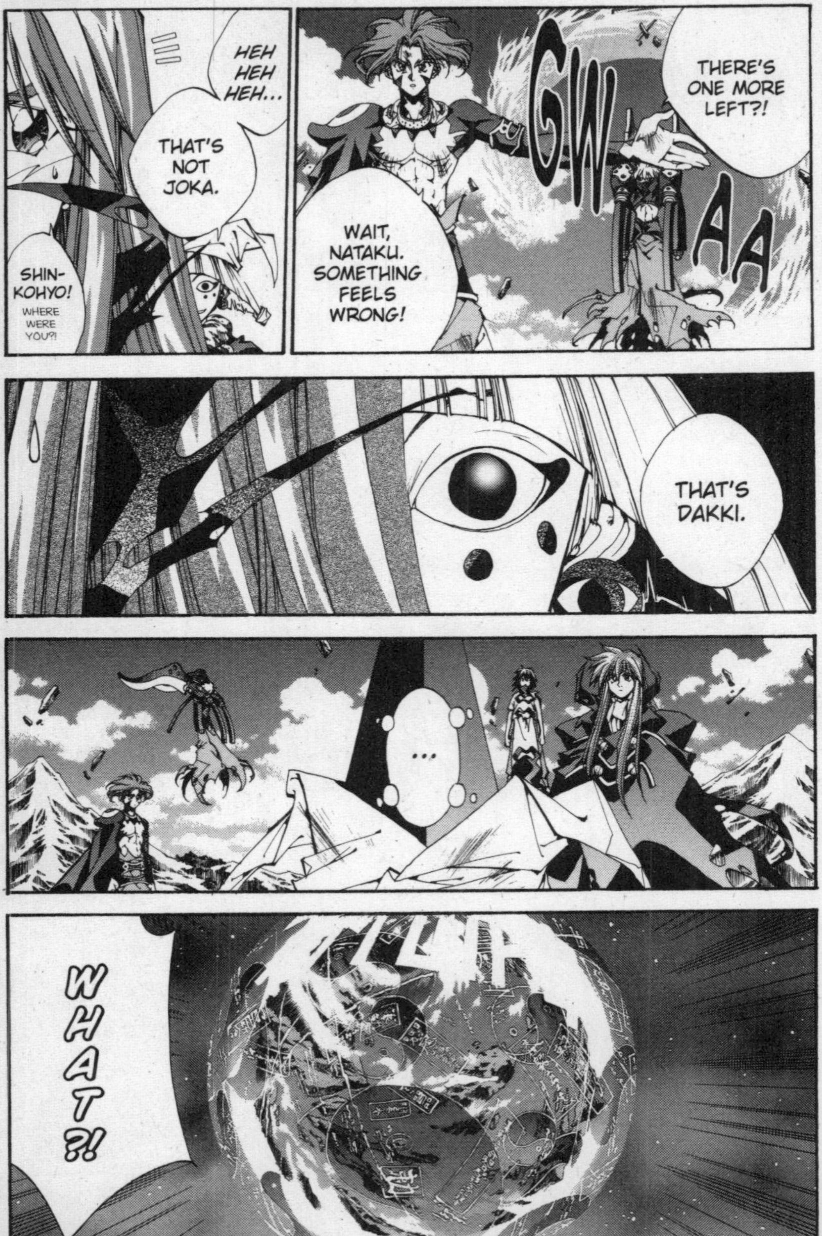
THERE'S ONE MORE LEFT?!
GWAA
WAIT, NATAKU. SOMETHING FEELS WRONG!
HEH HEH HEH...
THAT'S NOT JOKA.
SHIN-KOHYO!
WHERE WERE YOU?!
THAT'S DAKKI.
...
WHAT?!

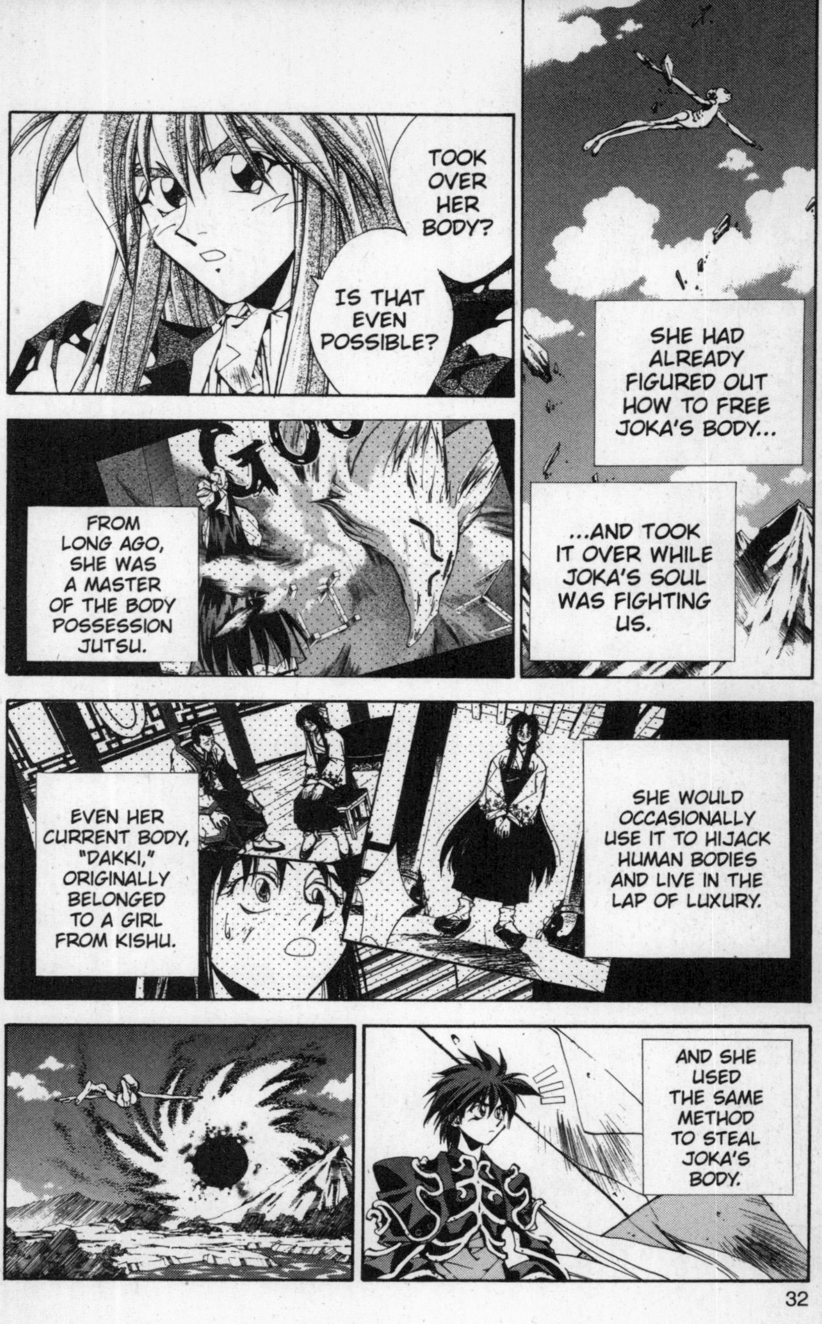
TOOK OVER HER BODY?
IS THAT EVEN POSSIBLE?
SHE HAD ALREADY FIGURED OUT HOW TO FREE JOKA'S BODY...
...AND TOOK IT OVER WHILE JOKA'S SOUL WAS FIGHTING US.
FROM LONG AGO, SHE WAS A MASTER OF THE BODY POSSESSION JUTSU.
SHE WOULD OCCASIONALLY USE IT TO HIJACK HUMAN BODIES AND LIVE IN THE LAP OF LUXURY.
EVEN HER CURRENT BODY, "DAKKI," ORIGINALLY BELONGED TO A GIRL FROM KISHU.
AND SHE USED THE SAME METHOD TO STEAL JOKA'S BODY.

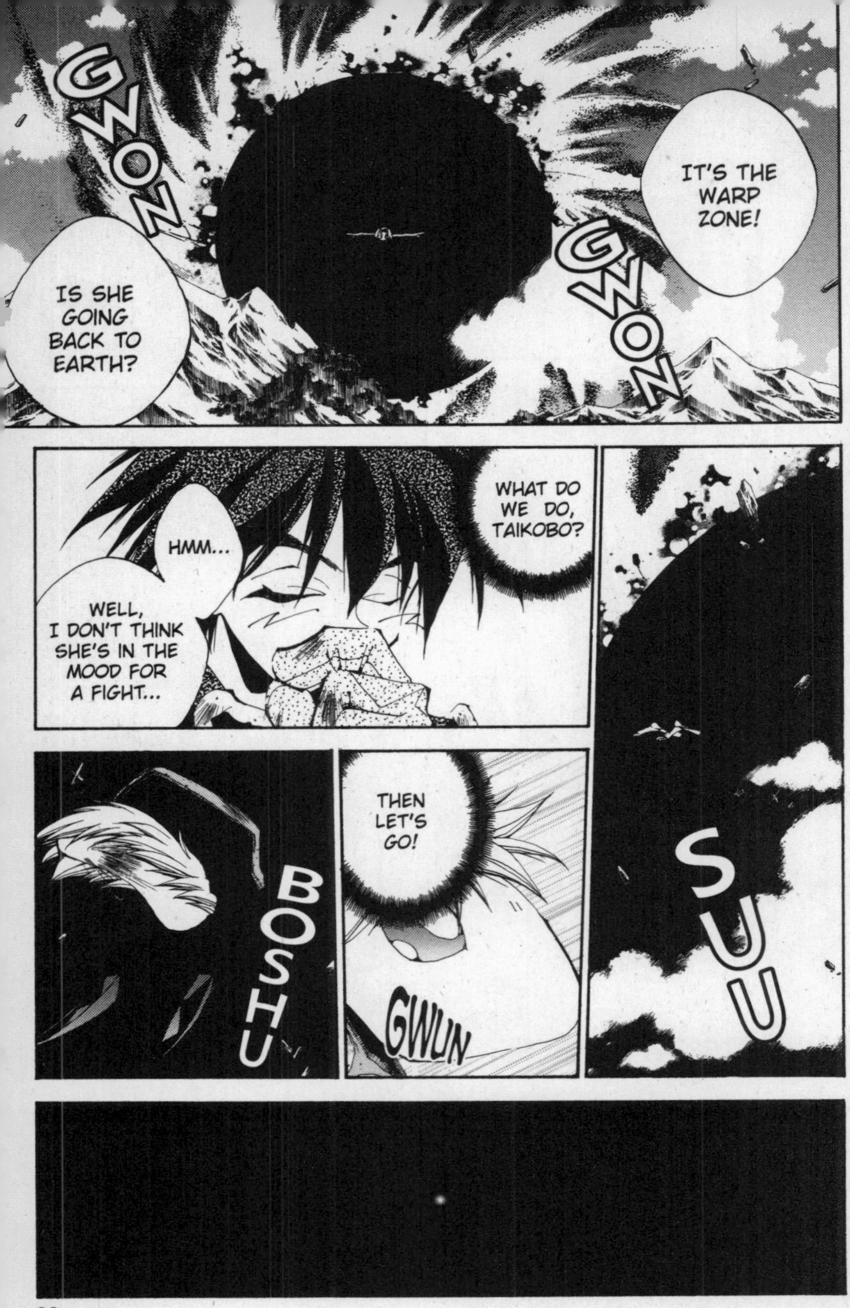
IT'S THE WARP ZONE!
GWON
GWON
GWON
IS SHE GOING BACK TO EARTH?
WHAT DO WE DO, TAIKOBO?
HMM...
WELL, I DON'T THINK SHE'S IN THE MOOD FOR A FIGHT...
THEN LET'S GO!
GWUN
BOSHU
SUU

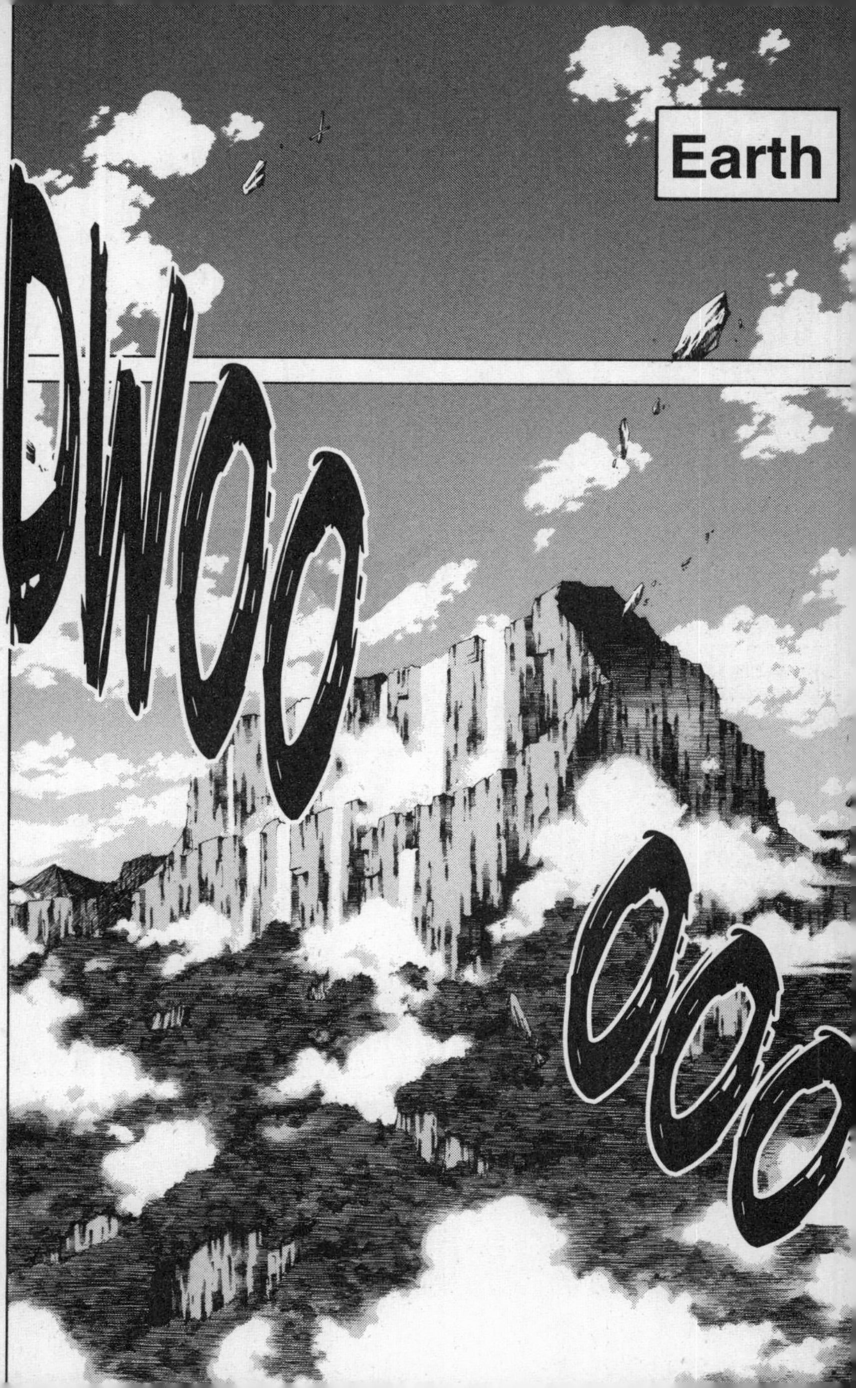
Earth
DWOO
OOOO

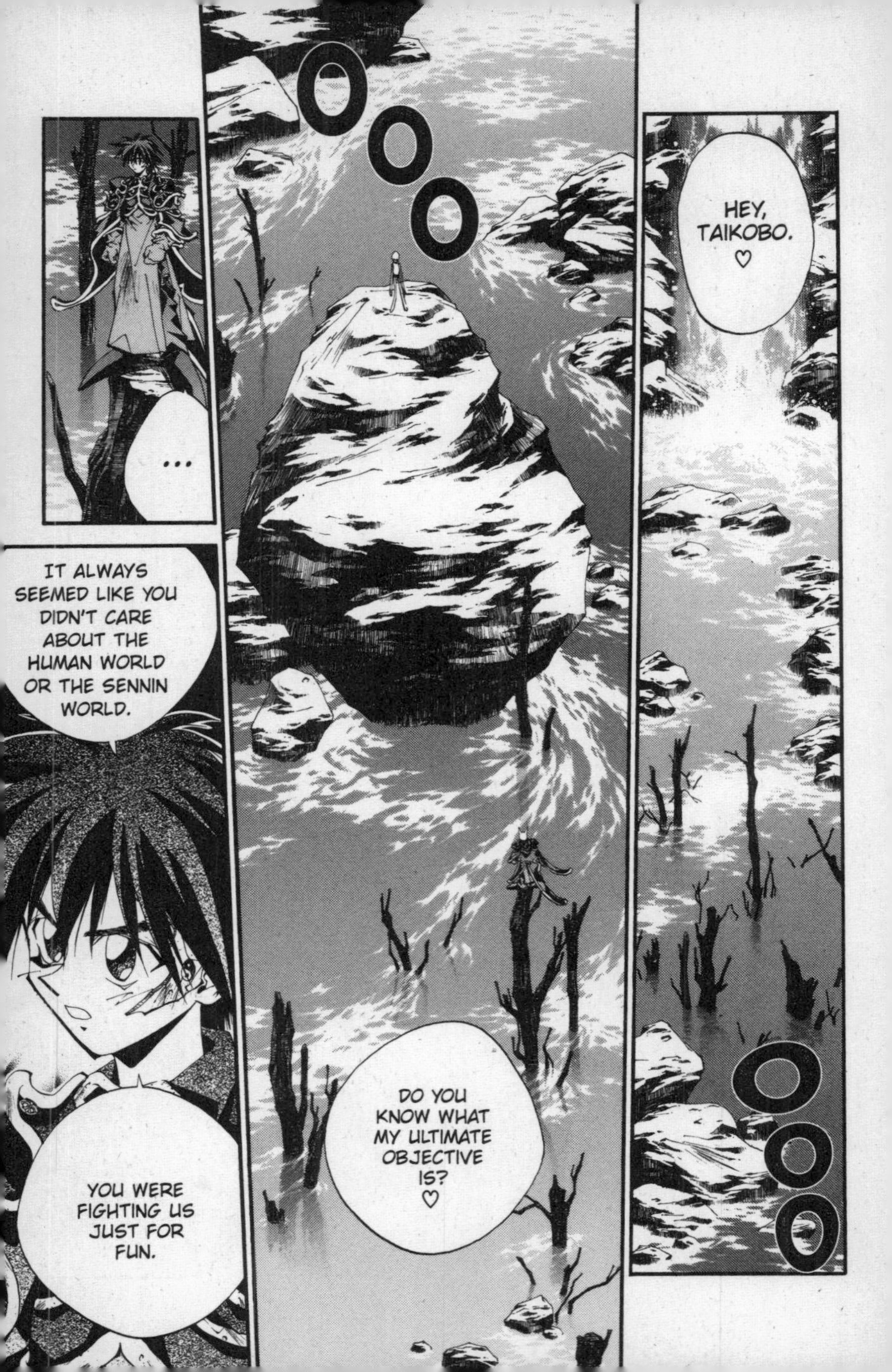
HEY, TAIKOBO. ♡
OOO
OOO
DO YOU KNOW WHAT MY ULTIMATE OBJECTIVE IS? ♡
...
IT ALWAYS SEEMED LIKE YOU DIDN'T CARE ABOUT THE HUMAN WORLD OR THE SENNIN WORLD.
YOU WERE FIGHTING US JUST FOR FUN.

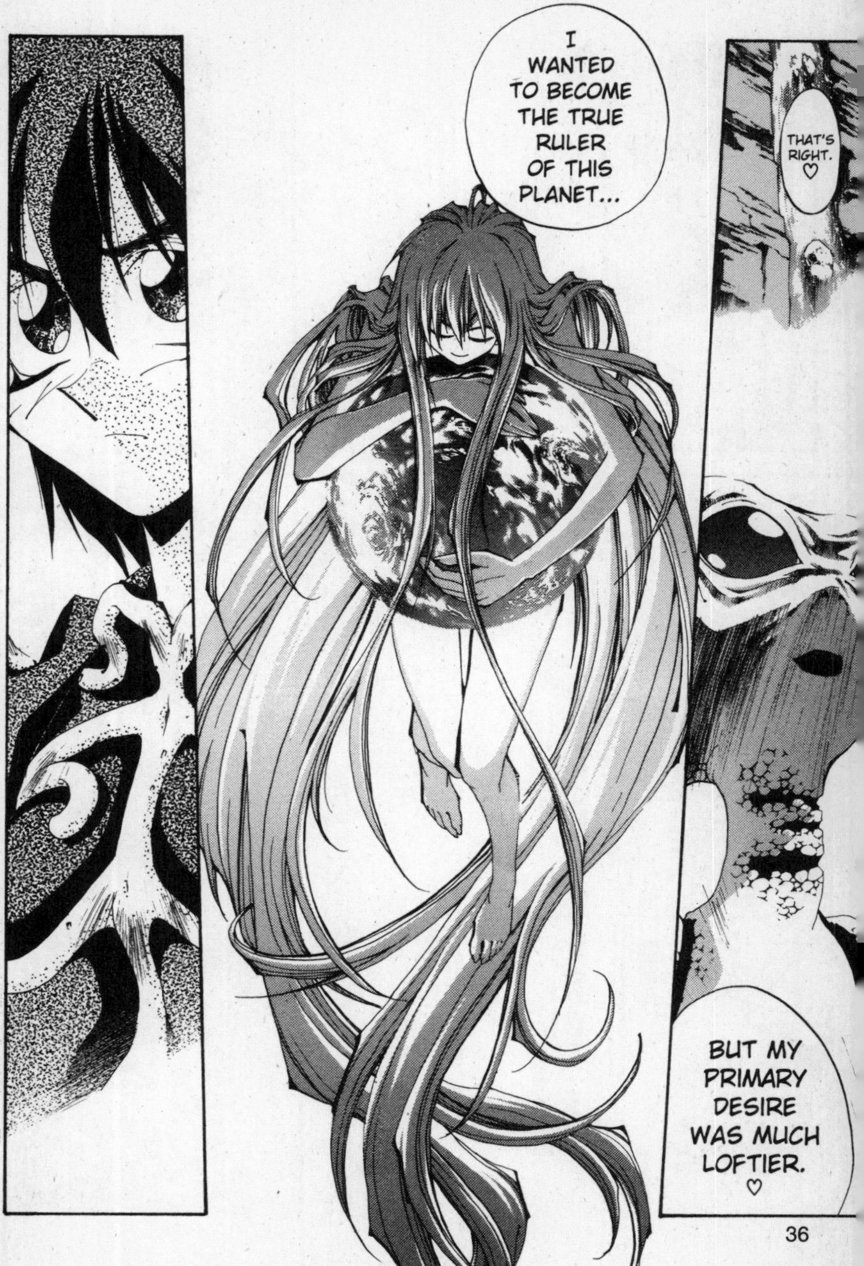
THAT'S RIGHT. ♡
I WANTED TO BECOME THE TRUE RULER OF THIS PLANET...
BUT MY PRIMARY DESIRE WAS MUCH LOFTIER. ♡

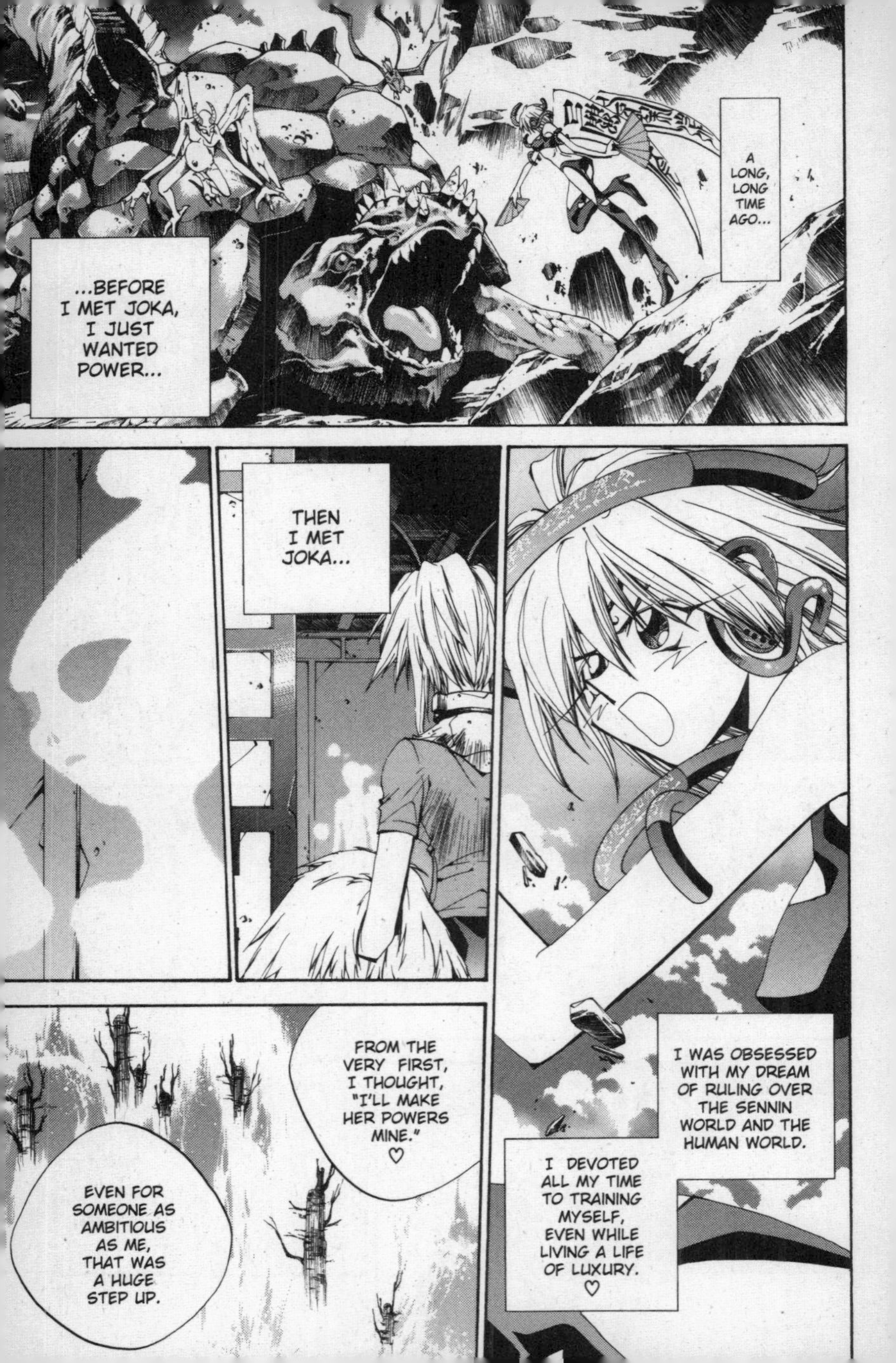
A LONG, LONG TIME AGO...
...BEFORE I MET JOKA, I JUST WANTED POWER...
I WAS OBSESSED WITH MY DREAM OF RULING OVER THE SENNIN WORLD AND THE HUMAN WORLD.
I DEVOTED ALL MY TIME TO TRAINING MYSELF, EVEN WHILE LIVING A LIFE OF LUXURY. ♡
THEN I MET JOKA...
FROM THE VERY FIRST, I THOUGHT, "I'LL MAKE HER POWERS MINE." ♡
EVEN FOR SOMEONE AS AMBITIOUS AS ME, THAT WAS A HUGE STEP UP.

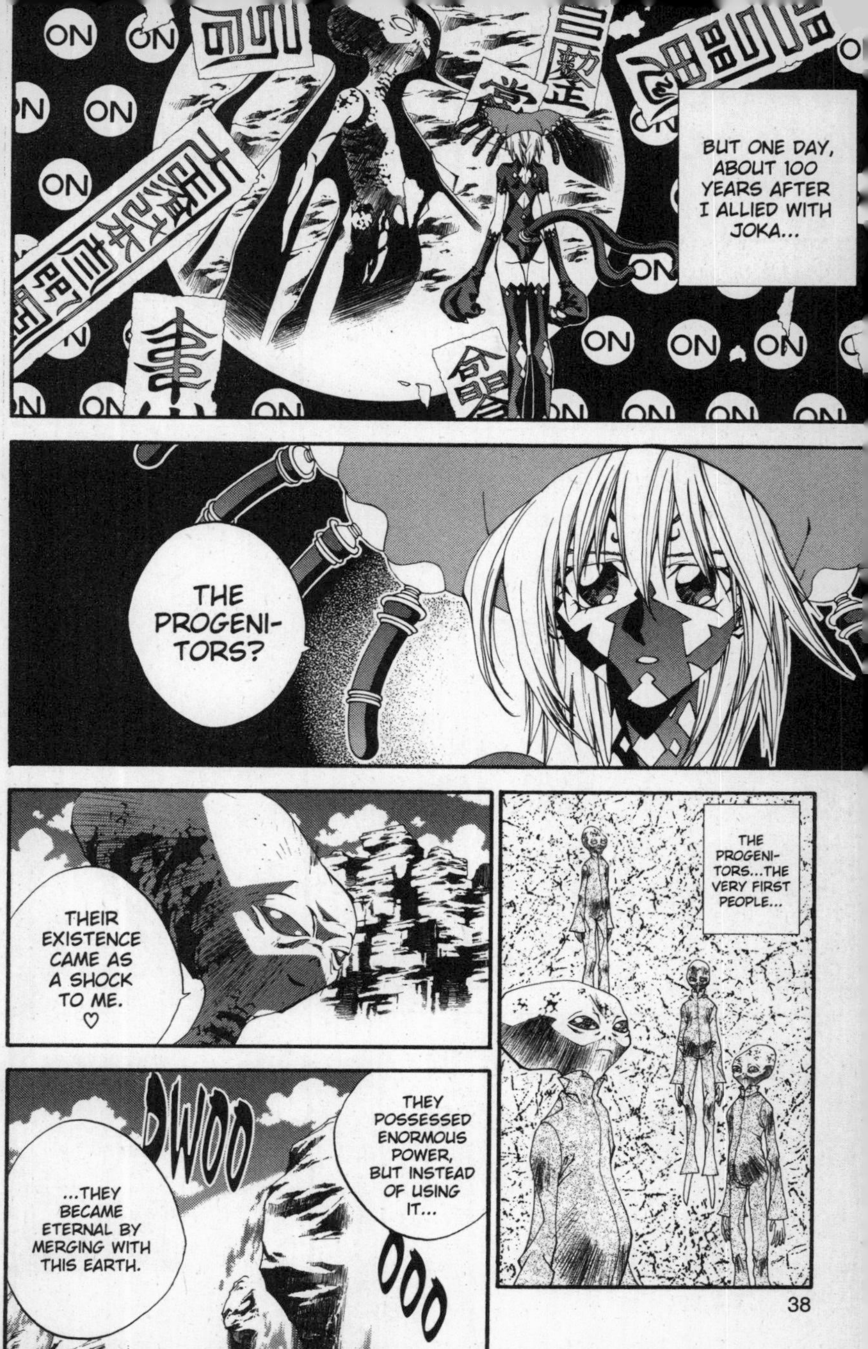
BUT ONE DAY, ABOUT 100 YEARS AFTER I ALLIED WITH JOKA...
THE PROGENI-TORS?
THE PROGENI-TORS...THE VERY FIRST PEOPLE...
THEIR EXISTENCE CAME AS A SHOCK TO ME. ♡
THEY POSSESSED ENORMOUS POWER, BUT INSTEAD OF USING IT...
DWOO
OOO
...THEY BECAME ETERNAL BY MERGING WITH THIS EARTH.

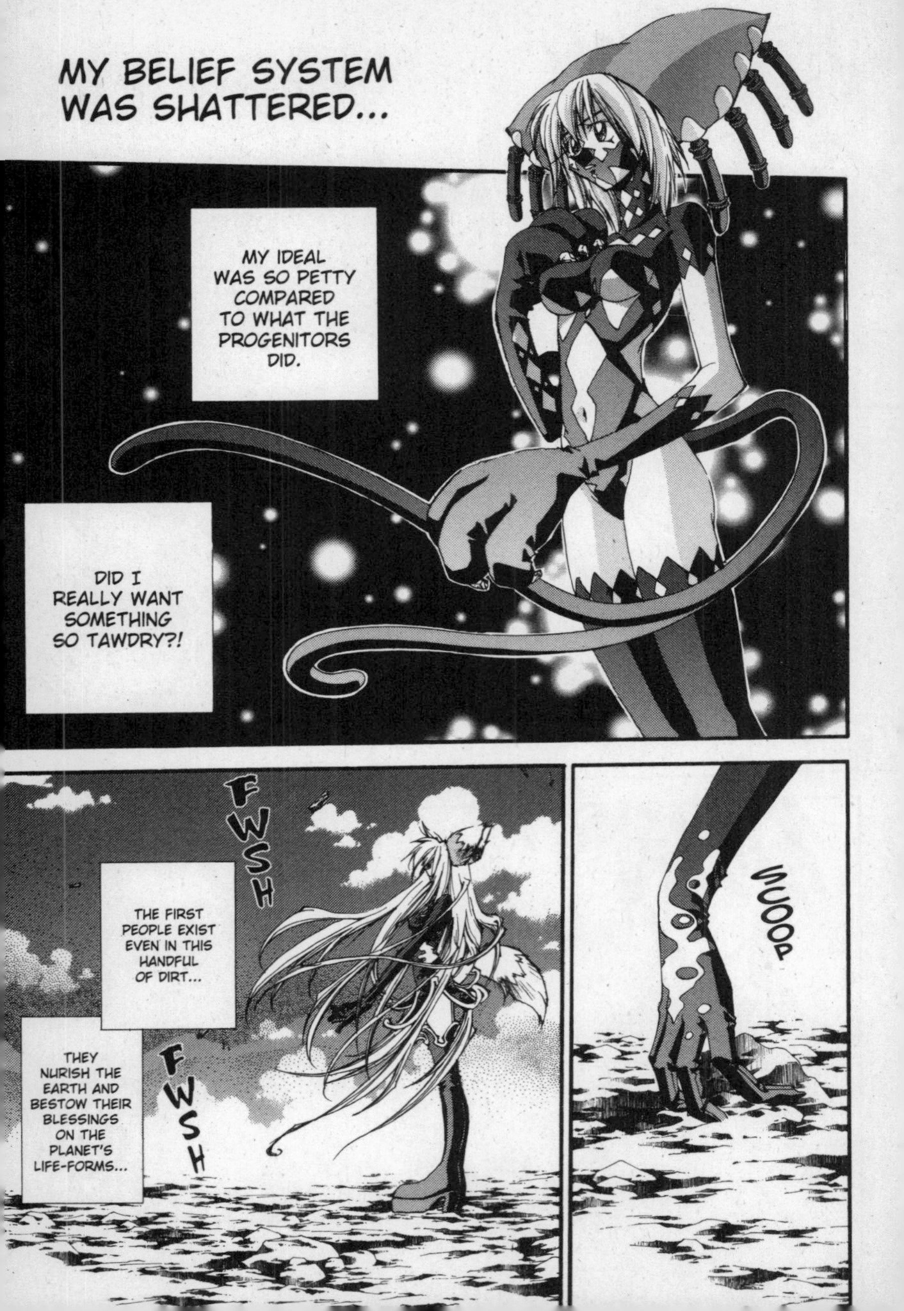
MY BELIEF SYSTEM WAS SHATTERED...
MY IDEAL WAS SO PETTY COMPARED TO WHAT THE PROGENITORS DID.
DID I REALLY WANT SOMETHING SO TAWDRY?!
SCOOP
FWSH
THE FIRST PEOPLE EXIST EVEN IN THIS HANDFUL OF DIRT...
FWSH
THEY NURISH THE EARTH AND BESTOW THEIR BLESSINGS ON THE PLANET'S LIFE-FORMS...

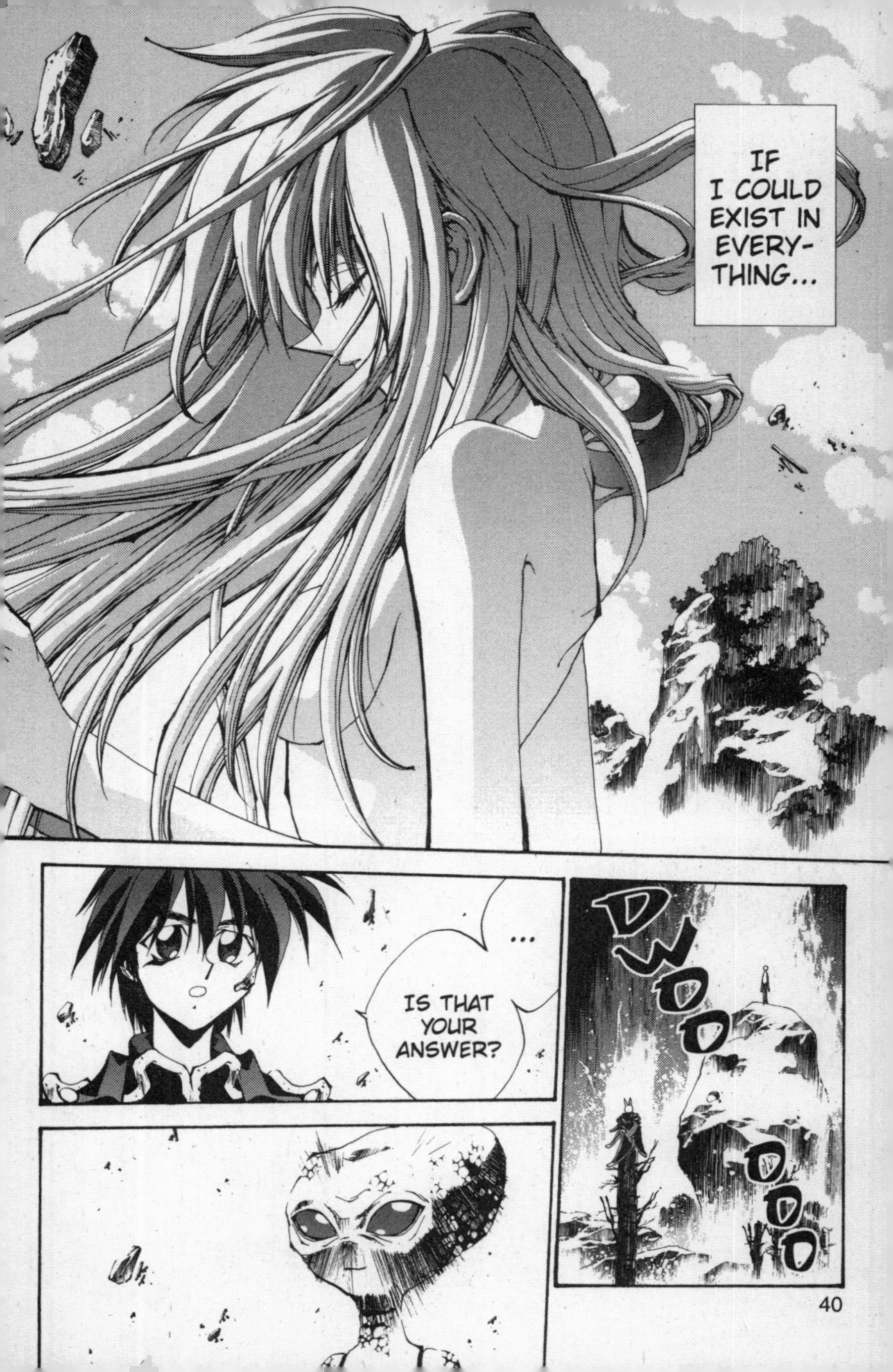
IF I COULD EXIST IN EVERY-THING...
...
IS THAT YOUR ANSWER?

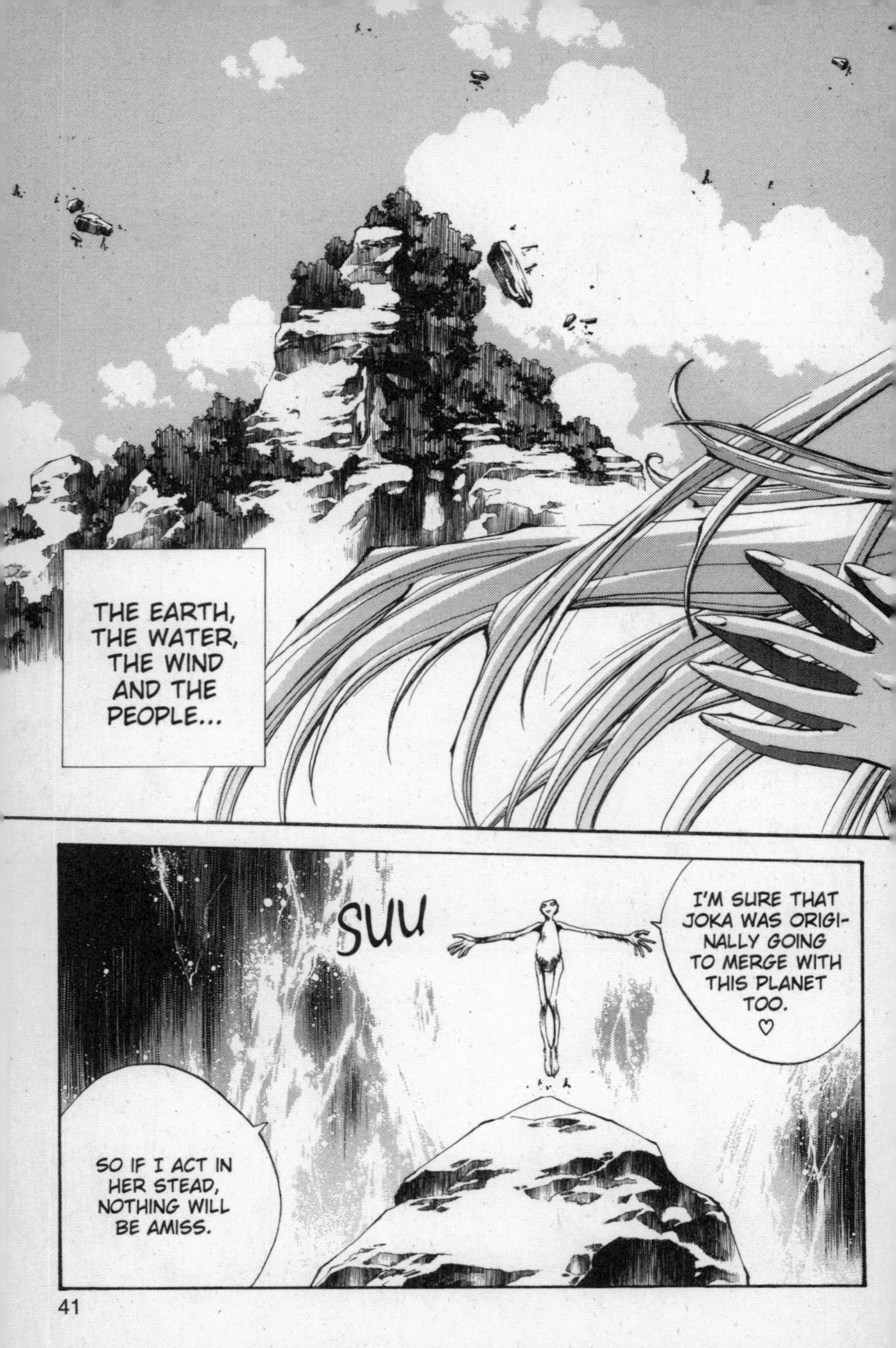
THE EARTH, THE WATER, THE WIND AND THE PEOPLE...
I'M SURE THAT JOKA WAS ORIGINALLY GOING TO MERGE WITH THIS PLANET TOO. ♡
SUU
SO IF I ACT IN HER STEAD, NOTHING WILL BE AMISS.

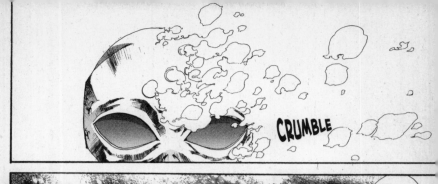

CRUMBLE

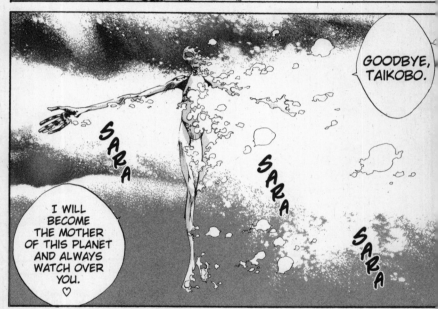

GOODBYE, TAIKOBO.

SARA

SARA

SARA

I WILL BECOME THE MOTHER OF THIS PLANET AND ALWAYS WATCH OVER YOU. ♡

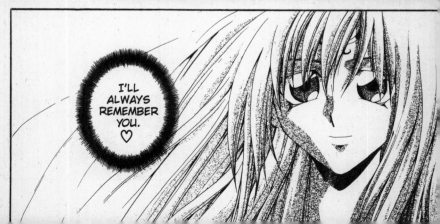

I'LL ALWAYS REMEMBER YOU. ♡

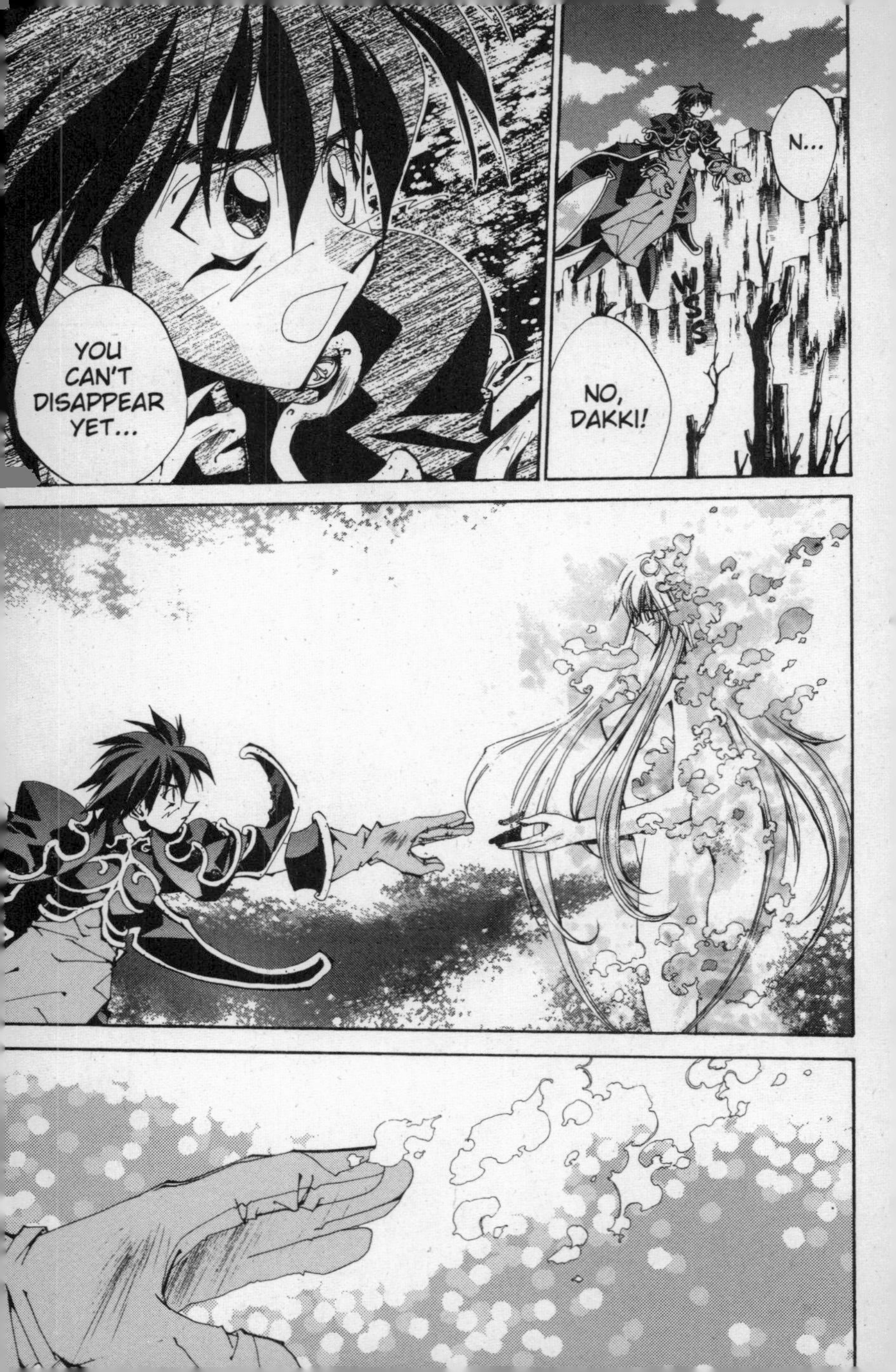
N...
WSS
NO, DAKKI!
YOU CAN'T DISAPPEAR YET...

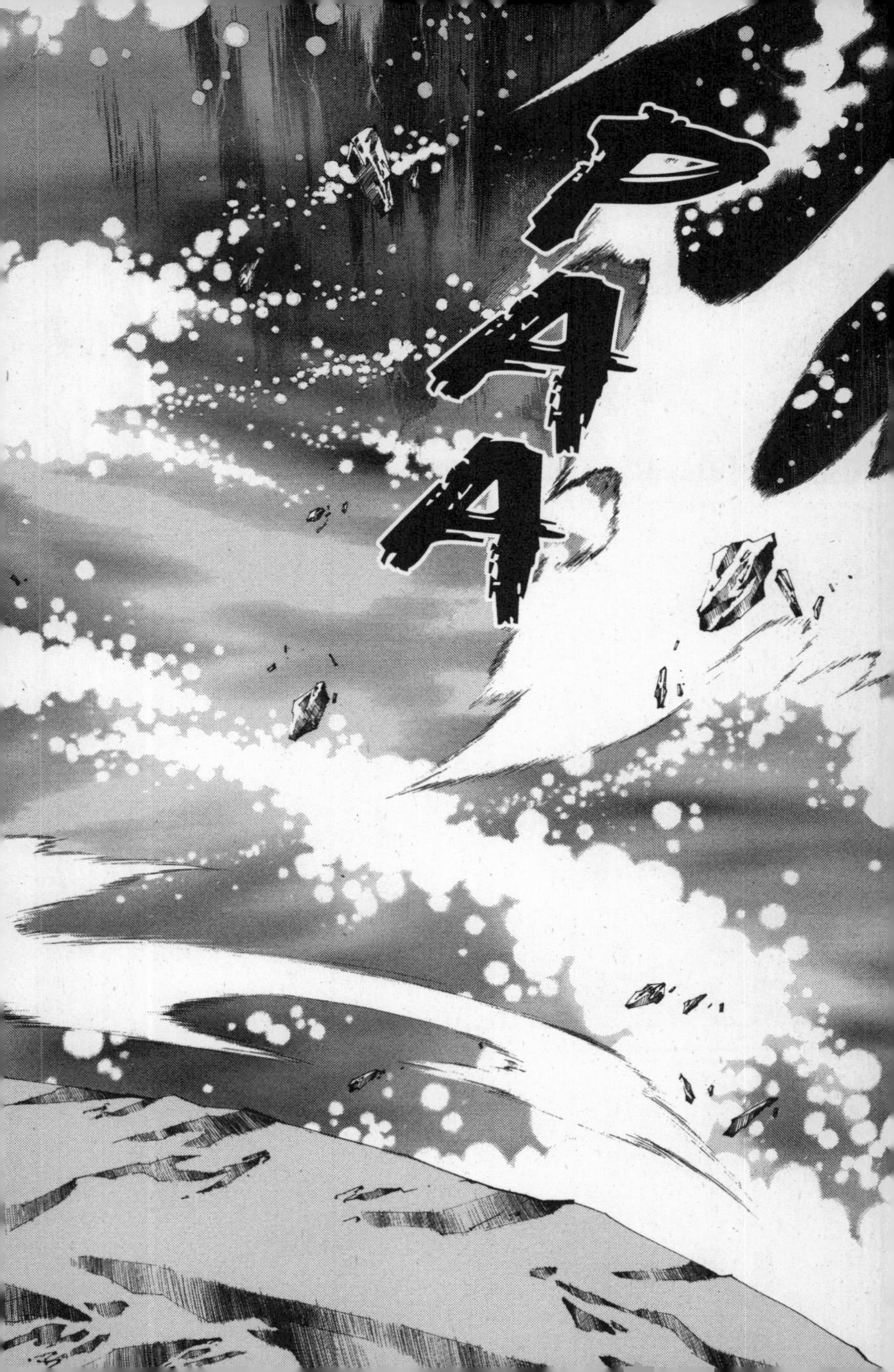
ドムム

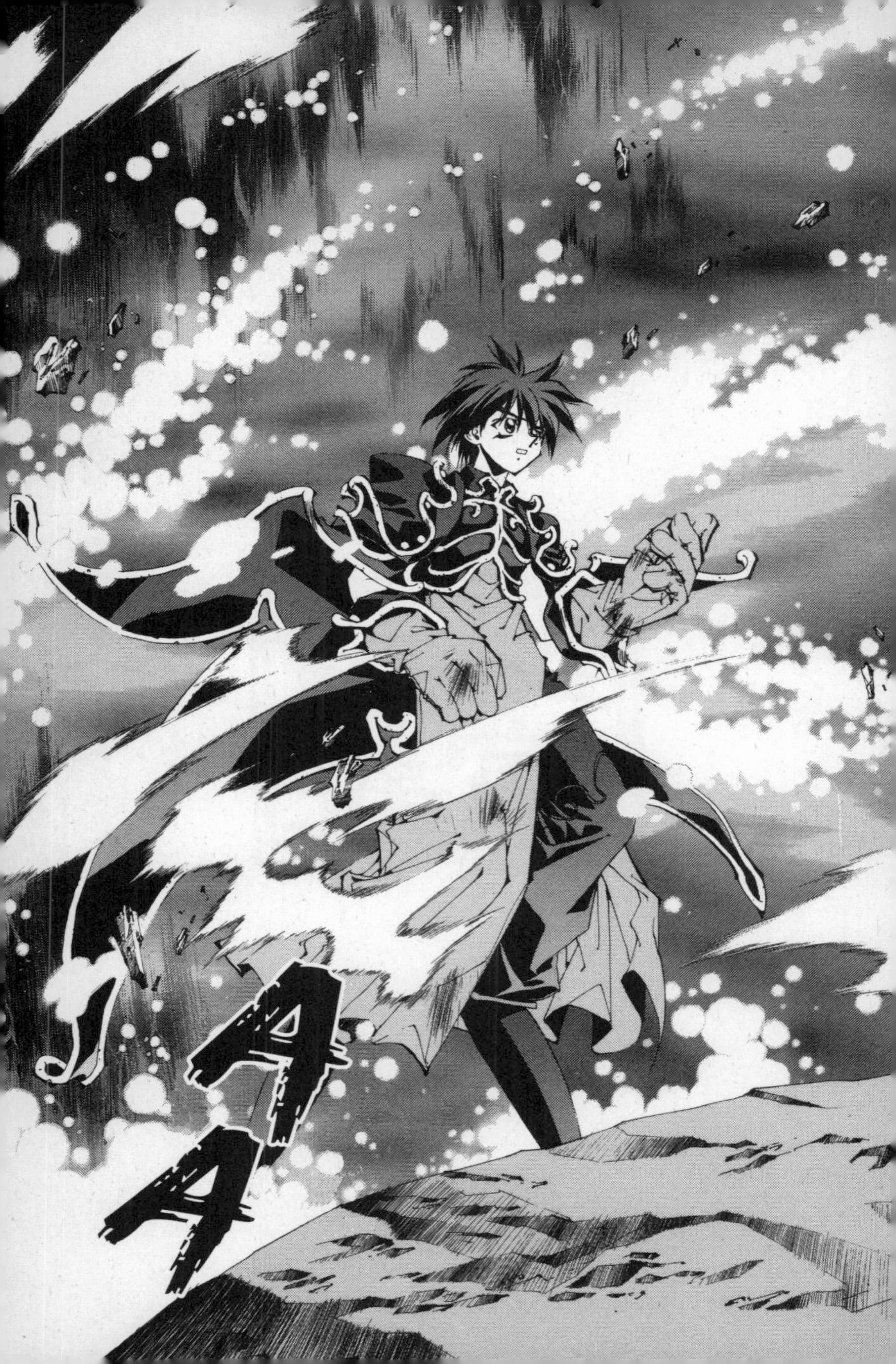

封神演義

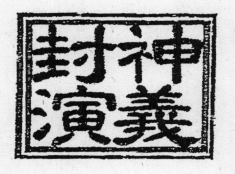

CHAPTER 198: THE GREAT MOTHER, PART 4
THE QUIET AWAKENING

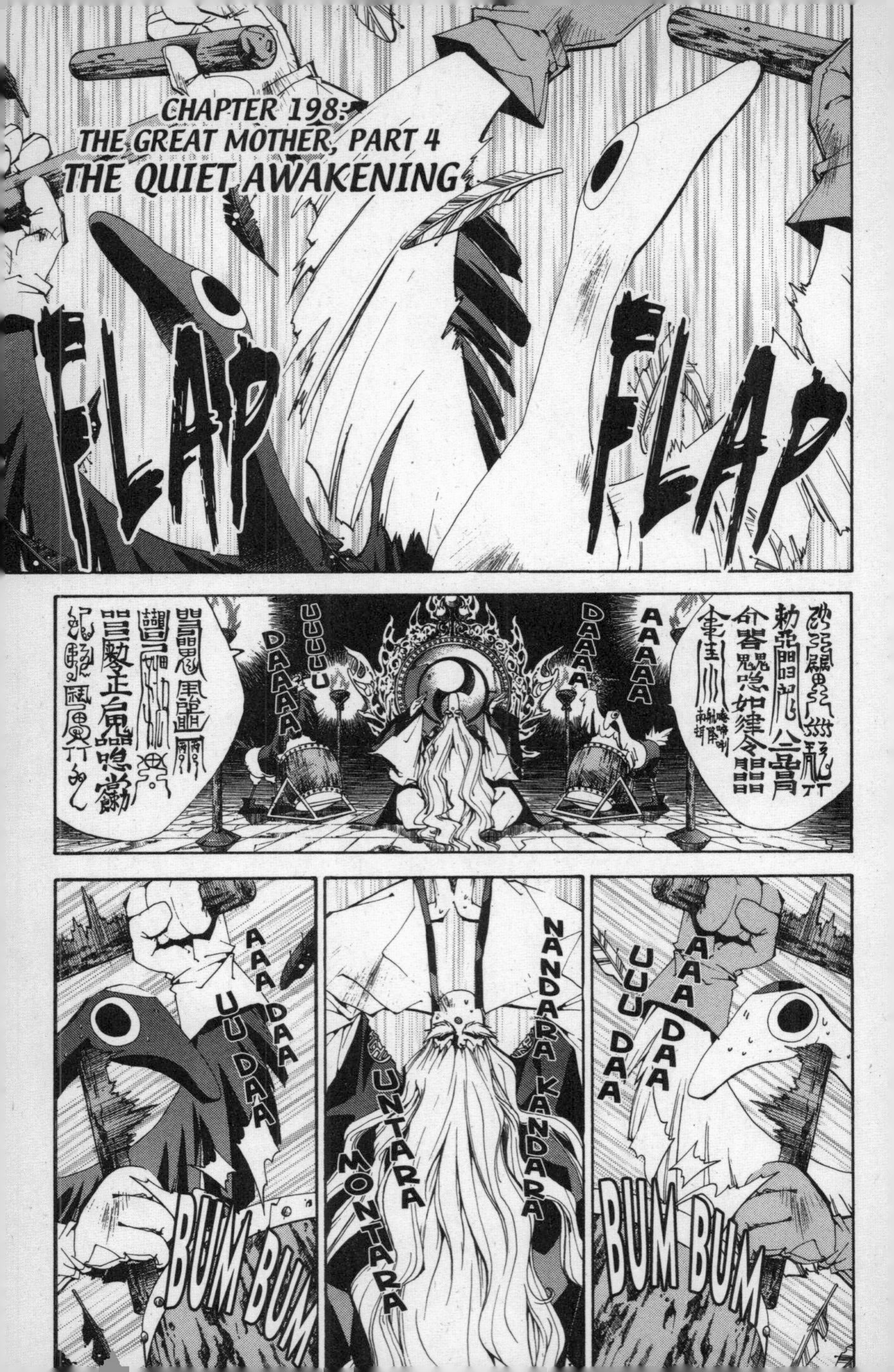
FLAP
FLAP
AAAAA
DAAAA
UUUUU
DAAAA
AAA DAA
UUU DAA
BUM BUM
NANDARA KANDARA
UNTARA
MONTARA
AAA DAA
UU DAA
BUM BUM

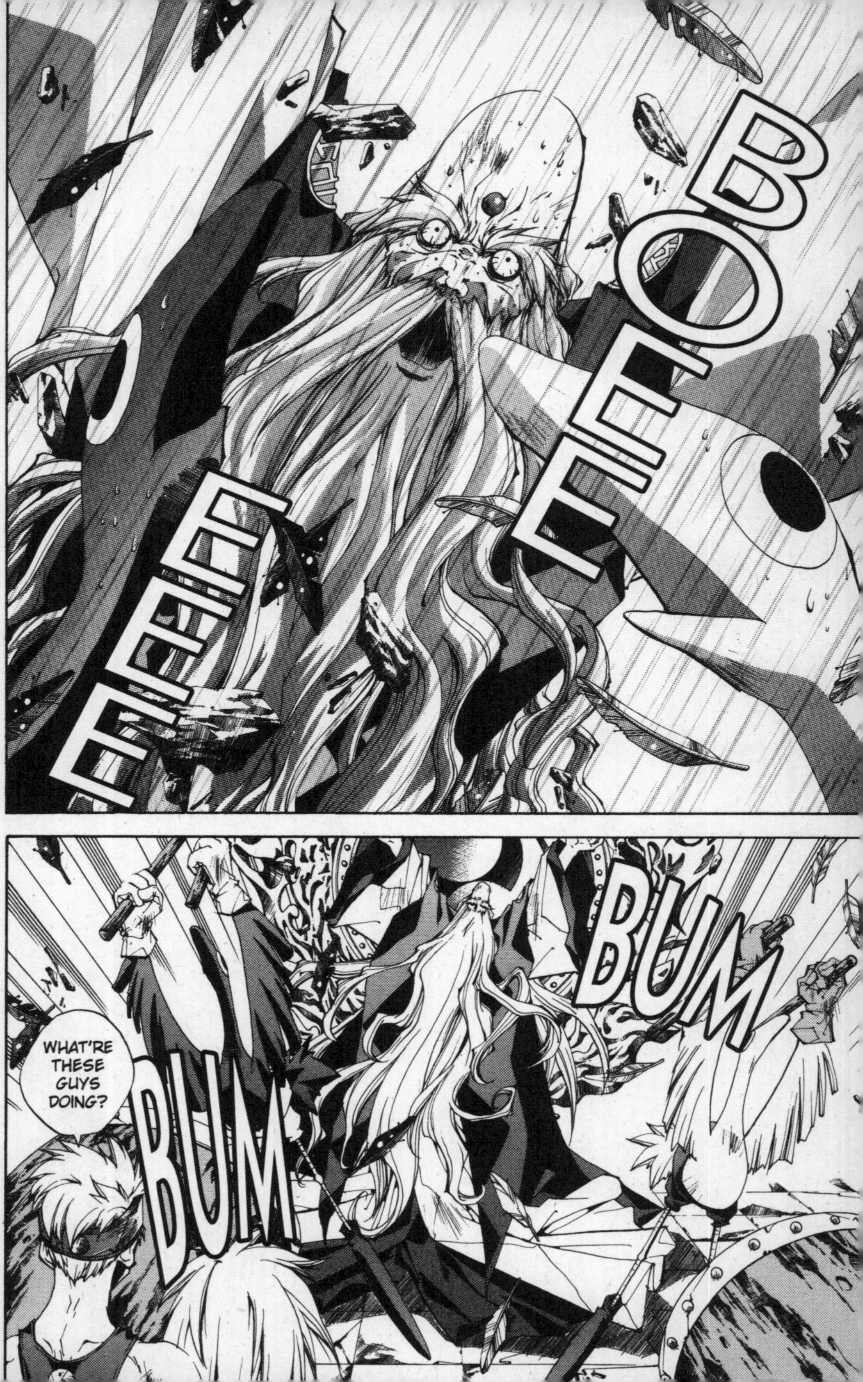
BOEEE
EEEE
BUM
WHAT'RE THESE GUYS DOING?
BUM

Chapter 198

THE GREAT MOTHER, PART 4
THE QUIET AWAKENING

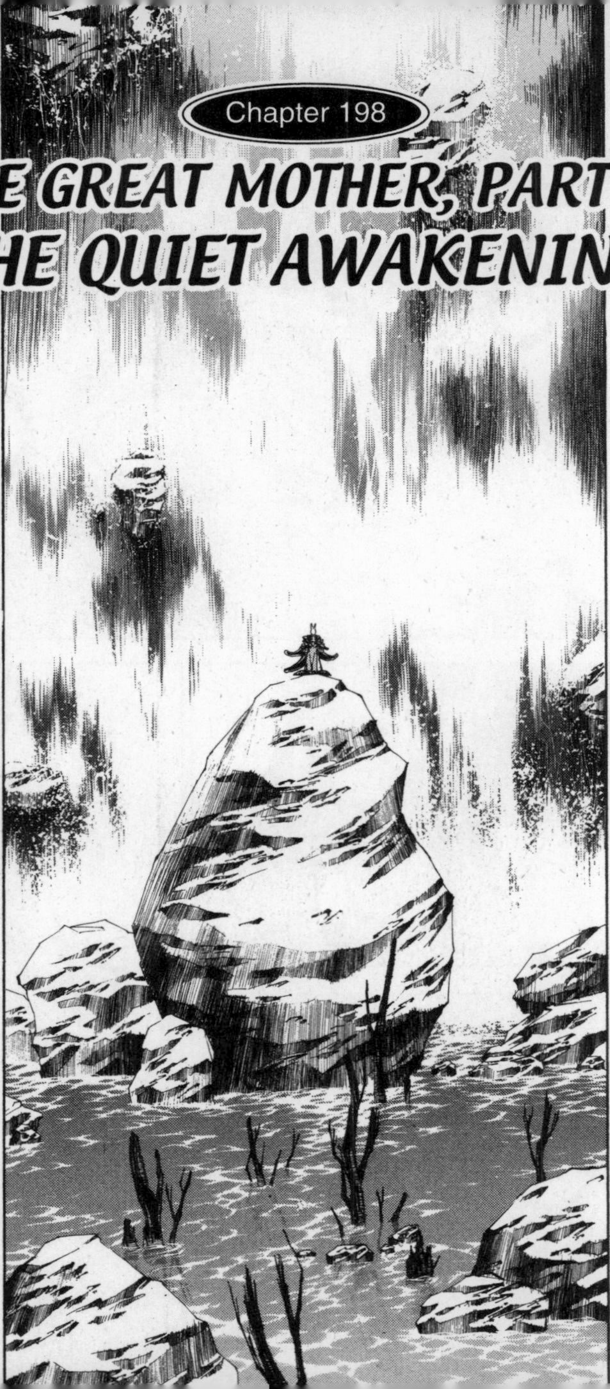

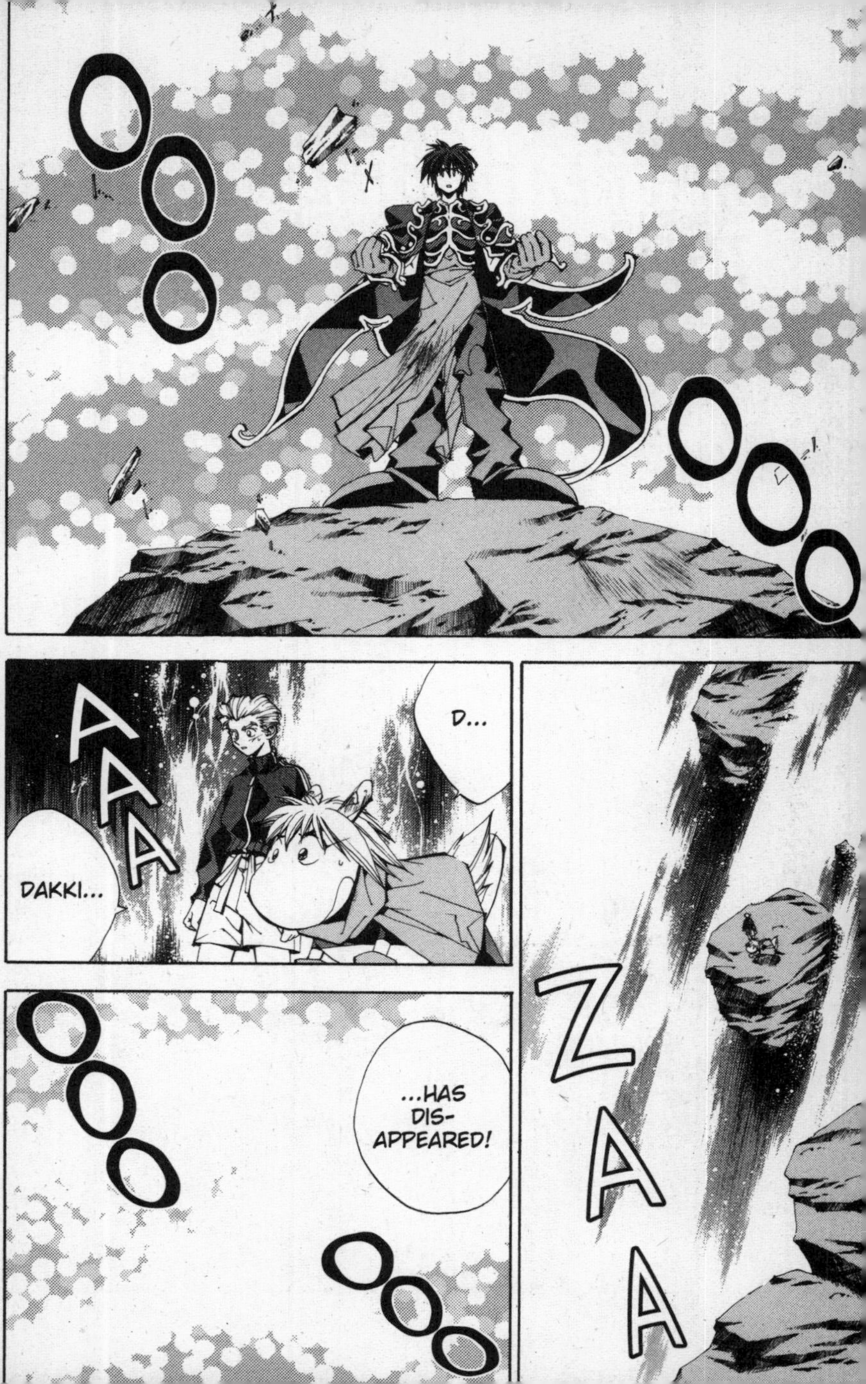
OOOOOOO
ZAAA
AAA
DAKKI...
D...
...HAS DIS-APPEARED!
OOOOOOO

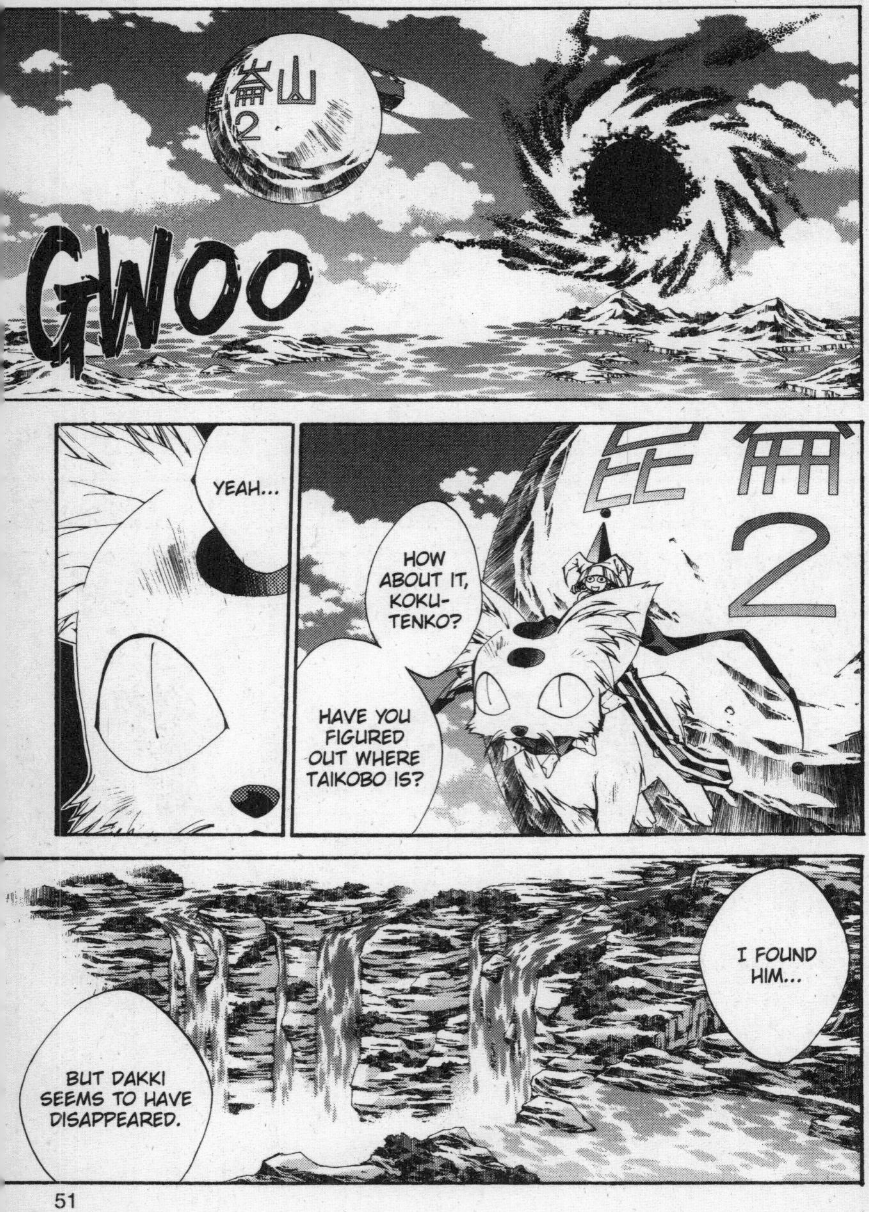
READ THIS WAY
GWOO
HOW ABOUT IT, KOKU-TENKO?
HAVE YOU FIGURED OUT WHERE TAIKOBO IS?
YEAH...
I FOUND HIM...
BUT DAKKI SEEMS TO HAVE DISAPPEARED.

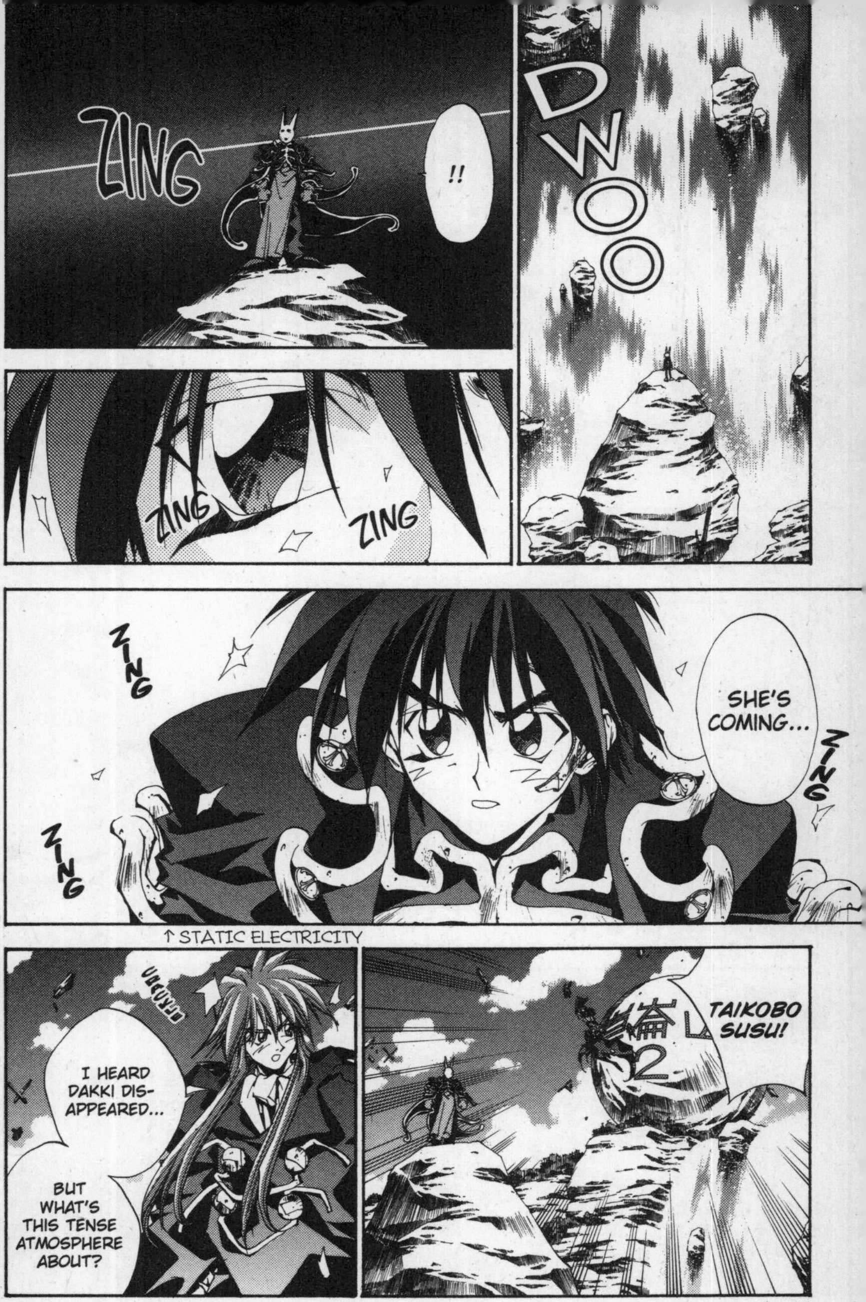

DWOOO
ZING
!!
ZING
ZING
ZING
SHE'S COMING...
ZING
ZING
↑ STATIC ELECTRICITY
TAIKOBO SUSU!
I HEARD DAKKI DIS-APPEARED...
BUT WHAT'S THIS TENSE ATMOSPHERE ABOUT?

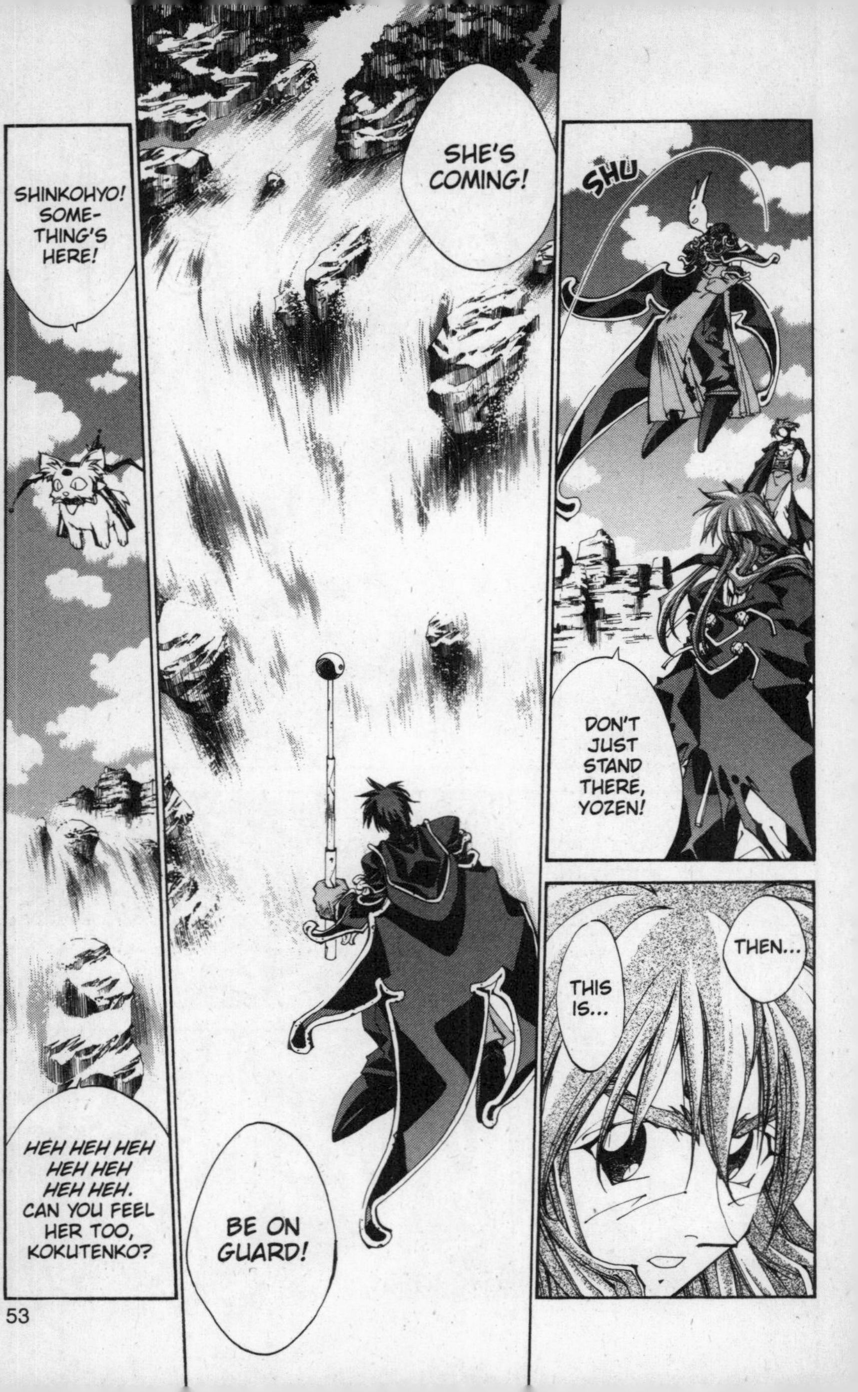
SHU
DON'T JUST STAND THERE, YOZEN!
THEN...
THIS IS...
SHE'S COMING!
BE ON GUARD!
SHINKOHYO! SOME-THING'S HERE!
HEH HEH HEH HEH HEH HEH HEH. CAN YOU FEEL HER TOO, KOKUTENKO?

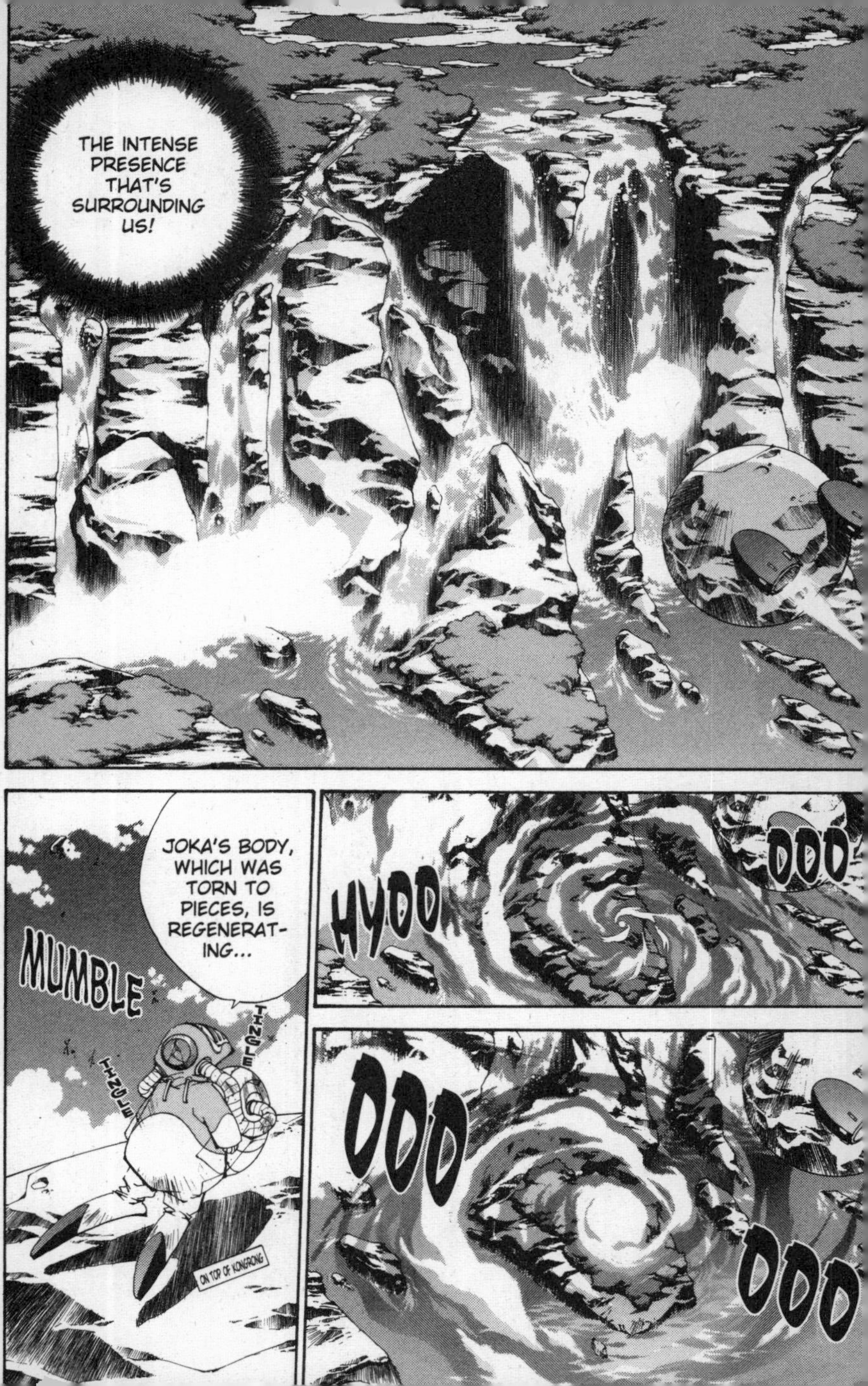
THE INTENSE PRESENCE THAT'S SURROUNDING US!
ODD
HYDD
JOKA'S BODY, WHICH WAS TORN TO PIECES, IS REGENERATING...
MUMBLE
TINGLE
TINGLE
ON TOP OF KONGRONG
DDD
DDD

READ THIS WAY

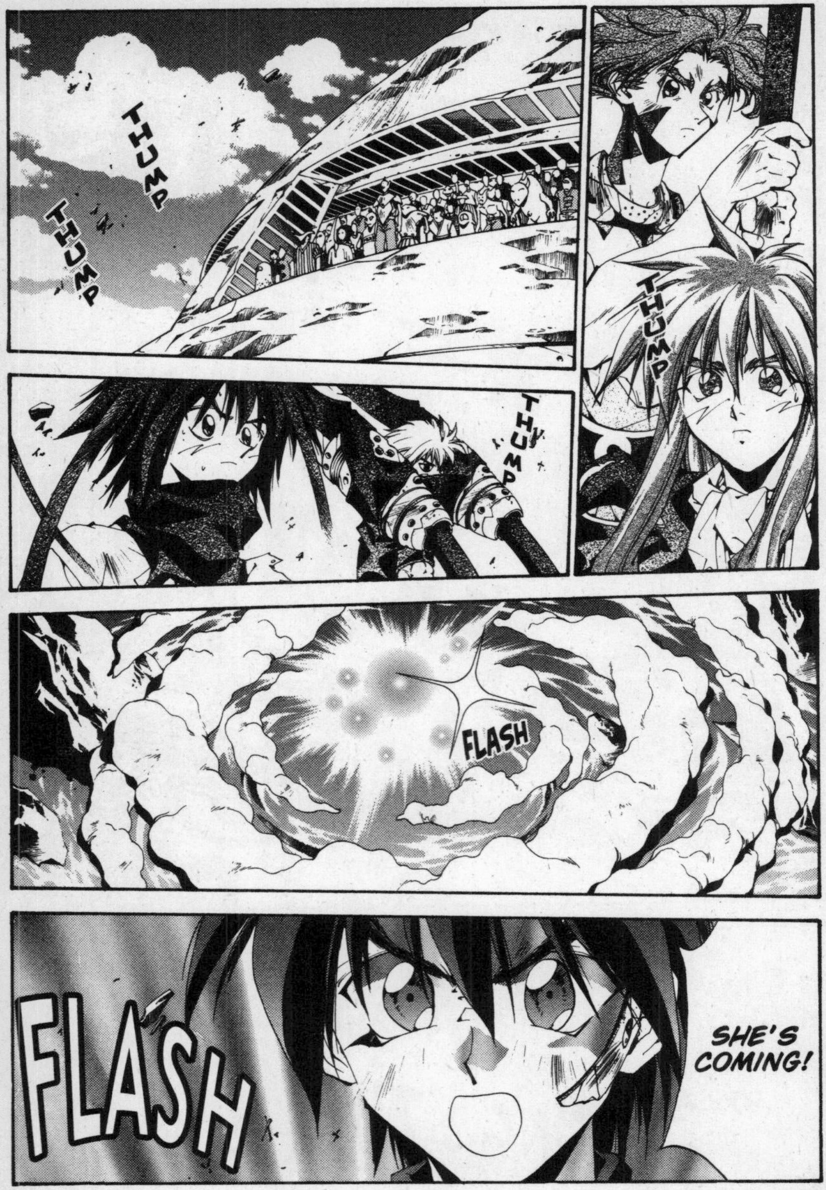
THUMP
THUMP
THUMP
THUMP
FLASH
FLASH
SHE'S COMING!

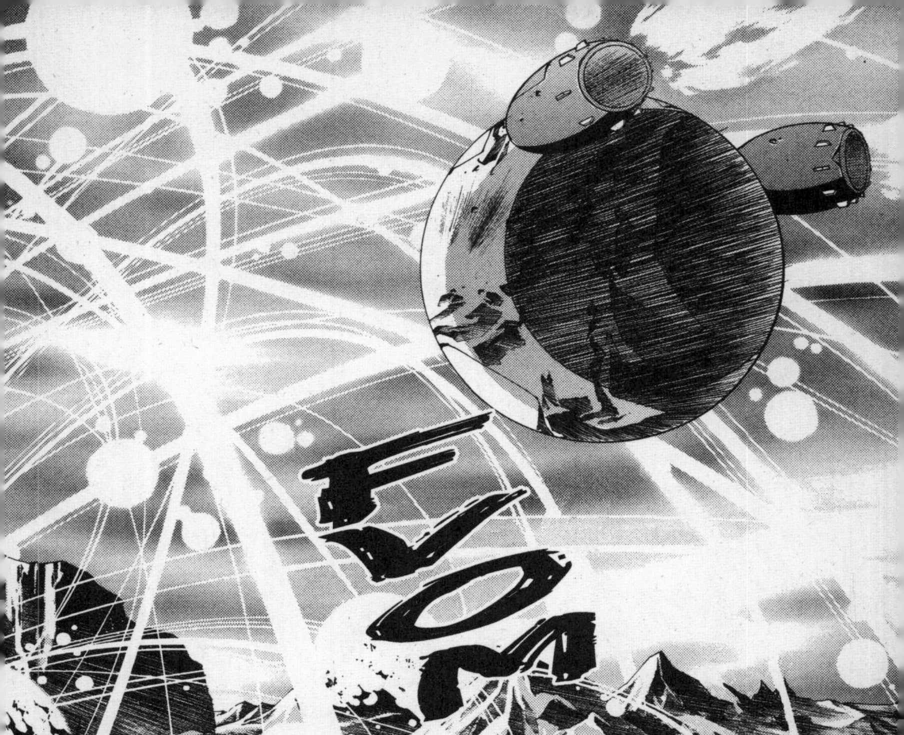

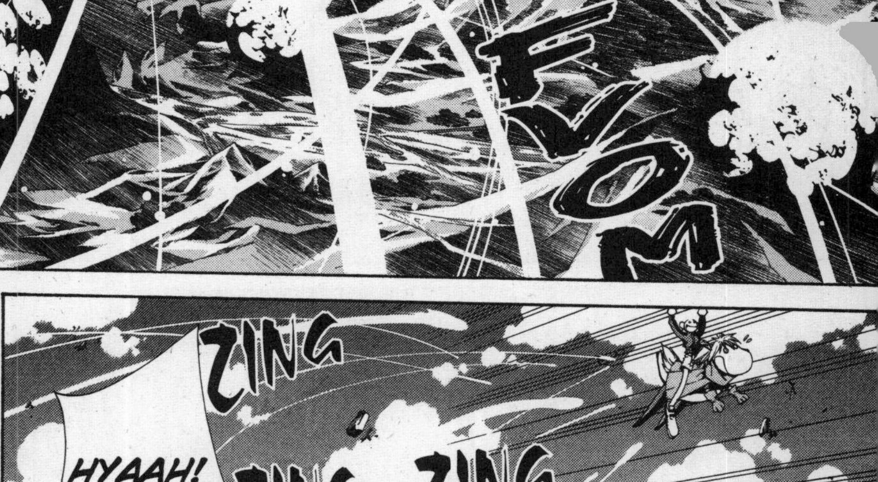
ZING
ZING ZING
HYAAH!

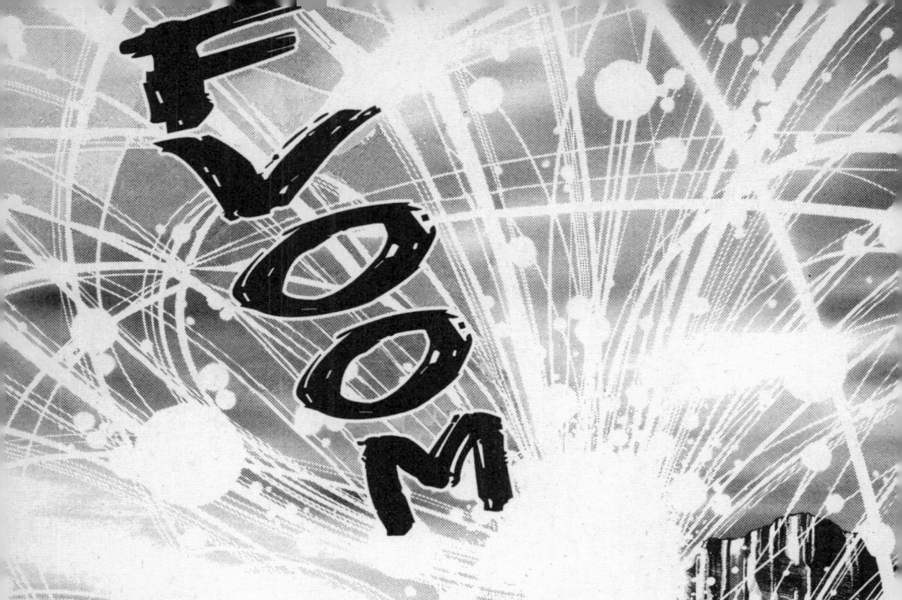
FOOM

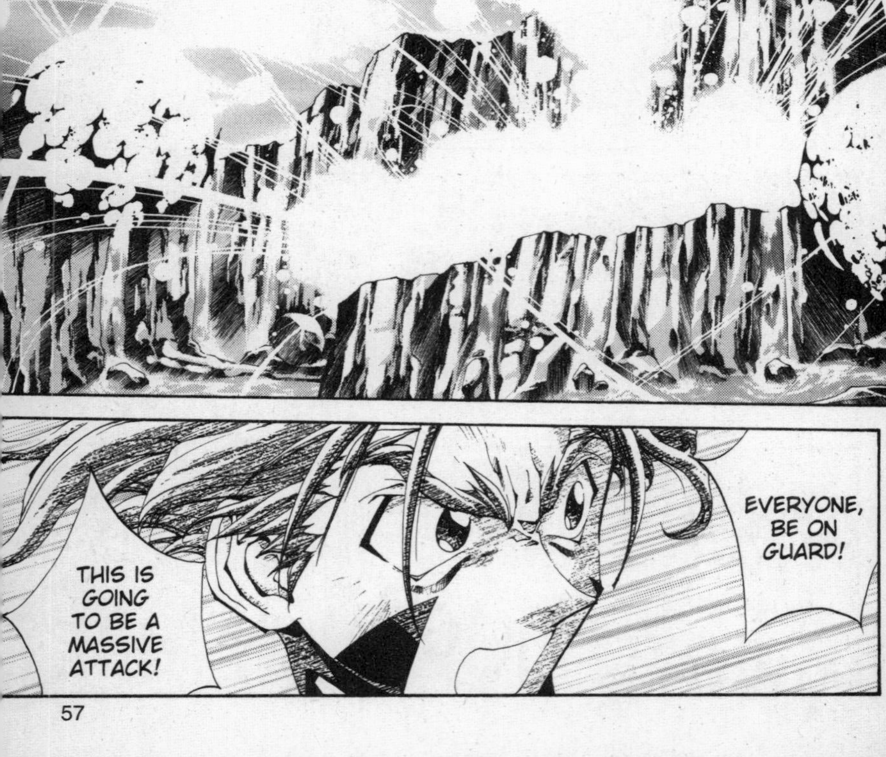
EVERYONE, BE ON GUARD!
THIS IS GOING TO BE A MASSIVE ATTACK!

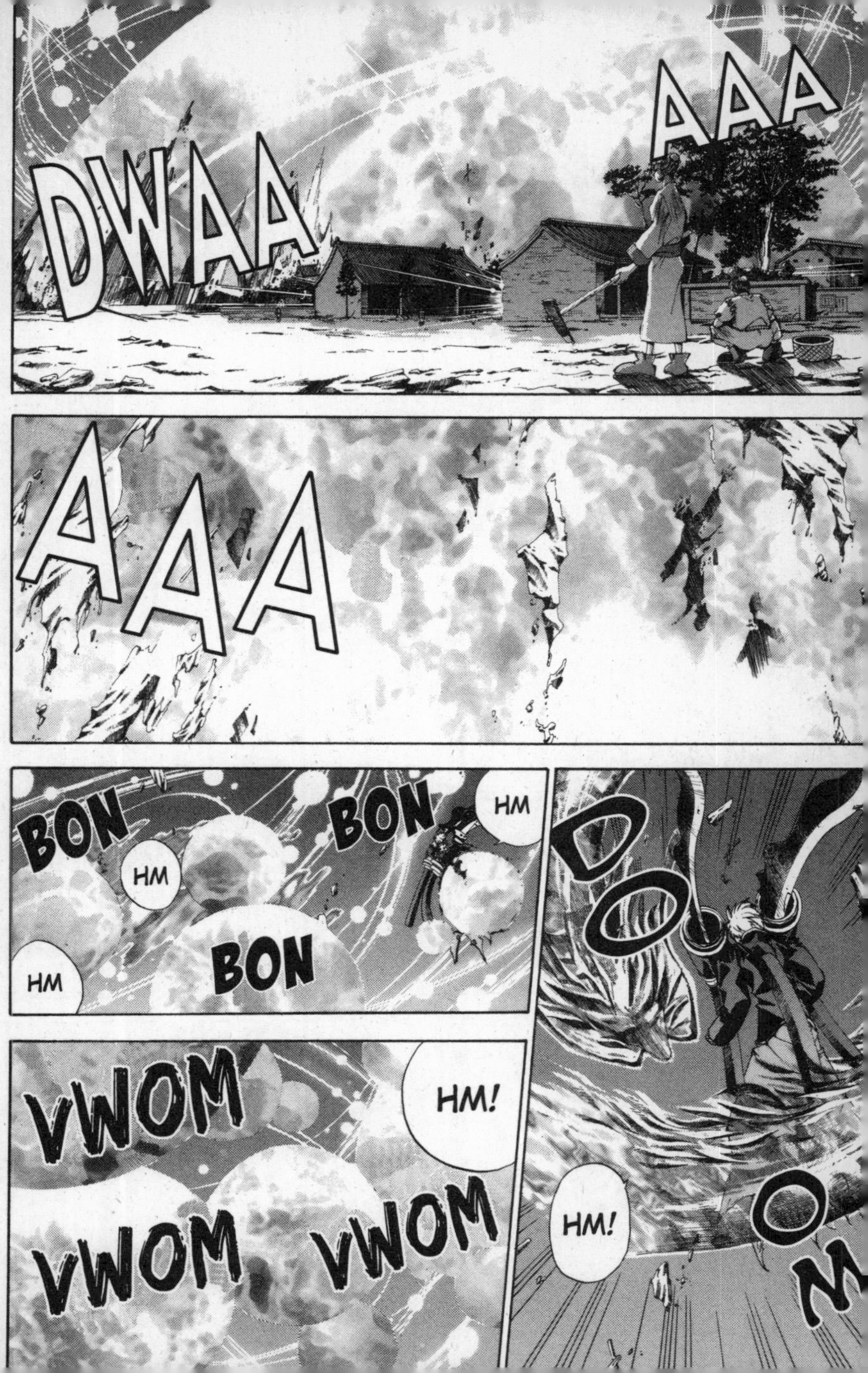
DWAA
AAA
AAA
DO
O
M
HM!
BON
HM
BON
HM
BON
HM
VWOM
HM!
VWOM
VWOM

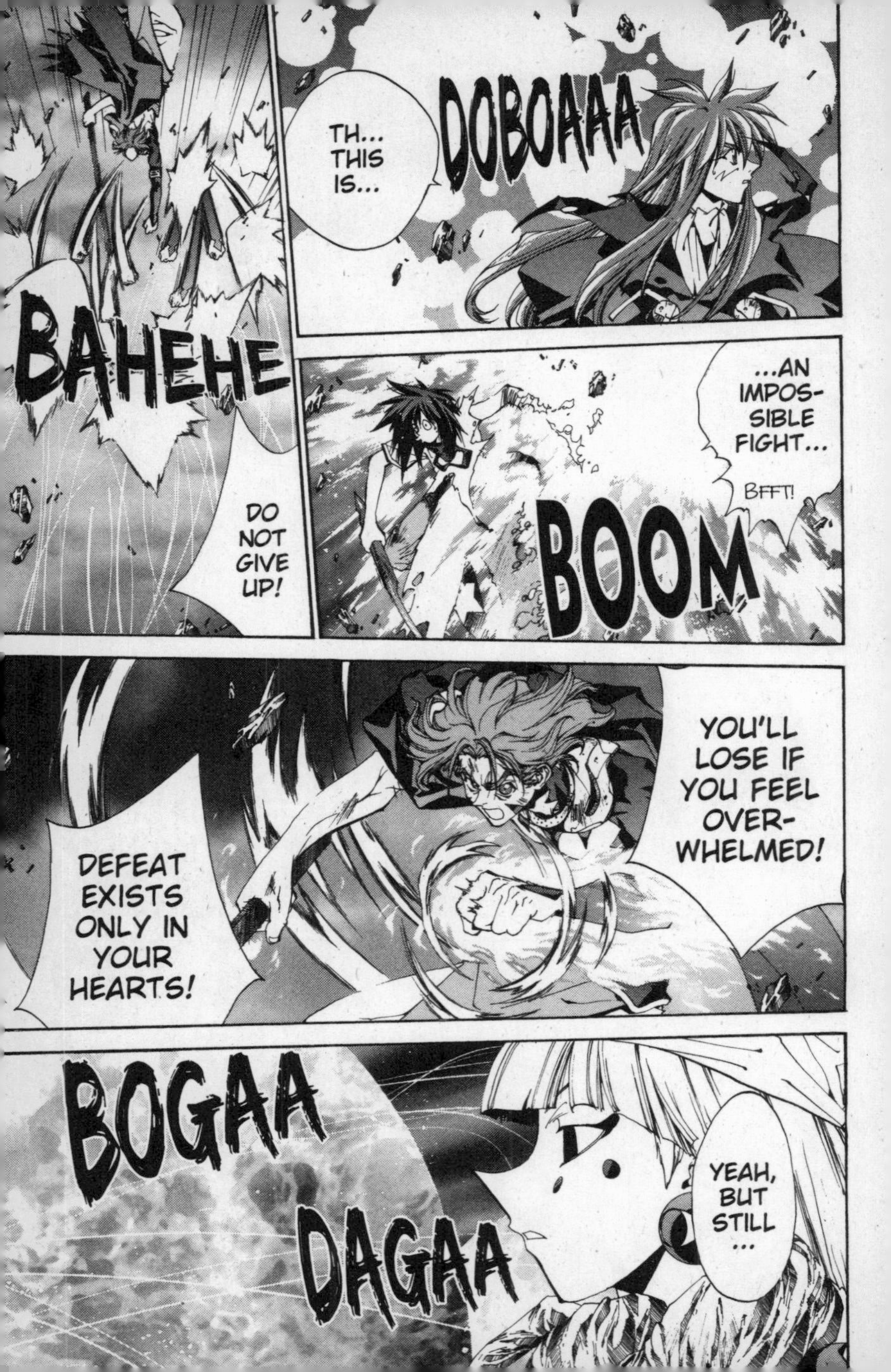
TH... THIS IS...
DOBOAAA
...AN IMPOSSIBLE FIGHT...
BFFT!
BOOM
BAHEHE
DO NOT GIVE UP!
YOU'LL LOSE IF YOU FEEL OVERWHELMED!
DEFEAT EXISTS ONLY IN YOUR HEARTS!
BOGAA
YEAH, BUT STILL...
DAGAA

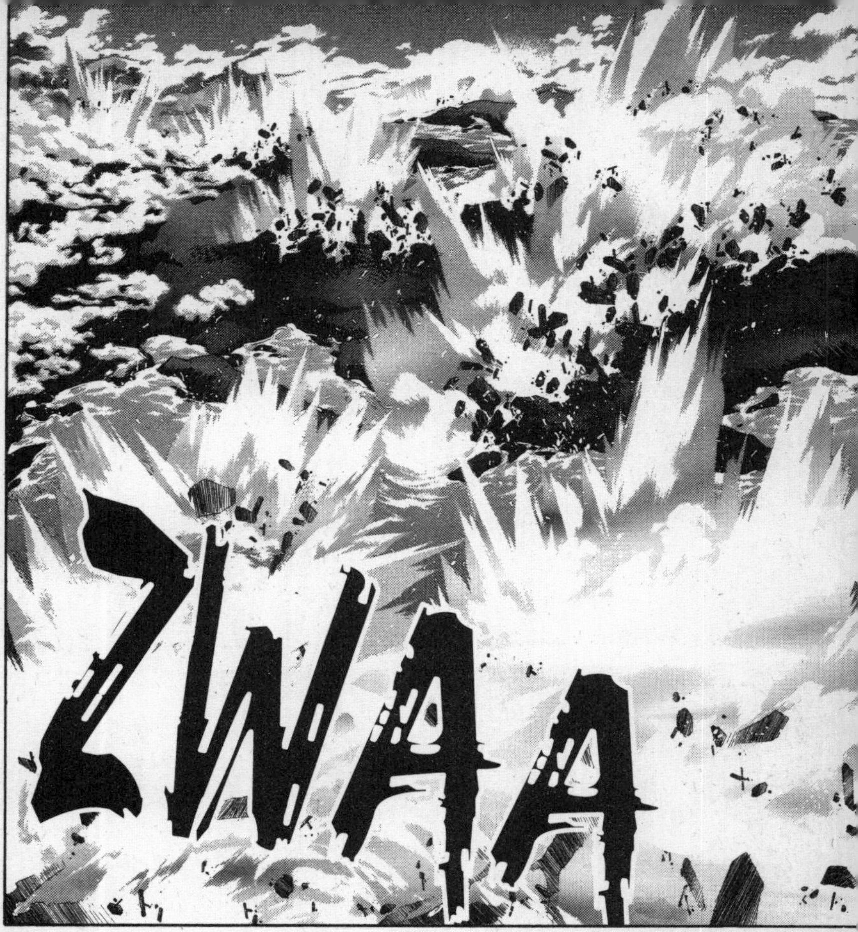
ZWAA

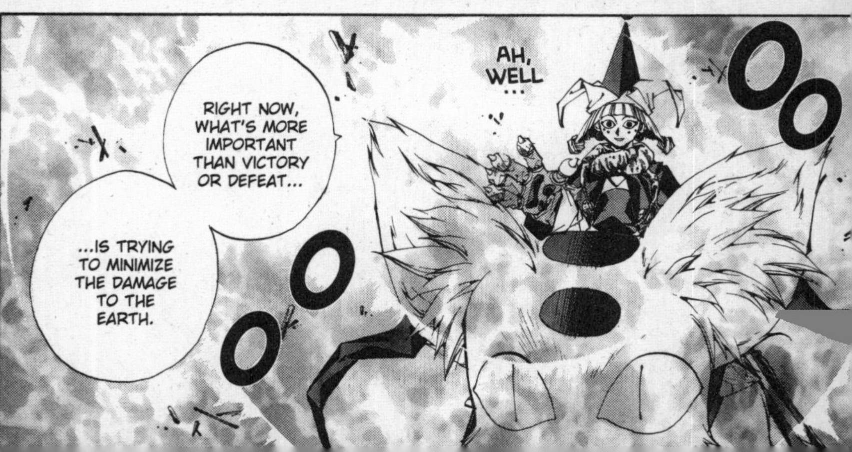
OOOO
AH, WELL...
RIGHT NOW, WHAT'S MORE IMPORTANT THAN VICTORY OR DEFEAT...
...IS TRYING TO MINIMIZE THE DAMAGE TO THE EARTH.

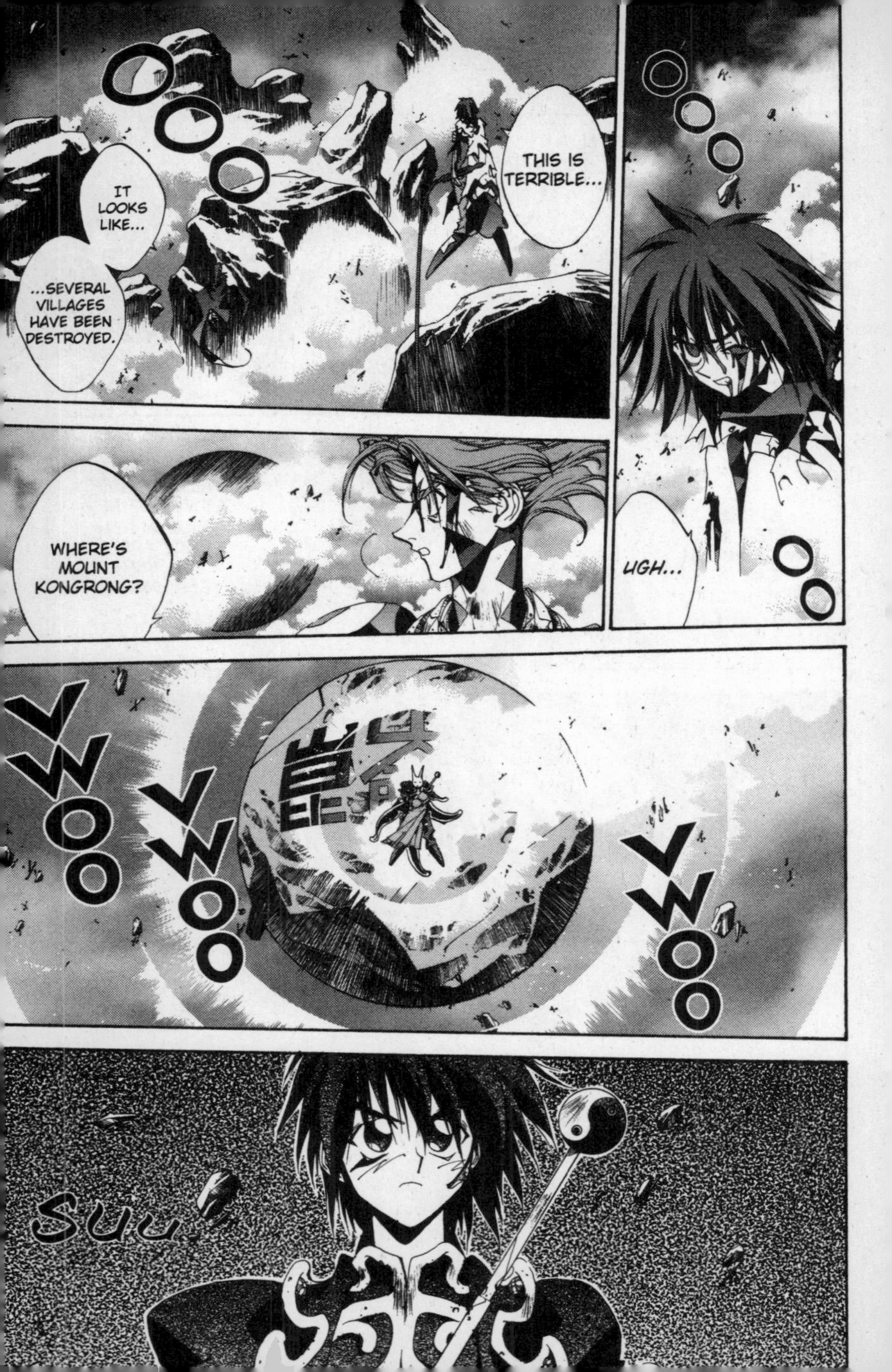

OOOO
UGH...
OO
THIS IS TERRIBLE...
OOOO
IT LOOKS LIKE...
...SEVERAL VILLAGES HAVE BEEN DESTROYED.
WHERE'S MOUNT KONGRONG?
VWOO
VWOO
VWOO
SUU

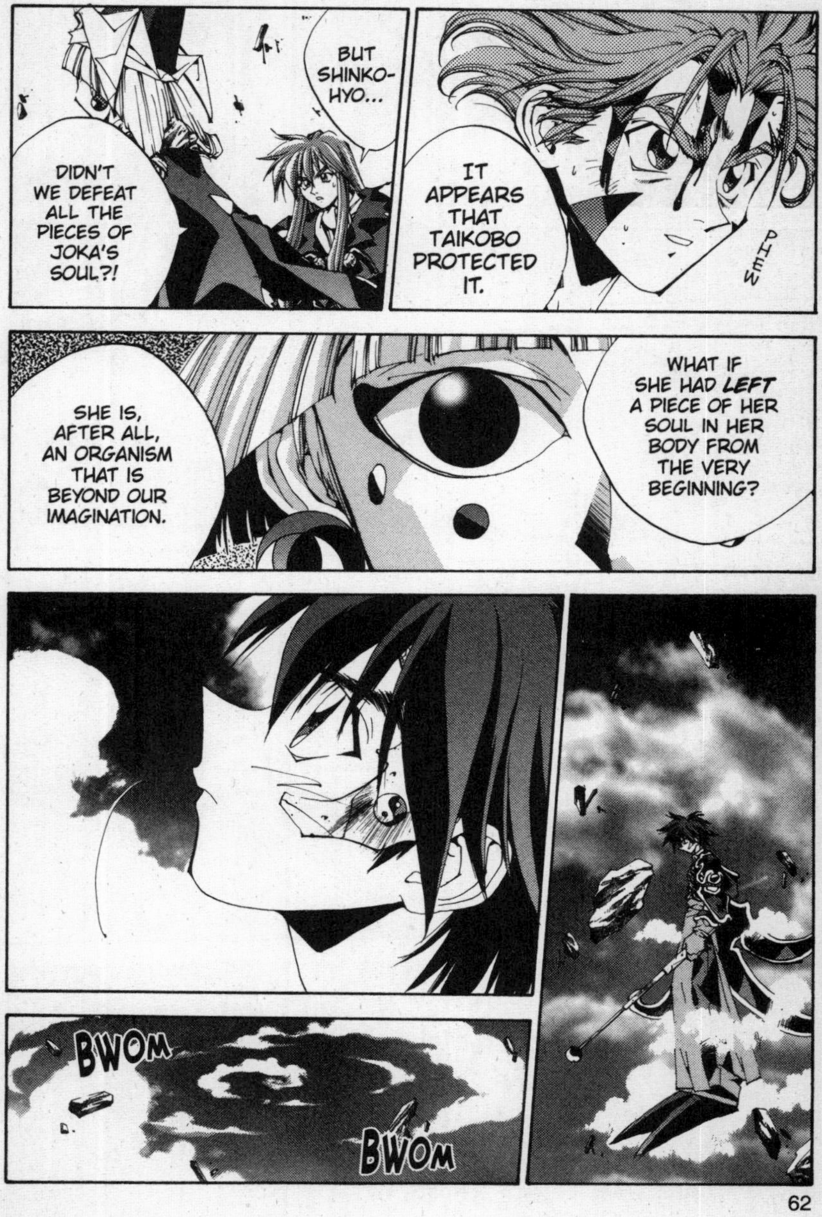
IT APPEARS THAT TAIKOBO PROTECTED IT.
PHEW
BUT SHINKO-HYO...
DIDN'T WE DEFEAT ALL THE PIECES OF JOKA'S SOUL?!
WHAT IF SHE HAD *LEFT* A PIECE OF HER SOUL IN HER BODY FROM THE VERY BEGINNING?
SHE IS, AFTER ALL, AN ORGANISM THAT IS BEYOND OUR IMAGINATION.
BWOM
BWOM

READ THIS WAY

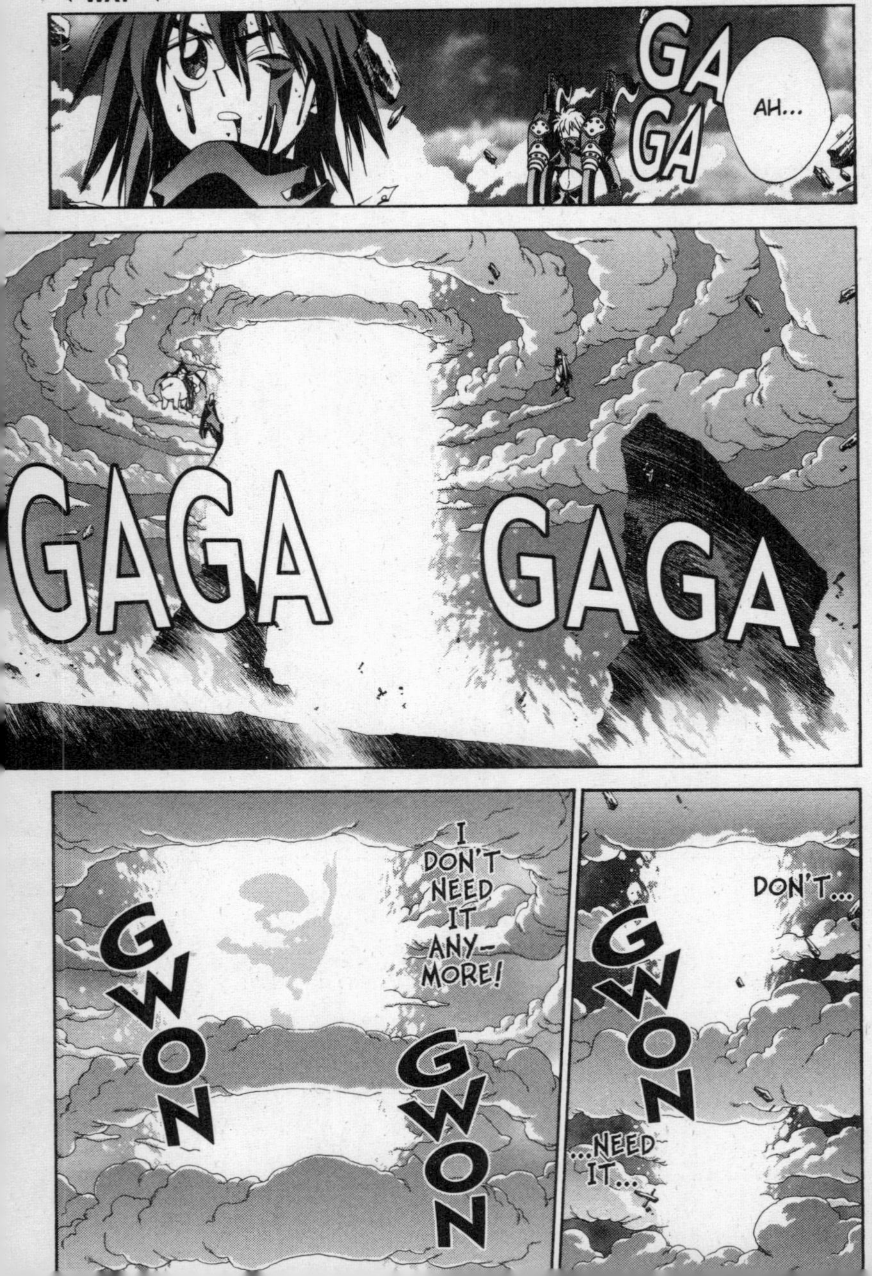
AH...
GA GA
GAGA
GAGA
DON'T...
GWON
...NEED IT...
I DON'T NEED IT ANY-MORE!
GWON
GWON

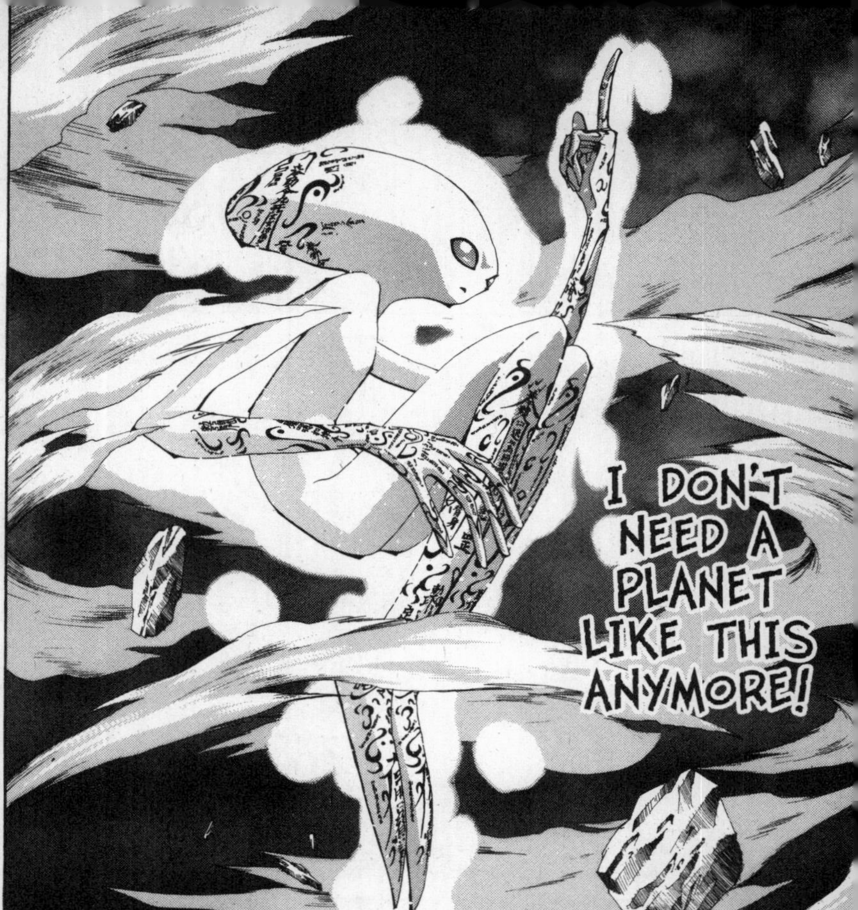
I DON'T NEED A PLANET LIKE THIS ANYMORE!
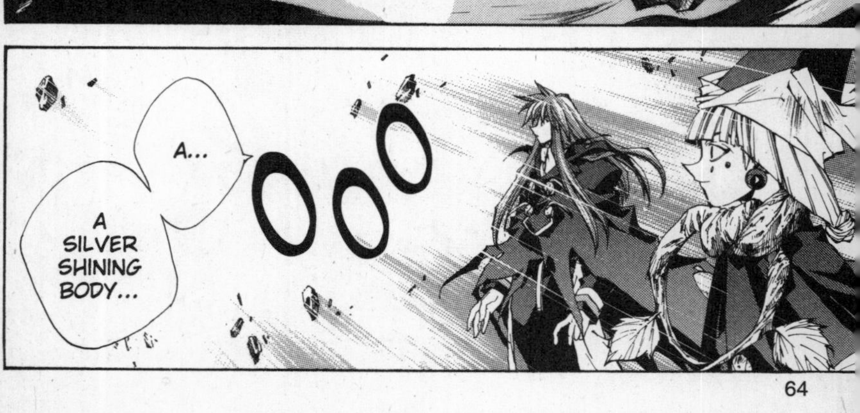
A...
A SILVER SHINING BODY...
OOO

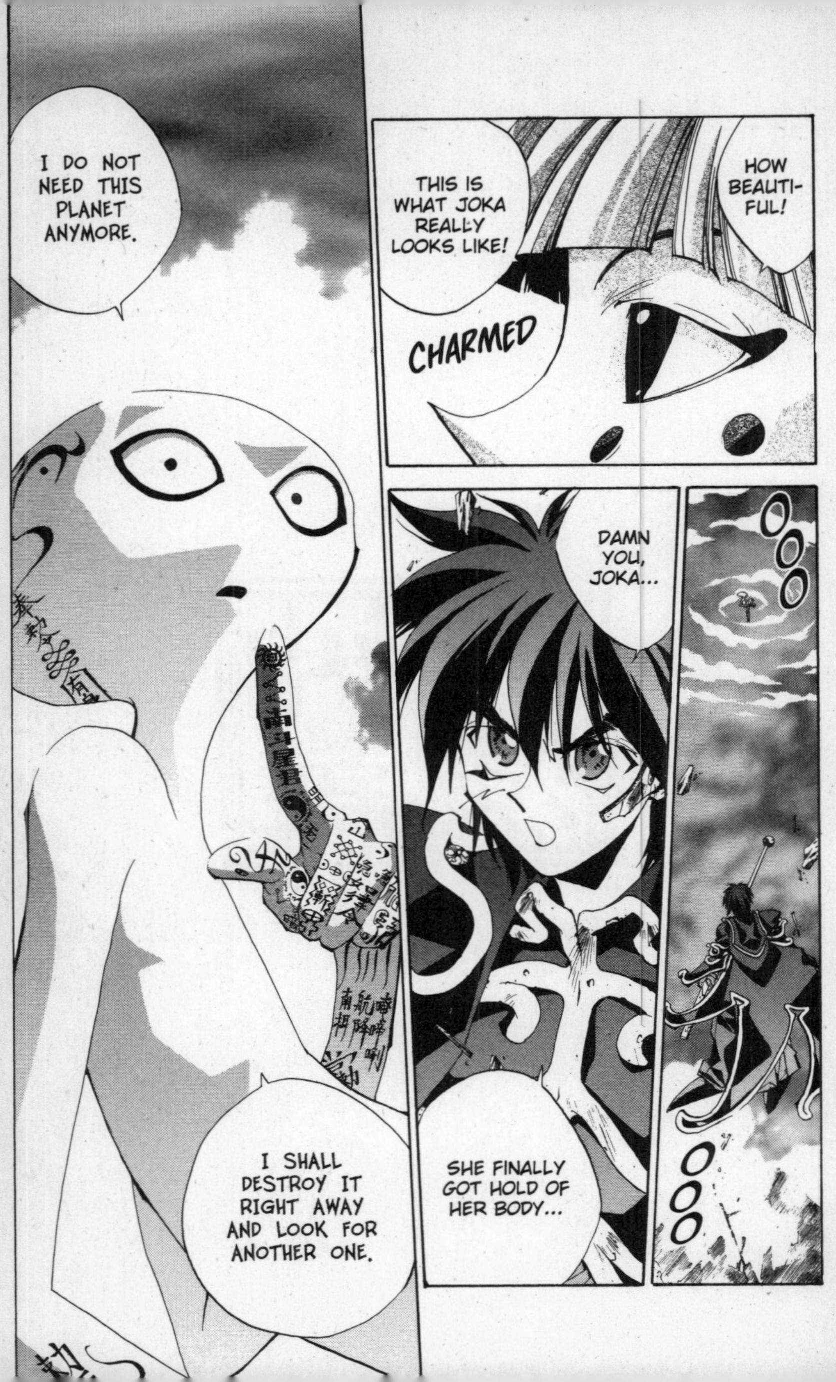
HOW BEAUTIFUL!
THIS IS WHAT JOKA REALLY LOOKS LIKE!
CHARMED
OOO
OOO
DAMN YOU, JOKA...
SHE FINALLY GOT HOLD OF HER BODY...
I DO NOT NEED THIS PLANET ANYMORE.
I SHALL DESTROY IT RIGHT AWAY AND LOOK FOR ANOTHER ONE.

封神演義

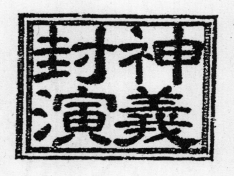

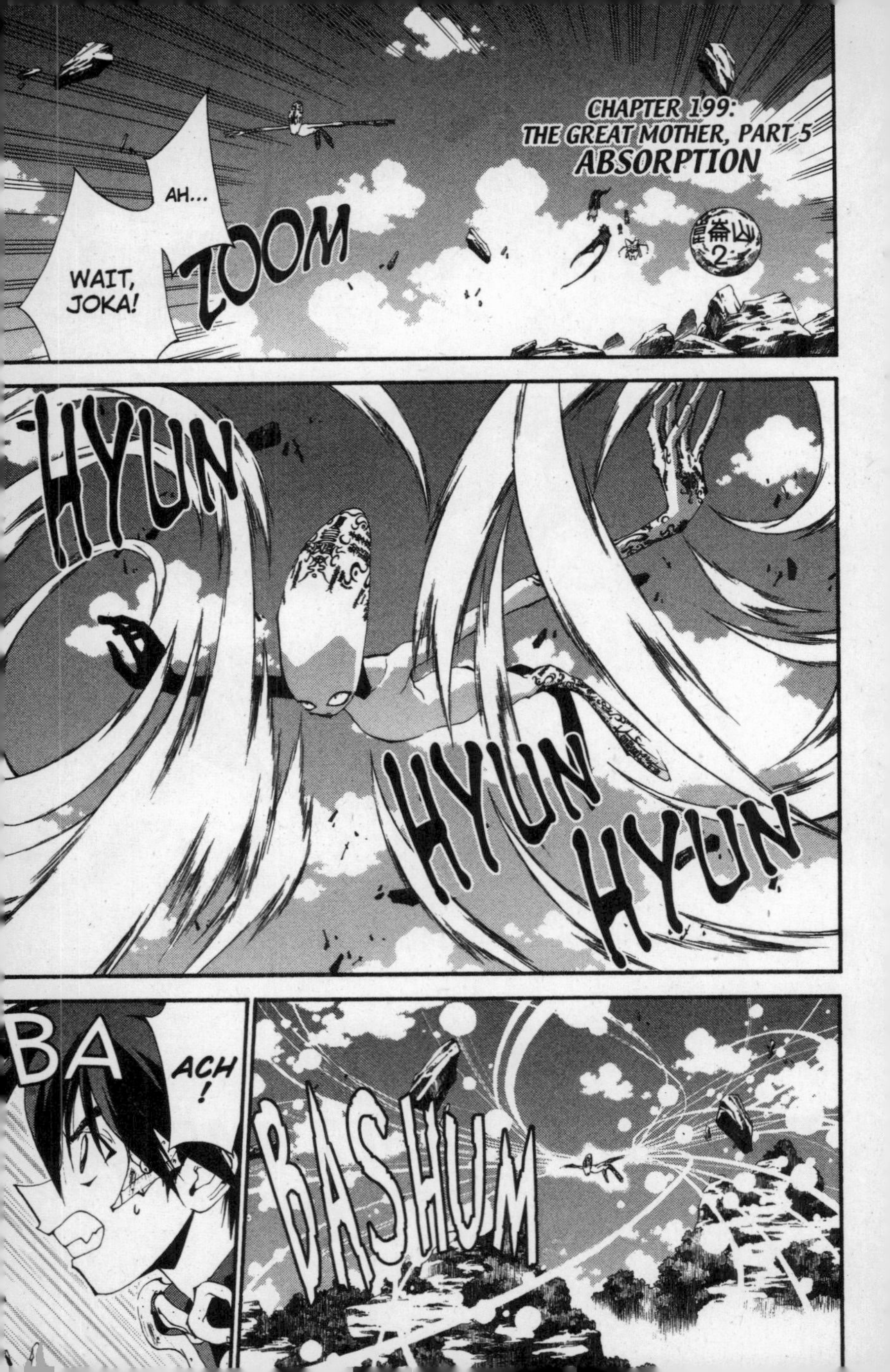
CHAPTER 199:
THE GREAT MOTHER, PART 5
ABSORPTION
ZOOM
AH...
WAIT, JOKA!
HYUN
HYUN
HYUN
BASHUM
BA
ACH!

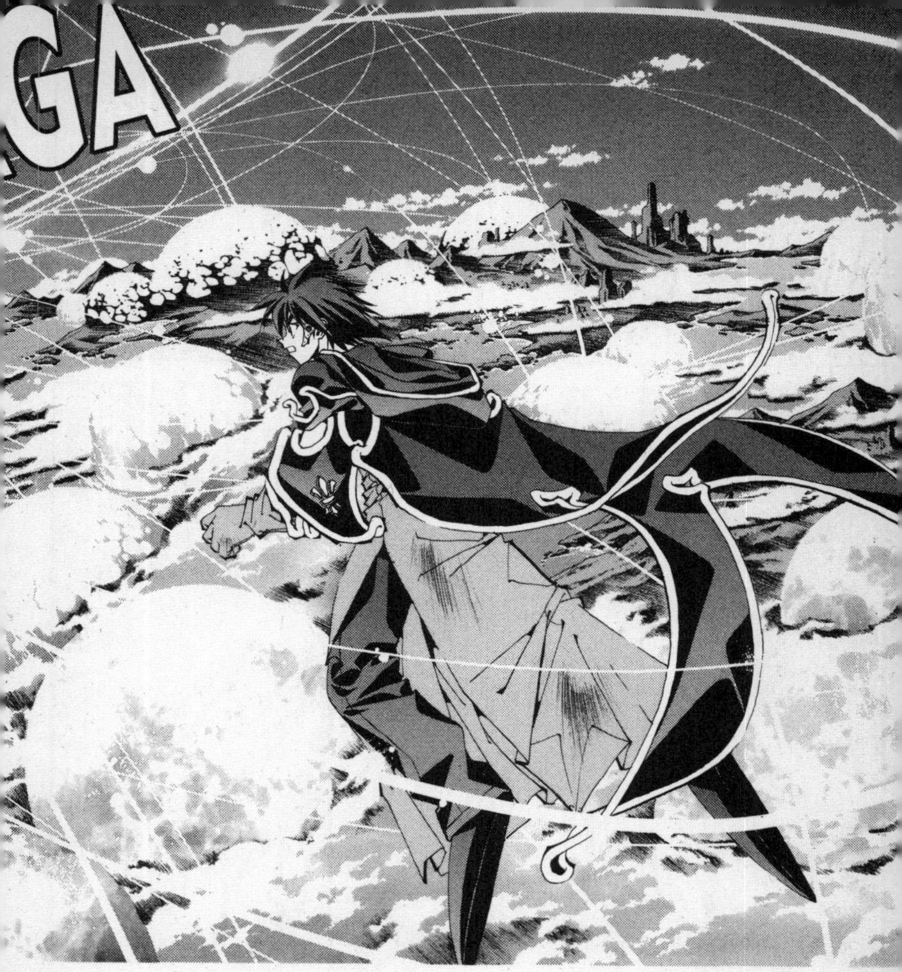

Chapter 199

THE GREAT MOTHER, PART 5
ABSORPTION

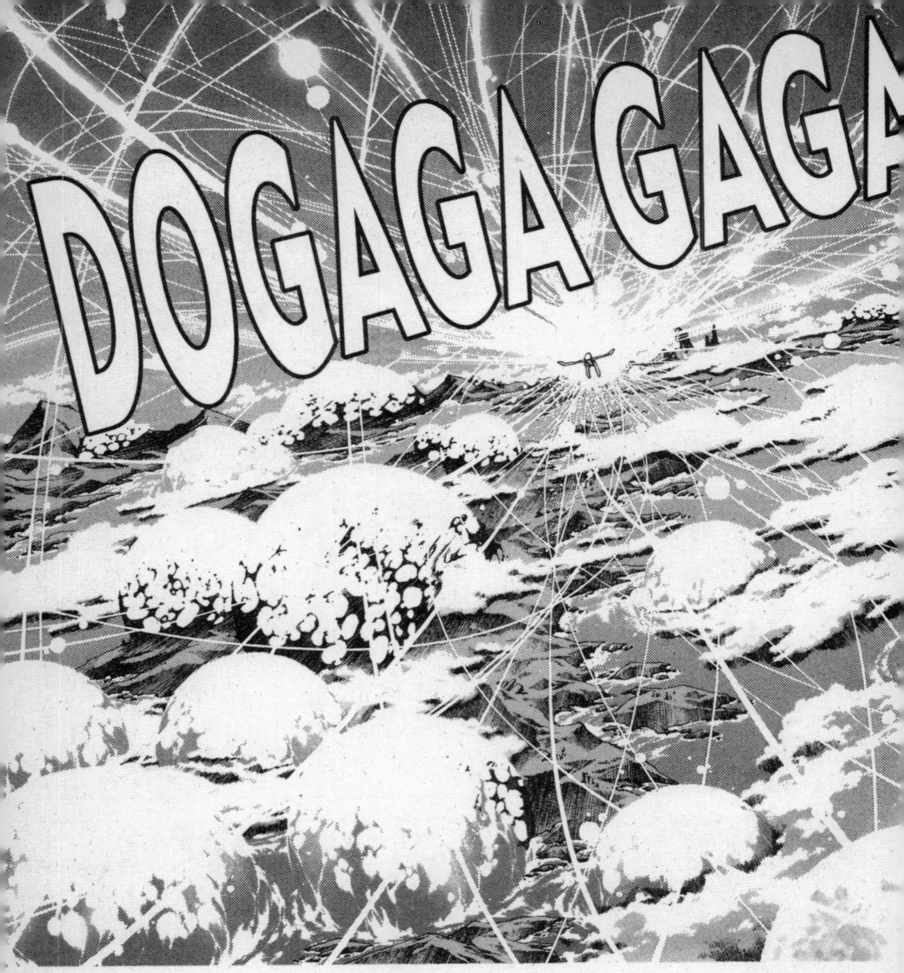
DOGAGA GAGA

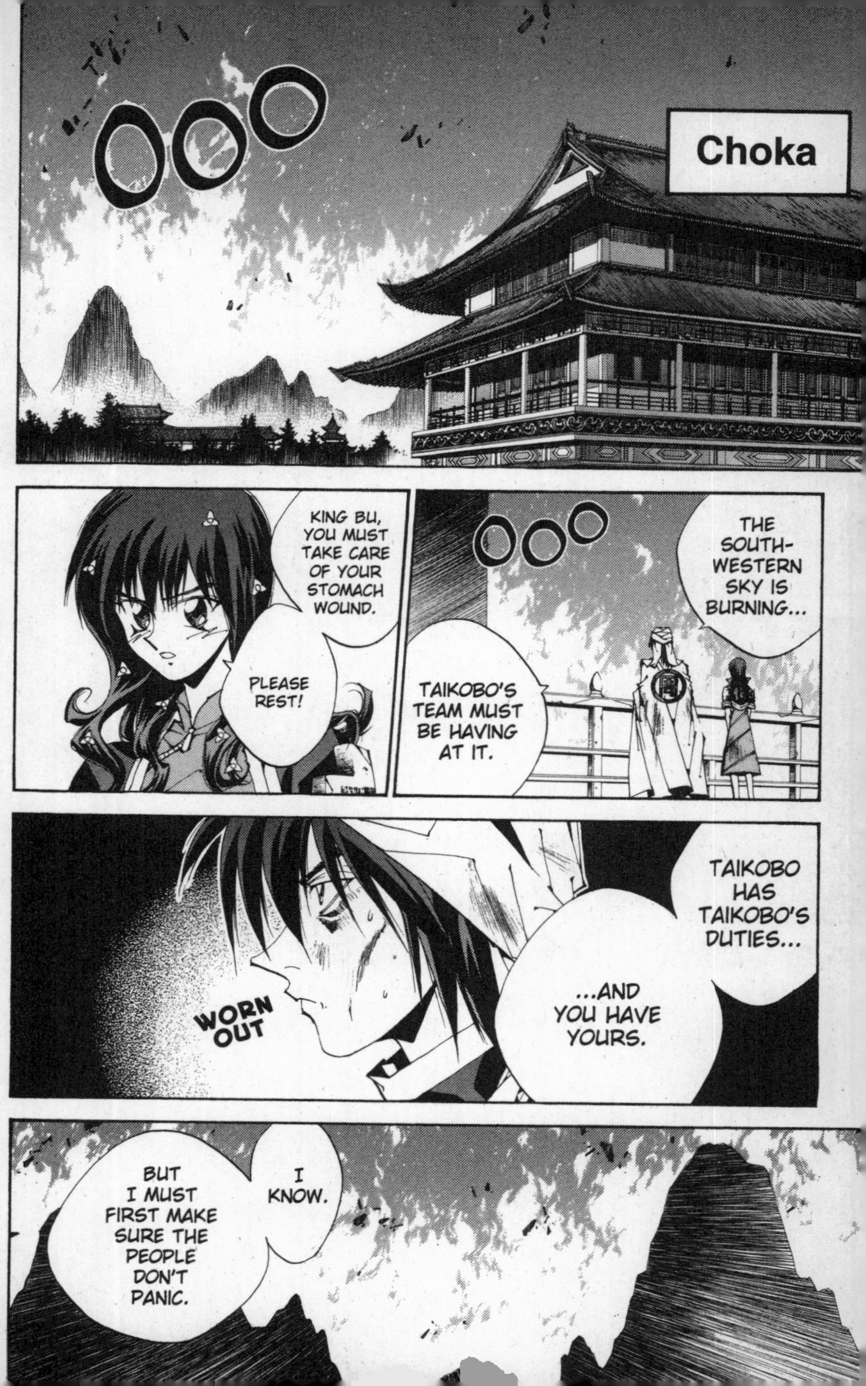
Choka
THE SOUTH-WESTERN SKY IS BURNING...
TAIKOBO'S TEAM MUST BE HAVING AT IT.
KING BU, YOU MUST TAKE CARE OF YOUR STOMACH WOUND.
PLEASE REST!
TAIKOBO HAS TAIKOBO'S DUTIES...
...AND YOU HAVE YOURS.
WORN OUT
I KNOW.
BUT I MUST FIRST MAKE SURE THE PEOPLE DON'T PANIC.

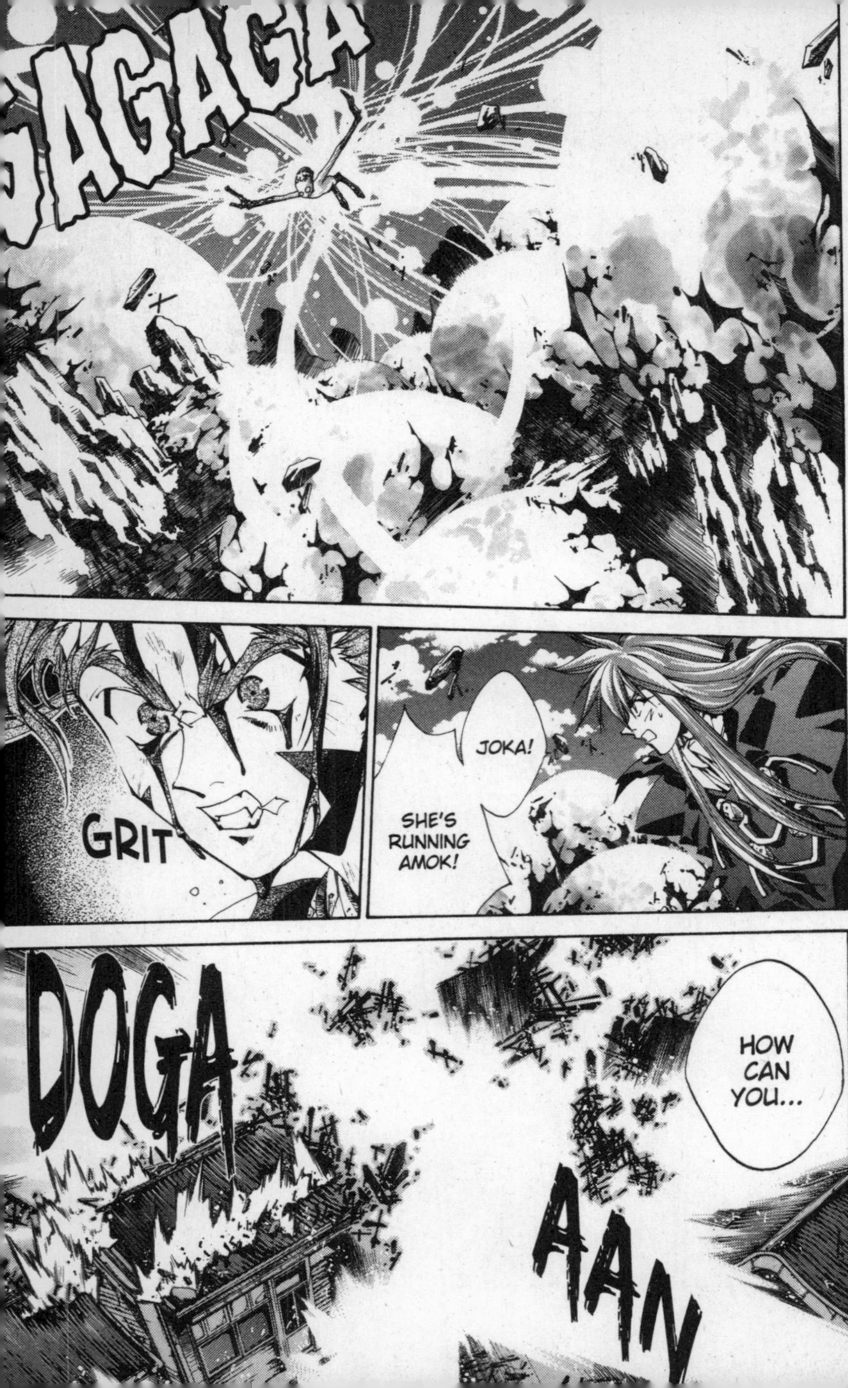
GAGAGA
JOKA!
SHE'S RUNNING AMOK!
GRIT
HOW CAN YOU...
DOGA
AAN

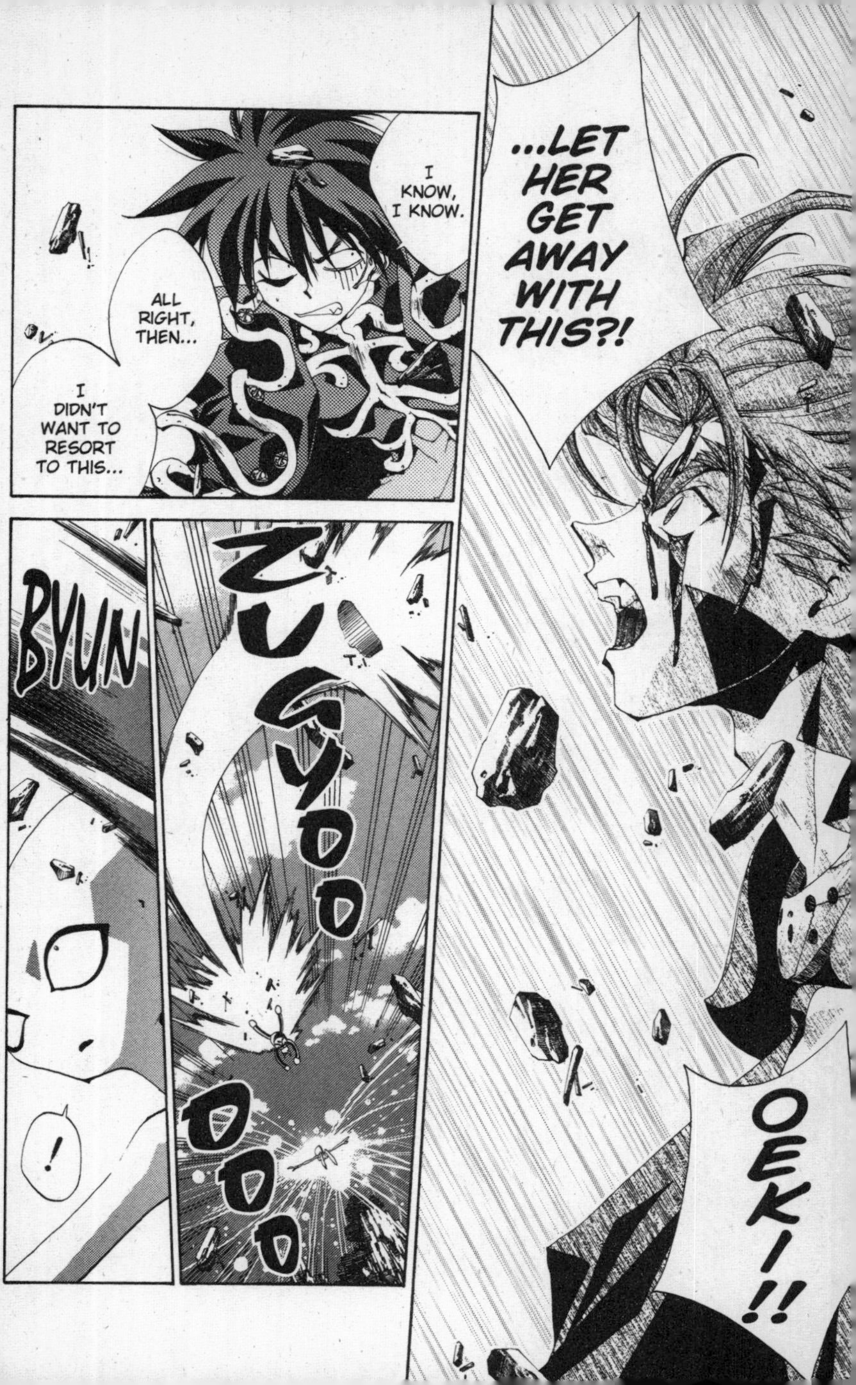
...LET HER GET AWAY WITH THIS?!
OEKI!!
I KNOW, I KNOW.
ALL RIGHT, THEN...
I DIDN'T WANT TO RESORT TO THIS...
BYUN
!

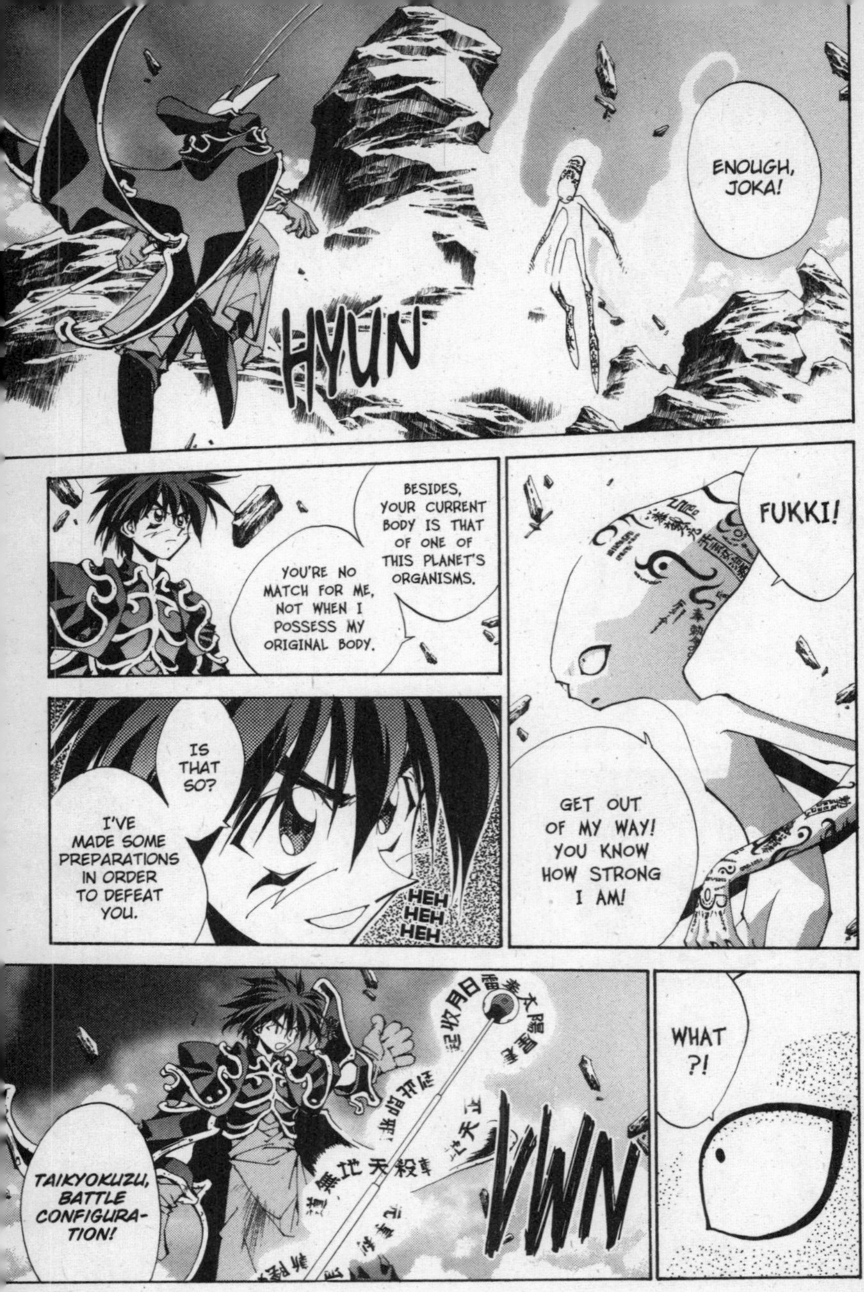
ENOUGH, JOKA!
HYUN
FUKKI!
GET OUT OF MY WAY! YOU KNOW HOW STRONG I AM!
BESIDES, YOUR CURRENT BODY IS THAT OF ONE OF THIS PLANET'S ORGANISMS.
YOU'RE NO MATCH FOR ME, NOT WHEN I POSSESS MY ORIGINAL BODY.
IS THAT SO?
I'VE MADE SOME PREPARATIONS IN ORDER TO DEFEAT YOU.
HEH HEH HEH
WHAT ?!
VWN
TAIKYOKUZU, BATTLE CONFIGURATION!

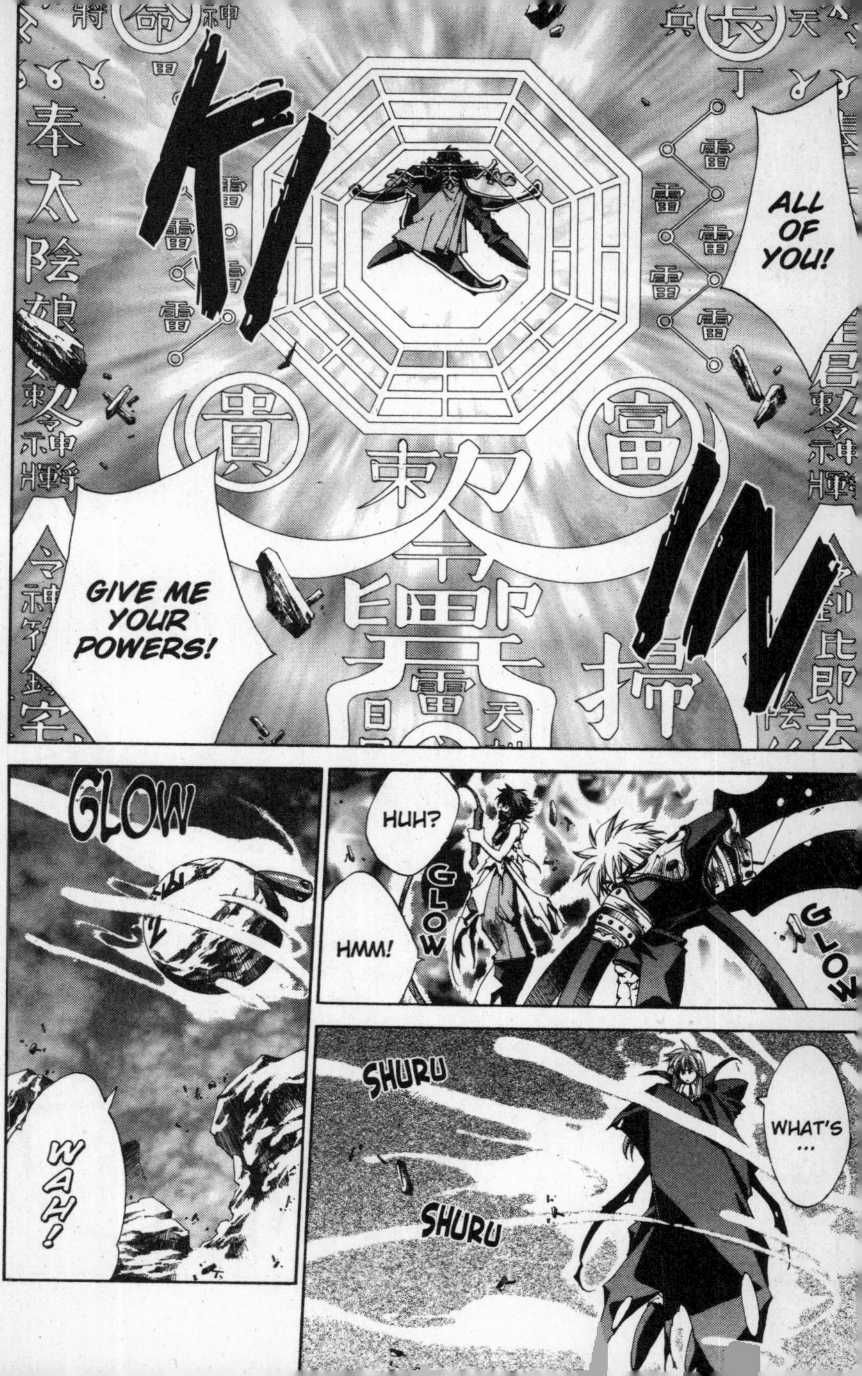
ALL OF YOU!
IN
KI
GIVE ME YOUR POWERS!
GLOW
HUH?
GLOW
HMM!
WHAT'S ...
SHURU
SHURU
GLOW
WAH!

READ THIS WAY

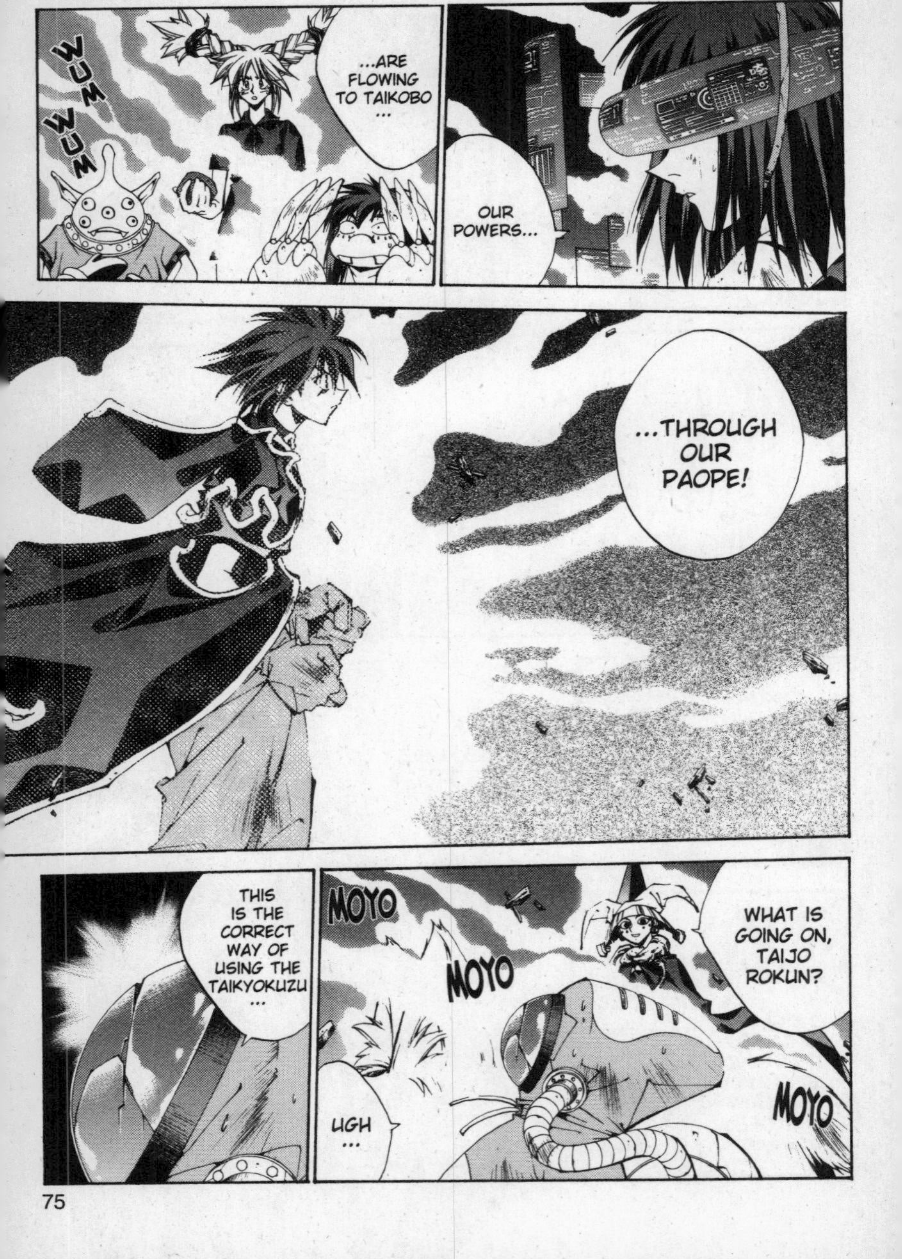
OUR POWERS...
...ARE FLOWING TO TAIKOBO ...
WUM WUM WUM
...THROUGH OUR PAOPE!
WHAT IS GOING ON, TAIJO ROKUN?
MOYO
MOYO
MOYO
UGH ...
THIS IS THE CORRECT WAY OF USING THE TAIKYOKUZU ...

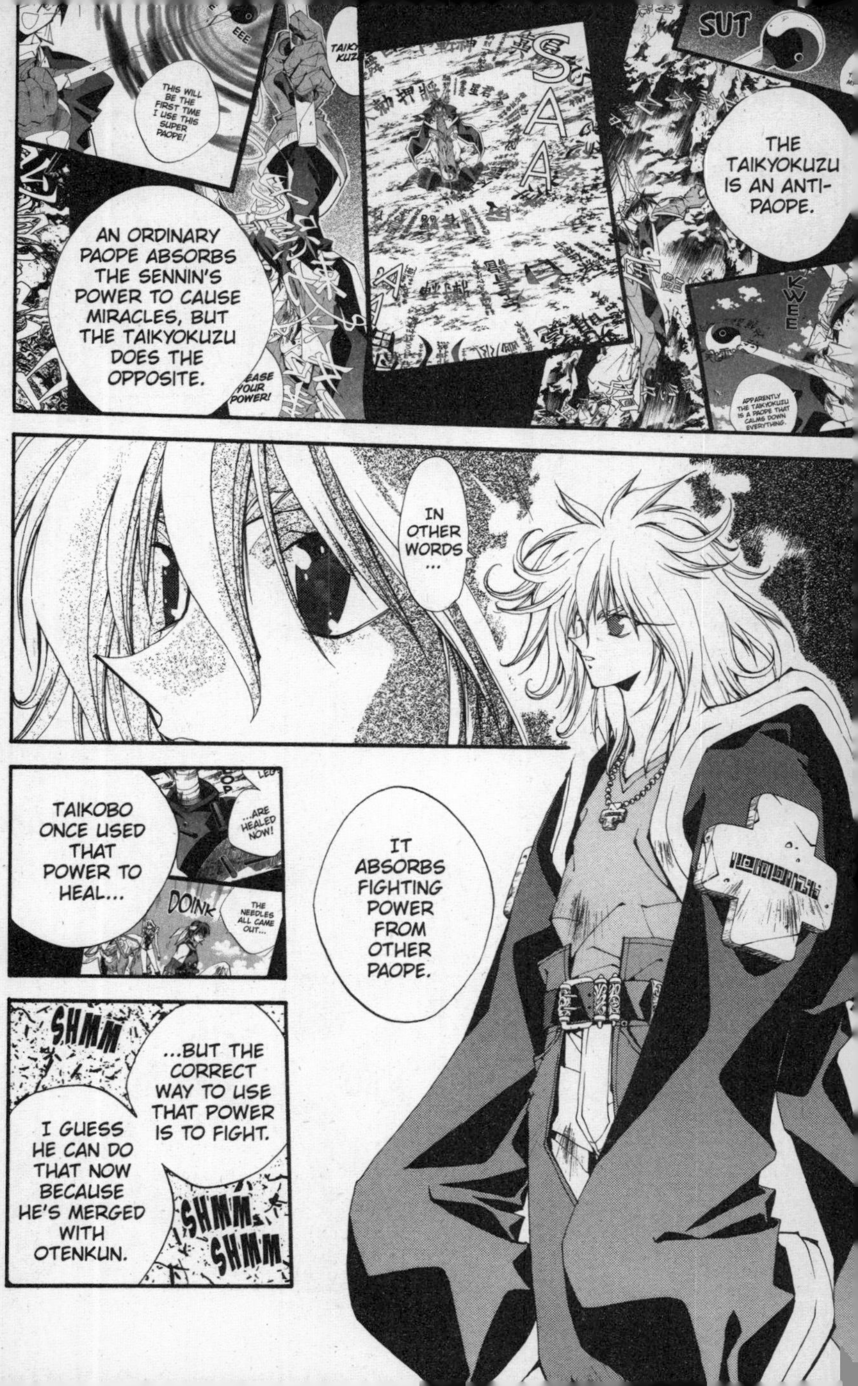
SUT
THE TAIKYOKUZU IS AN ANTI-PAOPE.
KWEE
APPARENTLY THE TAIKYOKUZU IS A PAOPE THAT CALMS DOWN EVERYTHING.
SAA
EEE
THIS WILL BE THE FIRST TIME I USE THIS SUPER PAOPE!
AN ORDINARY PAOPE ABSORBS THE SENNIN'S POWER TO CAUSE MIRACLES, BUT THE TAIKYOKUZU DOES THE OPPOSITE.
IN OTHER WORDS...
IT ABSORBS FIGHTING POWER FROM OTHER PAOPE.
...ARE HEALED NOW!
TAIKOBO ONCE USED THAT POWER TO HEAL...
DOINK
THE NEEDLES ALL CAME OUT...
SHMM
...BUT THE CORRECT WAY TO USE THAT POWER IS TO FIGHT.
I GUESS HE CAN DO THAT NOW BECAUSE HE'S MERGED WITH OTENKUN.
SHMM SHMM

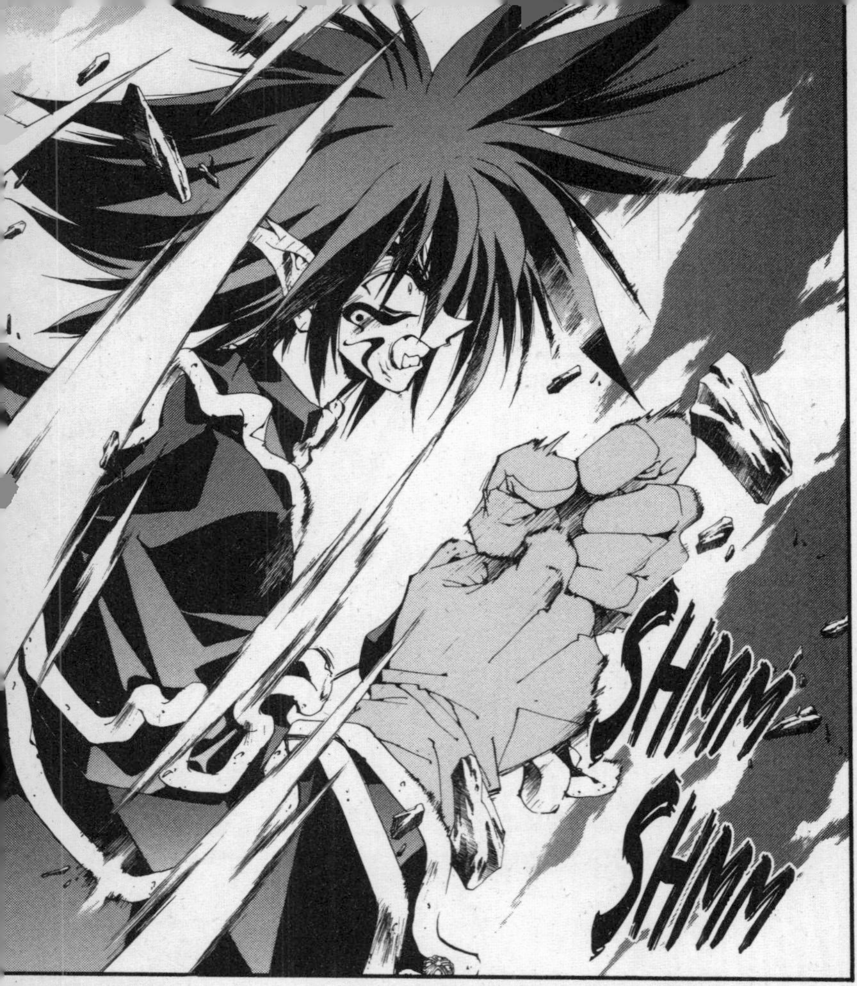
SHMM SHMM

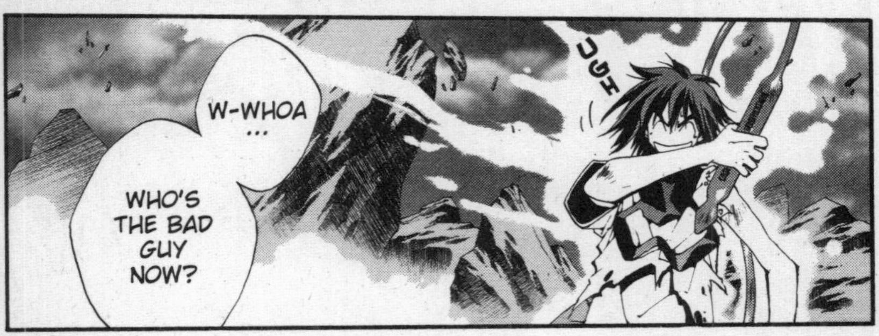
UGH
W-WHOA ...
WHO'S THE BAD GUY NOW?

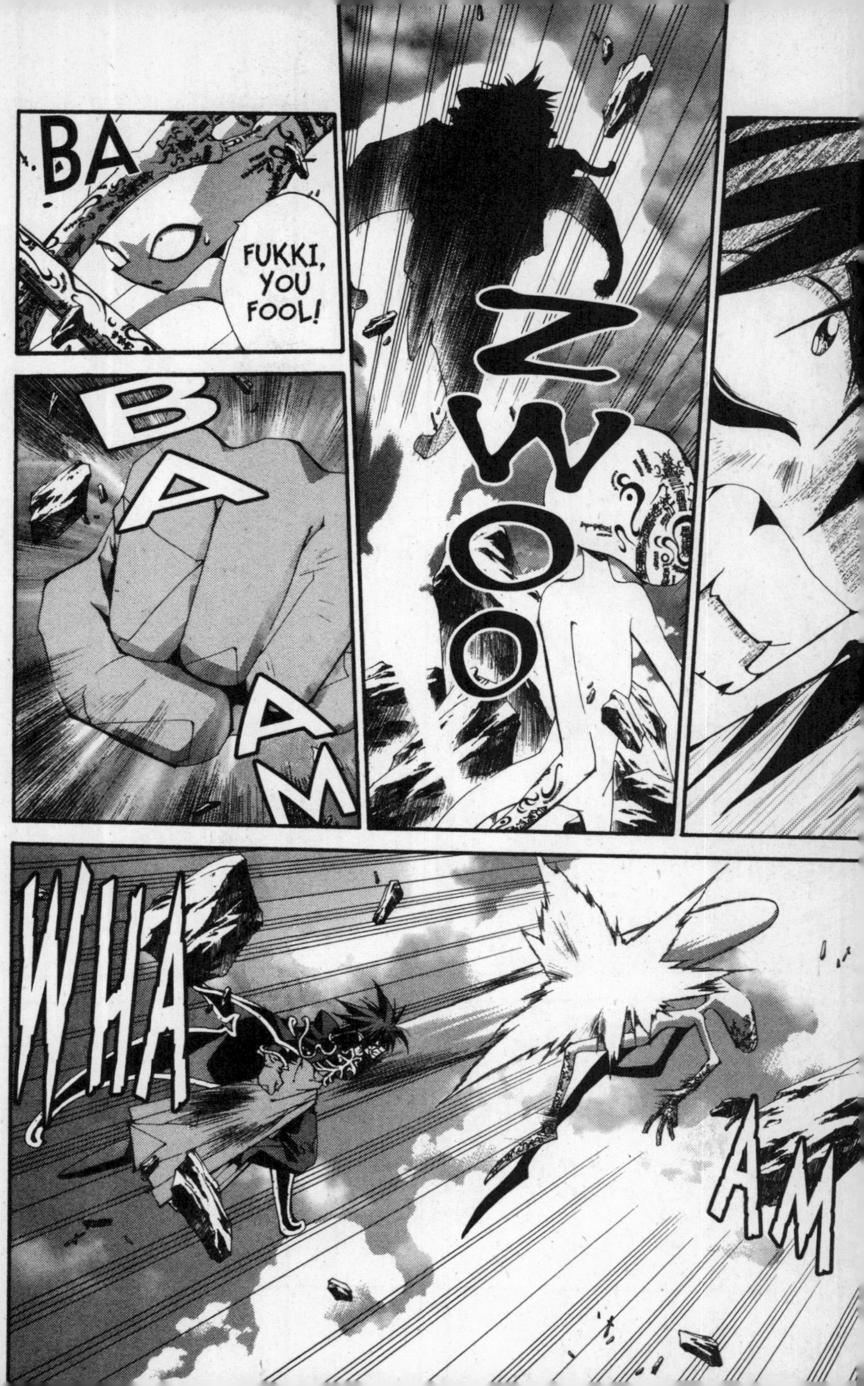

ZWOO
BA
FUKKI, YOU FOOL!
BAAM
WHA
AM

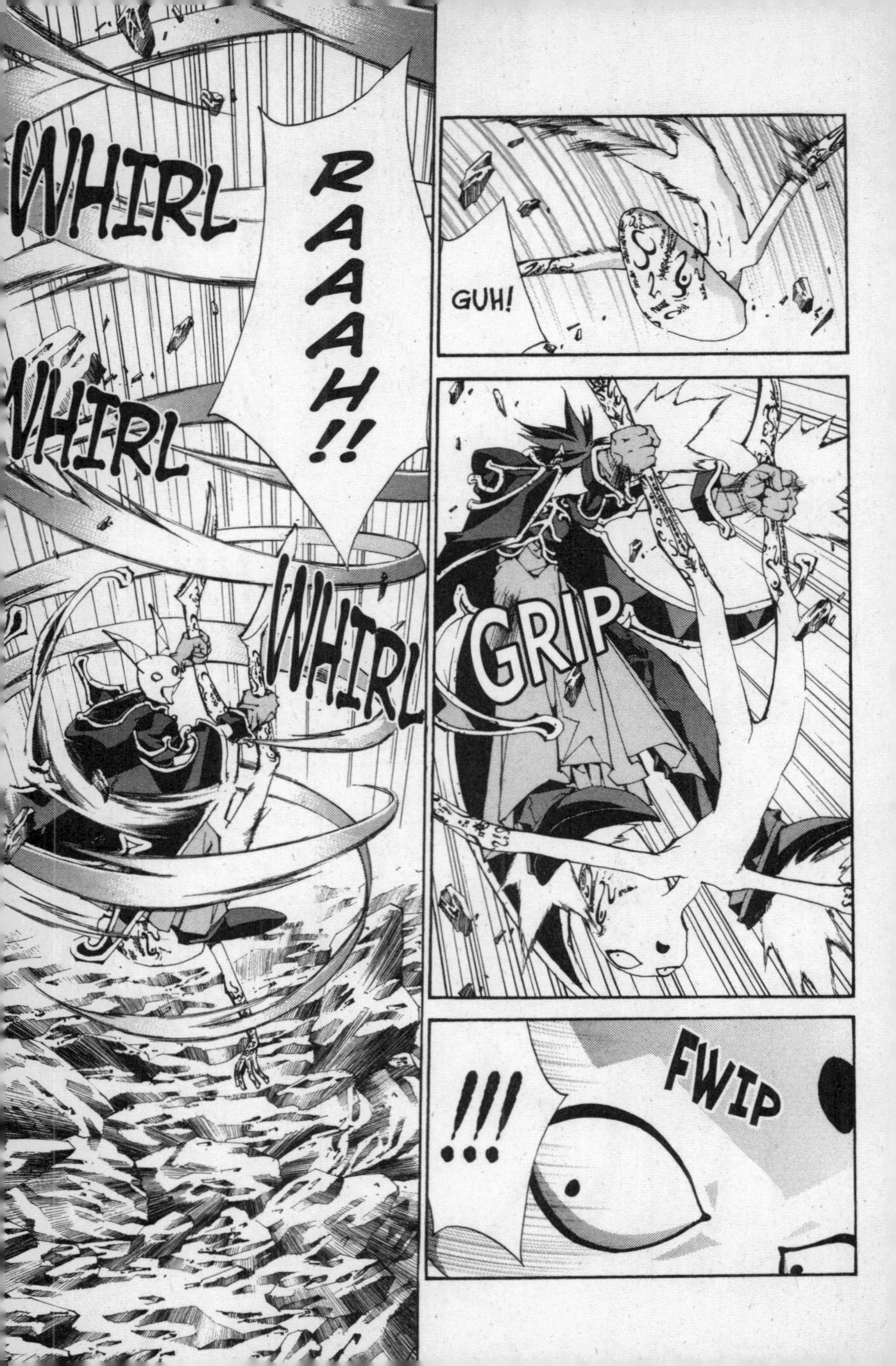
GUH!
GRIP
!!!
FWIP
WHIRL
RAAAAH!!
WHIRL
WHIRL

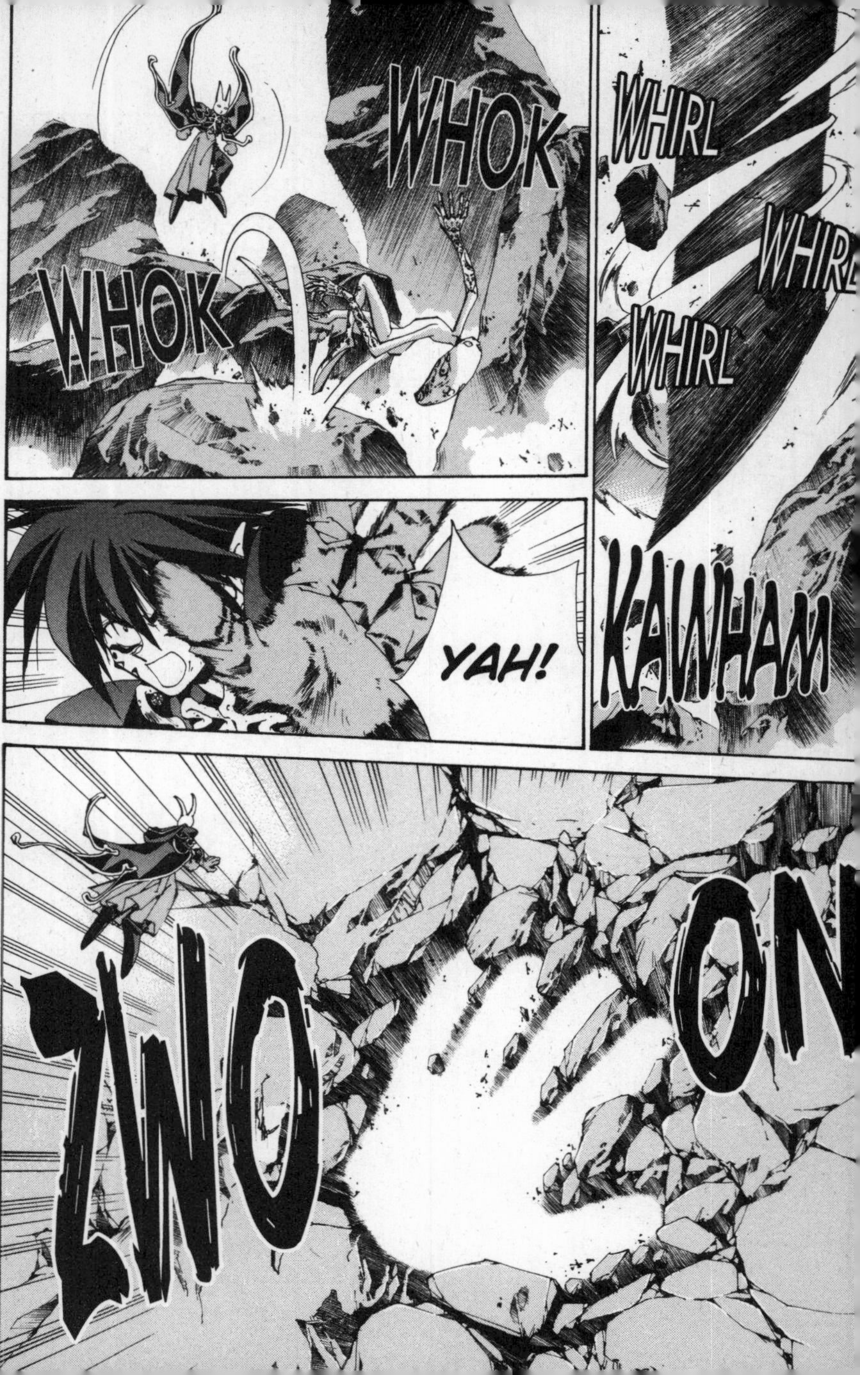
WHIRL
WHIRL
WHIRL
KAWHAM
WHOK
WHOK
YAH!
ZWOON

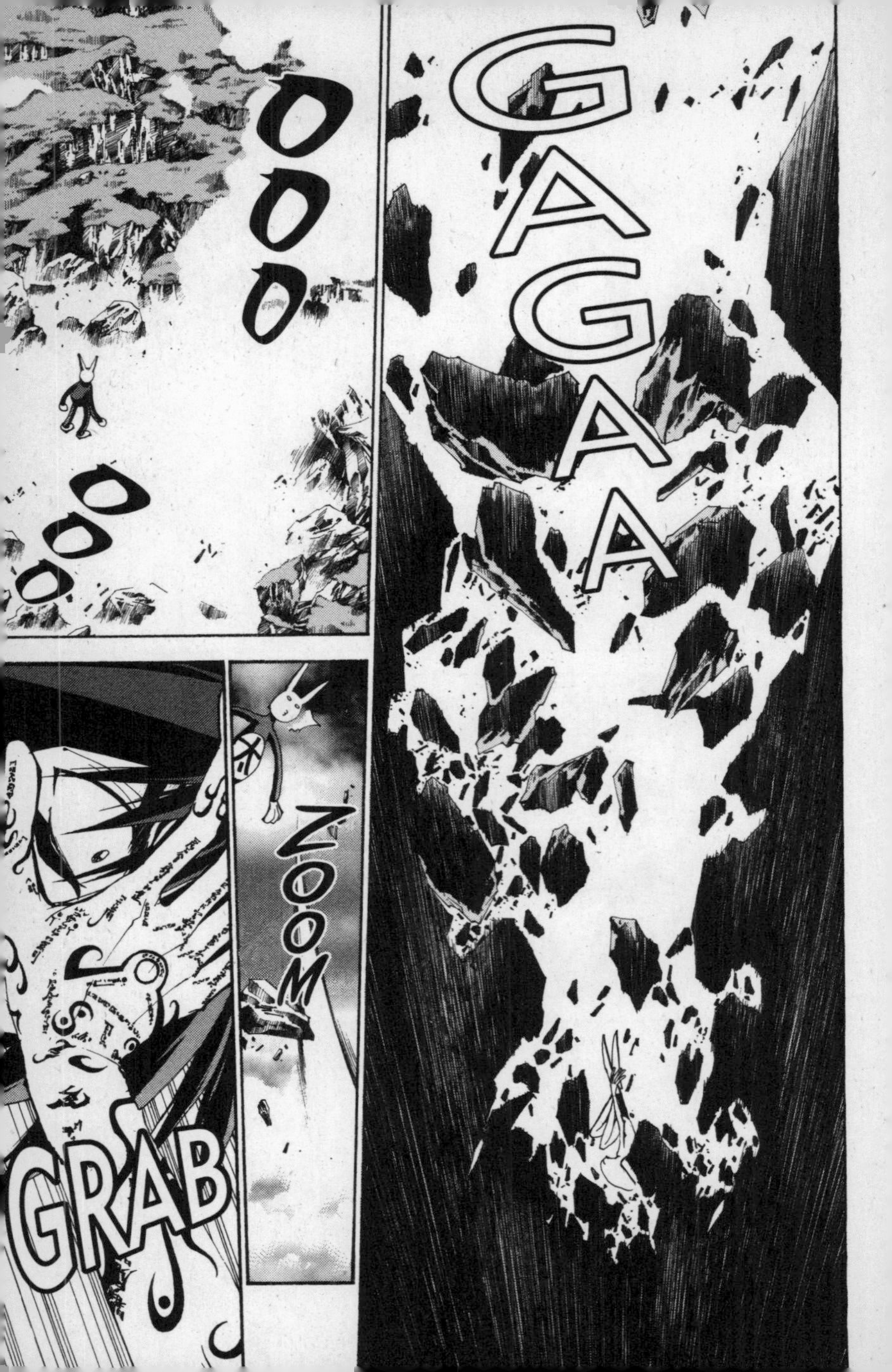
GAGAGA
ZOOM
GRAB

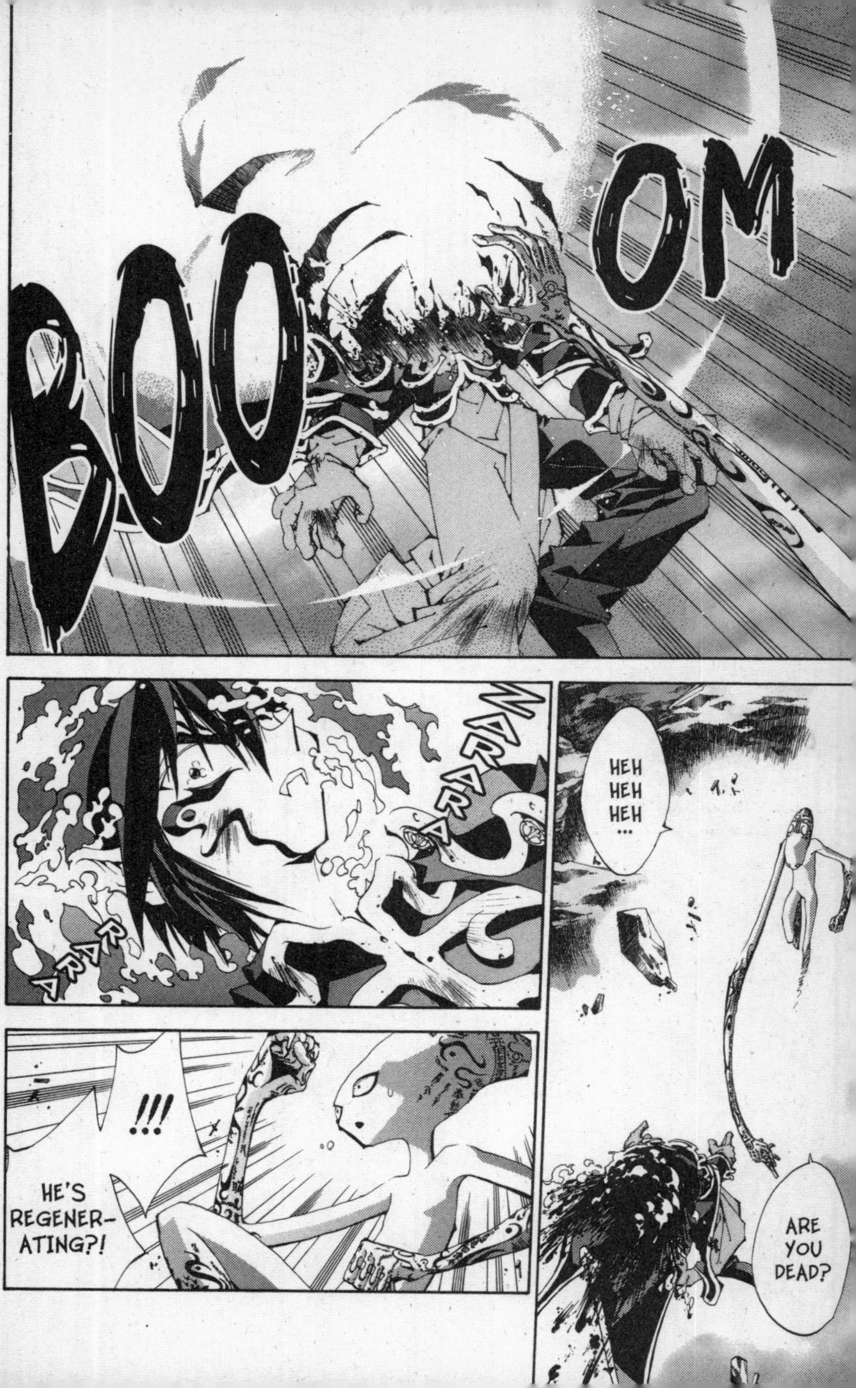
BOOOM
HEH HEH HEH...
ARE YOU DEAD?
ZARARARA
RARA
!!!
HE'S REGENER-ATING?!

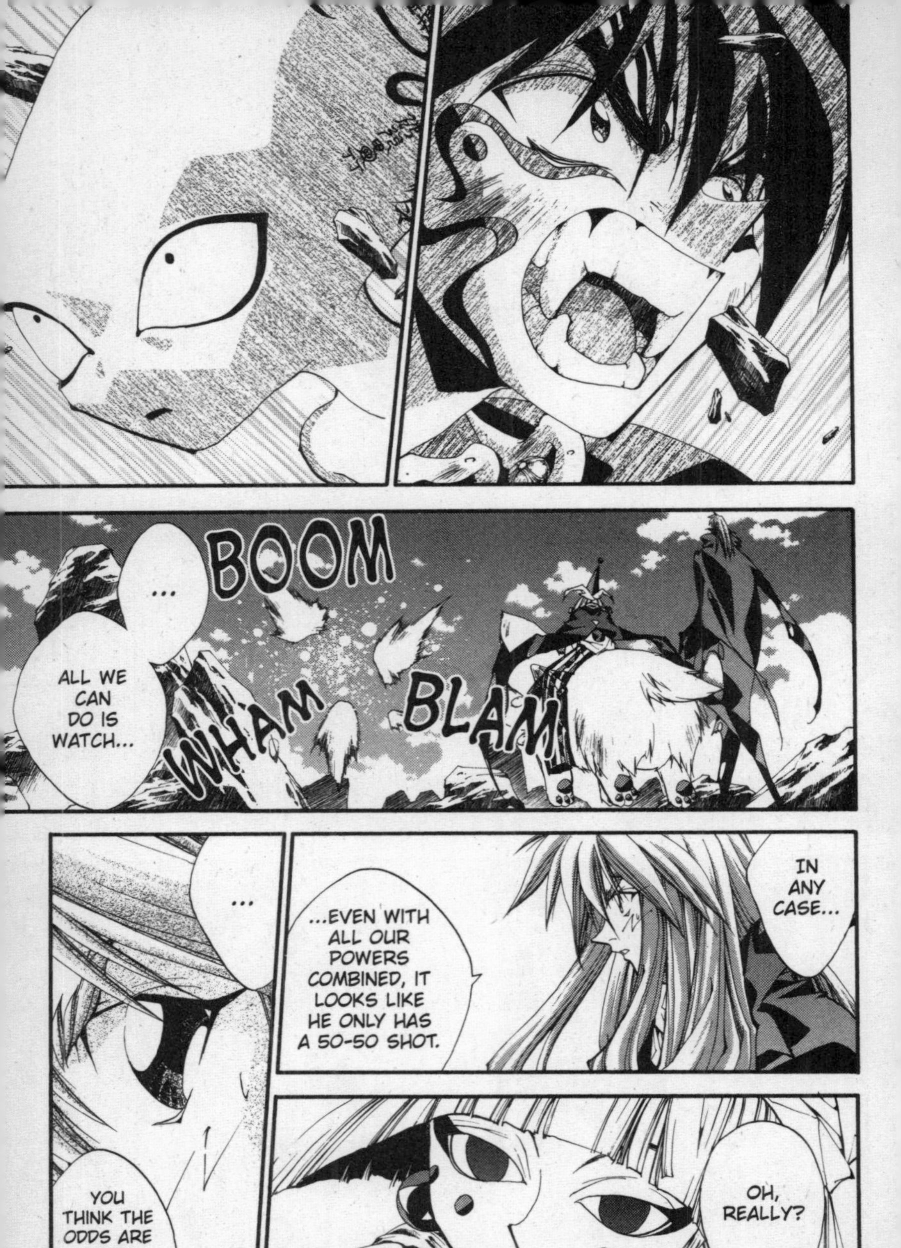
BOOM
...
ALL WE CAN DO IS WATCH...
BLAM
WHAM
IN ANY CASE...
...EVEN WITH ALL OUR POWERS COMBINED, IT LOOKS LIKE HE ONLY HAS A 50-50 SHOT.
OH, REALLY?
...
YOU THINK THE ODDS ARE EVEN?

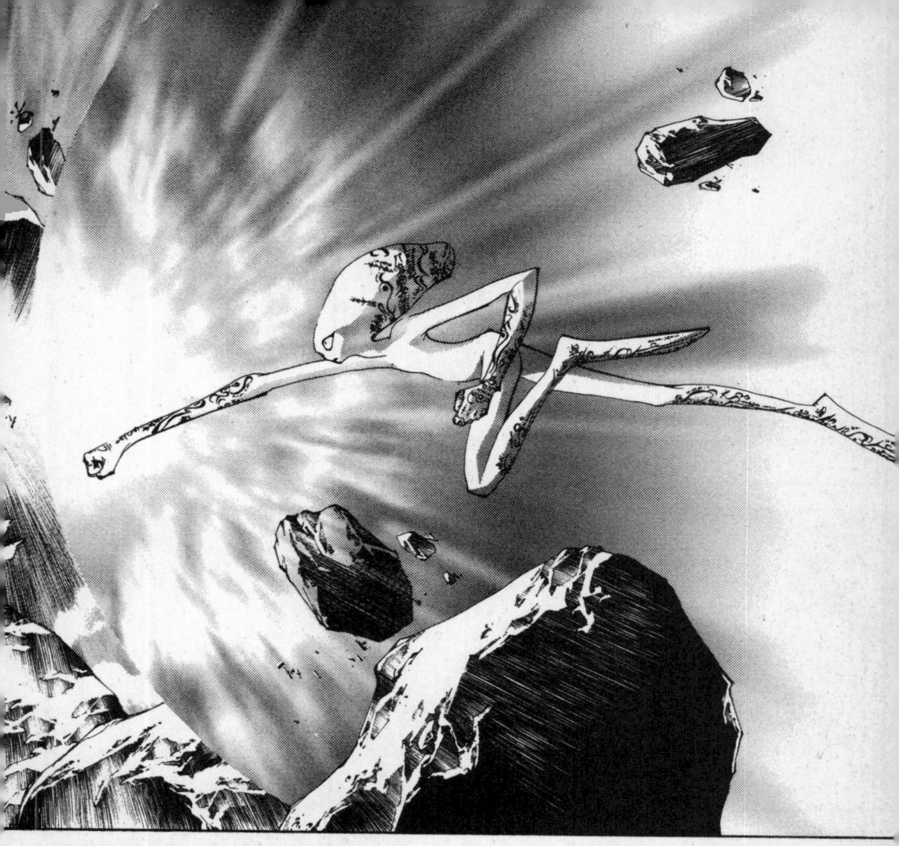

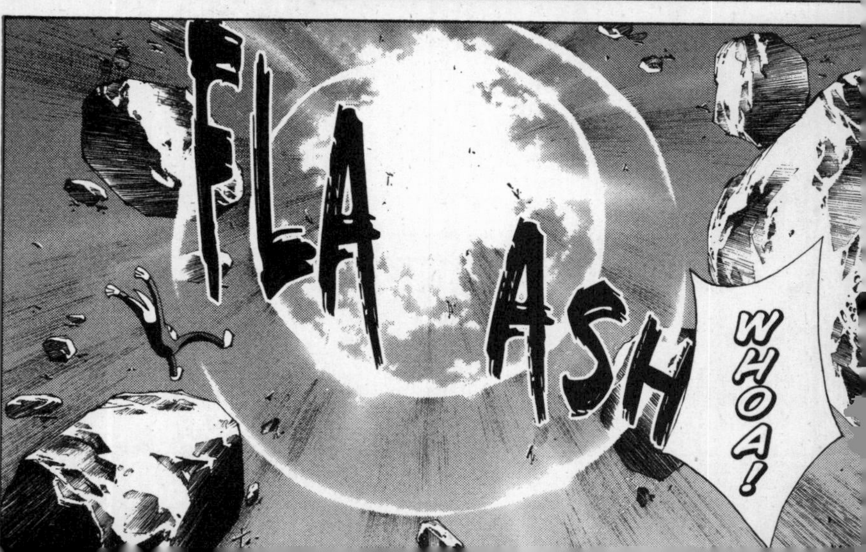
FLA ASH
WHOA!

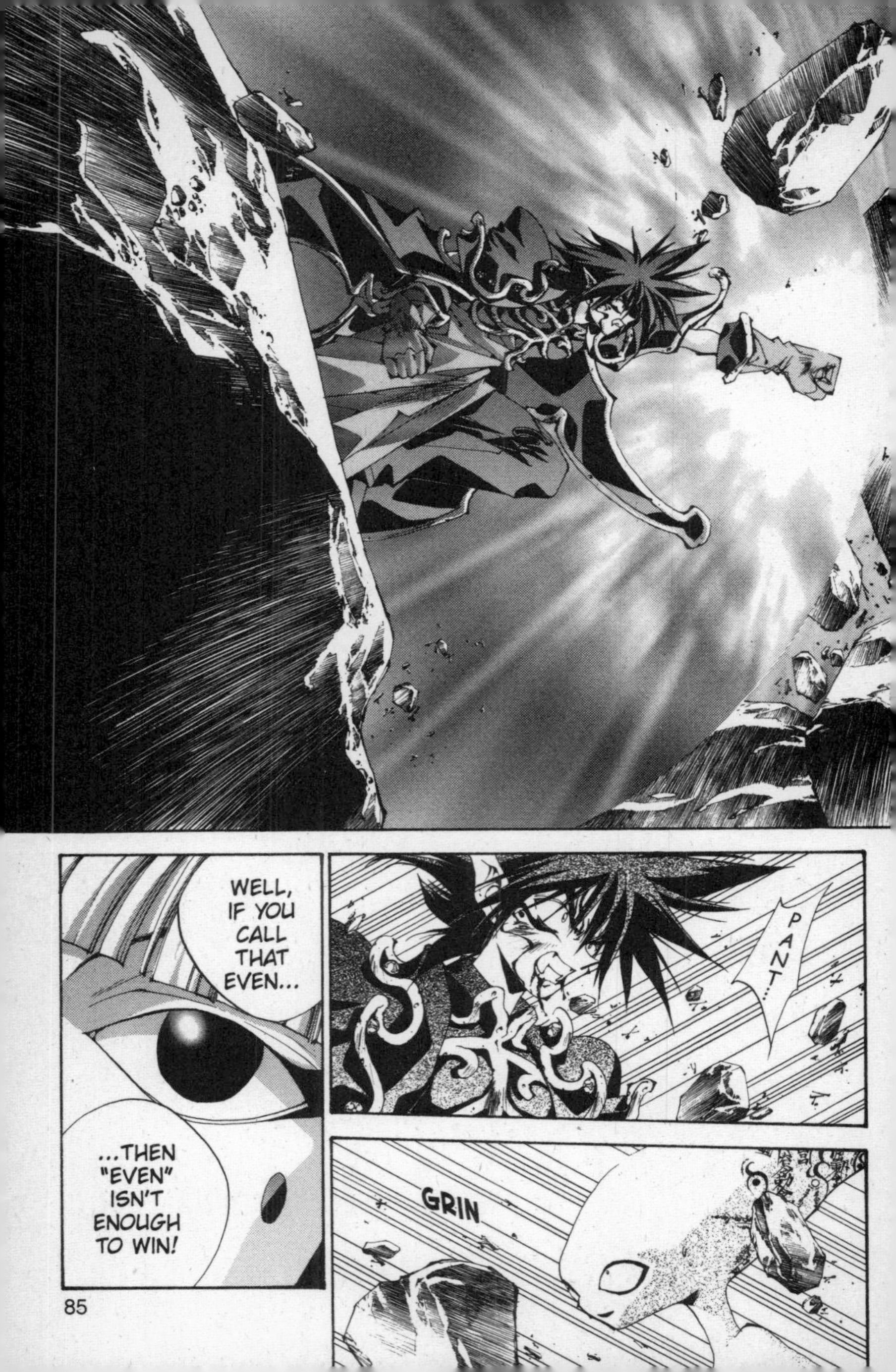
PANT...
GRIN
WELL, IF YOU CALL THAT EVEN...
...THEN "EVEN" ISN'T ENOUGH TO WIN!

封神演義

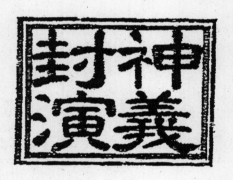

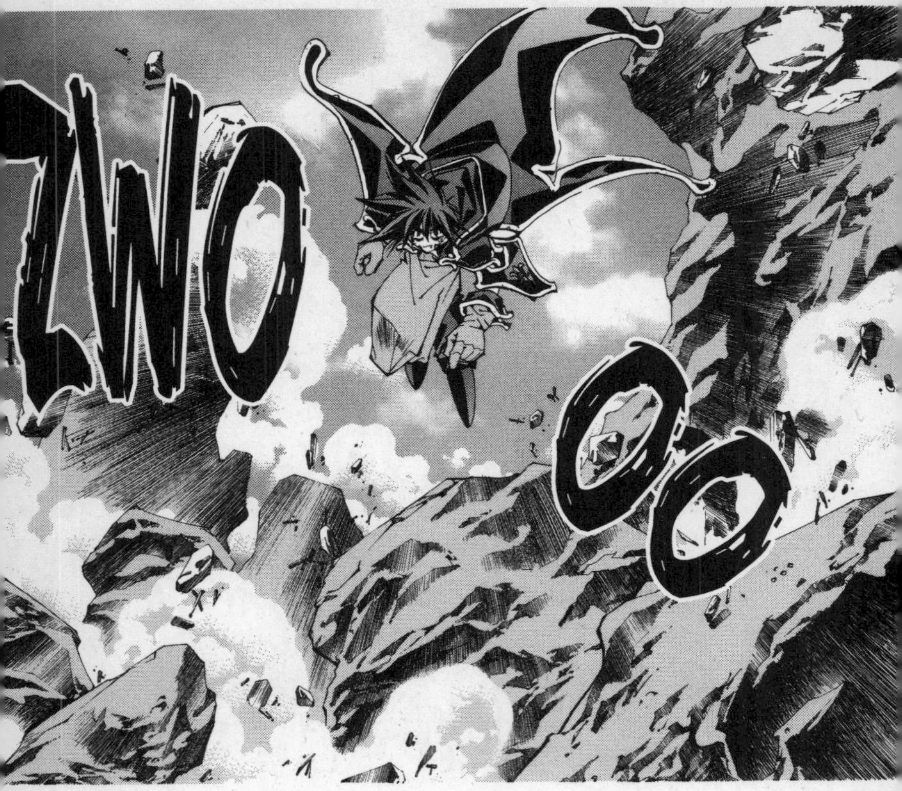
ZWOOOO

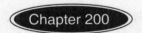

Chapter 200

THE HOSHINDAI IS SET FREE!

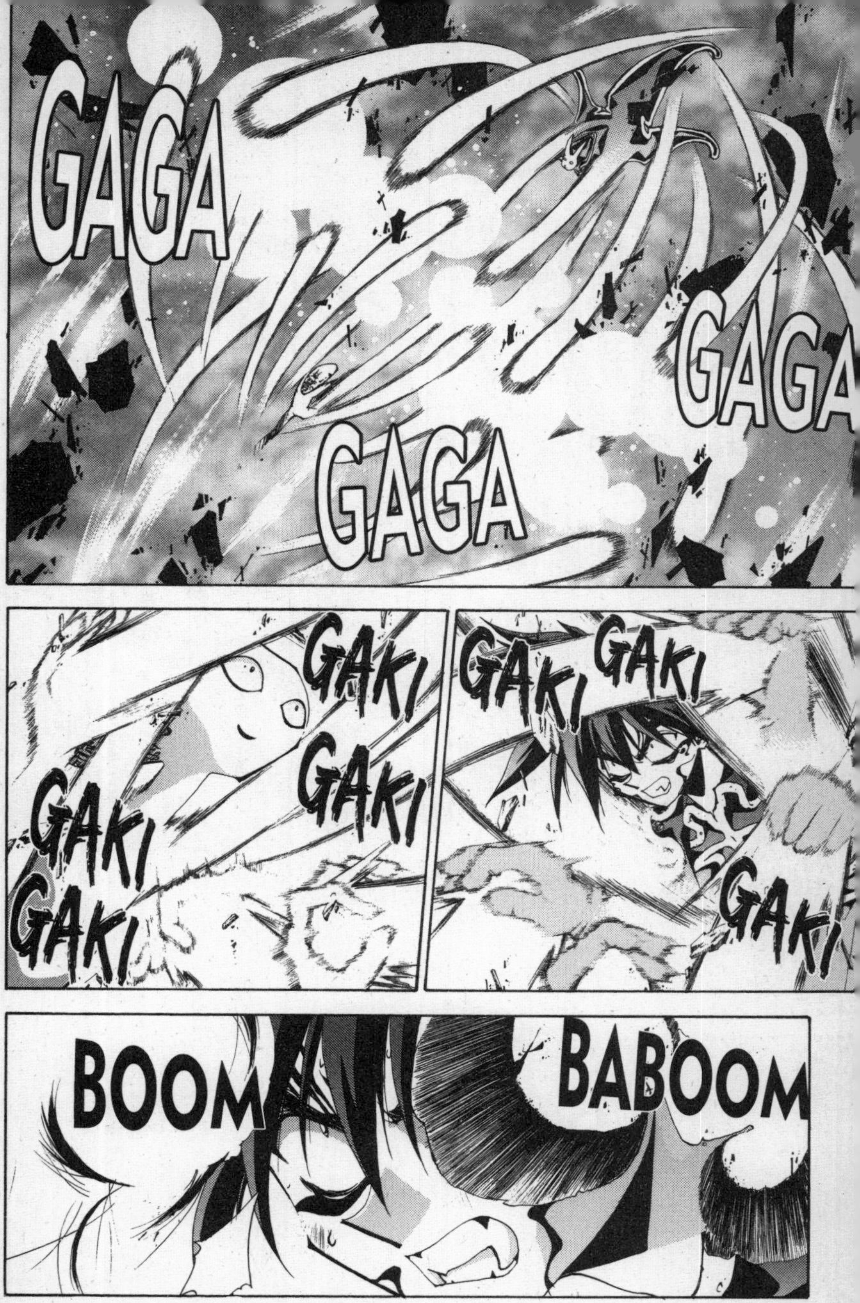
GAGA
GAGA
GAGA
GAKI
GAKI
GAKI
GAKI
GAKI
GAKI
GAKI
BABOOM
BOOM

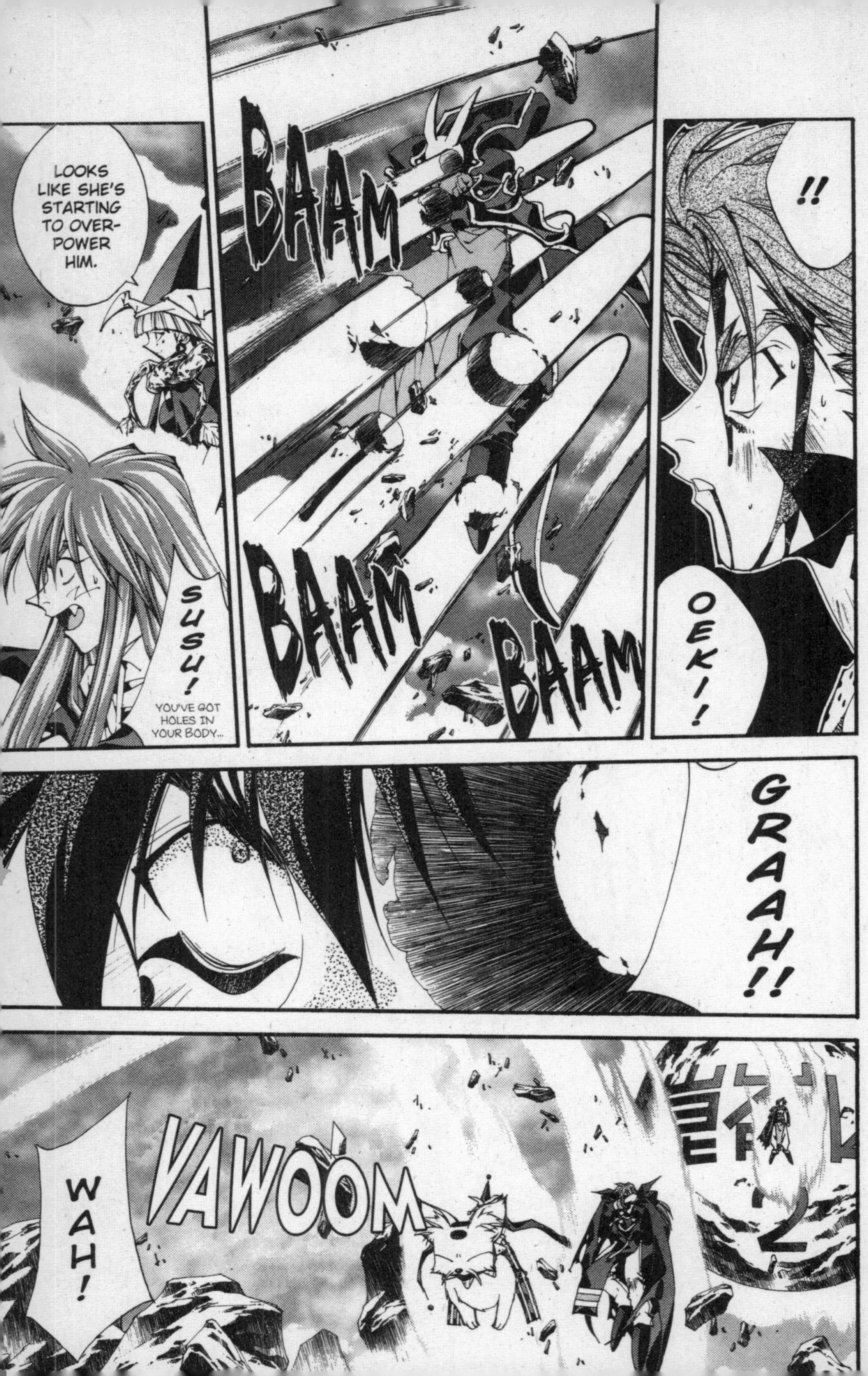
!!
OEKI!
BAAM
BAAM
BAAM
LOOKS LIKE SHE'S STARTING TO OVER-POWER HIM.
SUSU!
YOU'VE GOT HOLES IN YOUR BODY...
GRAAAH!!
VAWOOM
WAH!

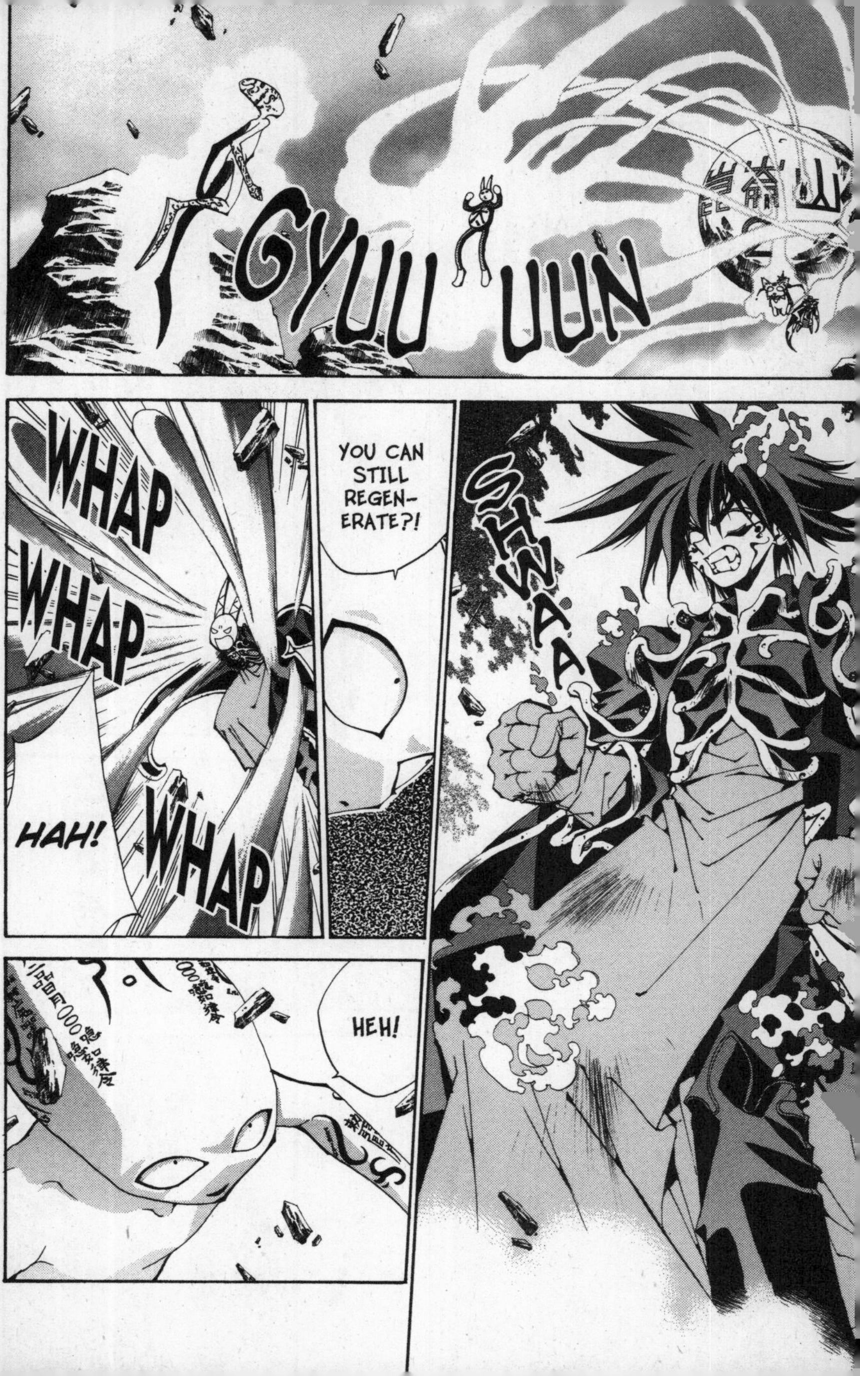

GYUU UUN
SHWAA
YOU CAN STILL REGENERATE?!
WHAP WHAP WHAP
HAH!
HEH!

READ THIS WAY

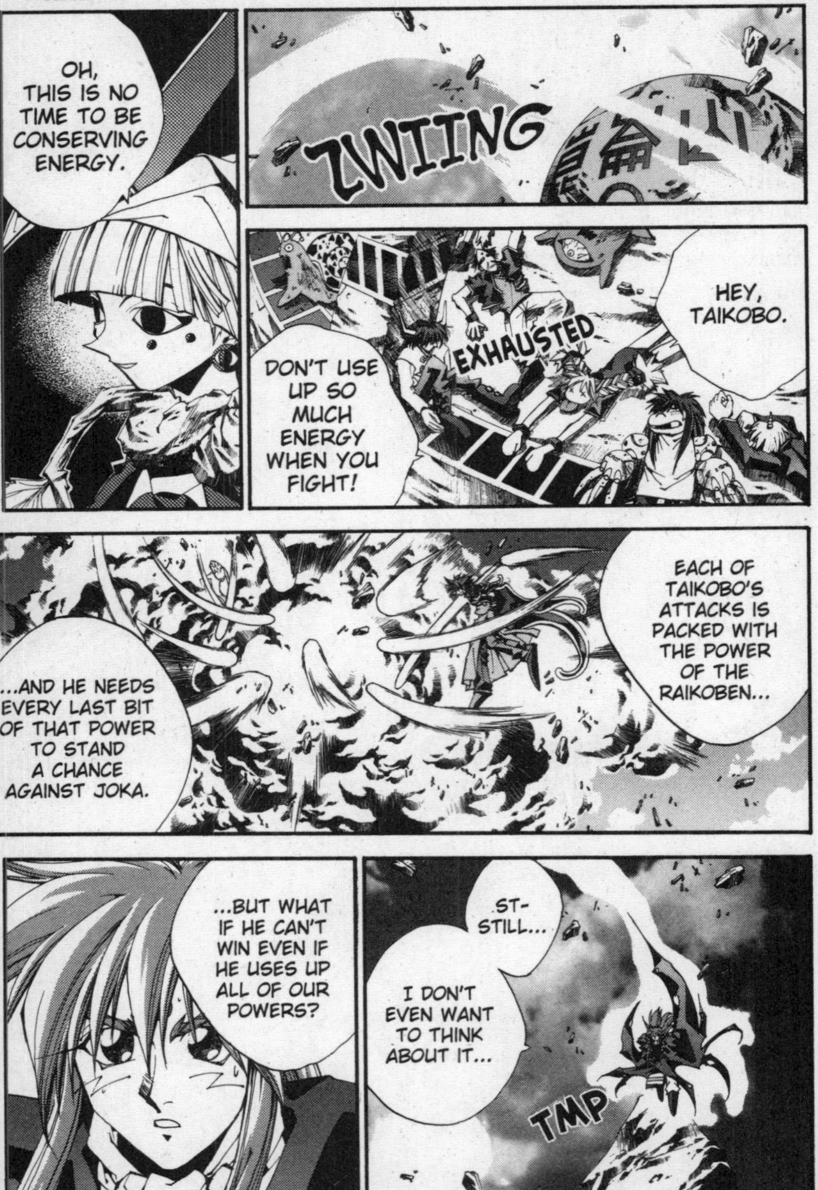
ZWIING
HEY, TAIKOBO.
DON'T USE UP SO MUCH ENERGY WHEN YOU FIGHT!
EXHAUSTED
OH, THIS IS NO TIME TO BE CONSERVING ENERGY.
EACH OF TAIKOBO'S ATTACKS IS PACKED WITH THE POWER OF THE RAIKOBEN...
...AND HE NEEDS EVERY LAST BIT OF THAT POWER TO STAND A CHANCE AGAINST JOKA.
ST- STILL...
I DON'T EVEN WANT TO THINK ABOUT IT...
TMP
...BUT WHAT IF HE CAN'T WIN EVEN IF HE USES UP ALL OF OUR POWERS?

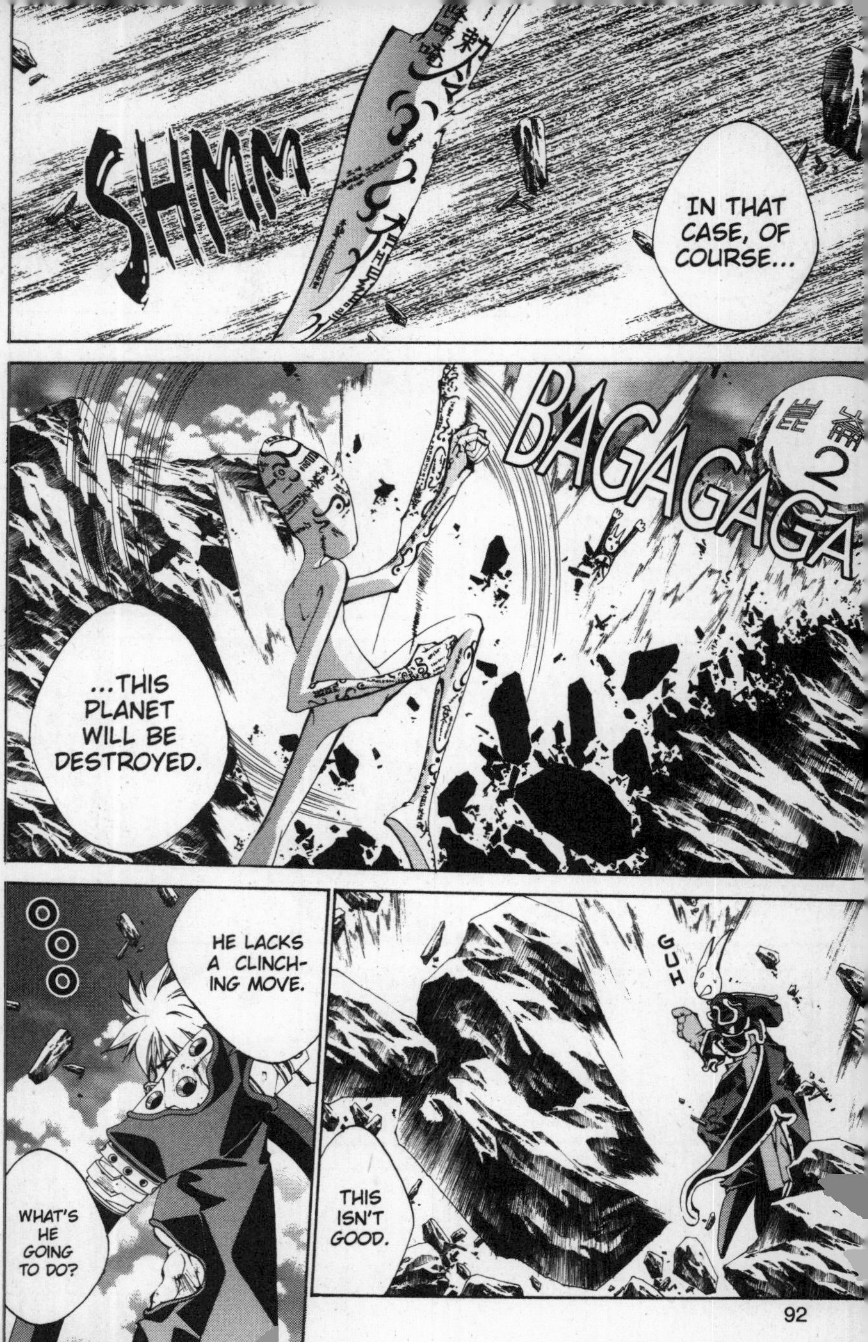
IN THAT CASE, OF COURSE...
SHMM
BAGAGAGA
...THIS PLANET WILL BE DESTROYED.
GUH
THIS ISN'T GOOD.
HE LACKS A CLINCHING MOVE.
WHAT'S HE GOING TO DO?

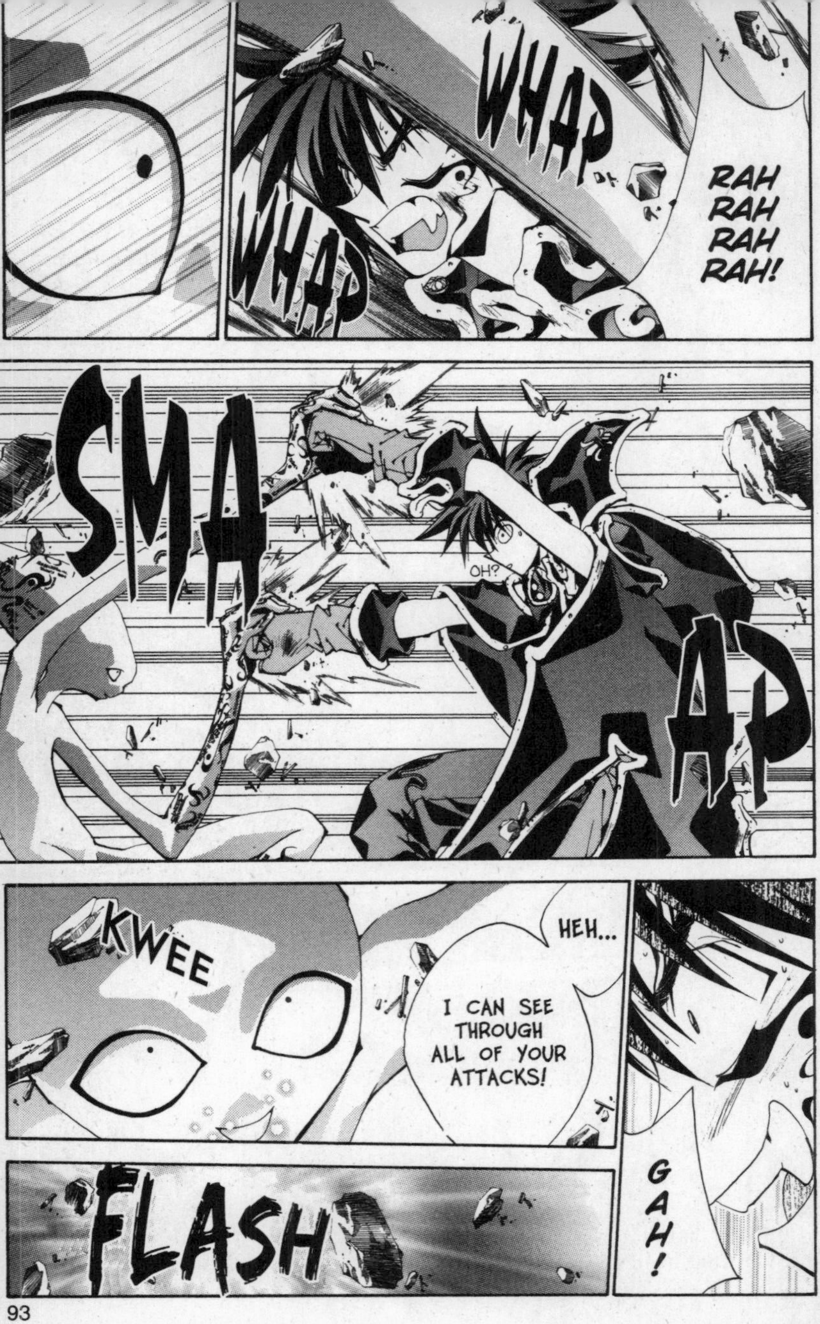
WHAP
WHAP
RAH RAH RAH RAH!
SMA
AP
OH?
GAH!
HEH...
I CAN SEE THROUGH ALL OF YOUR ATTACKS!
KWEE
FLASH

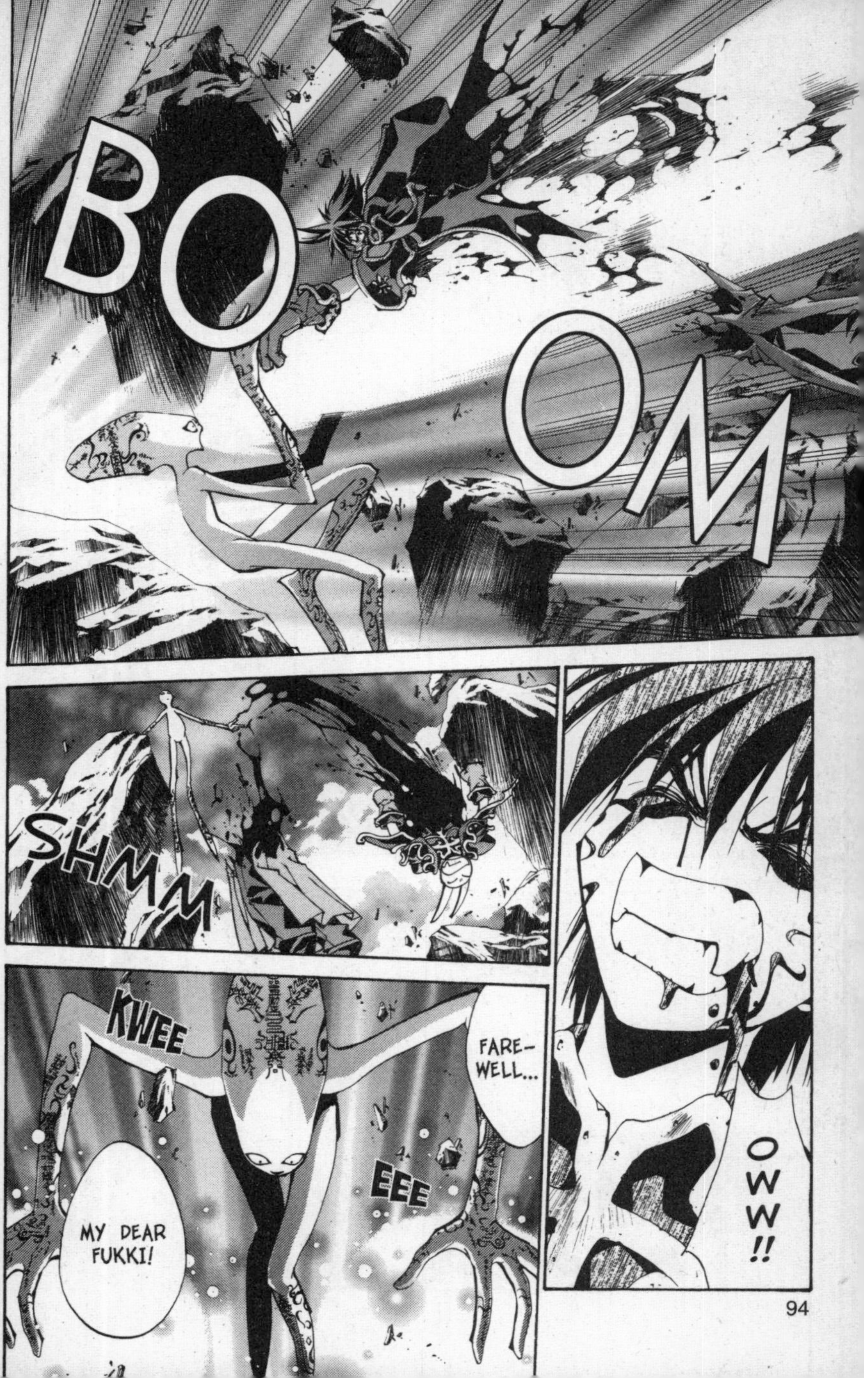
BOOM
OWW!!
SHMM
FARE-WELL...
KWEE
EEE
MY DEAR FUKKI!

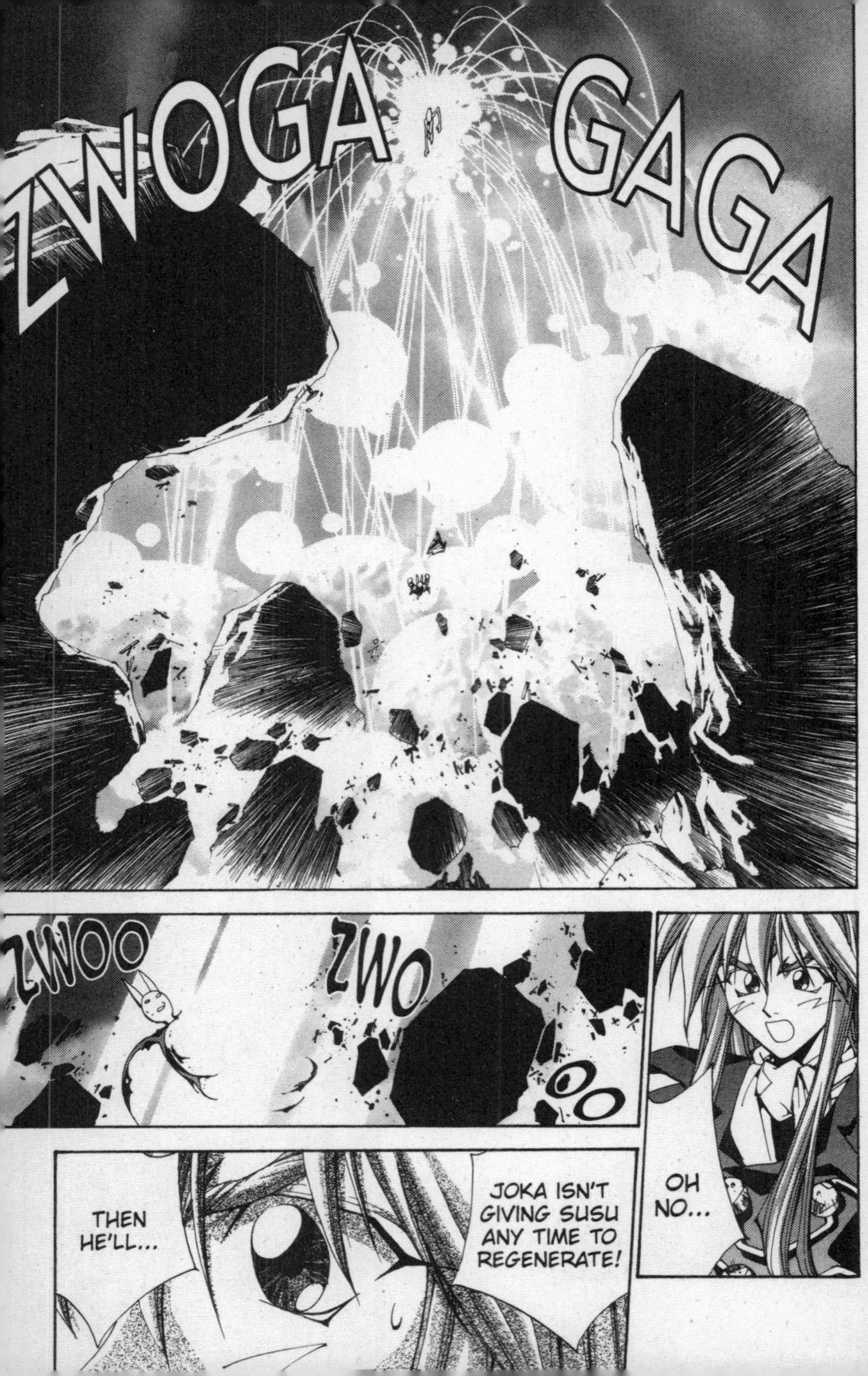
ZWOGA GAGA
OH NO...
ZWOO ZWO OO
JOKA ISN'T GIVING SUSU ANY TIME TO REGENERATE!
THEN HE'LL...

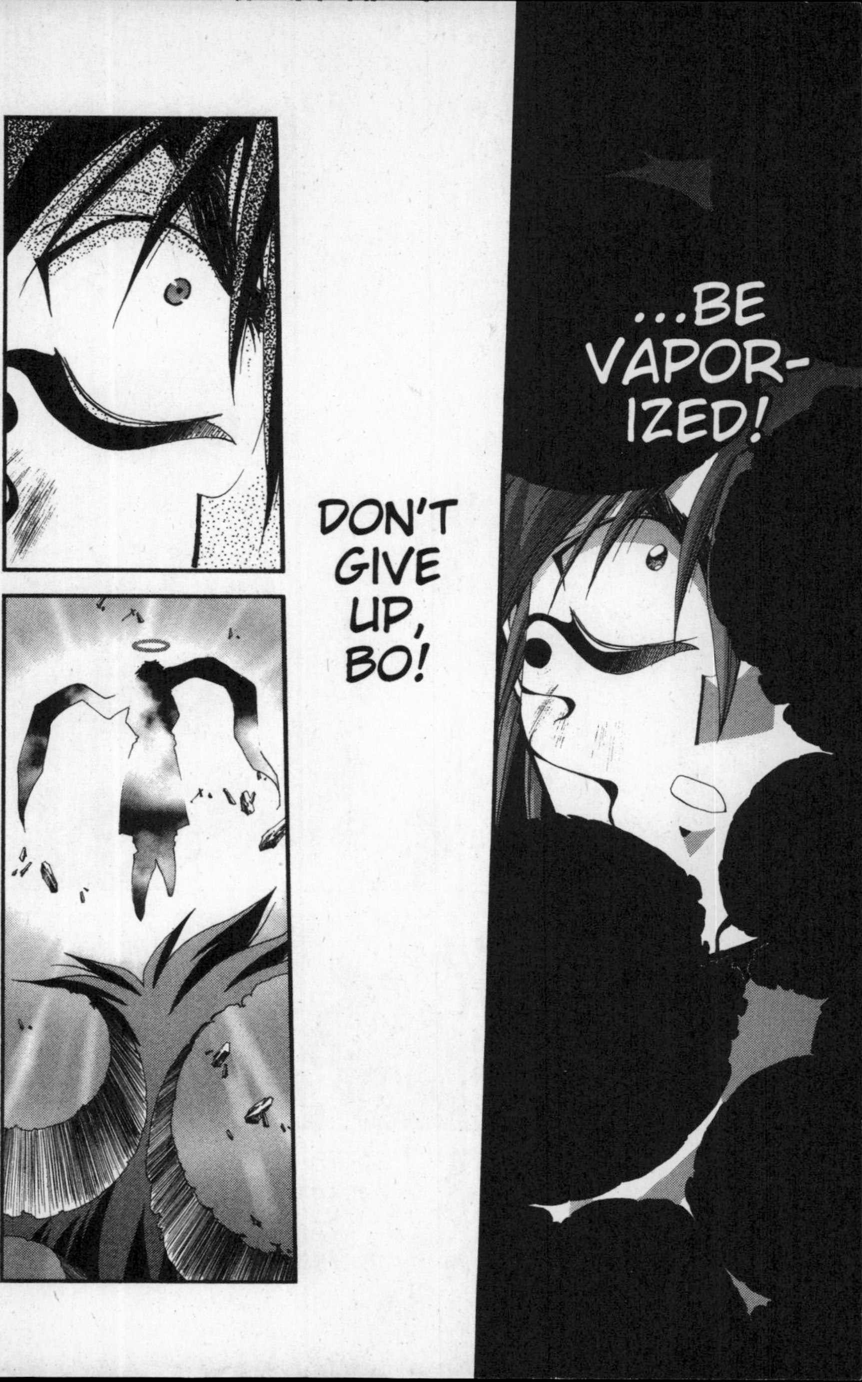
...BE VAPOR-IZED!
DON'T GIVE UP, BO!

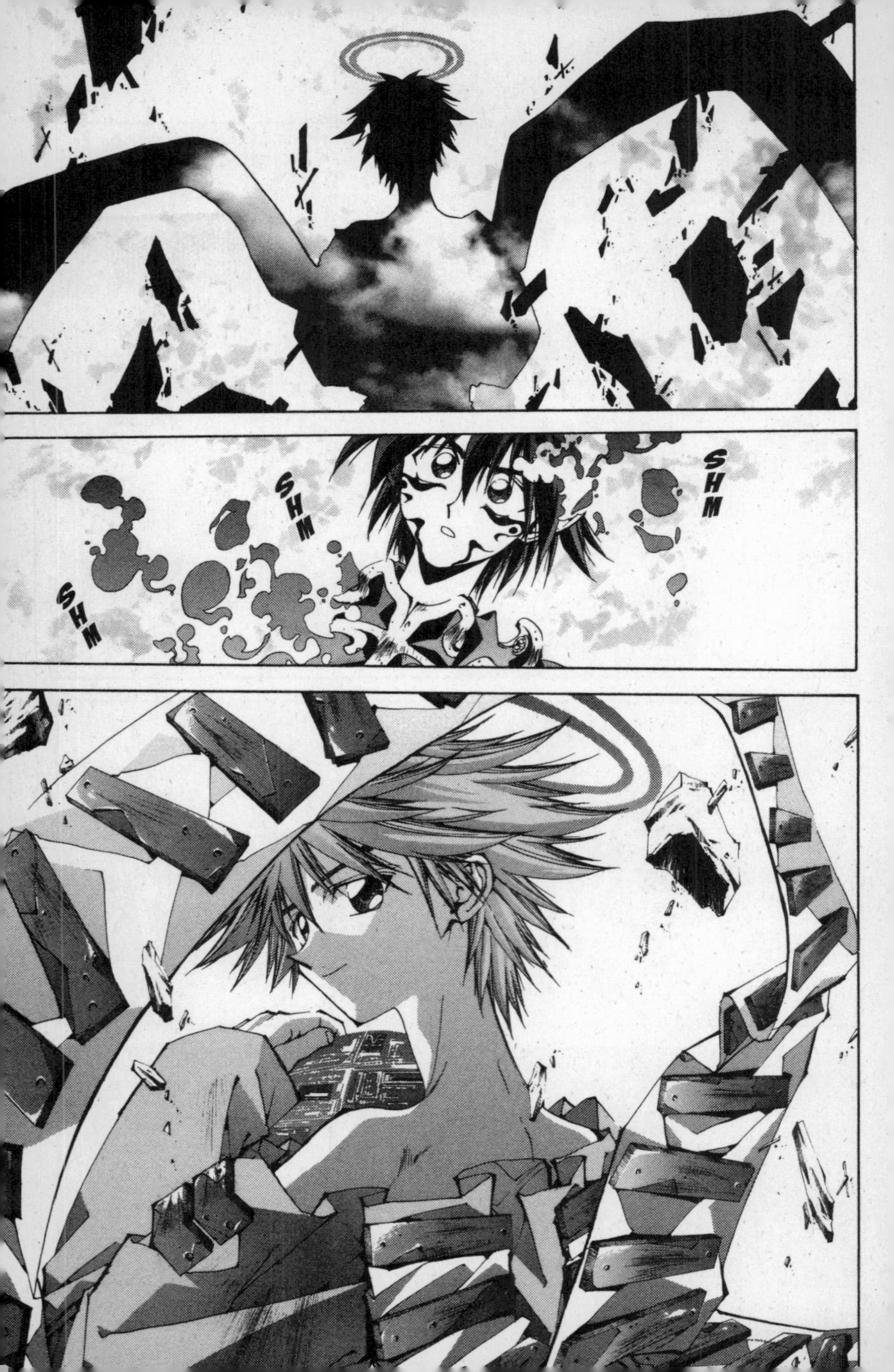
SHM
SHM
SHM

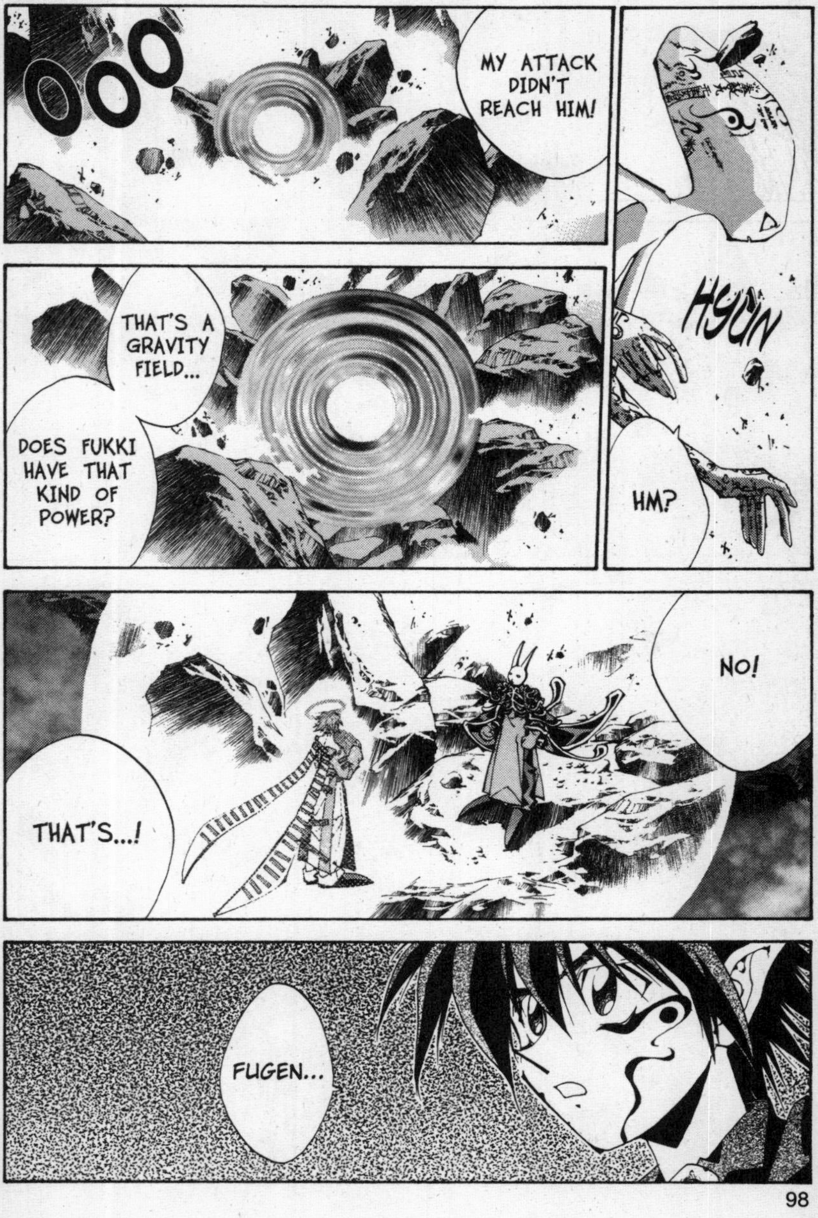
HYUN
HM?
OOO
MY ATTACK DIDN'T REACH HIM!
THAT'S A GRAVITY FIELD...
DOES FUKKI HAVE THAT KIND OF POWER?
NO!
THAT'S...!
FUGEN...

READ THIS WAY

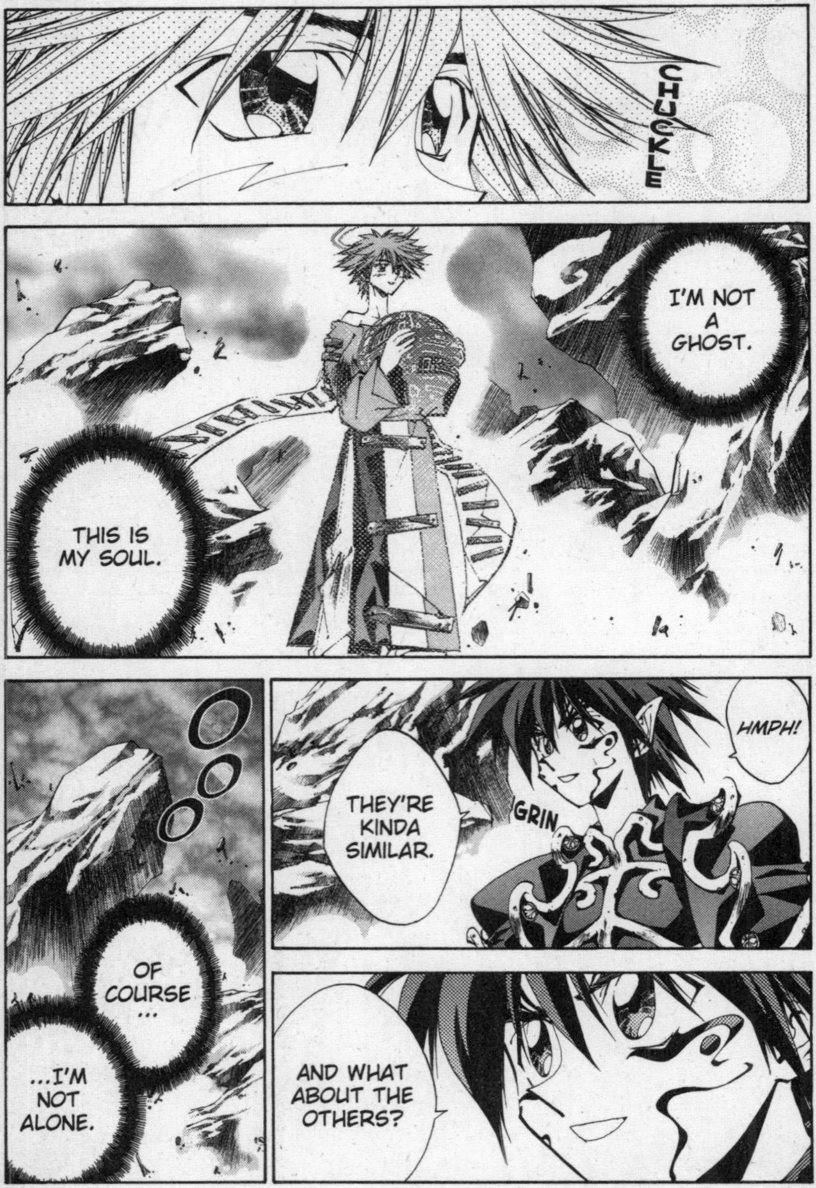
CHUCKLE
I'M NOT A GHOST.
THIS IS MY SOUL.
HMPH!
GRIN
THEY'RE KINDA SIMILAR.
AND WHAT ABOUT THE OTHERS?
OF COURSE...
...I'M NOT ALONE.

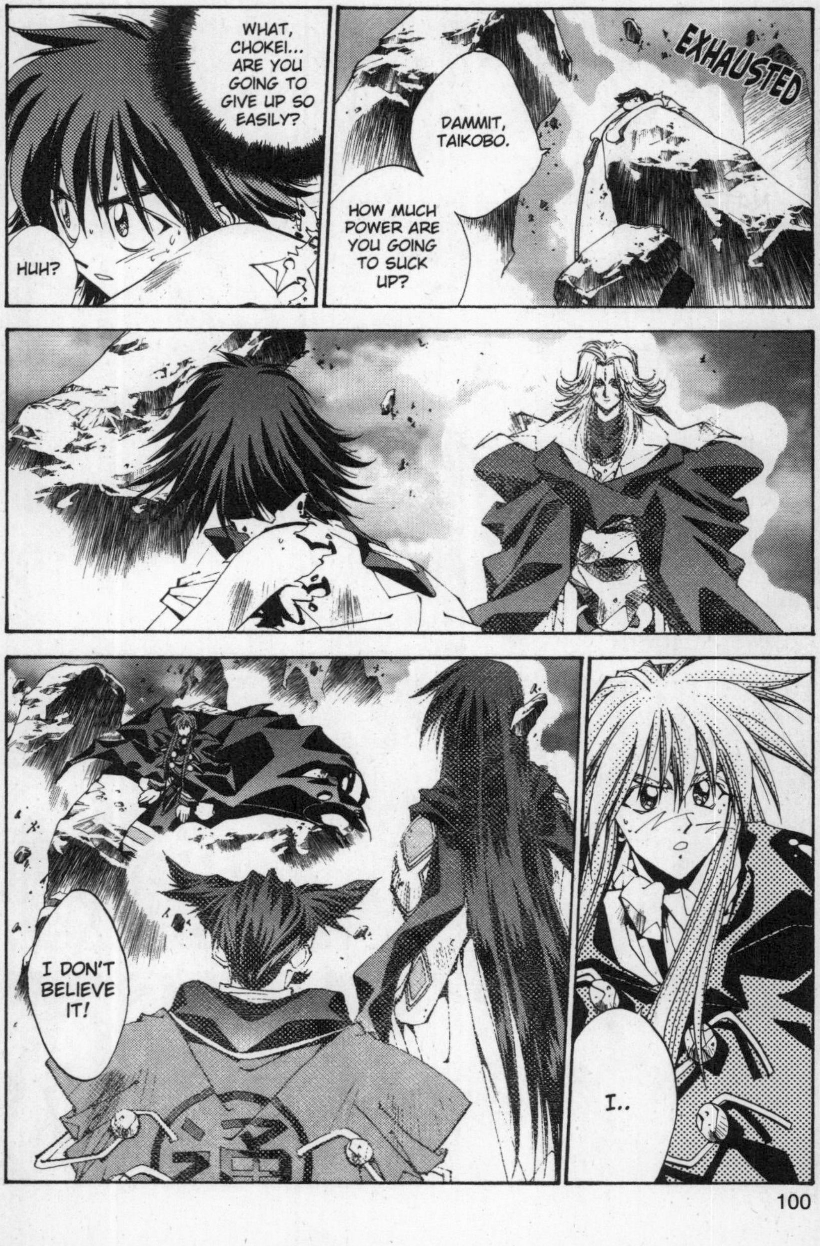
EXHAUSTED
DAMMIT, TAIKOBO.
HOW MUCH POWER ARE YOU GOING TO SUCK UP?
WHAT, CHOKEI... ARE YOU GOING TO GIVE UP SO EASILY?
HUH?
I..
I DON'T BELIEVE IT!

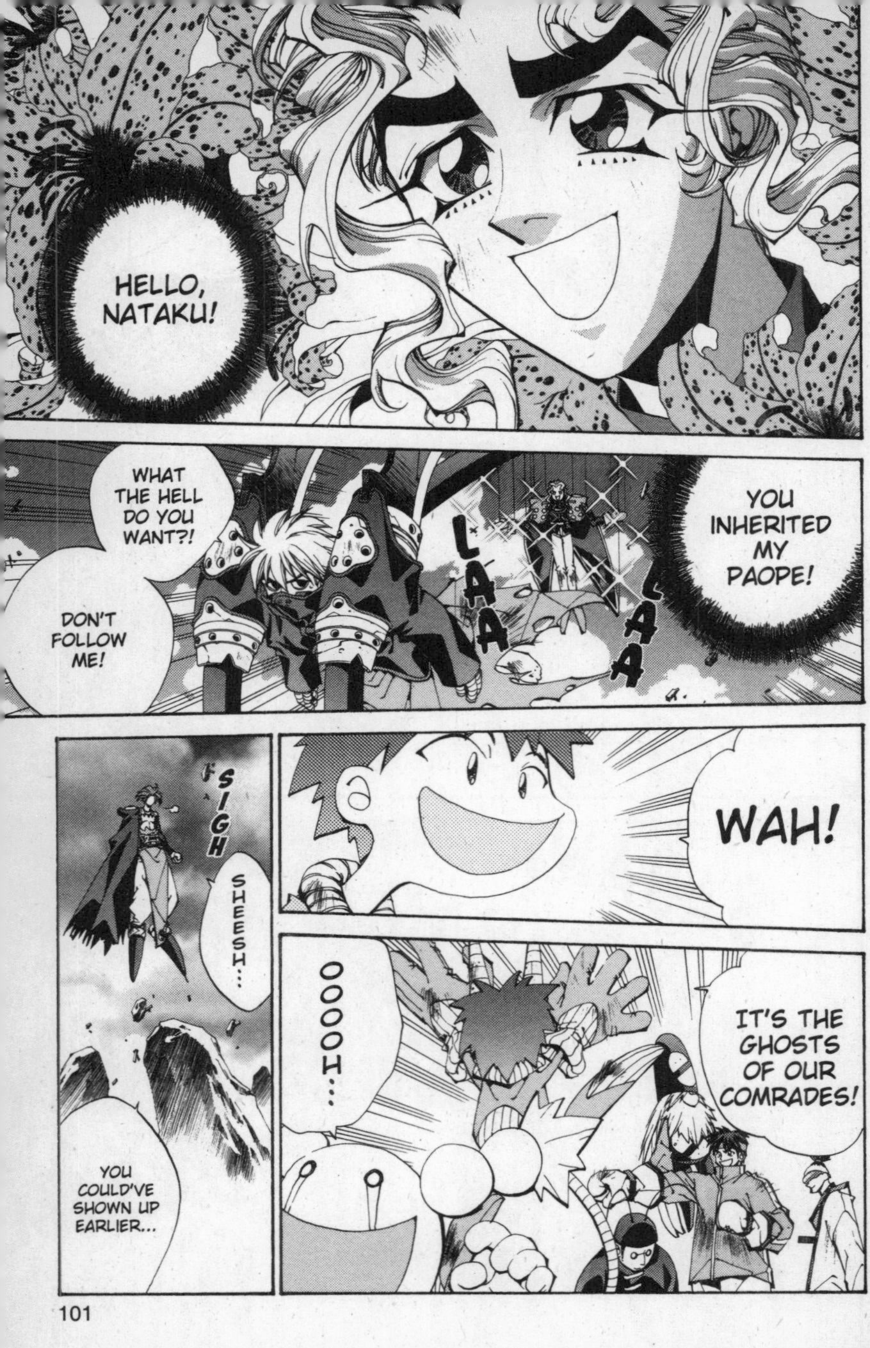
HELLO, NATAKU!
YOU INHERITED MY PAOPE!
LAAA
LAAA
WHAT THE HELL DO YOU WANT?!
DON'T FOLLOW ME!
WAH!
IT'S THE GHOSTS OF OUR COMRADES!
OOOOOH...
SIGH
SHEESH...
YOU COULD'VE SHOWN UP EARLIER...

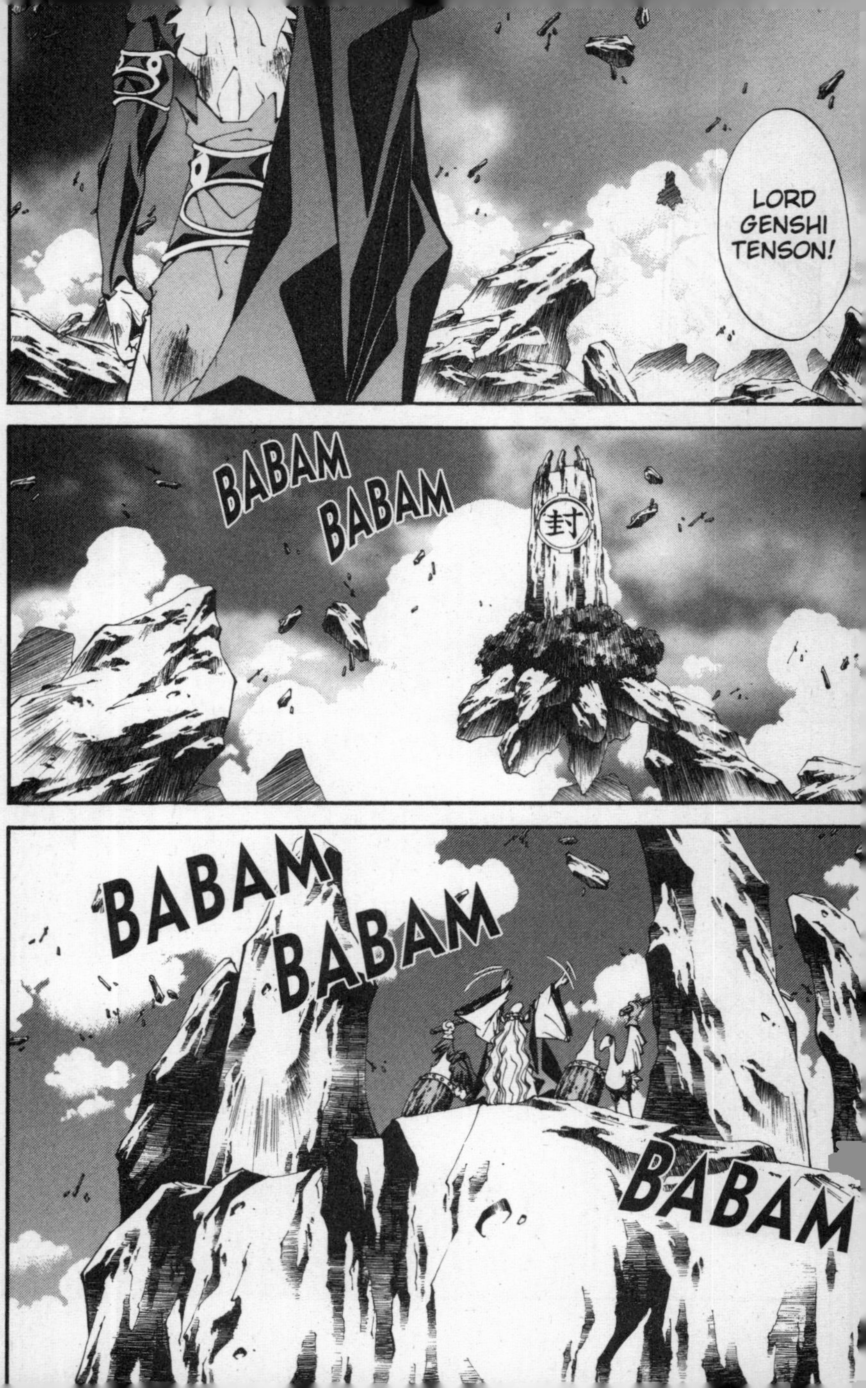
LORD GENSHI TENSON!
BABAM
BABAM
封
BABAM
BABAM
BABAM

READ THIS WAY

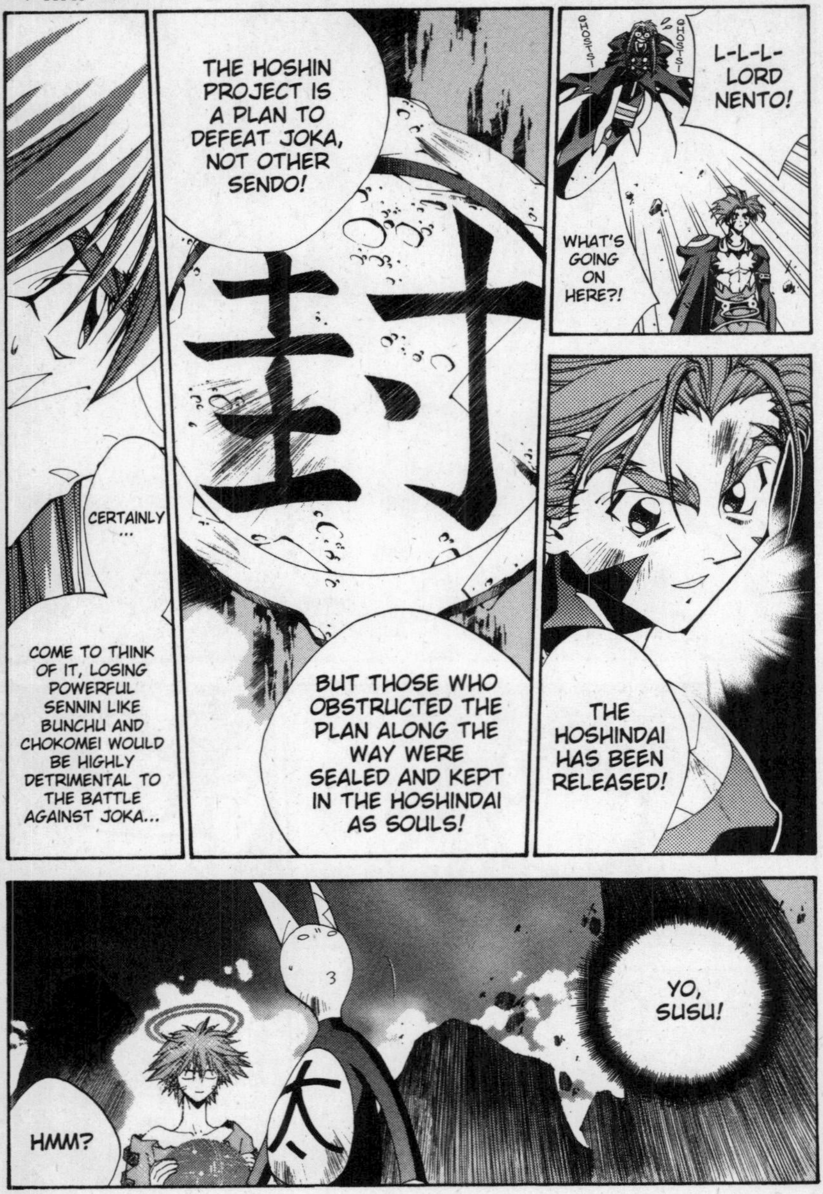
L-L-L-LORD NENTO!
GHOSTS!
GHOSTS!
WHAT'S GOING ON HERE?!
THE HOSHINDAI HAS BEEN RELEASED!
THE HOSHIN PROJECT IS A PLAN TO DEFEAT JOKA, NOT OTHER SENDO!
BUT THOSE WHO OBSTRUCTED THE PLAN ALONG THE WAY WERE SEALED AND KEPT IN THE HOSHINDAI AS SOULS!
CERTAINLY...
COME TO THINK OF IT, LOSING POWERFUL SENNIN LIKE BUNCHU AND CHOKOMEI WOULD BE HIGHLY DETRIMENTAL TO THE BATTLE AGAINST JOKA...
YO, SUSU!
HMM?

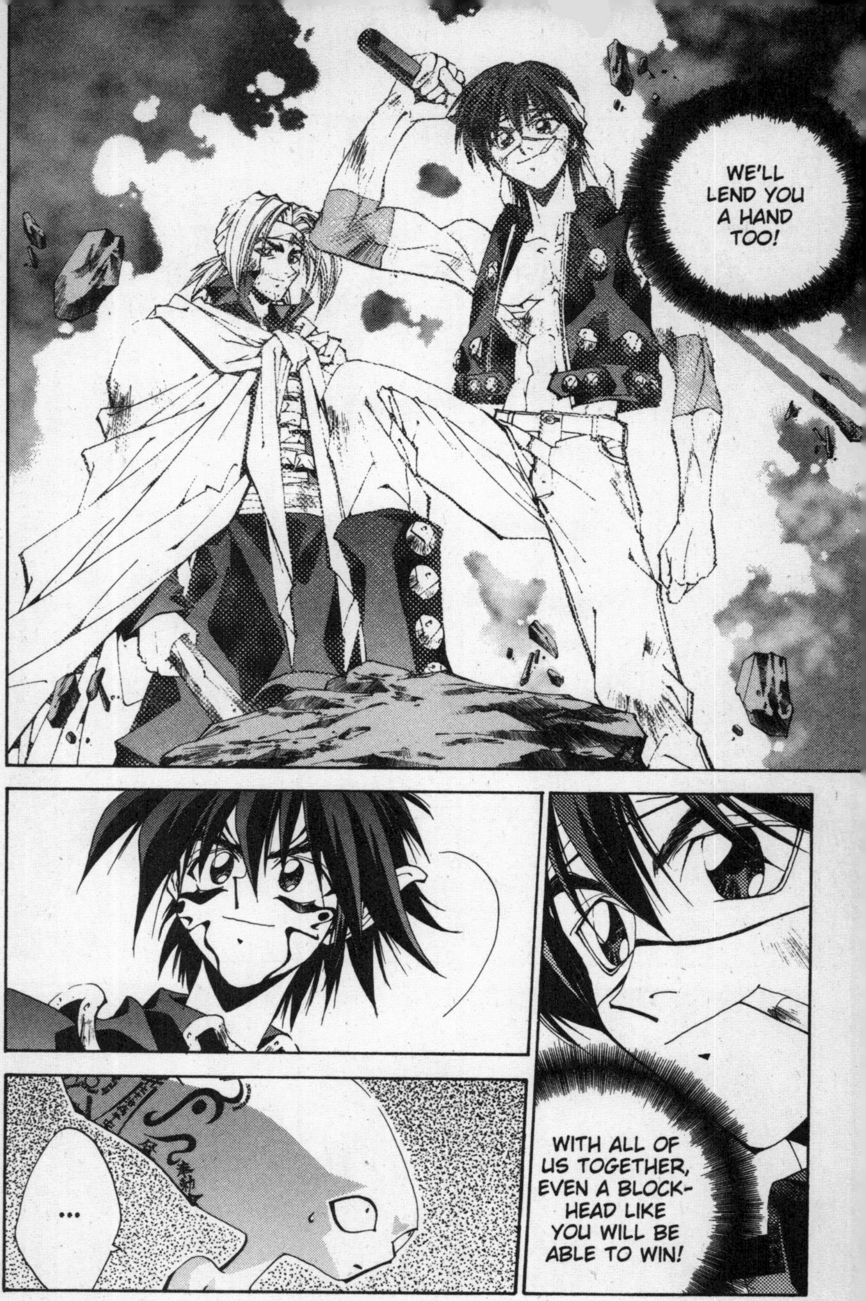
WE'LL LEND YOU A HAND TOO!
WITH ALL OF US TOGETHER, EVEN A BLOCK-HEAD LIKE YOU WILL BE ABLE TO WIN!
...

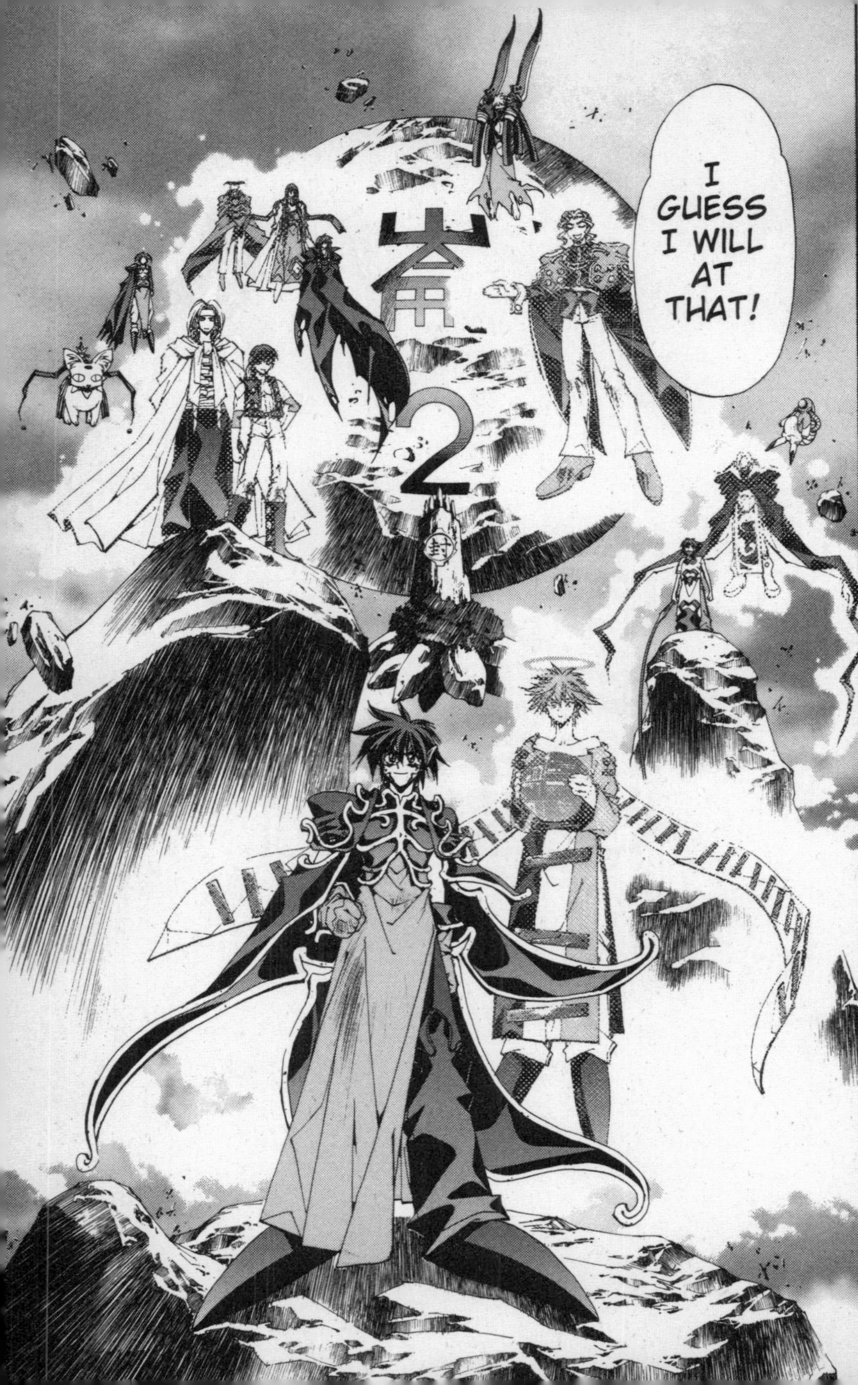
I GUESS I WILL AT THAT!

封神演義

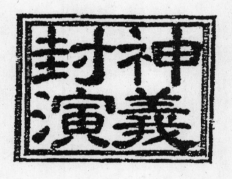

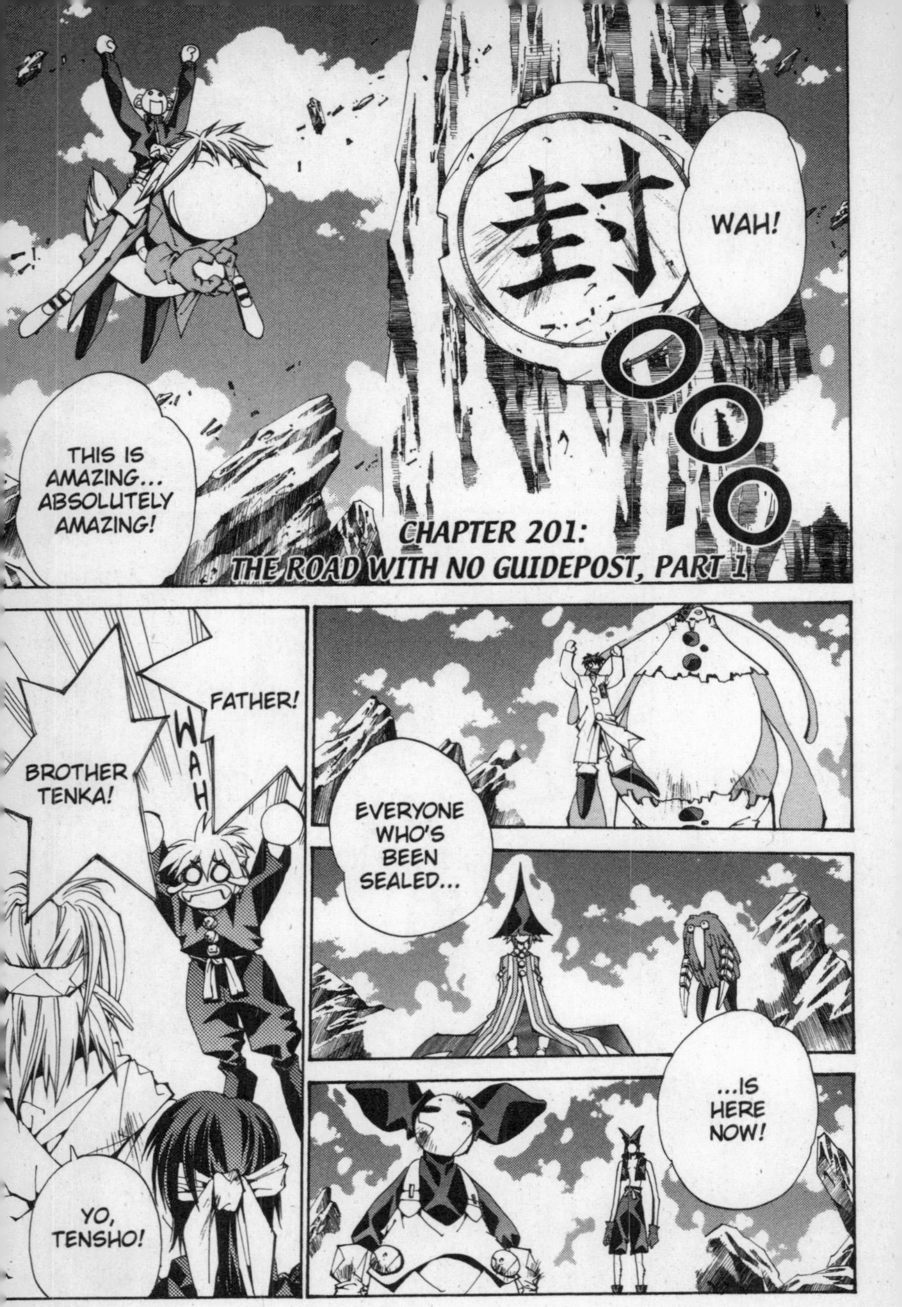
封
WAH!
OOOO
THIS IS AMAZING... ABSOLUTELY AMAZING!
CHAPTER 201:
THE ROAD WITH NO GUIDEPOST, PART 1
EVERYONE WHO'S BEEN SEALED...
...IS HERE NOW!
FATHER!
WAH
BROTHER TENKA!
YO, TENSHO!

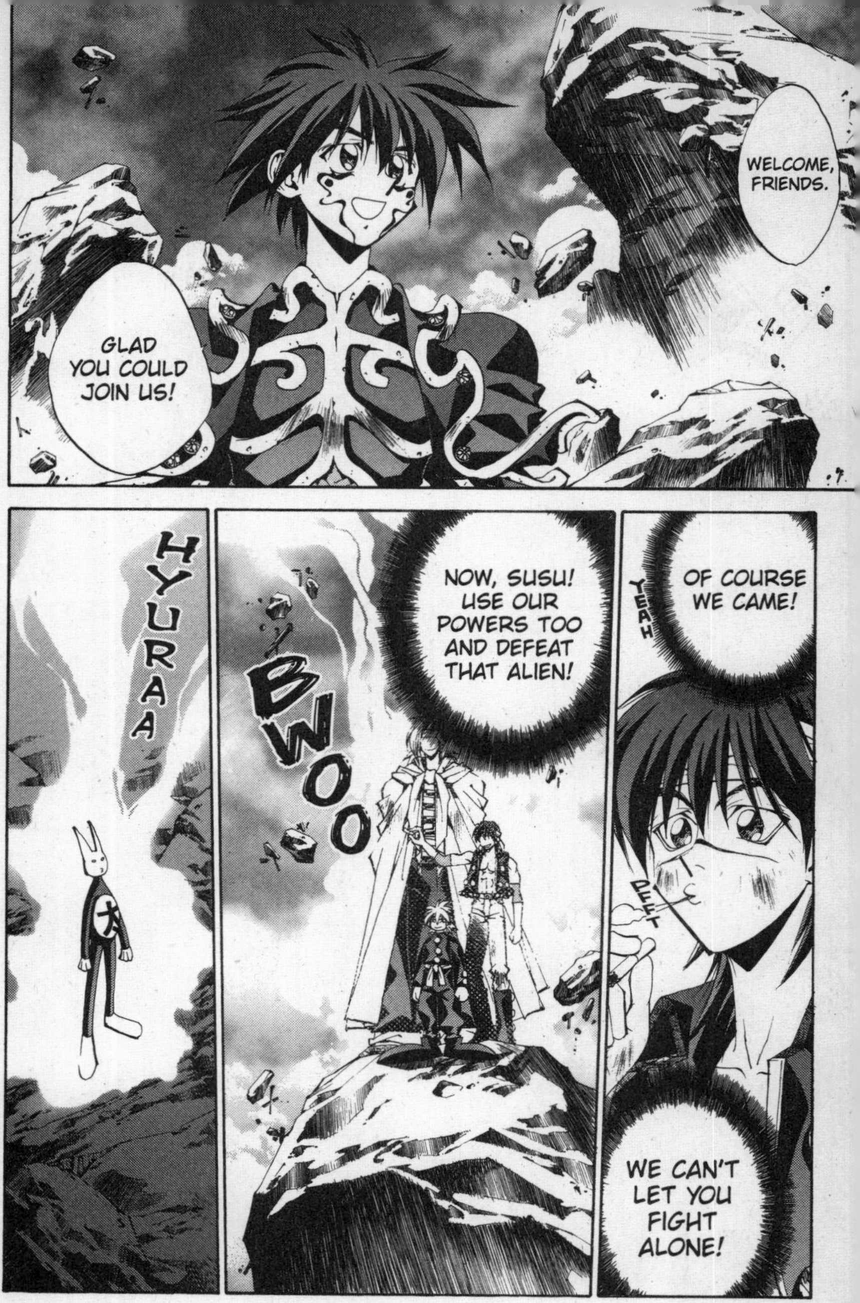
WELCOME, FRIENDS.
GLAD YOU COULD JOIN US!
YEAH
OF COURSE WE CAME!
PFFT
WE CAN'T LET YOU FIGHT ALONE!
NOW, SUSU! USE OUR POWERS TOO AND DEFEAT THAT ALIEN!
BWOO
HYURAA

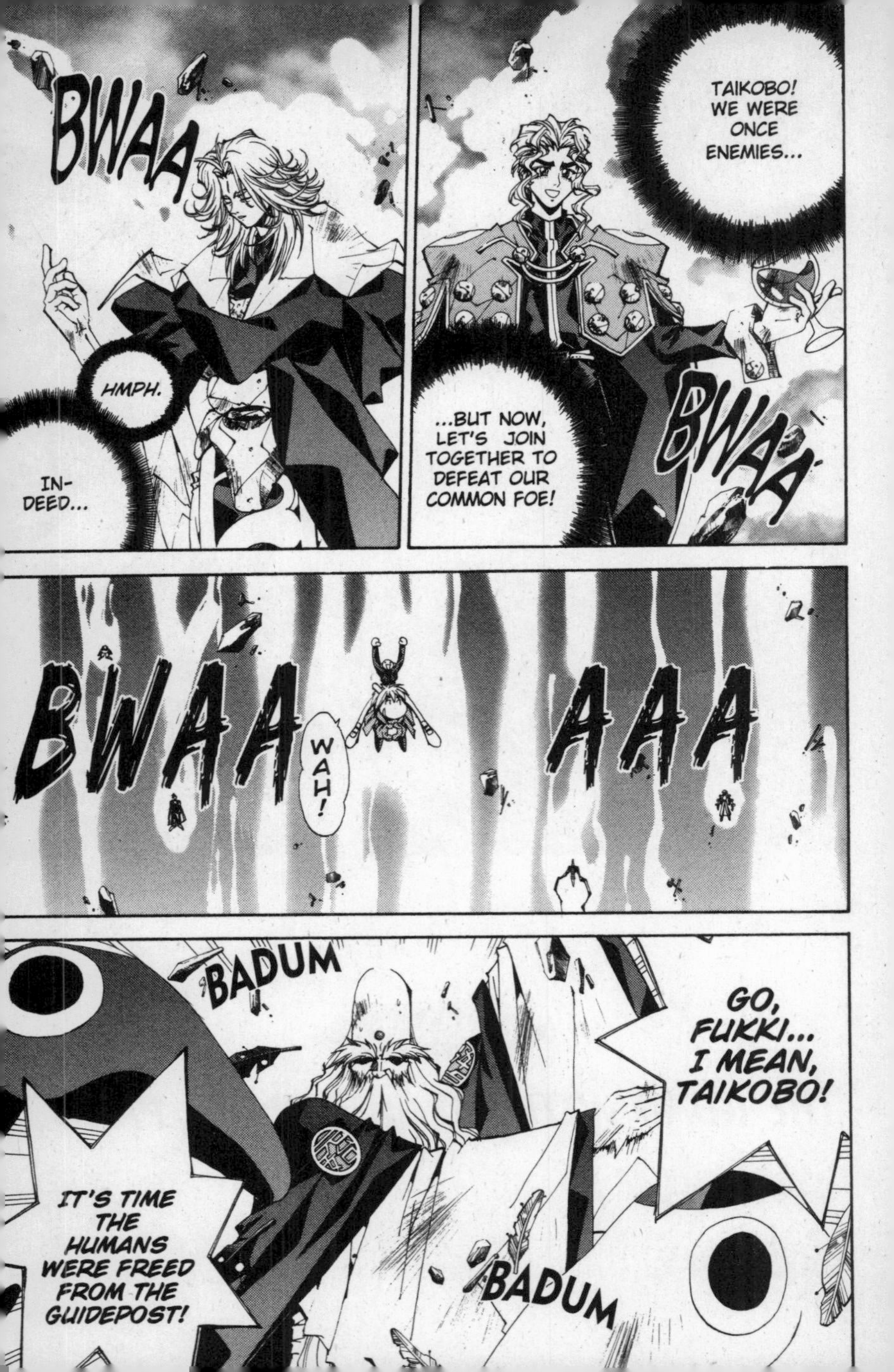
TAIKOBO! WE WERE ONCE ENEMIES...
...BUT NOW, LET'S JOIN TOGETHER TO DEFEAT OUR COMMON FOE!
BWAA
BWAA
HMPH.
IN-DEED...
BWAA AAA
WAH!
BADUM
GO, FUKKI... I MEAN, TAIKOBO!
IT'S TIME THE HUMANS WERE FREED FROM THE GUIDEPOST!
BADUM

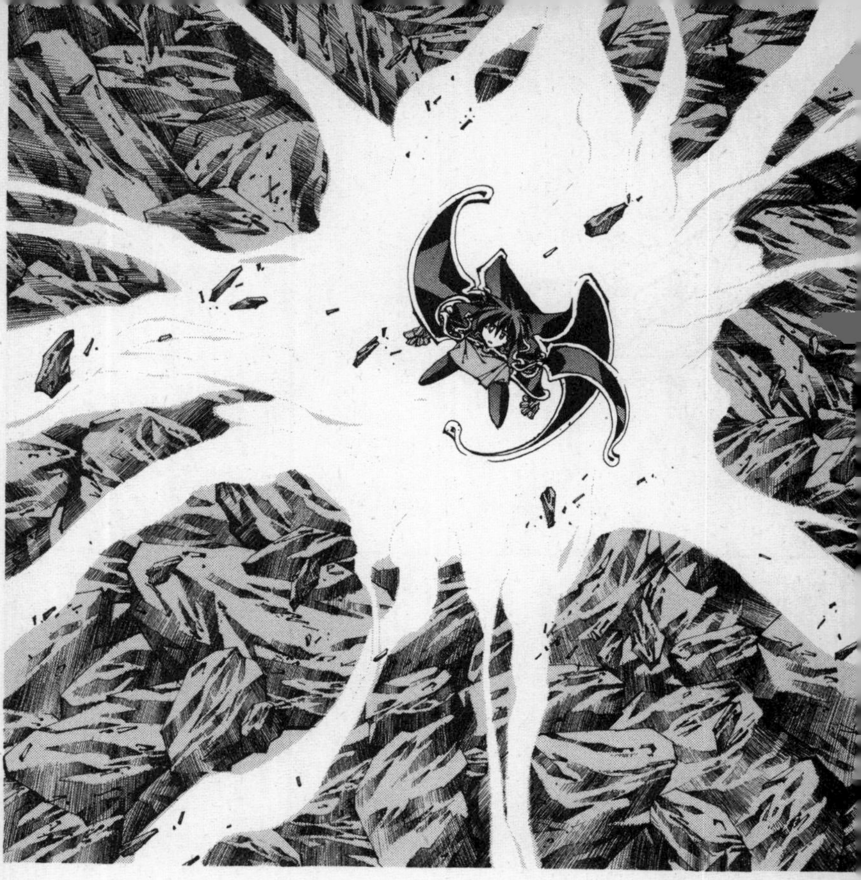

Chapter 201

THE ROAD WITH NO GUIDEPOST, PART 1

READ THIS WAY

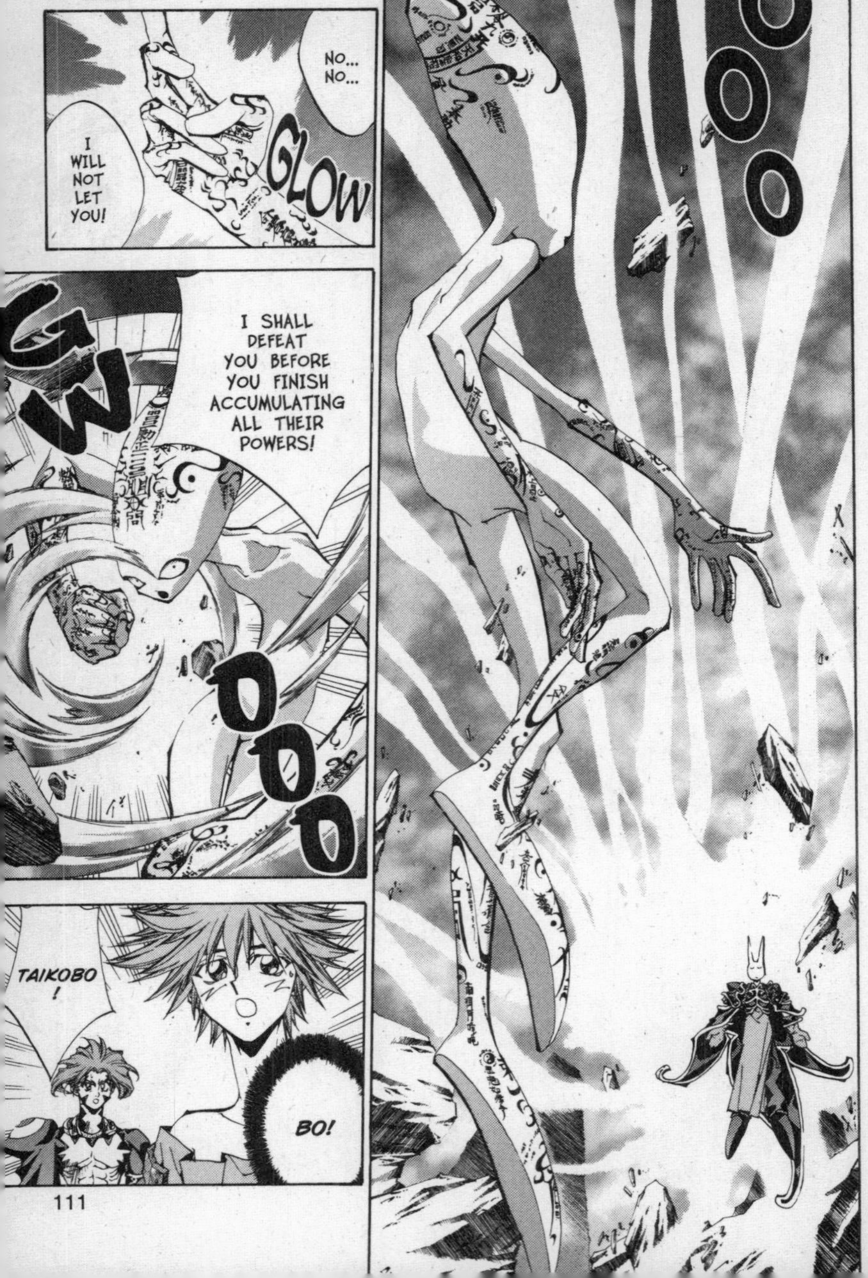
OOO
NO... NO...
GLOW
I WILL NOT LET YOU!
I SHALL DEFEAT YOU BEFORE YOU FINISH ACCUMULATING ALL THEIR POWERS!
GW
DODO
BO!
TAIKOBO!

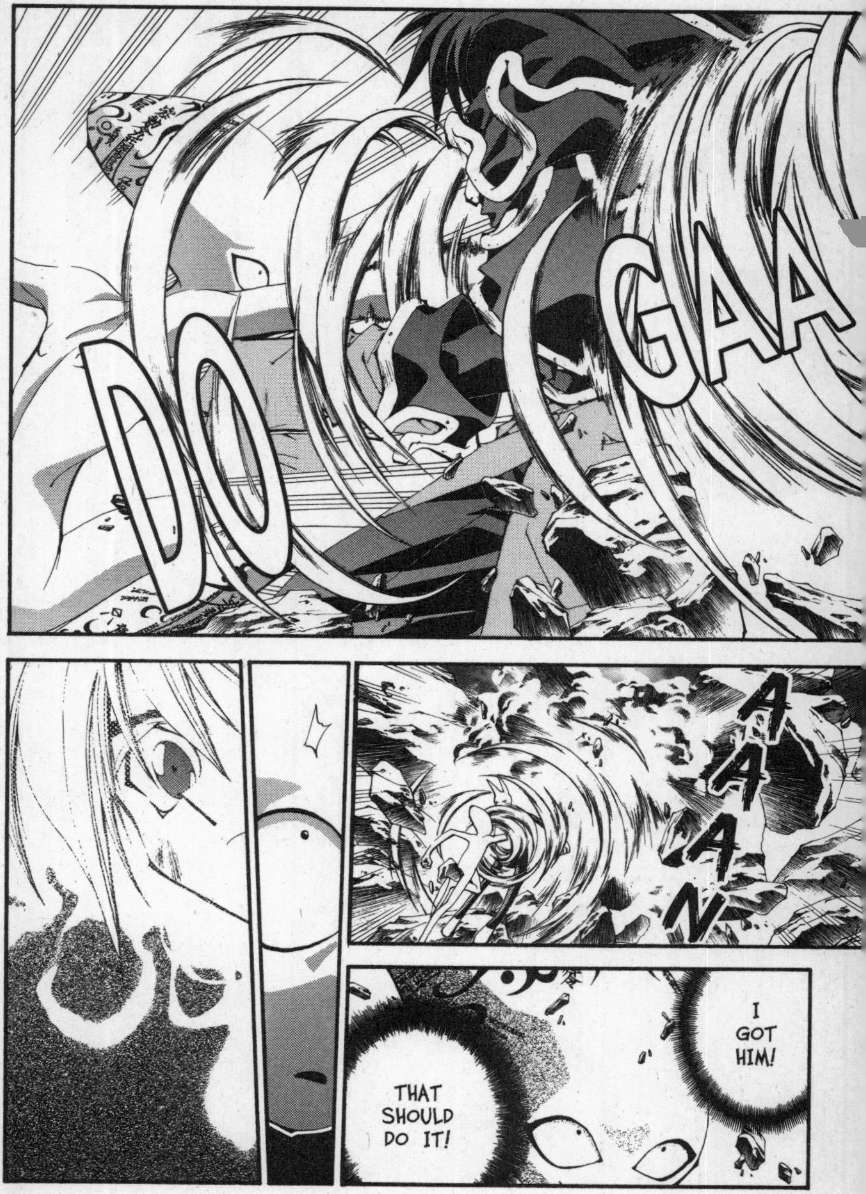
GAA
DO
AAAAN
I GOT HIM!
THAT SHOULD DO IT!

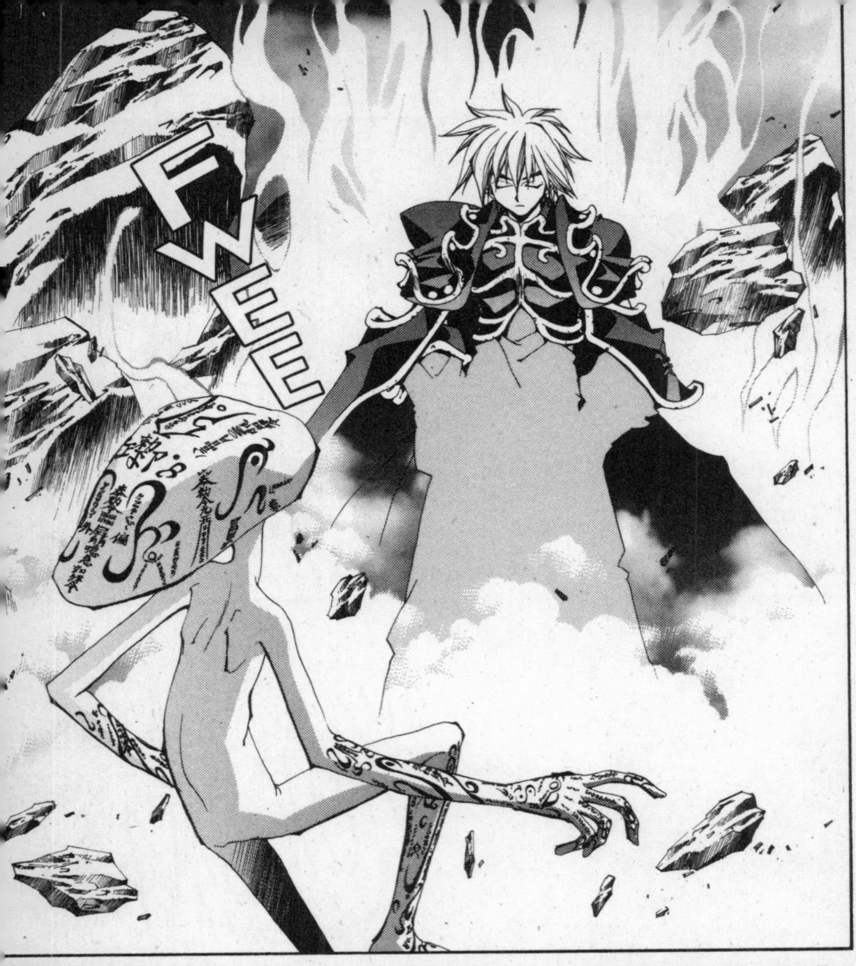
FWEEE
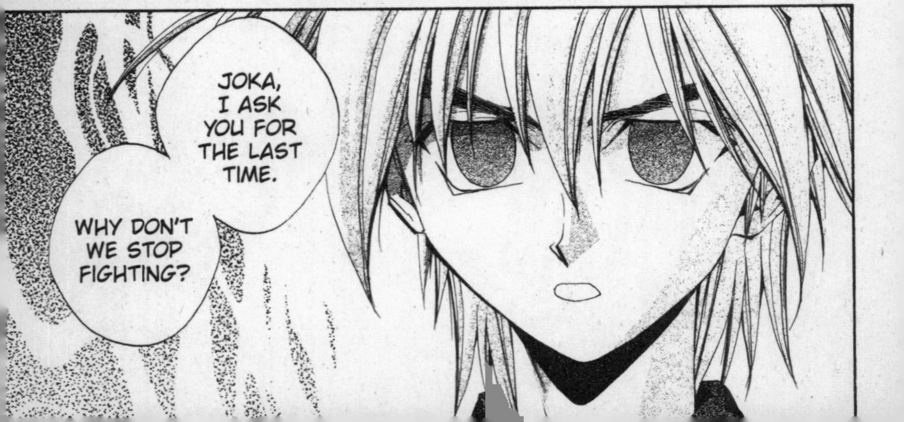
JOKA, I ASK YOU FOR THE LAST TIME.
WHY DON'T WE STOP FIGHTING?

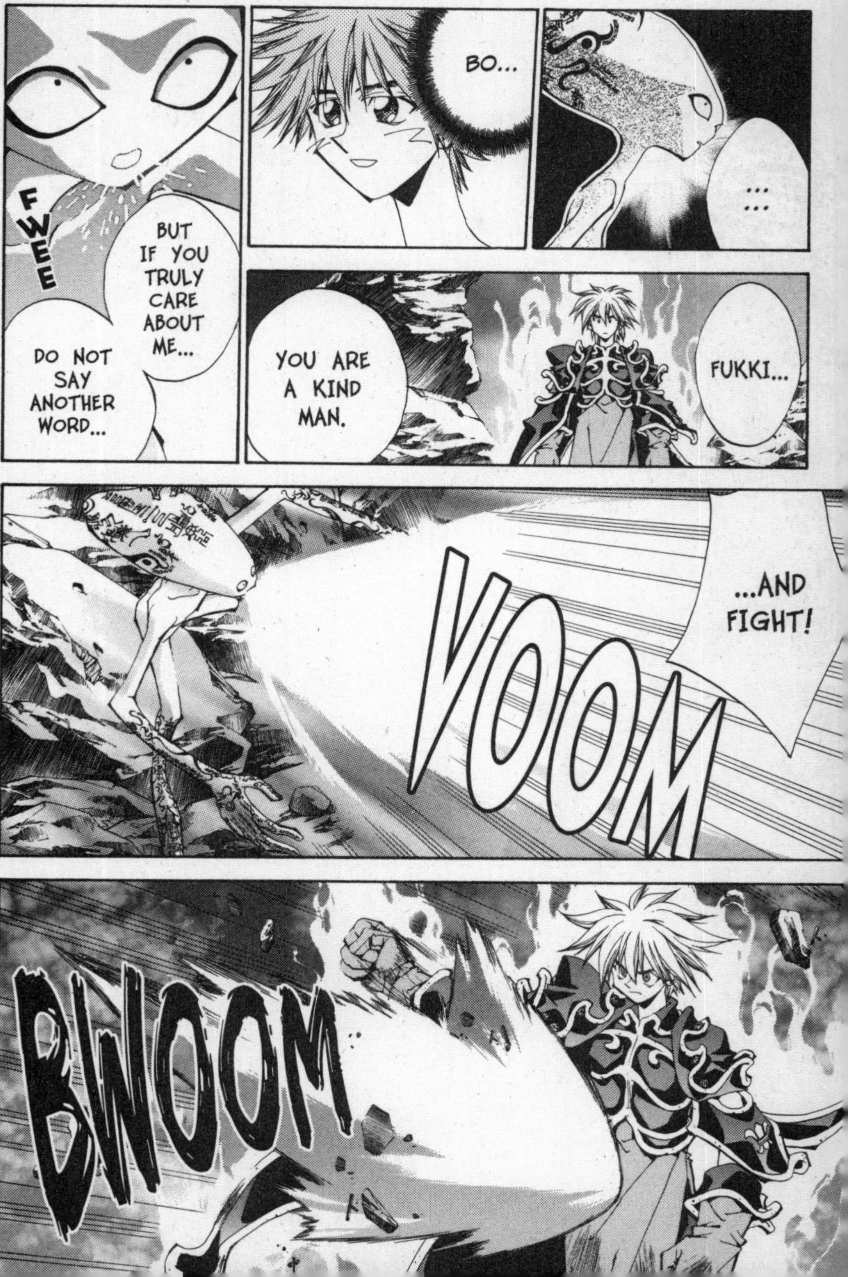
……
……
BO...
FUKKI...
YOU ARE A KIND MAN.
FWEE
BUT IF YOU TRULY CARE ABOUT ME...
DO NOT SAY ANOTHER WORD...
...AND FIGHT!
VOOM
BWOOM

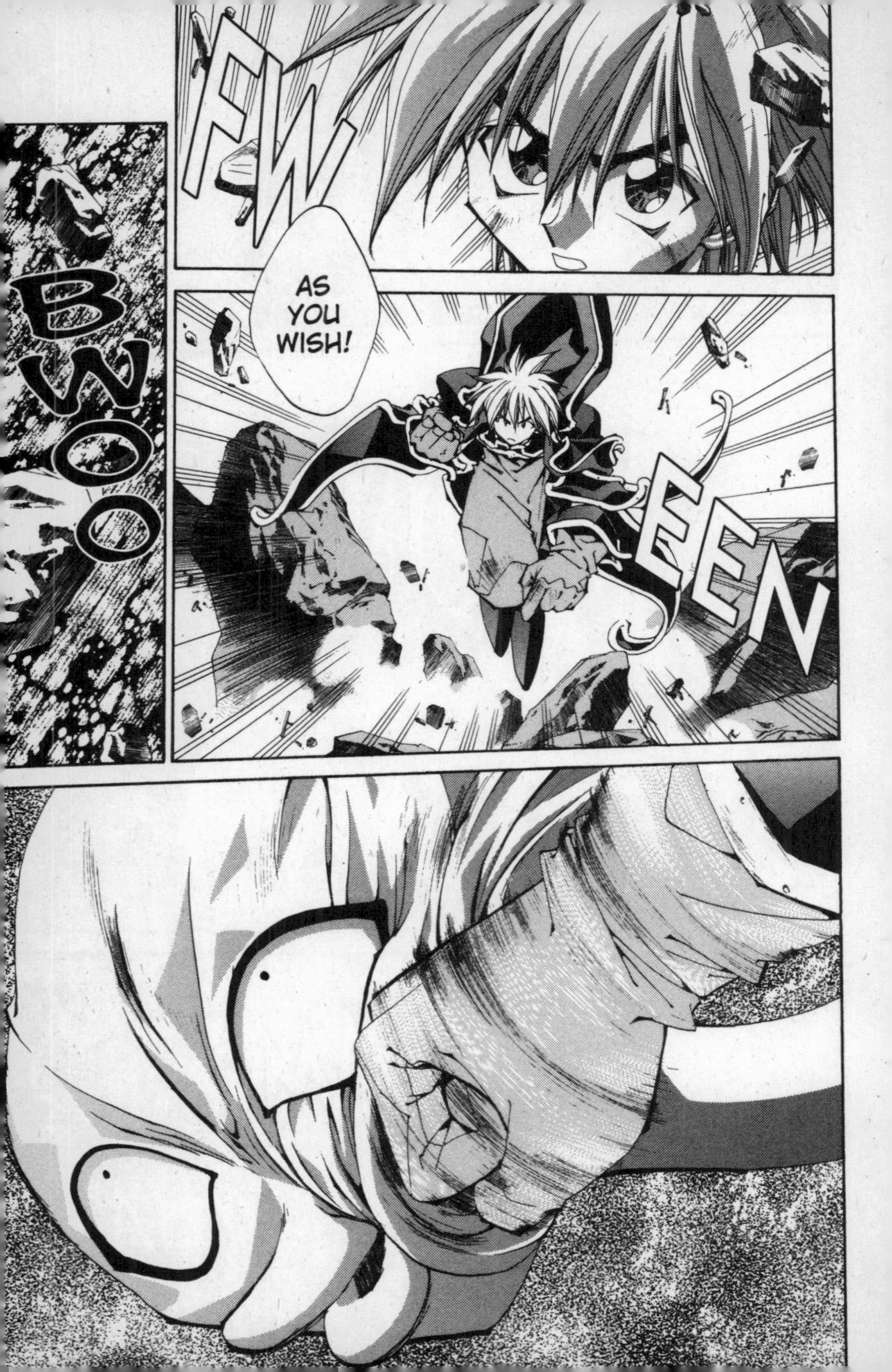
FW
AS YOU WISH!
EEN
BWOO

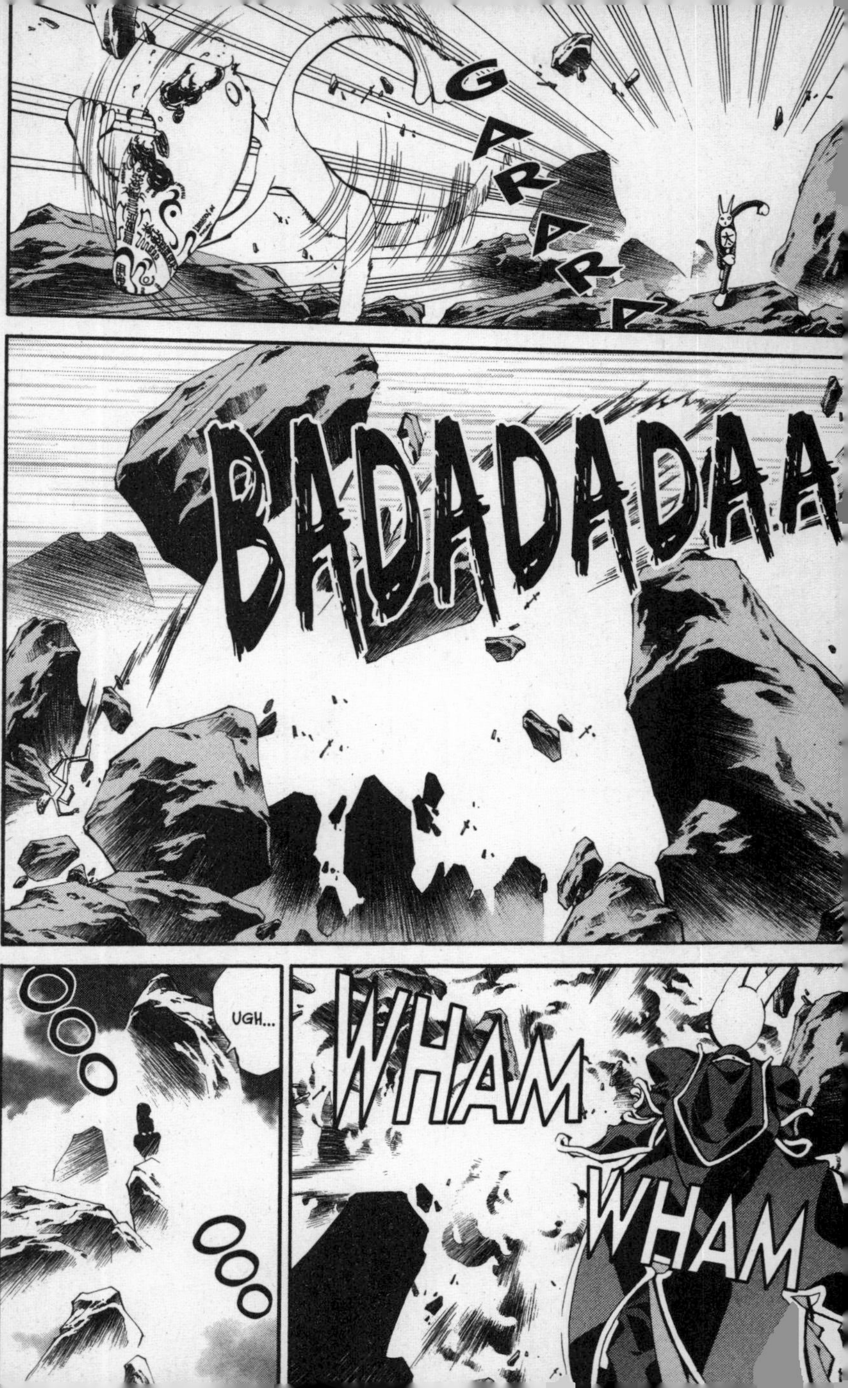
GARARA
BADADADAA
WHAM
WHAM
UGH...

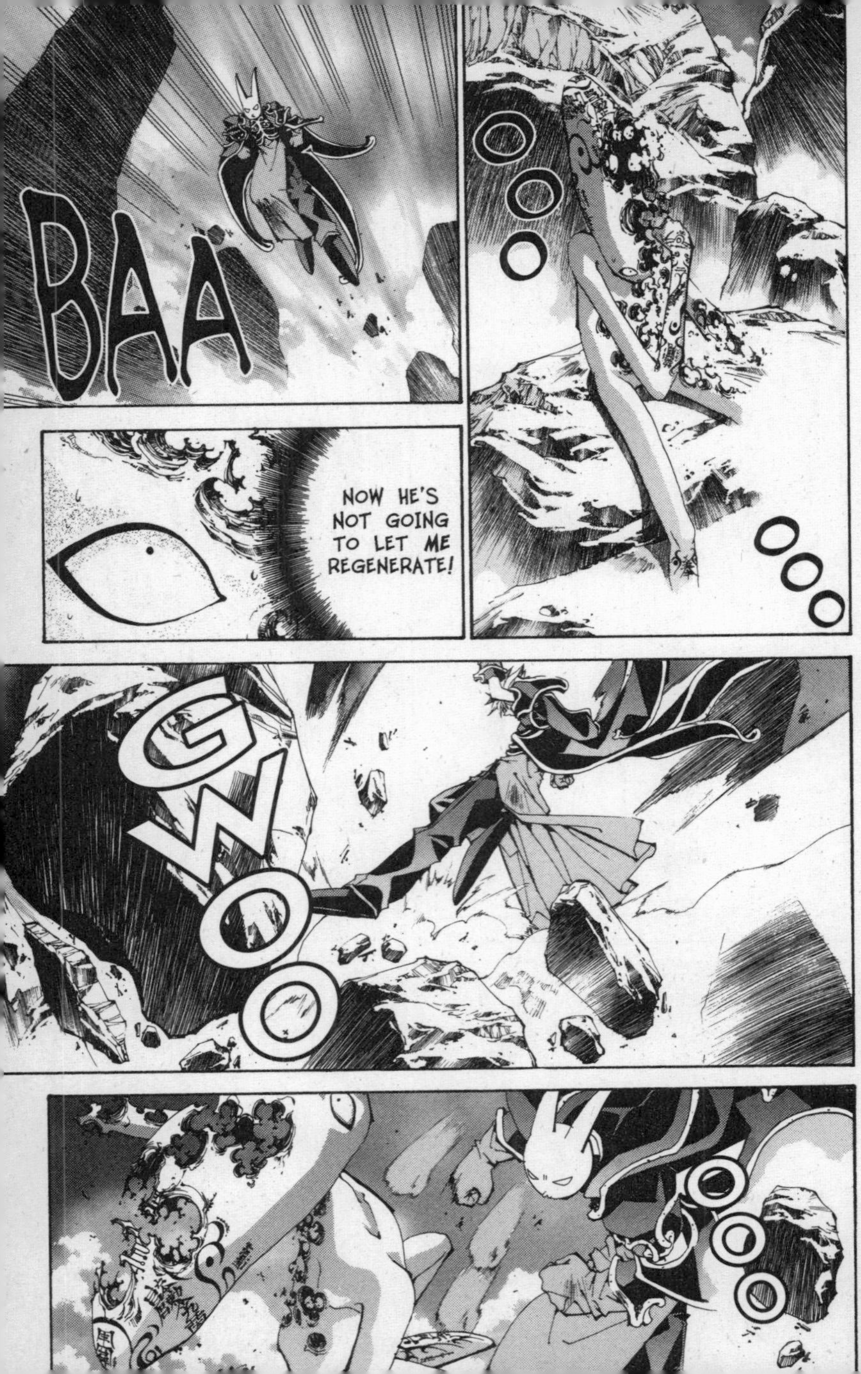
OOOO
OOO
BAA
NOW HE'S NOT GOING TO LET ME REGENERATE!
GWOO
OOOO

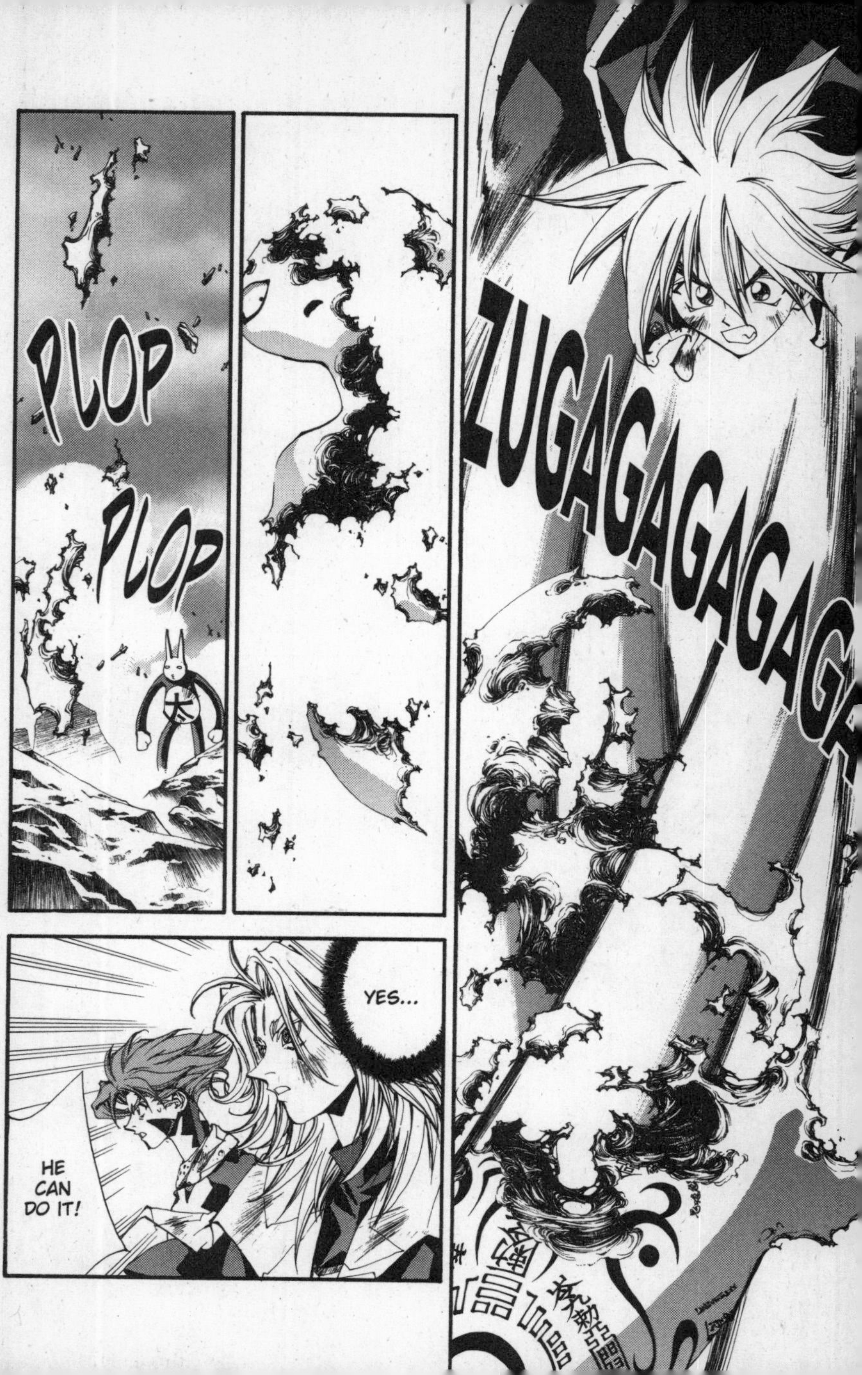
ZUGAGAGAGAGA
PLOP
PLOP
YES...
HE CAN DO IT!

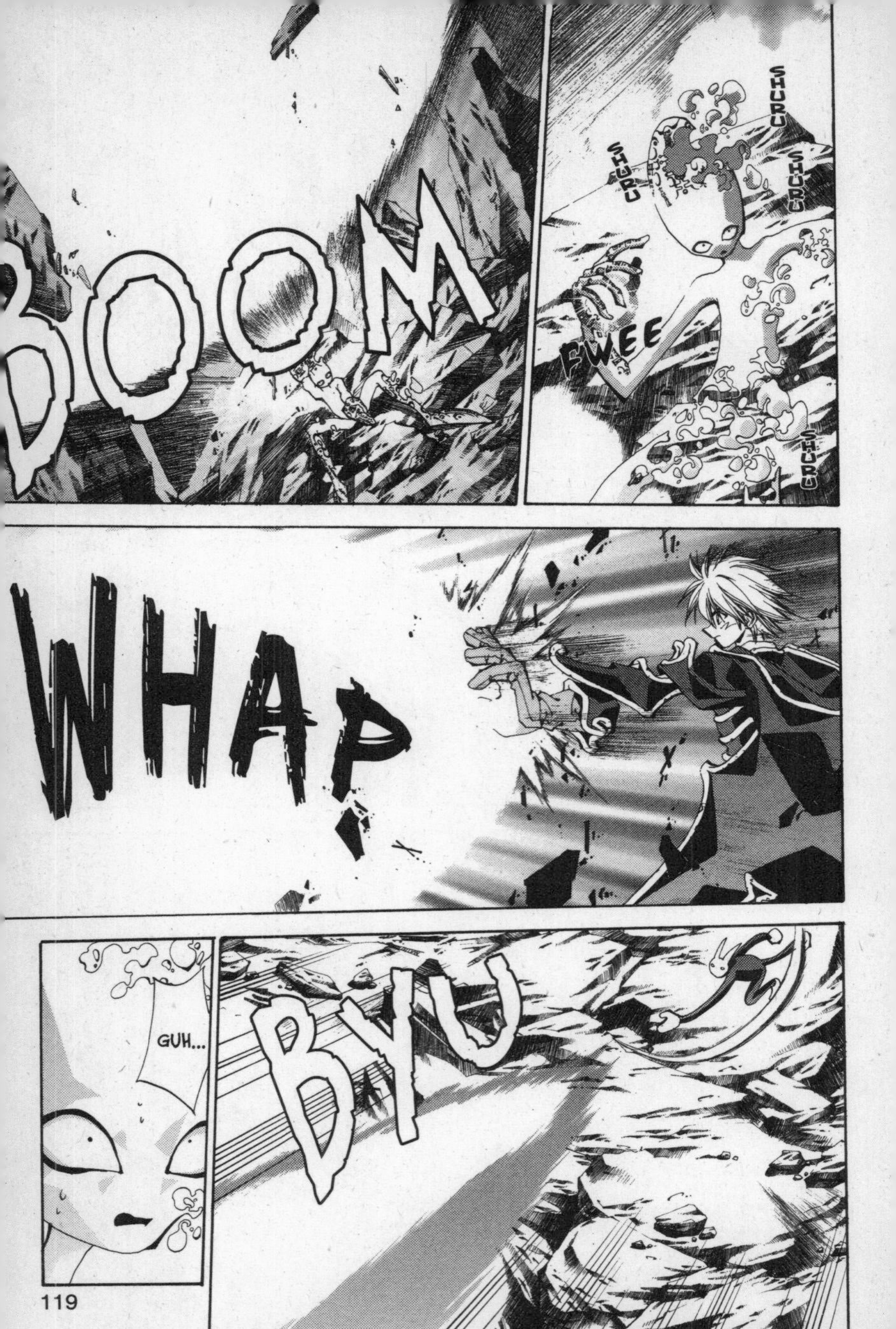
SHURU
SHURU
SHURU
SHURU
FWEE
BOOM
WHAP
BYU
GUH...

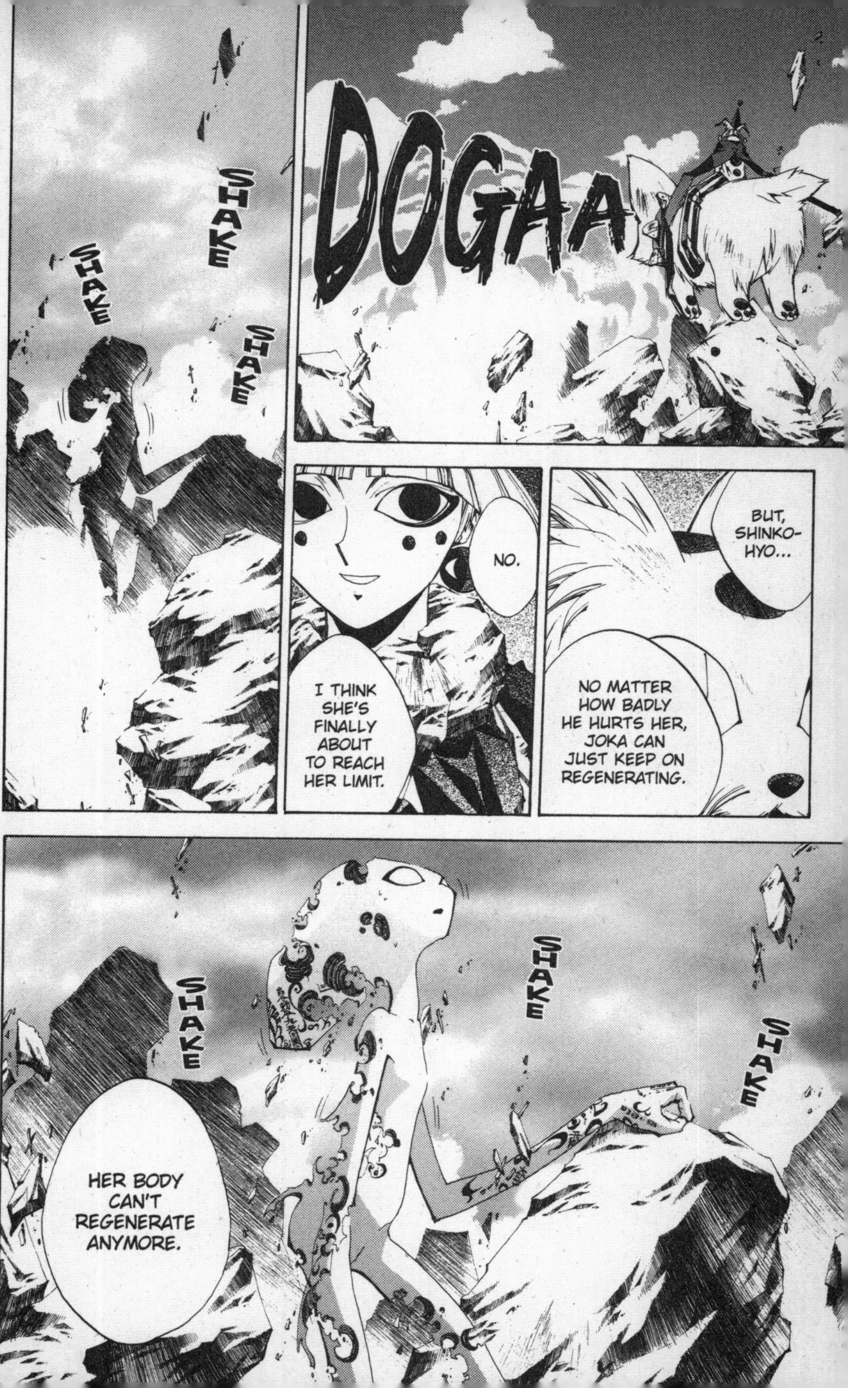
DOGAA
BUT, SHINKO-HYO...
NO MATTER HOW BADLY HE HURTS HER, JOKA CAN JUST KEEP ON REGENERATING.
NO.
I THINK SHE'S FINALLY ABOUT TO REACH HER LIMIT.
SHAKE
SHAKE
SHAKE
SHAKE
SHAKE
SHAKE
HER BODY CAN'T REGENERATE ANYMORE.

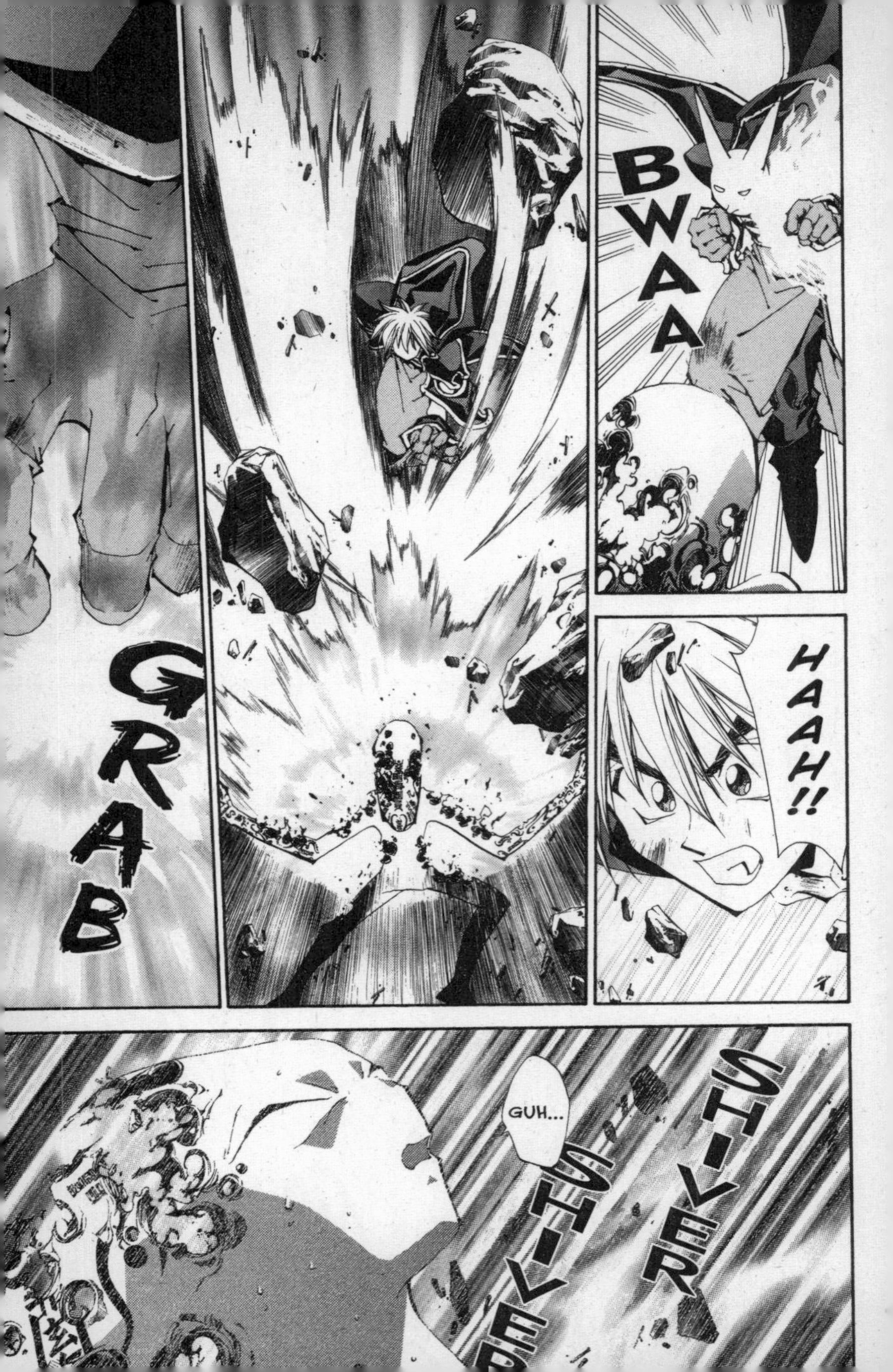
BWAA
HAAAH!!
GRAB
SHIVER
SHIVE
GUH...

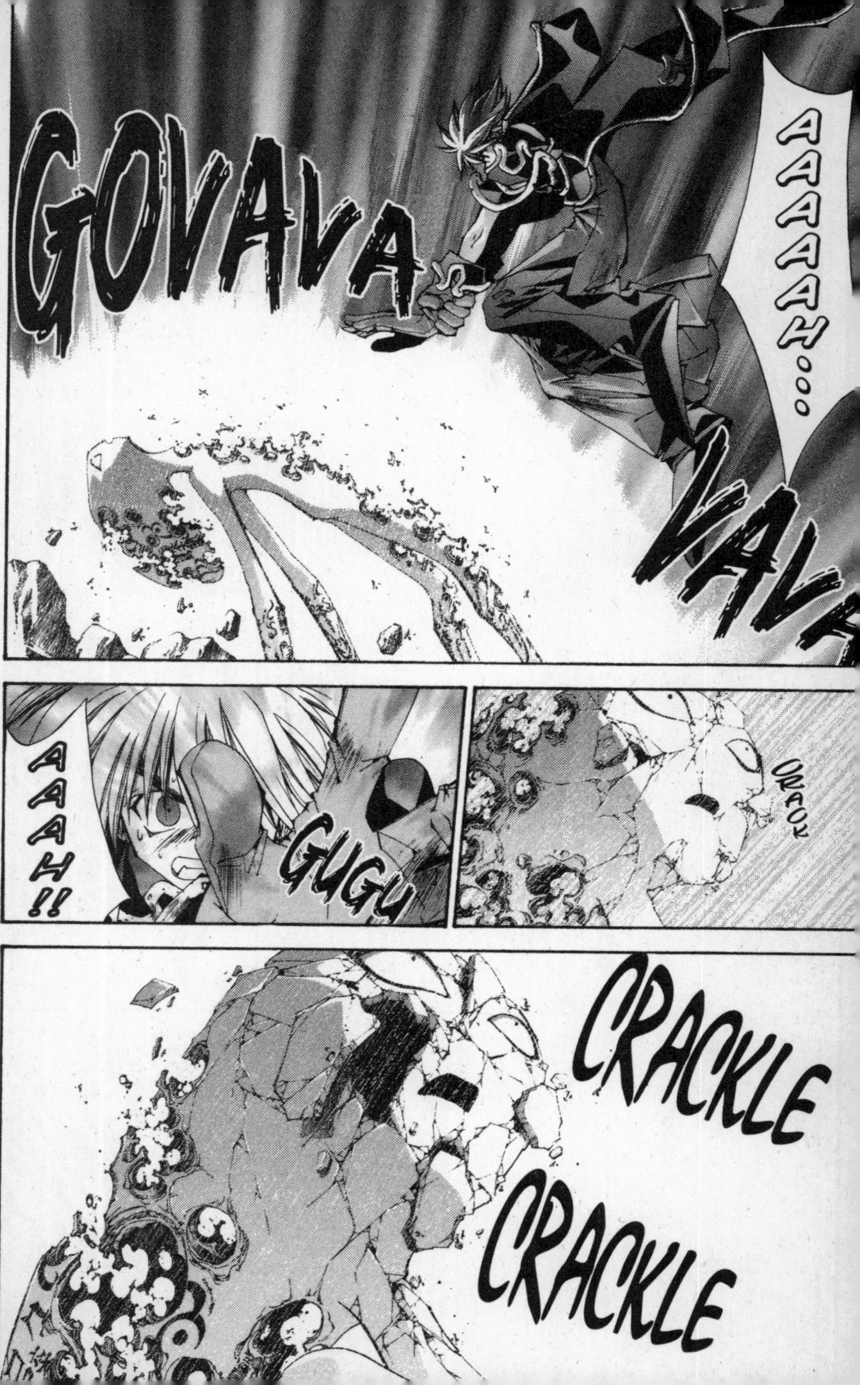
AAAAAAH...
GOVAVA
VAVA
CRACK
AAAAH!!
GUGU
CRACKLE
CRACKLE

READ THIS WAY

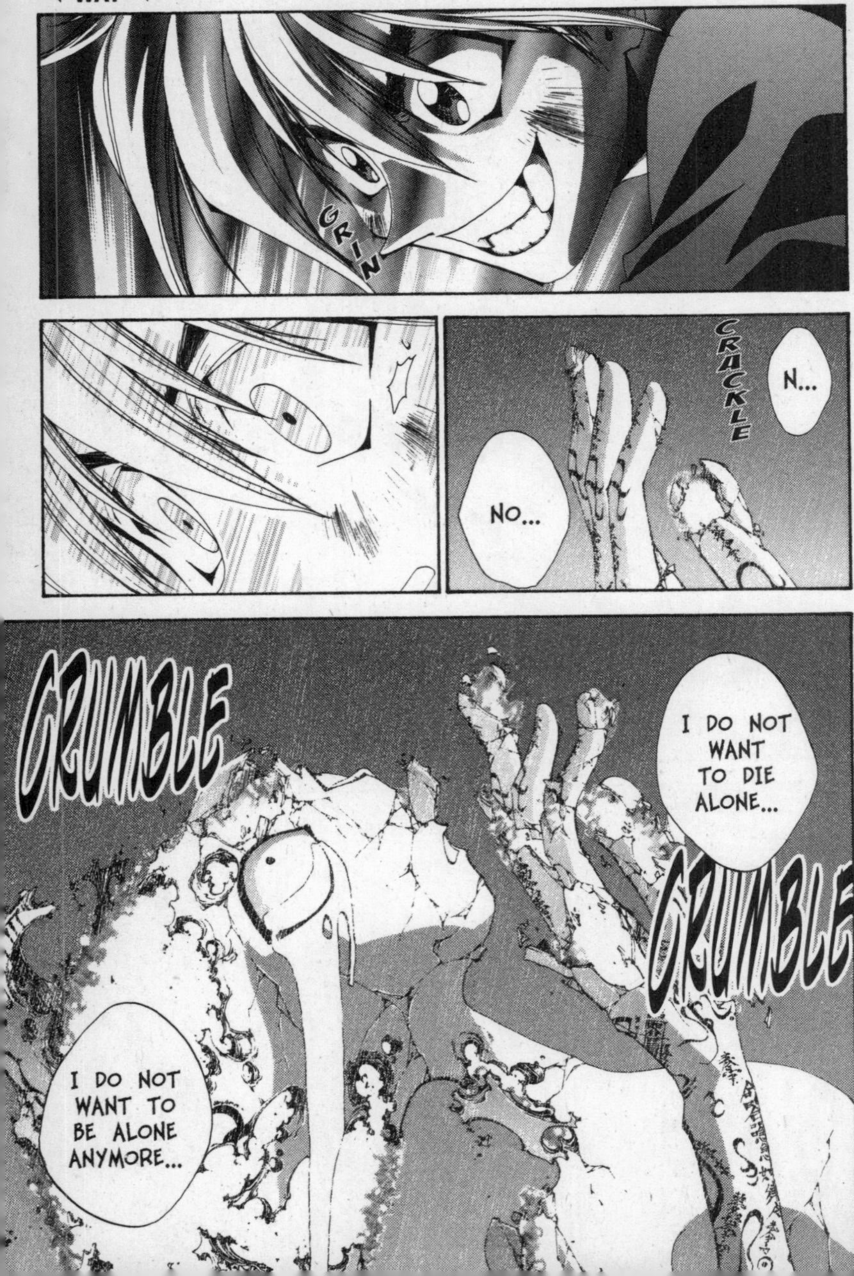
GRIN
CRACKLE
N...
NO...
I DO NOT WANT TO DIE ALONE...
CRUMBLE
CRUMBLE
I DO NOT WANT TO BE ALONE ANYMORE...

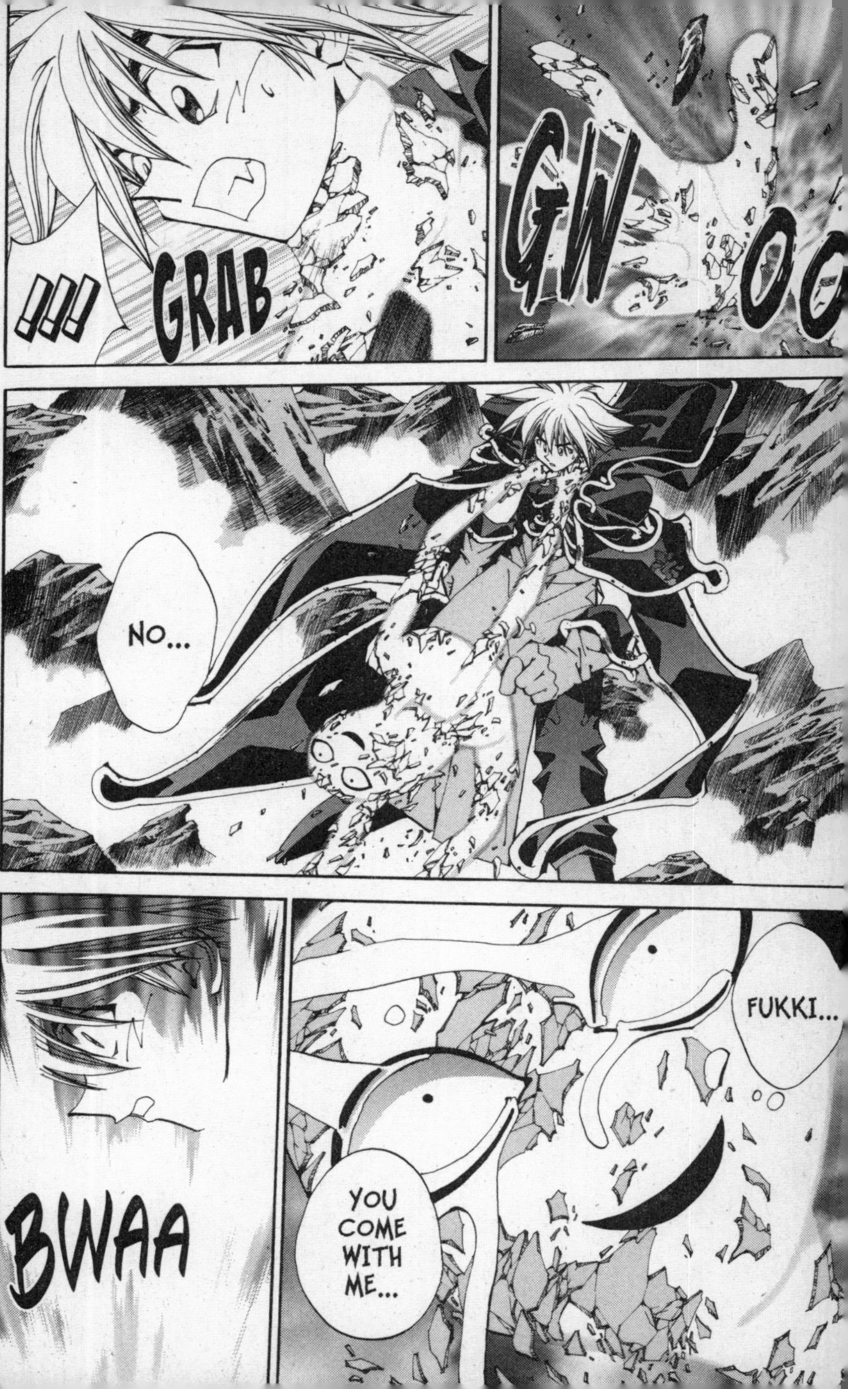
GWOO
!!!
GRAB
NO...
FUKKI...
YOU COME WITH ME...
BWAA

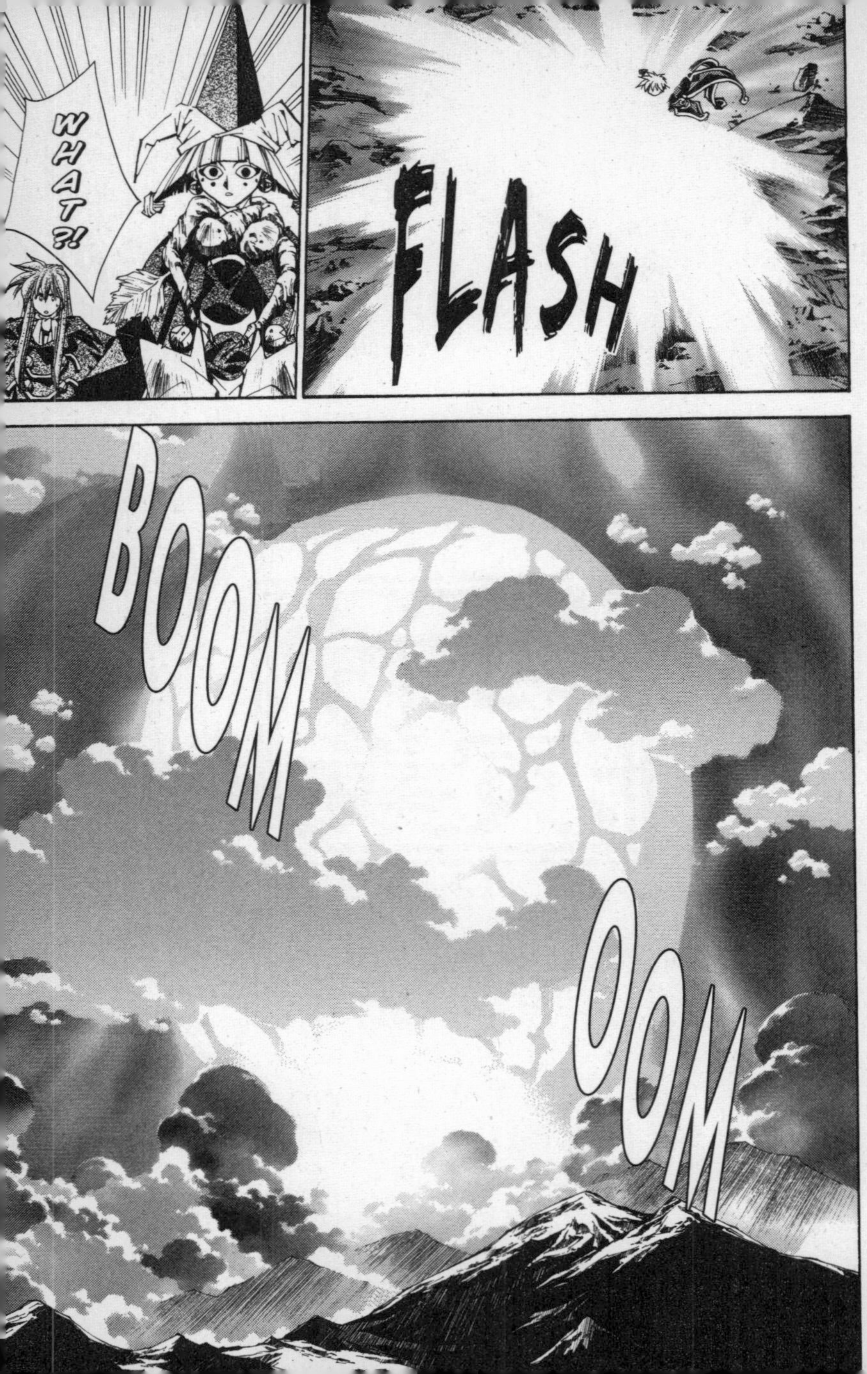
FLASH
WHAT?!
BOOM
OOM

封神演義

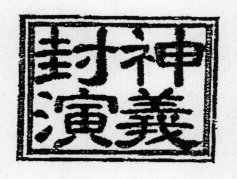

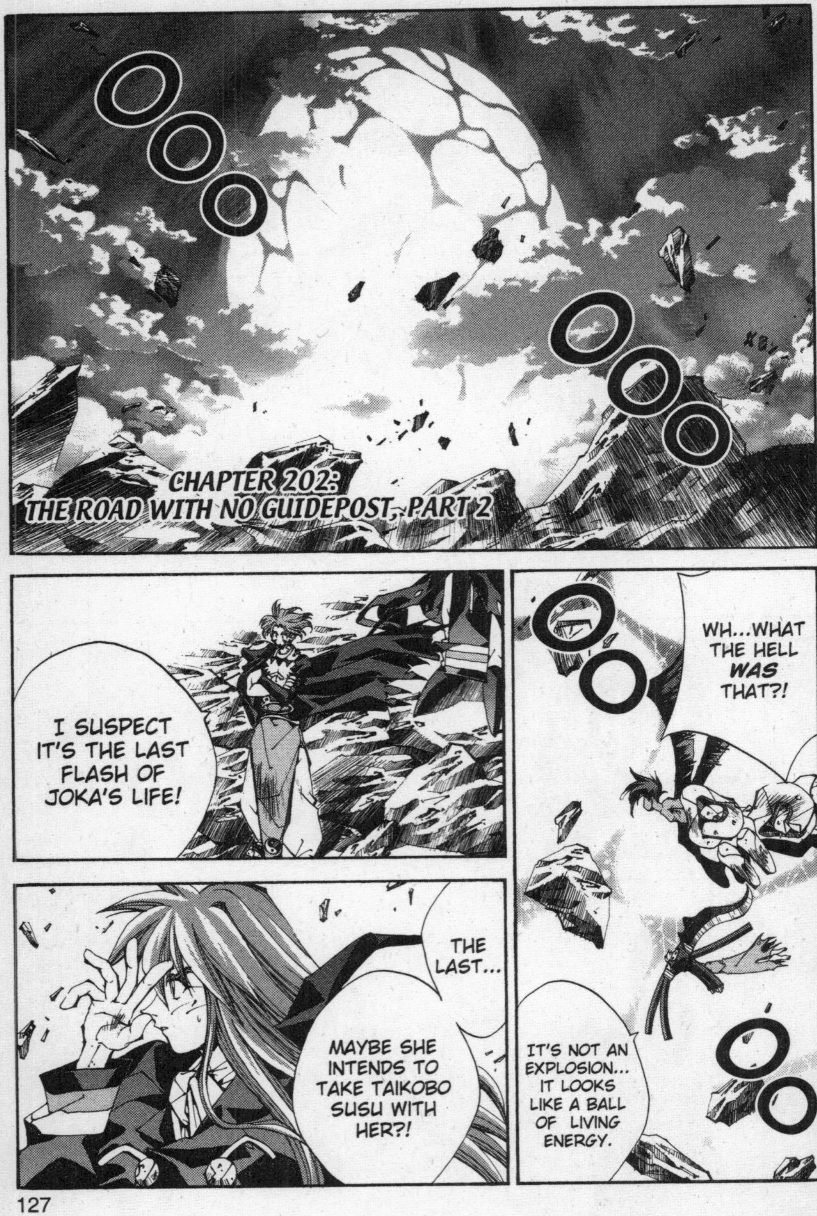
CHAPTER 202:
THE ROAD WITH NO GUIDEPOST, PART 2
WH...WHAT THE HELL WAS THAT?!
IT'S NOT AN EXPLOSION... IT LOOKS LIKE A BALL OF LIVING ENERGY.
I SUSPECT IT'S THE LAST FLASH OF JOKA'S LIFE!
THE LAST...
MAYBE SHE INTENDS TO TAKE TAIKOBO SUSU WITH HER?!

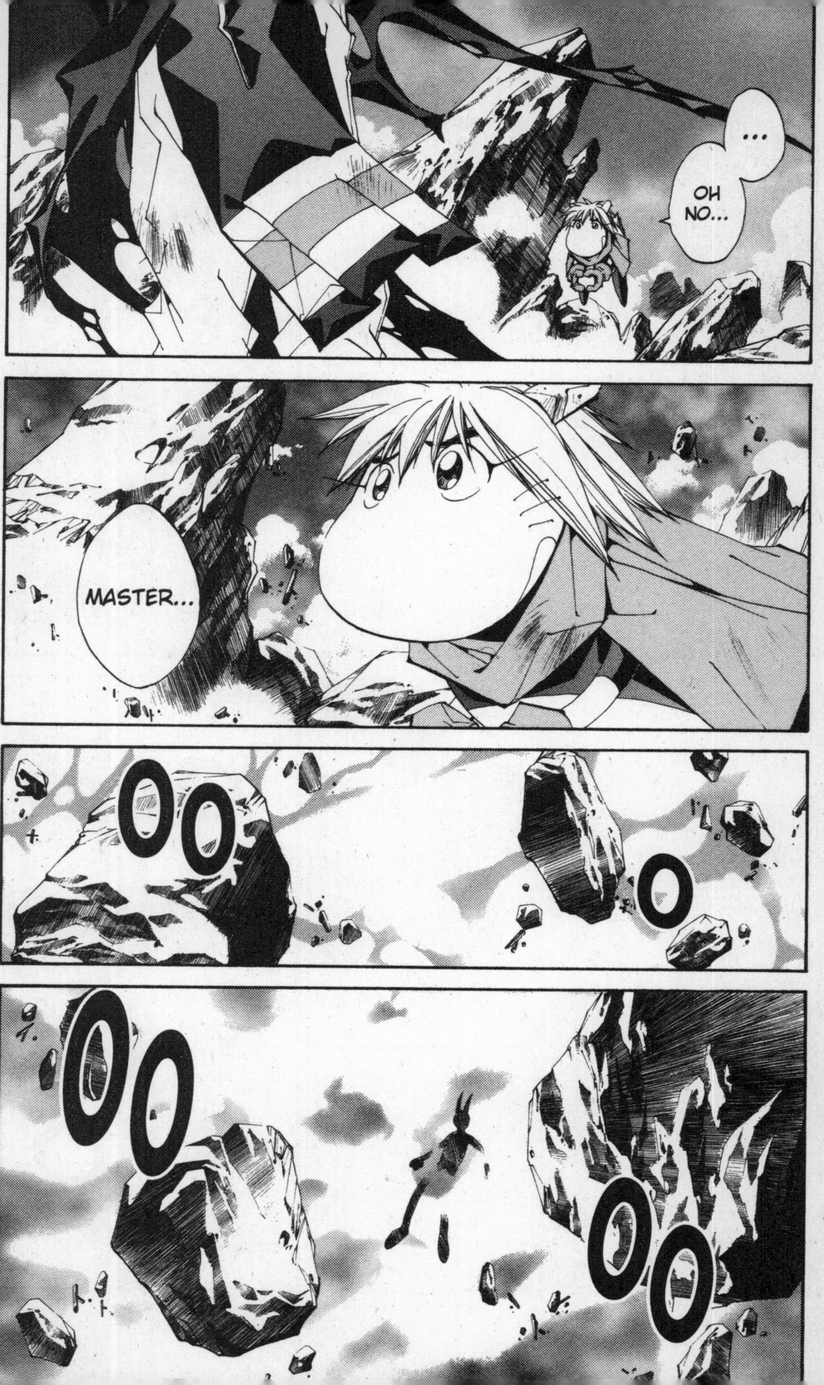
...
OH NO...
MASTER...
OOO
OOO

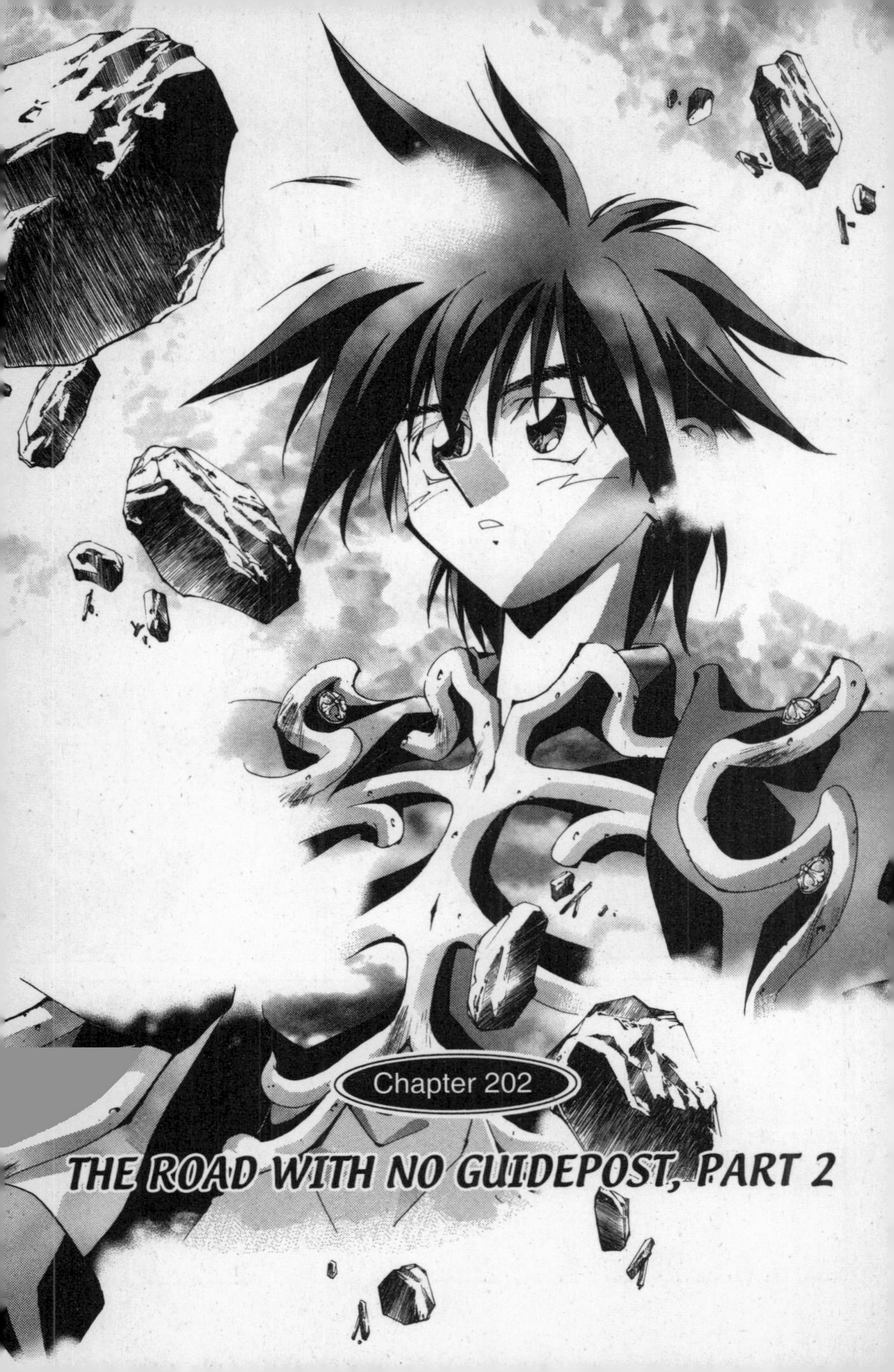
Chapter 202
THE ROAD WITH NO GUIDEPOST, PART 2

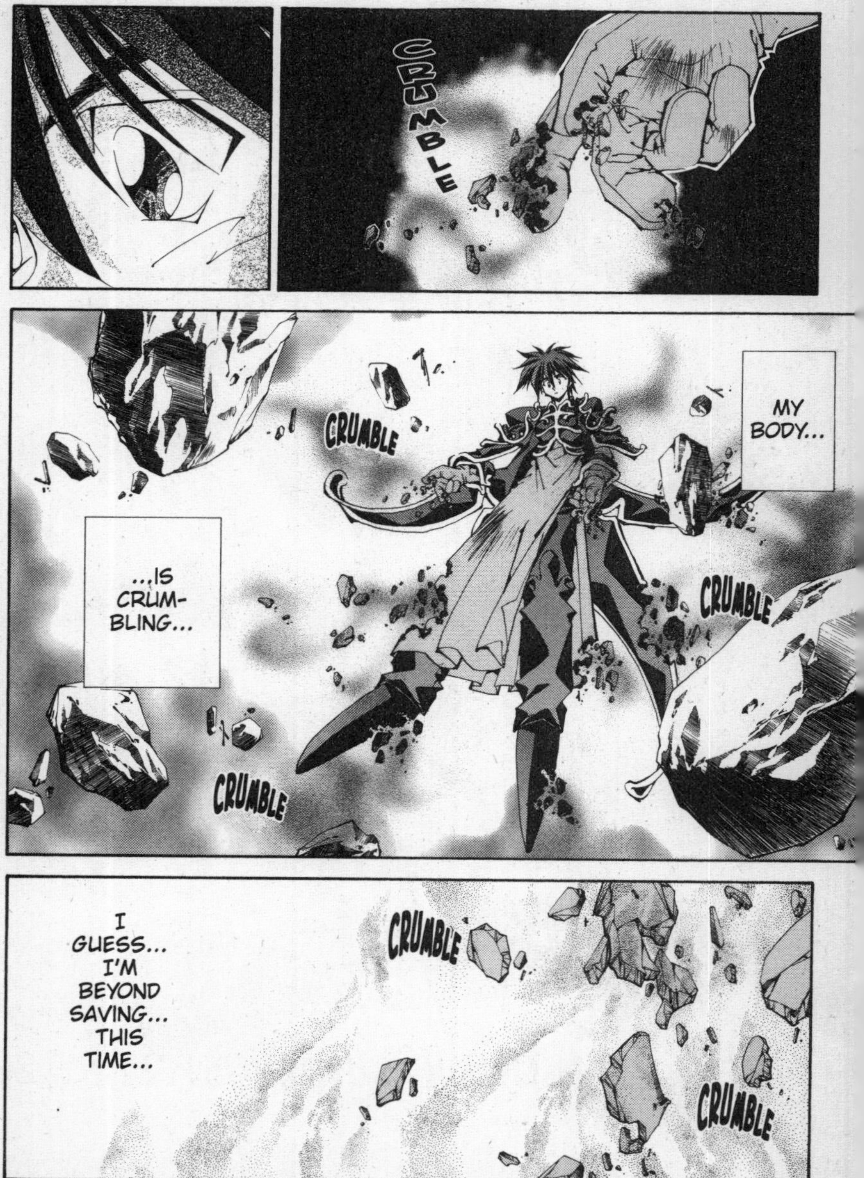
CRUMBLE
MY BODY...
CRUMBLE
...IS CRUM-BLING...
CRUMBLE
CRUMBLE
I GUESS... I'M BEYOND SAVING... THIS TIME...
CRUMBLE
CRUMBLE

READ THIS WAY

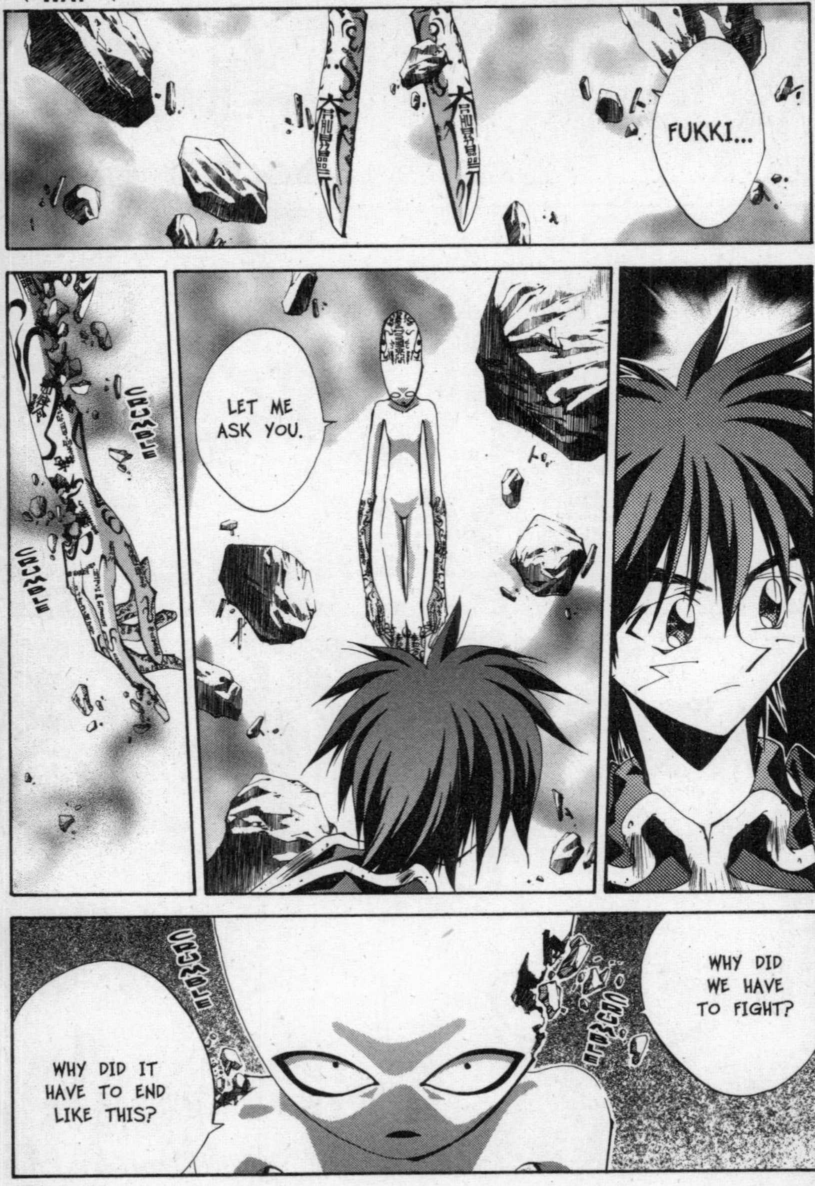
FUKKI...
LET ME ASK YOU.
CRUMBLE
CRUMBLE
WHY DID WE HAVE TO FIGHT?
CRUMBLE
CRUMBLE
WHY DID IT HAVE TO END LIKE THIS?

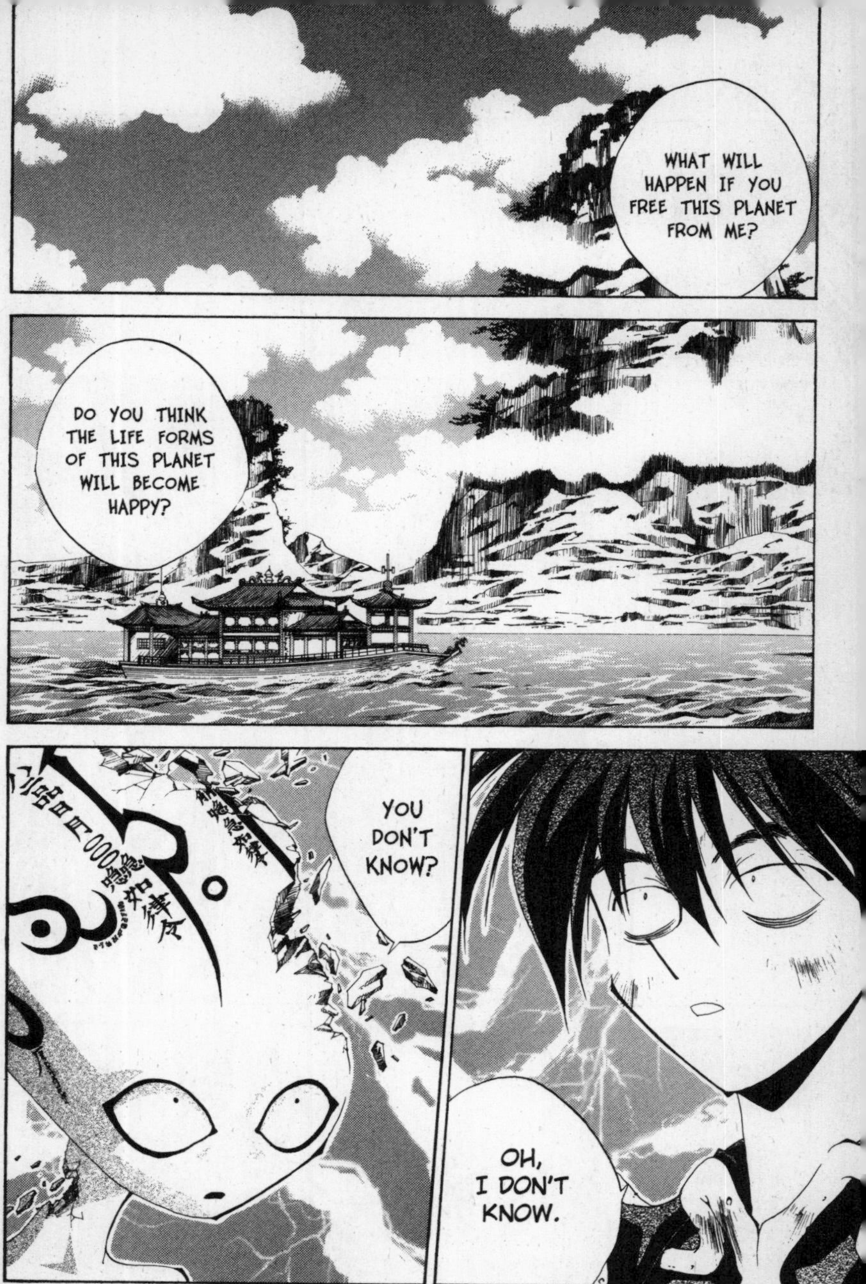
WHAT WILL HAPPEN IF YOU FREE THIS PLANET FROM ME?
DO YOU THINK THE LIFE FORMS OF THIS PLANET WILL BECOME HAPPY?
OH, I DON'T KNOW.
YOU DON'T KNOW?

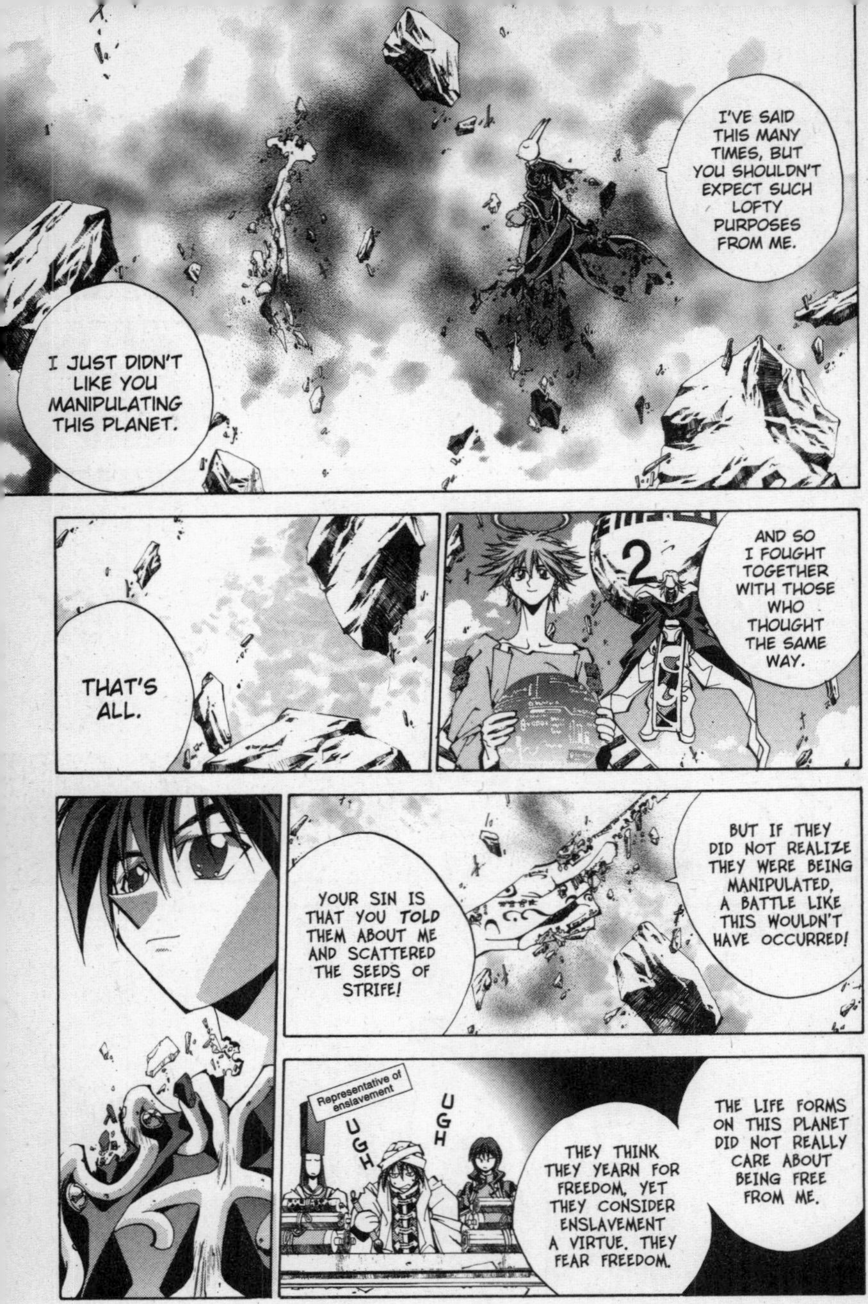
I'VE SAID THIS MANY TIMES, BUT YOU SHOULDN'T EXPECT SUCH LOFTY PURPOSES FROM ME.
I JUST DIDN'T LIKE YOU MANIPULATING THIS PLANET.
AND SO I FOUGHT TOGETHER WITH THOSE WHO THOUGHT THE SAME WAY.
2
THAT'S ALL.
BUT IF THEY DID NOT REALIZE THEY WERE BEING MANIPULATED, A BATTLE LIKE THIS WOULDN'T HAVE OCCURRED!
YOUR SIN IS THAT YOU *TOLD* THEM ABOUT ME AND SCATTERED THE SEEDS OF STRIFE!
THE LIFE FORMS ON THIS PLANET DID NOT REALLY CARE ABOUT BEING FREE FROM ME.
UGH
UGH
Representative of enslavement
THEY THINK THEY YEARN FOR FREEDOM, YET THEY CONSIDER ENSLAVEMENT A VIRTUE. THEY FEAR FREEDOM.

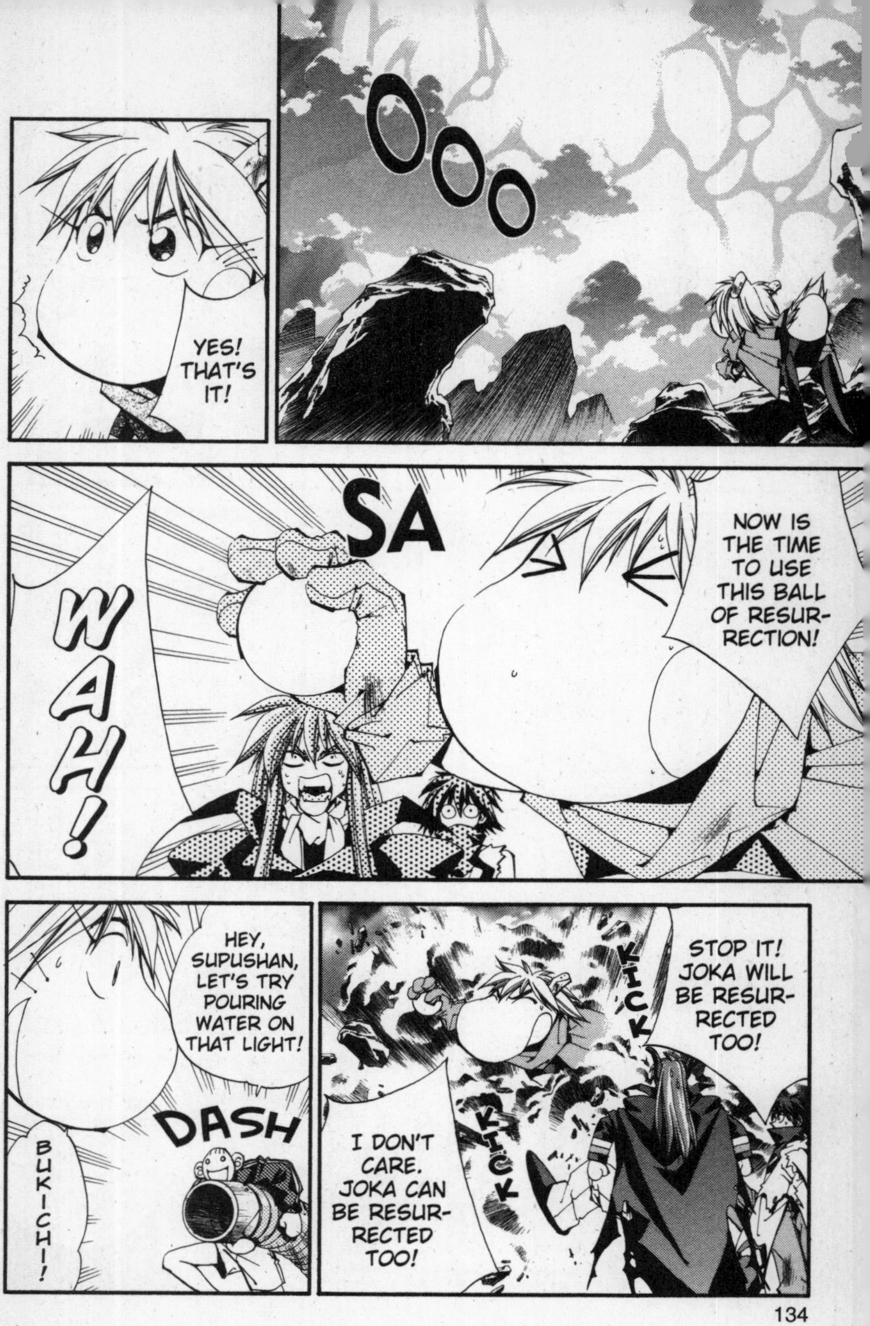
OOO
YES! THAT'S IT!
SA
NOW IS THE TIME TO USE THIS BALL OF RESURRECTION!
WAH!
STOP IT! JOKA WILL BE RESURRECTED TOO!
KICK
KICK
I DON'T CARE. JOKA CAN BE RESURRECTED TOO!
HEY, SUPUSHAN, LET'S TRY POURING WATER ON THAT LIGHT!
DASH
BUKICHI!

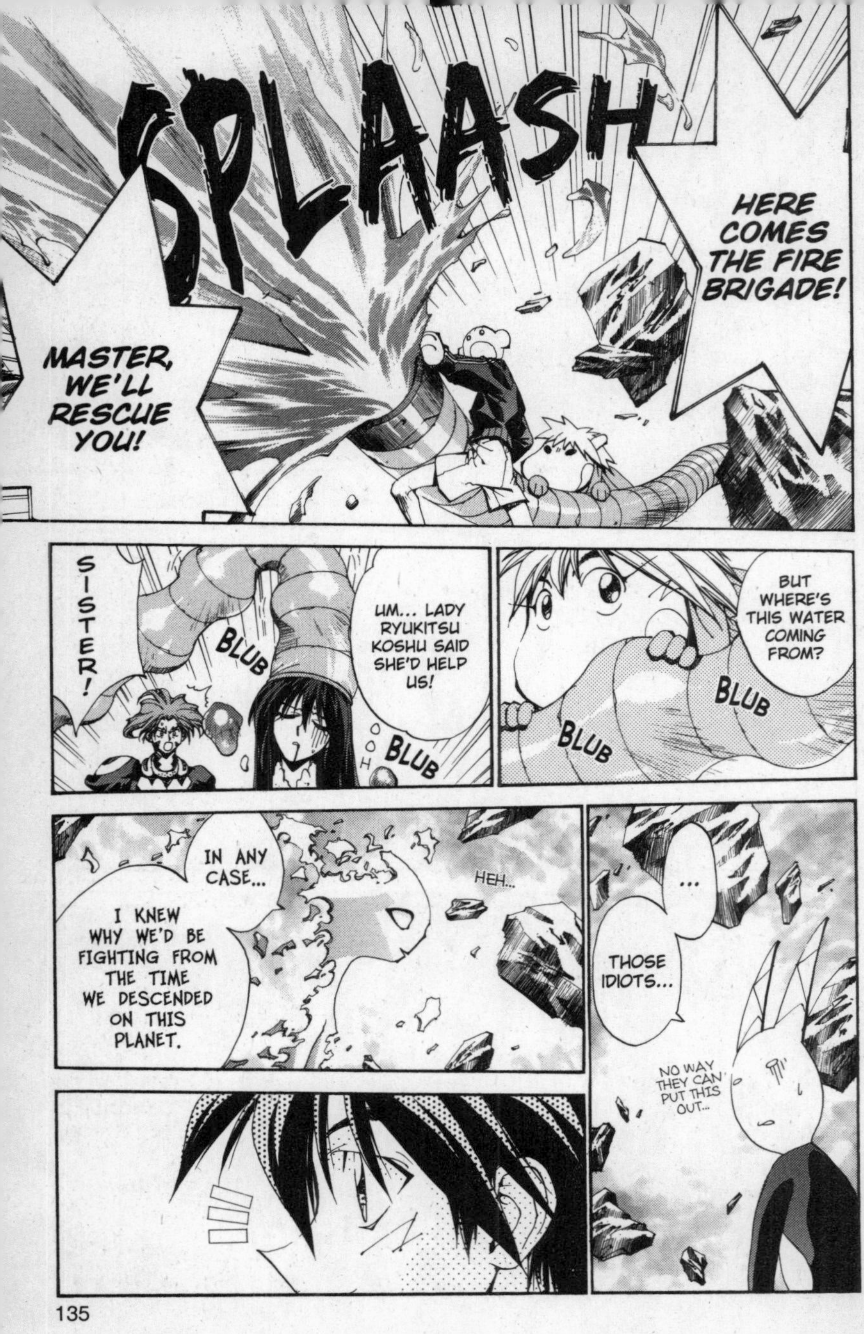
SPLAASH
HERE COMES THE FIRE BRIGADE!
MASTER, WE'LL RESCUE YOU!
BUT WHERE'S THIS WATER COMING FROM?
BLUB
BLUB
UM... LADY RYUKITSU KOSHU SAID SHE'D HELP US!
SISTER!
BLUB
OOH
BLUB
...
THOSE IDIOTS...
NO WAY THEY CAN PUT THIS OUT...
IN ANY CASE...
I KNEW WHY WE'D BE FIGHTING FROM THE TIME WE DESCENDED ON THIS PLANET.
HEH...

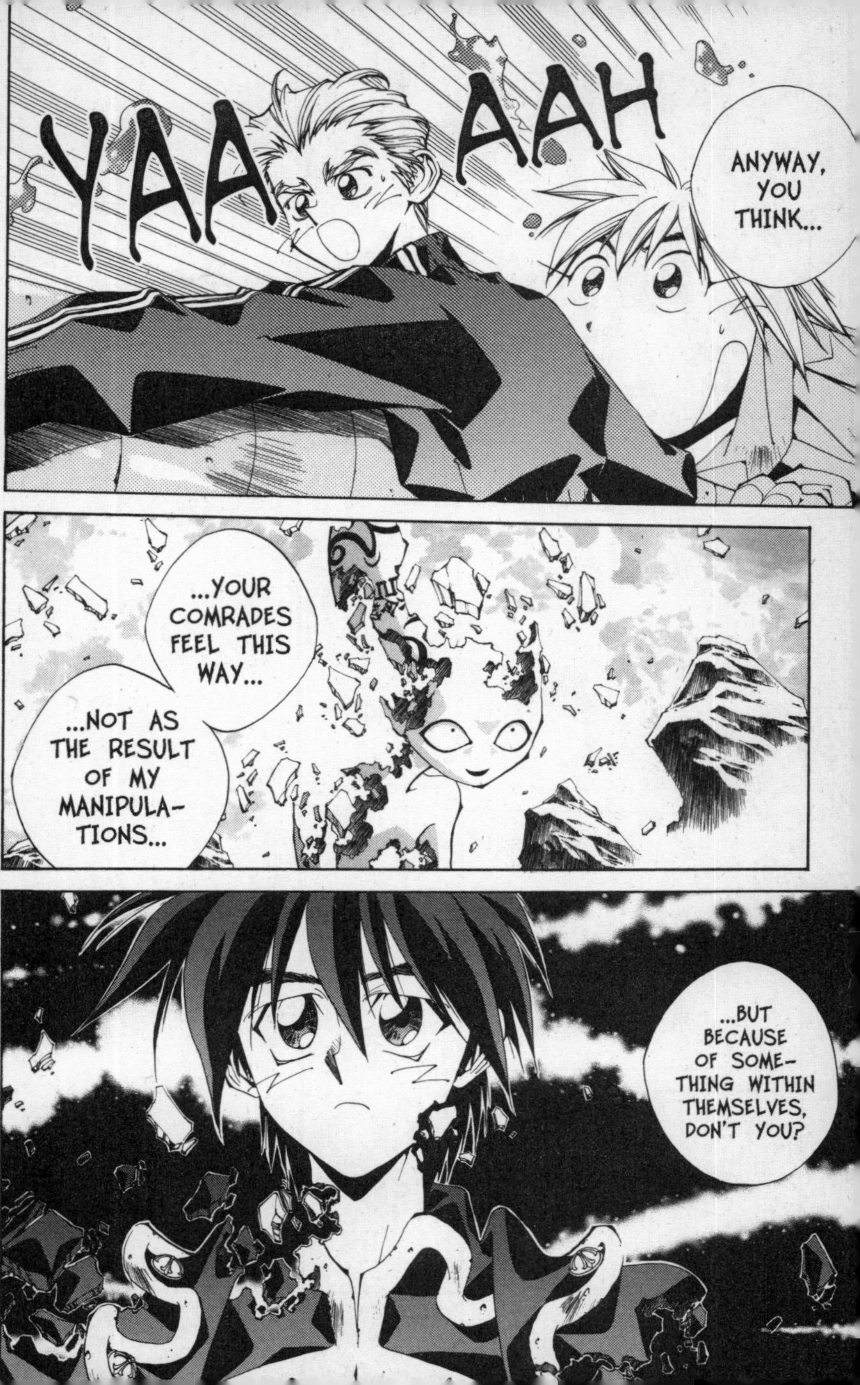
YAAAAAH
ANYWAY, YOU THINK...
...YOUR COMRADES FEEL THIS WAY...
...NOT AS THE RESULT OF MY MANIPULA-TIONS...
...BUT BECAUSE OF SOME-THING WITHIN THEMSELVES, DON'T YOU?

READ THIS WAY

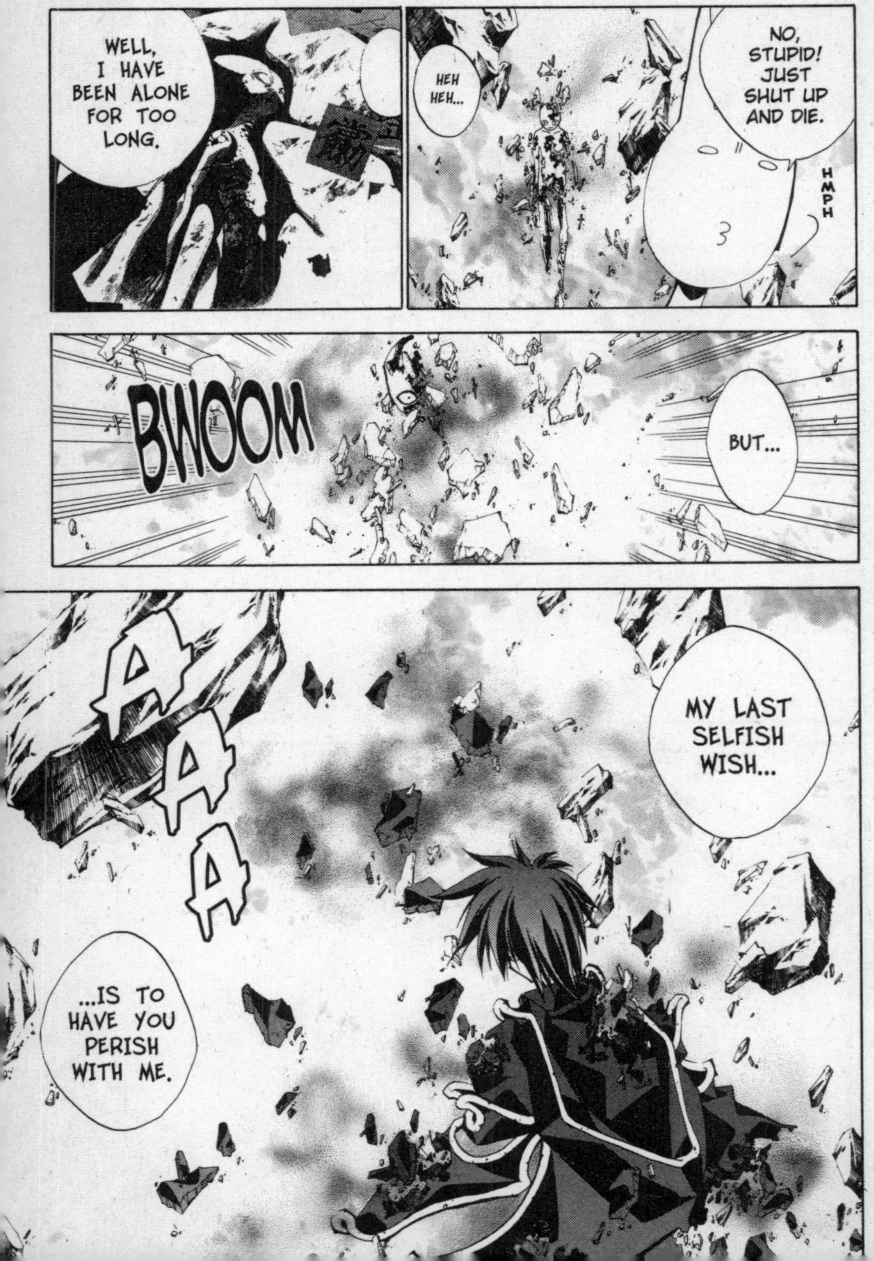
NO, STUPID! JUST SHUT UP AND DIE.
HMPH
HEH HEH...
WELL, I HAVE BEEN ALONE FOR TOO LONG.
BUT...
BWOOM
MY LAST SELFISH WISH...
AAAA
...IS TO HAVE YOU PERISH WITH ME.

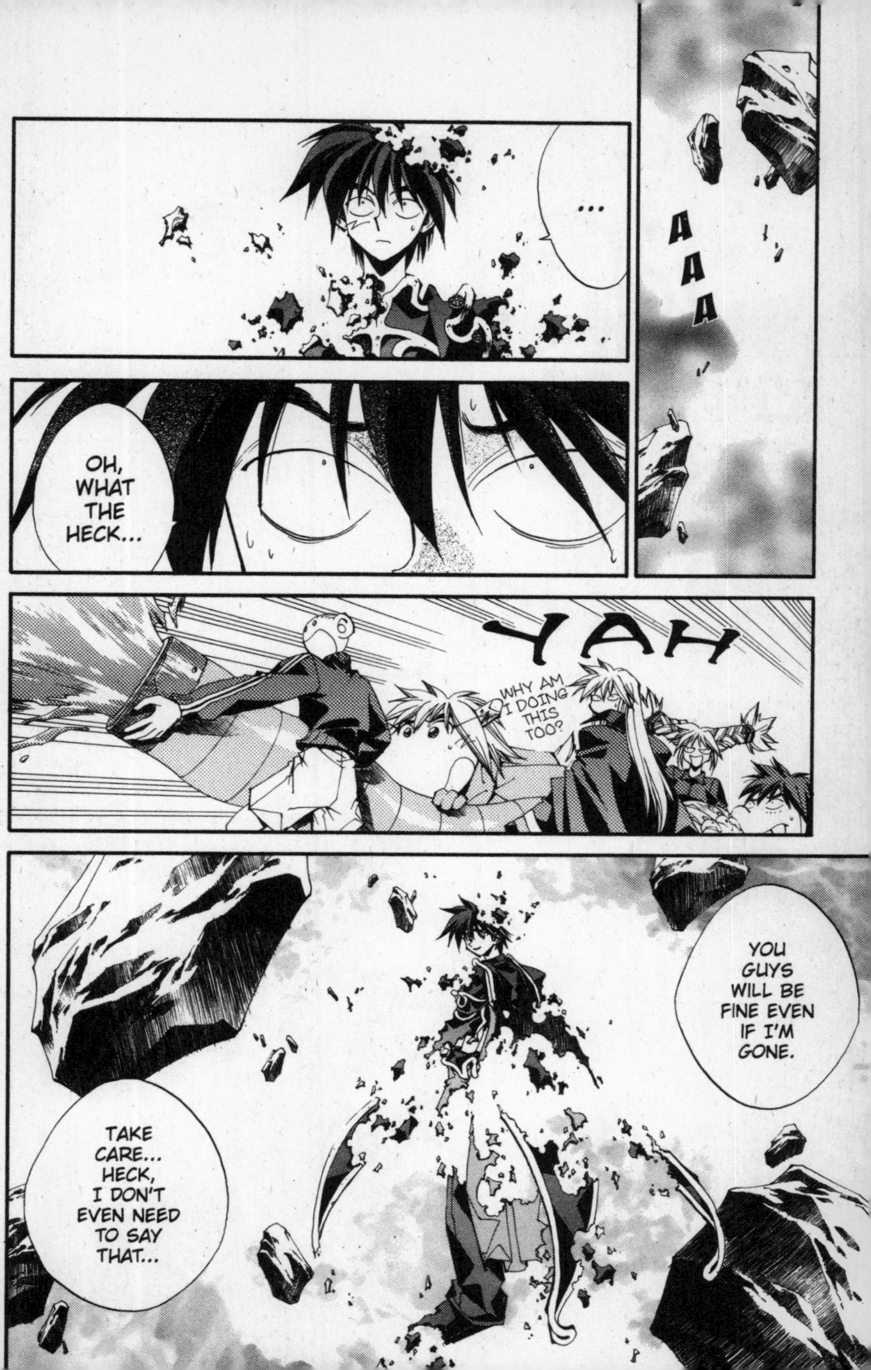
AAA
...
OH, WHAT THE HECK...
YAH
WHY AM I DOING THIS TOO?
YOU GUYS WILL BE FINE EVEN IF I'M GONE.
TAKE CARE... HECK, I DON'T EVEN NEED TO SAY THAT...

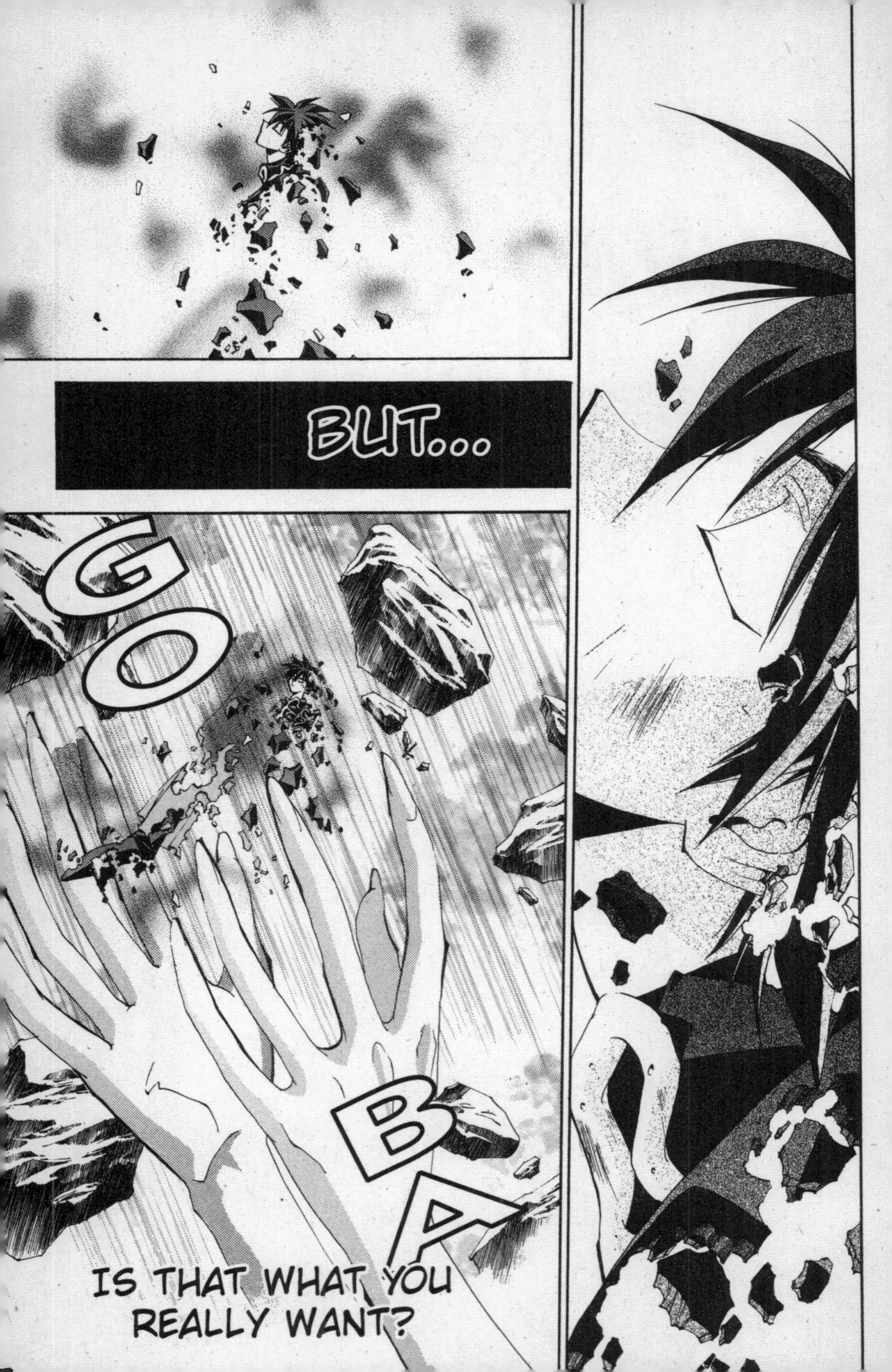
BUT...
GO
BA
IS THAT WHAT YOU REALLY WANT?

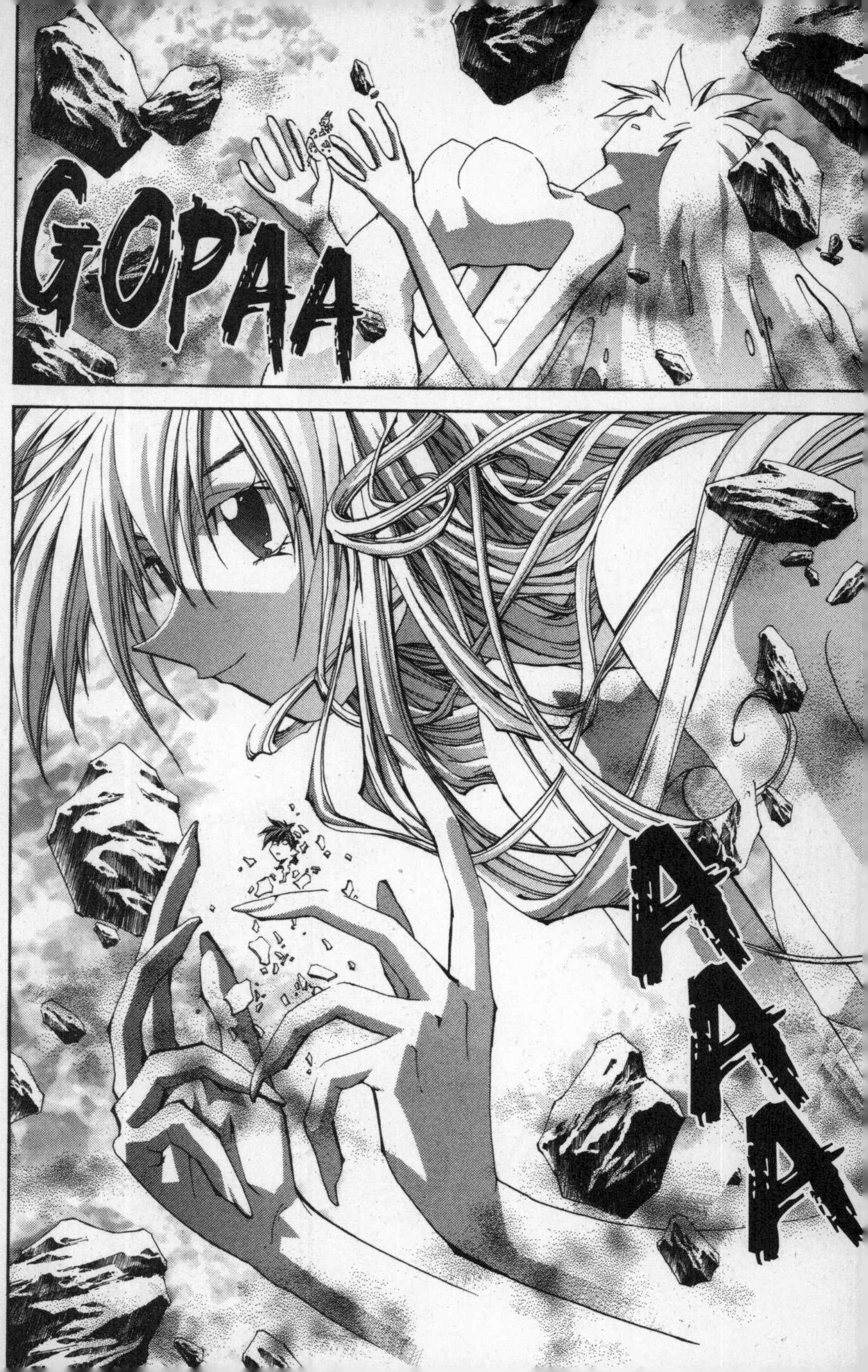
GOPAA
AAA

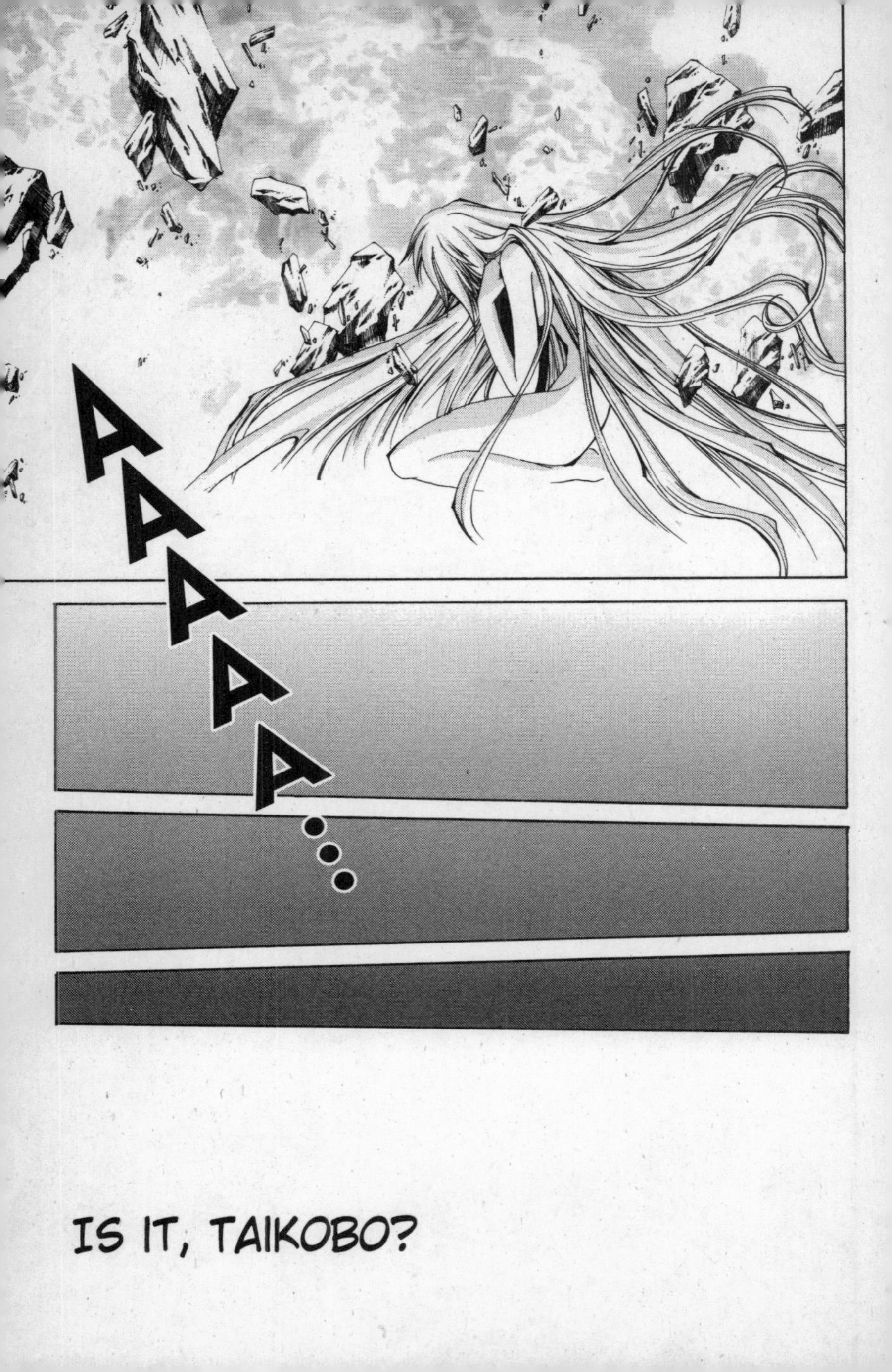
AAAAA...
IS IT, TAIKOBO?

EVENTUALLY...

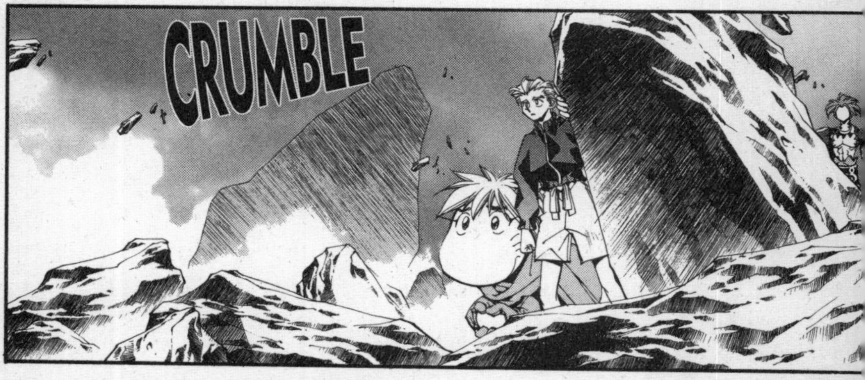
CRUMBLE

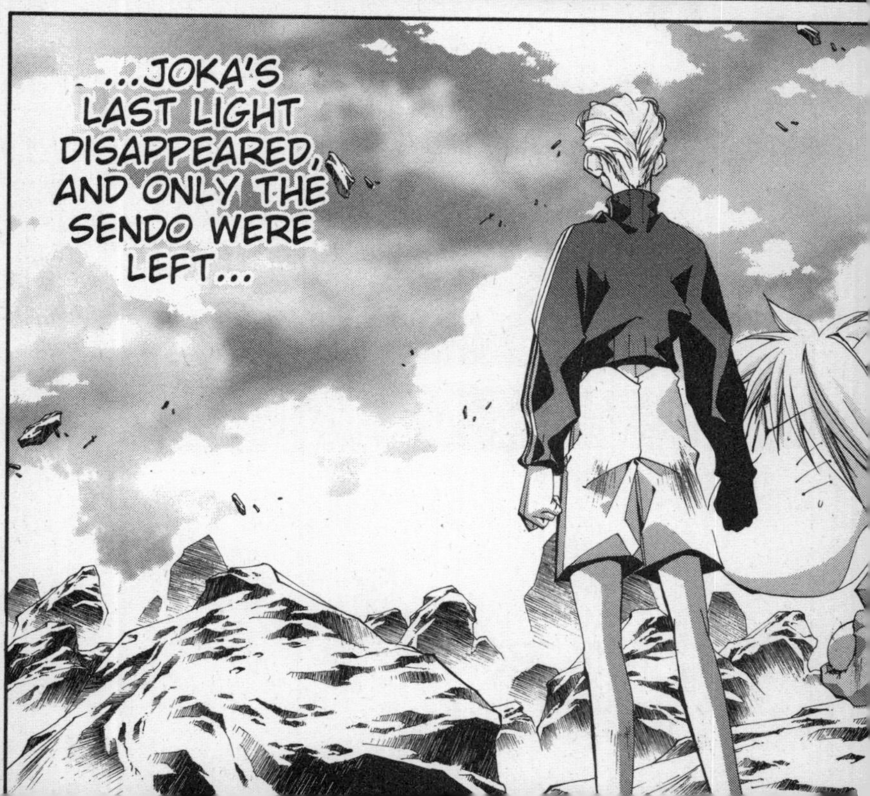
...JOKA'S LAST LIGHT DISAPPEARED, AND ONLY THE SENDO WERE LEFT...

READ THIS WAY

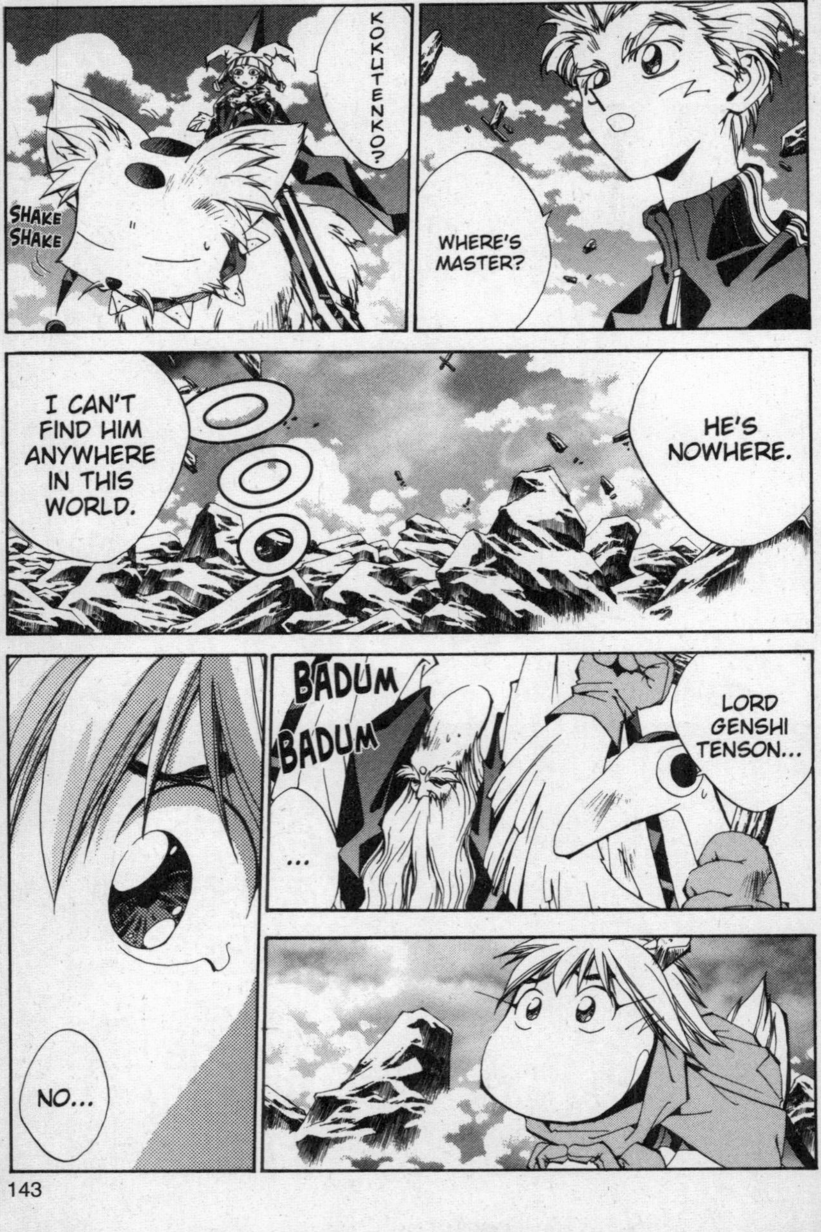
WHERE'S MASTER?
KOKUTENKO?
SHAKE SHAKE
HE'S NOWHERE.
I CAN'T FIND HIM ANYWHERE IN THIS WORLD.
LORD GENSHI TENSON...
BADUM
BADUM
...
NO...

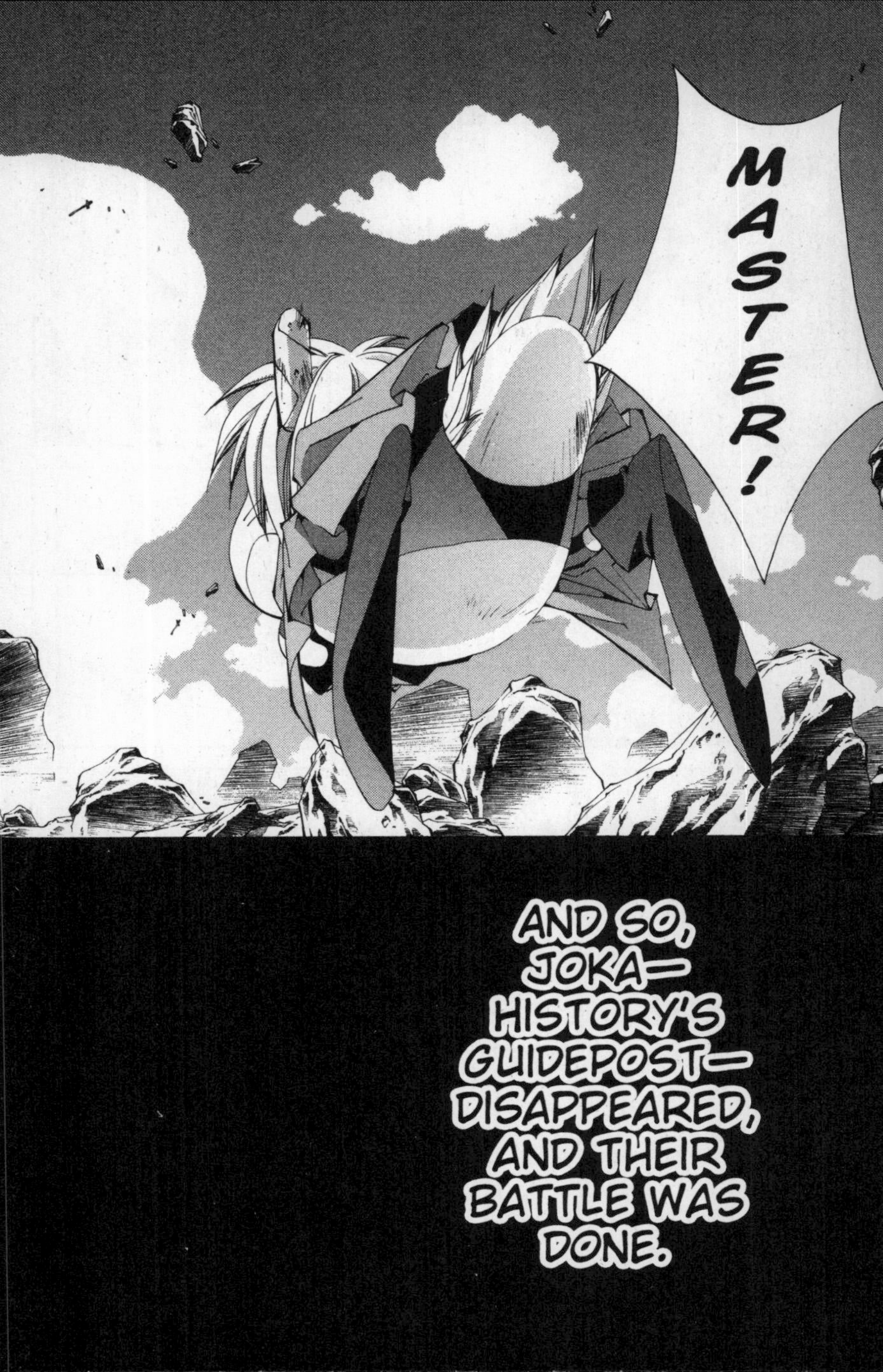
MASTER!
AND SO, JOKA— HISTORY'S GUIDEPOST— DISAPPEARED, AND THEIR BATTLE WAS DONE.

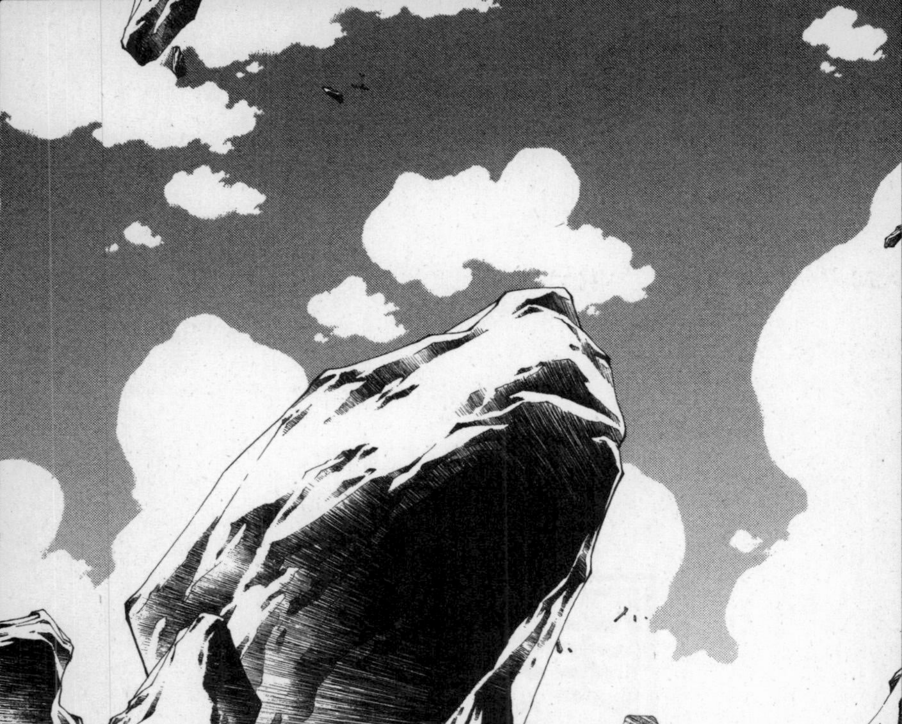

THIS MEANT THAT THE ERA OF MYTHS, THE ROOT OF THIS PLANET'S HISTORY, WAS OVER.

封神演義

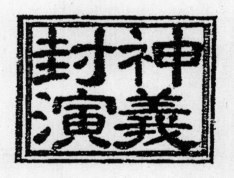

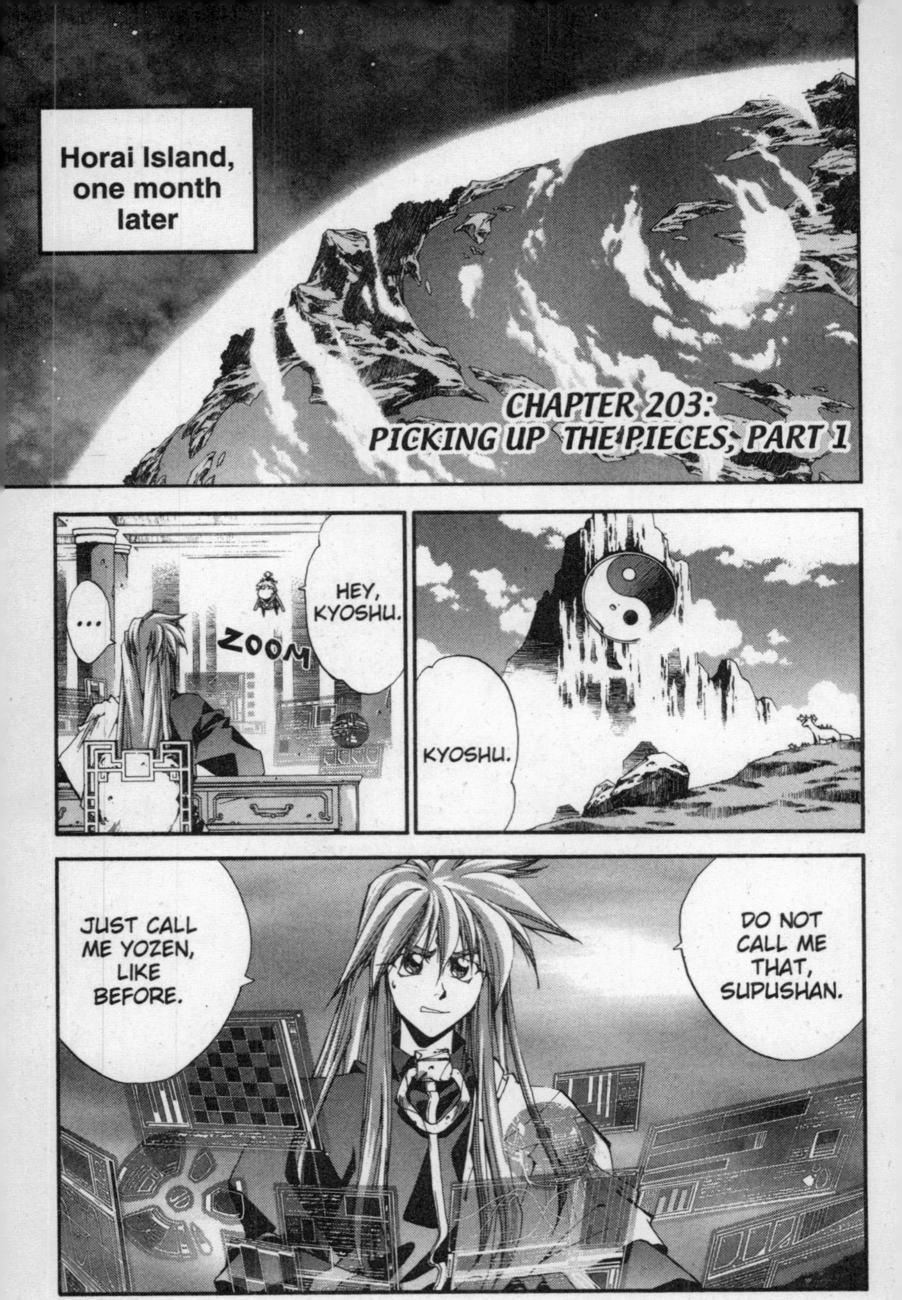
Horai Island, one month later
CHAPTER 203: PICKING UP THE PIECES, PART 1
KYOSHU.
HEY, KYOSHU.
ZOOM
...
DO NOT CALL ME THAT, SUPUSHAN.
JUST CALL ME YOZEN, LIKE BEFORE.

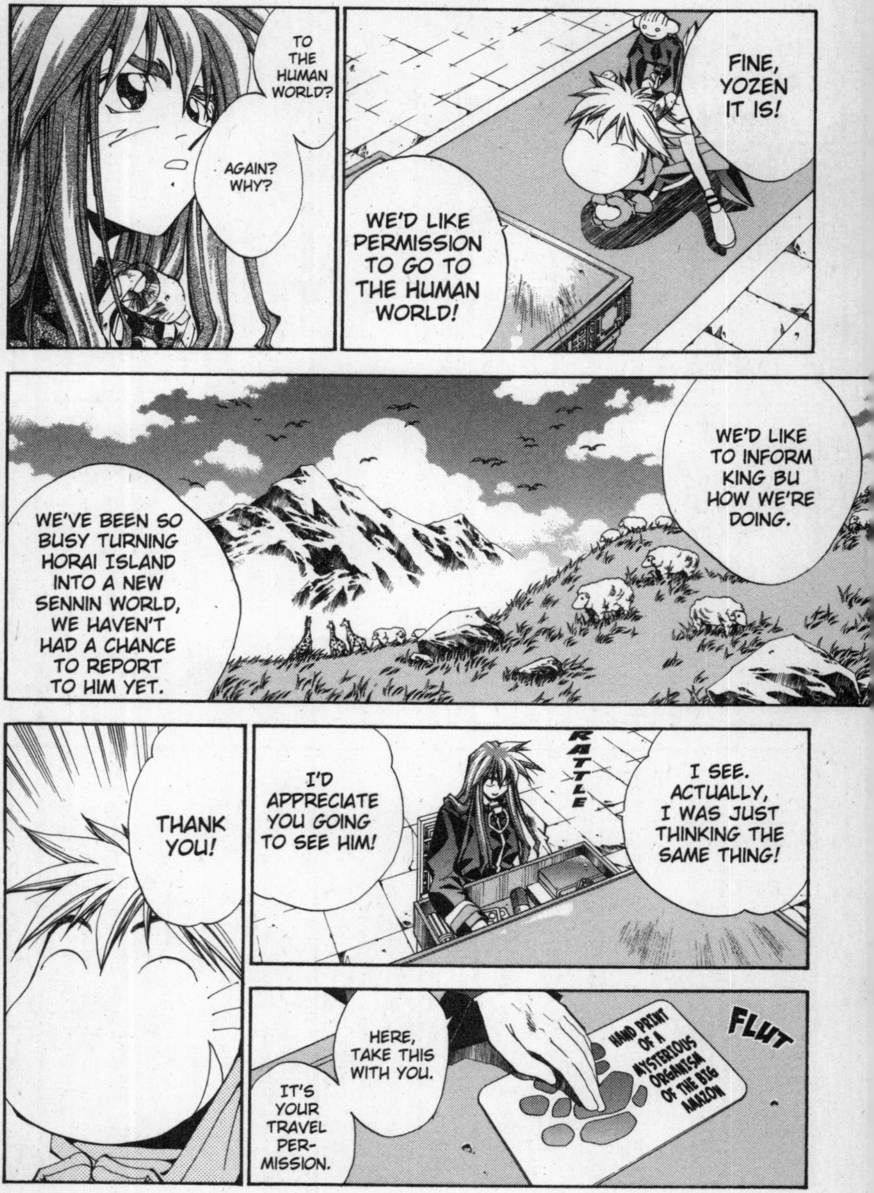
FINE, YOZEN IT IS!
WE'D LIKE PERMISSION TO GO TO THE HUMAN WORLD!
TO THE HUMAN WORLD?
AGAIN? WHY?
WE'D LIKE TO INFORM KING BU HOW WE'RE DOING.
WE'VE BEEN SO BUSY TURNING HORAI ISLAND INTO A NEW SENNIN WORLD, WE HAVEN'T HAD A CHANCE TO REPORT TO HIM YET.
I SEE. ACTUALLY, I WAS JUST THINKING THE SAME THING!
RATTLE
I'D APPRECIATE YOU GOING TO SEE HIM!
FLUT
HAND PRINT OF A MYSTERIOUS ORGANISM OF THE BIG AMAZON
HERE, TAKE THIS WITH YOU.
IT'S YOUR TRAVEL PERMISSION.
THANK YOU!

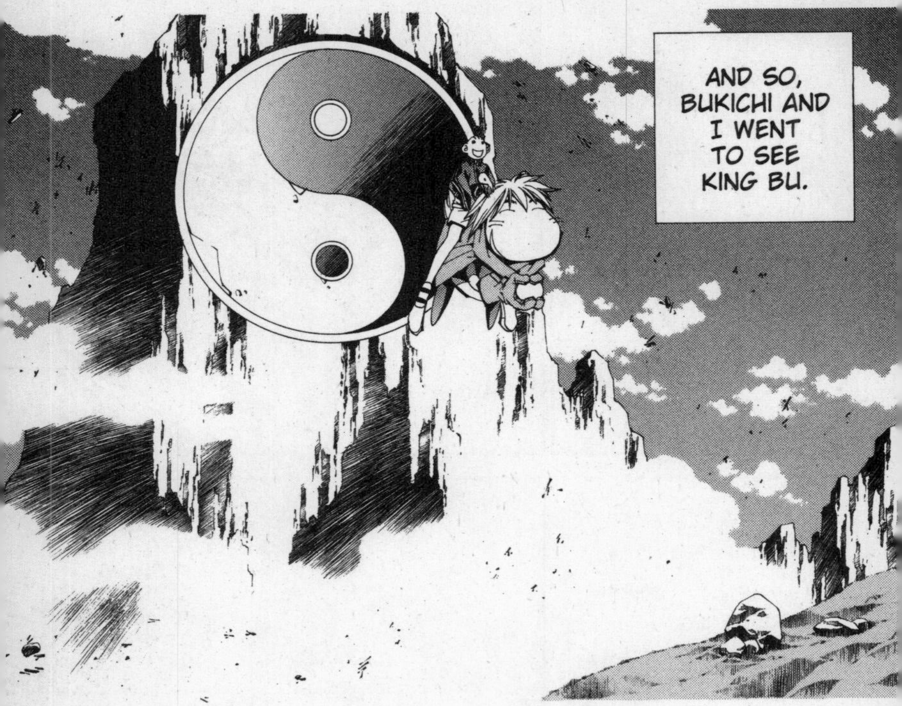
AND SO, BUKICHI AND I WENT TO SEE KING BU.

Chapter 203

PICKING UP THE PIECES, PART 1

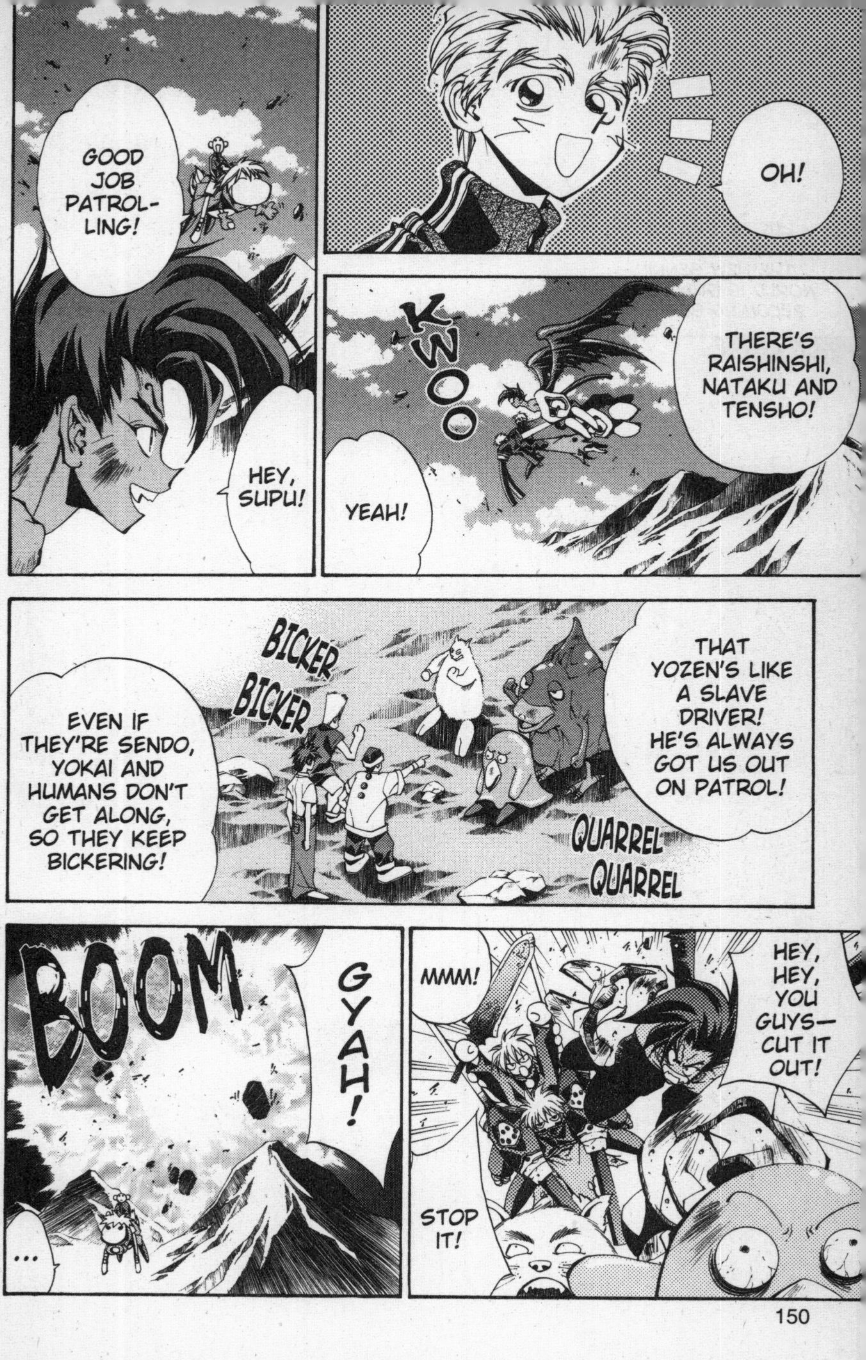
OH!
KWOO
THERE'S RAISHINSHI, NATAKU AND TENSHO!
YEAH!
GOOD JOB PATROL-LING!
HEY, SUPU!
THAT YOZEN'S LIKE A SLAVE DRIVER! HE'S ALWAYS GOT US OUT ON PATROL!
BICKER BICKER
EVEN IF THEY'RE SENDO, YOKAI AND HUMANS DON'T GET ALONG, SO THEY KEEP BICKERING!
QUARREL QUARREL
HEY, HEY, YOU GUYS— CUT IT OUT!
MMMM!
STOP IT!
GYAH!
BOOM
...

THERE'RE STILL A LOT OF PROBLEMS TO DEAL WITH, BUT THE NEW SENNIN WORLD IS GRADUALLY BECOMING BETTER.

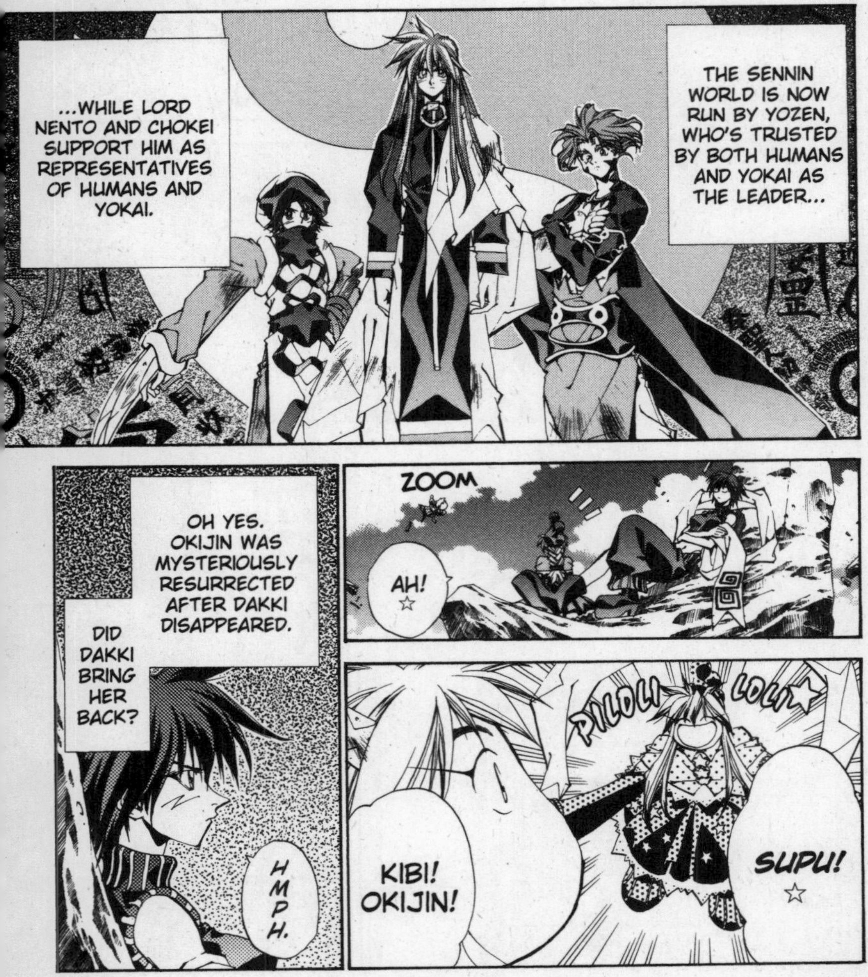
THE SENNIN WORLD IS NOW RUN BY YOZEN, WHO'S TRUSTED BY BOTH HUMANS AND YOKAI AS THE LEADER...
...WHILE LORD NENTO AND CHOKEI SUPPORT HIM AS REPRESENTATIVES OF HUMANS AND YOKAI.
ZOOM
AH! ☆
PILOLI LOLI☆
SUPU! ☆
KIBI! OKIJIN!
OH YES. OKIJIN WAS MYSTERIOUSLY RESURRECTED AFTER DAKKI DISAPPEARED.
DID DAKKI BRING HER BACK?
HMPH.

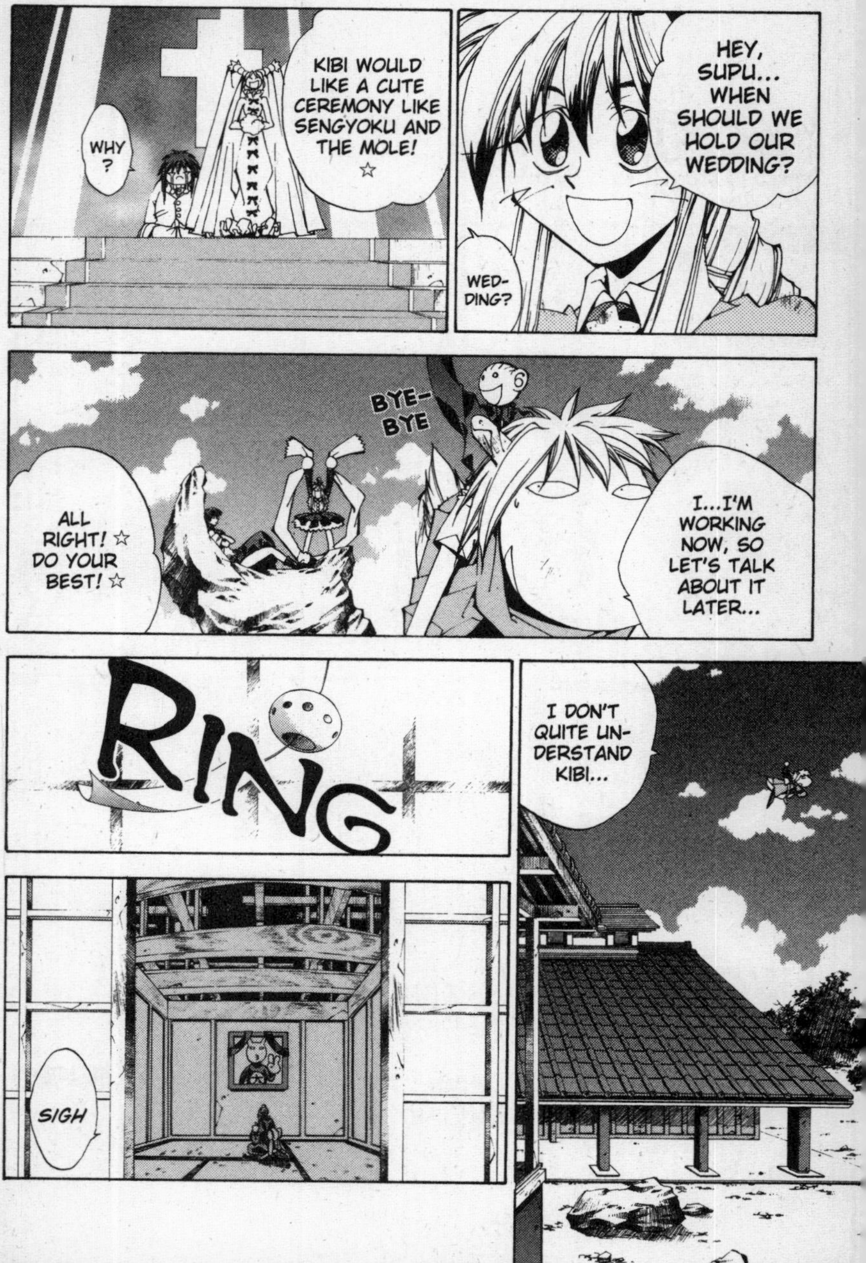
HEY, SUPU... WHEN SHOULD WE HOLD OUR WEDDING?
WED-DING?
KIBI WOULD LIKE A CUTE CEREMONY LIKE SENGYOKU AND THE MOLE! ☆
WHY?
I...I'M WORKING NOW, SO LET'S TALK ABOUT IT LATER...
BYE-BYE
ALL RIGHT! ☆ DO YOUR BEST! ☆
I DON'T QUITE UN-DERSTAND KIBI...
RING
SIGH

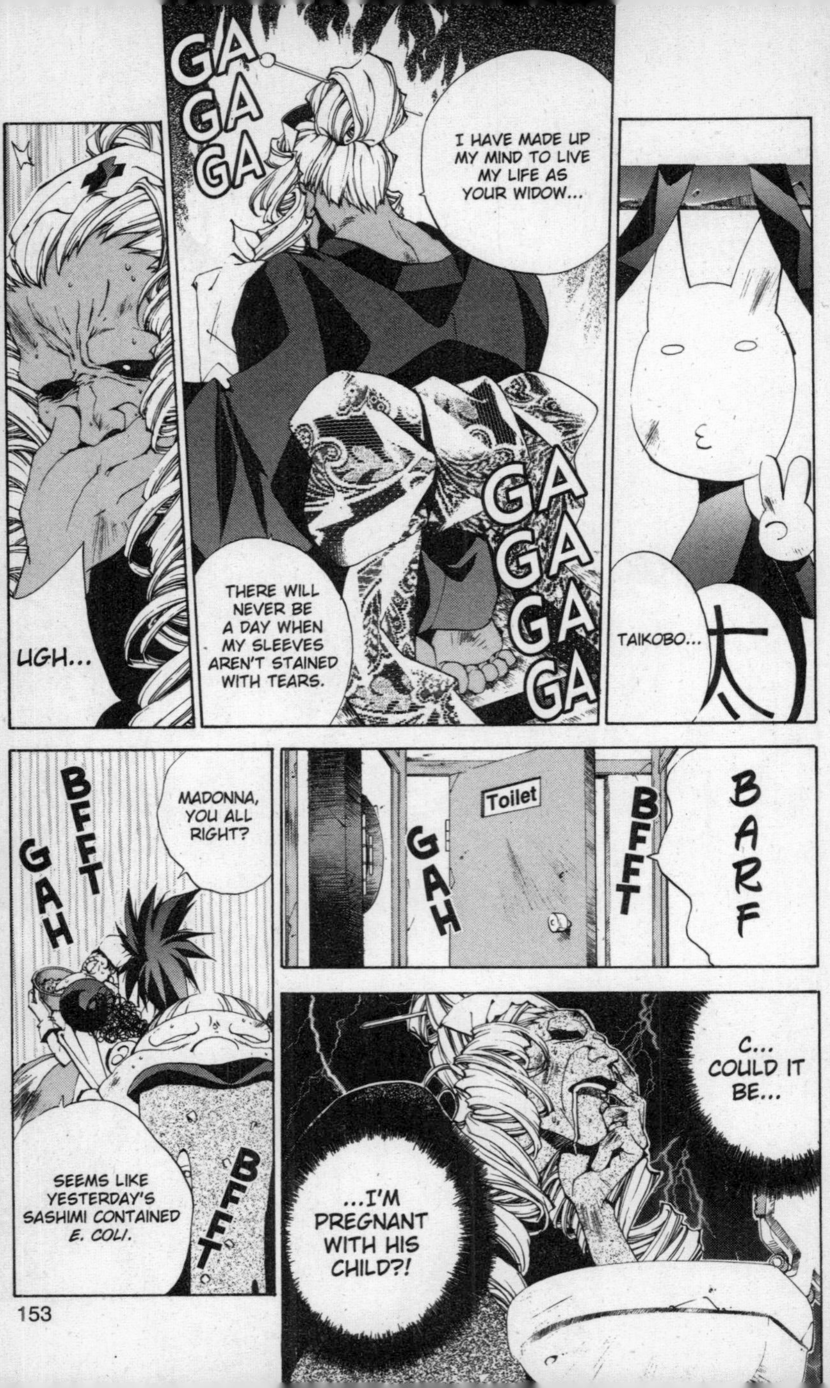

TAIKOBO...
太
I HAVE MADE UP MY MIND TO LIVE MY LIFE AS YOUR WIDOW...
GA GA GA
GA GA GA GA
THERE WILL NEVER BE A DAY WHEN MY SLEEVES AREN'T STAINED WITH TEARS.
UGH...
BARF
BFFT
Toilet
GAH
C... COULD IT BE...
...I'M PREGNANT WITH HIS CHILD?!
MADONNA, YOU ALL RIGHT?
BFFT
GAH
SEEMS LIKE YESTERDAY'S SASHIMI CONTAINED *E. COLI*.
BFFT

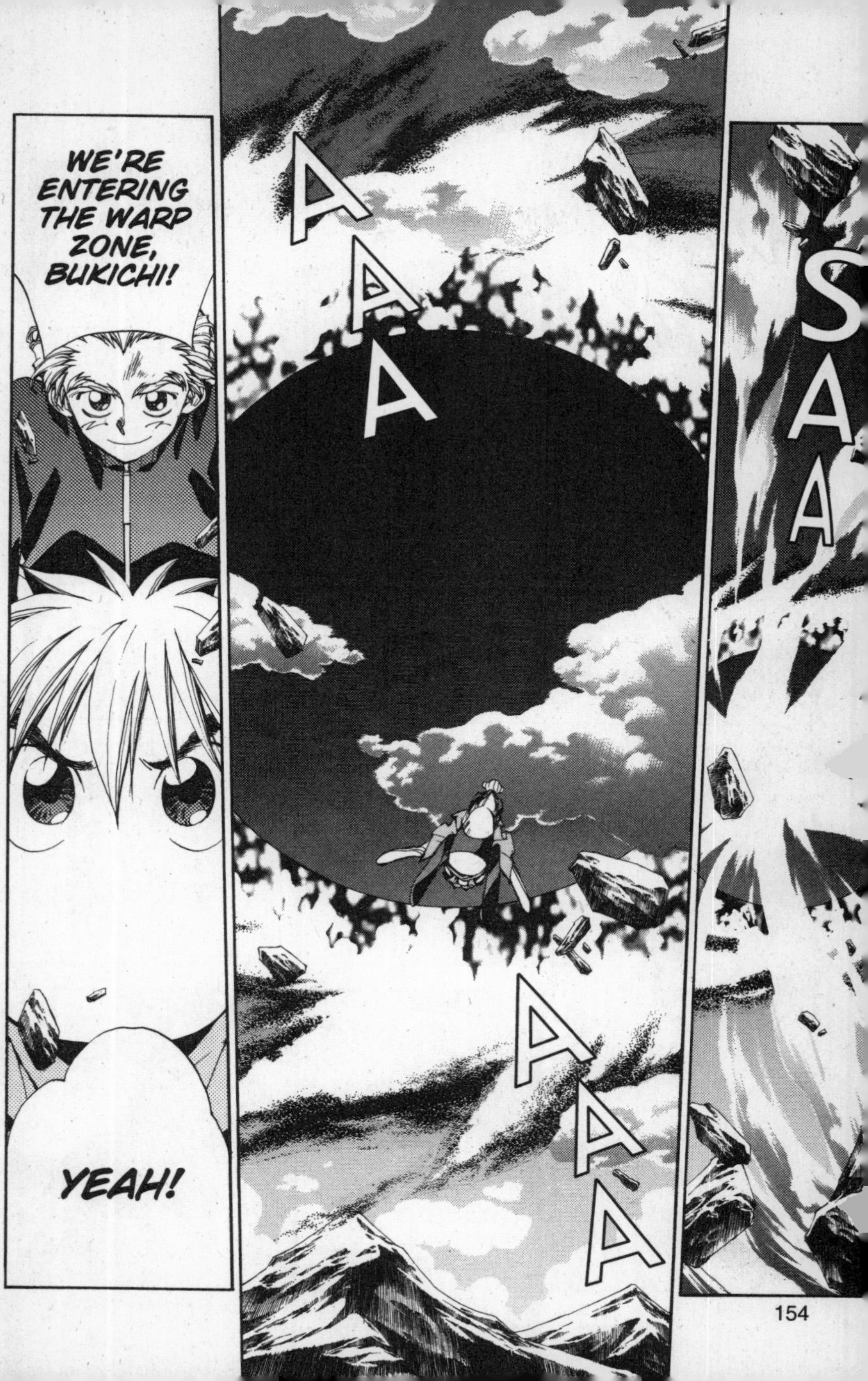
SAAA
AAA
AAAA
WE'RE ENTERING THE WARP ZONE, BUKICHI!
YEAH!

READ THIS WAY

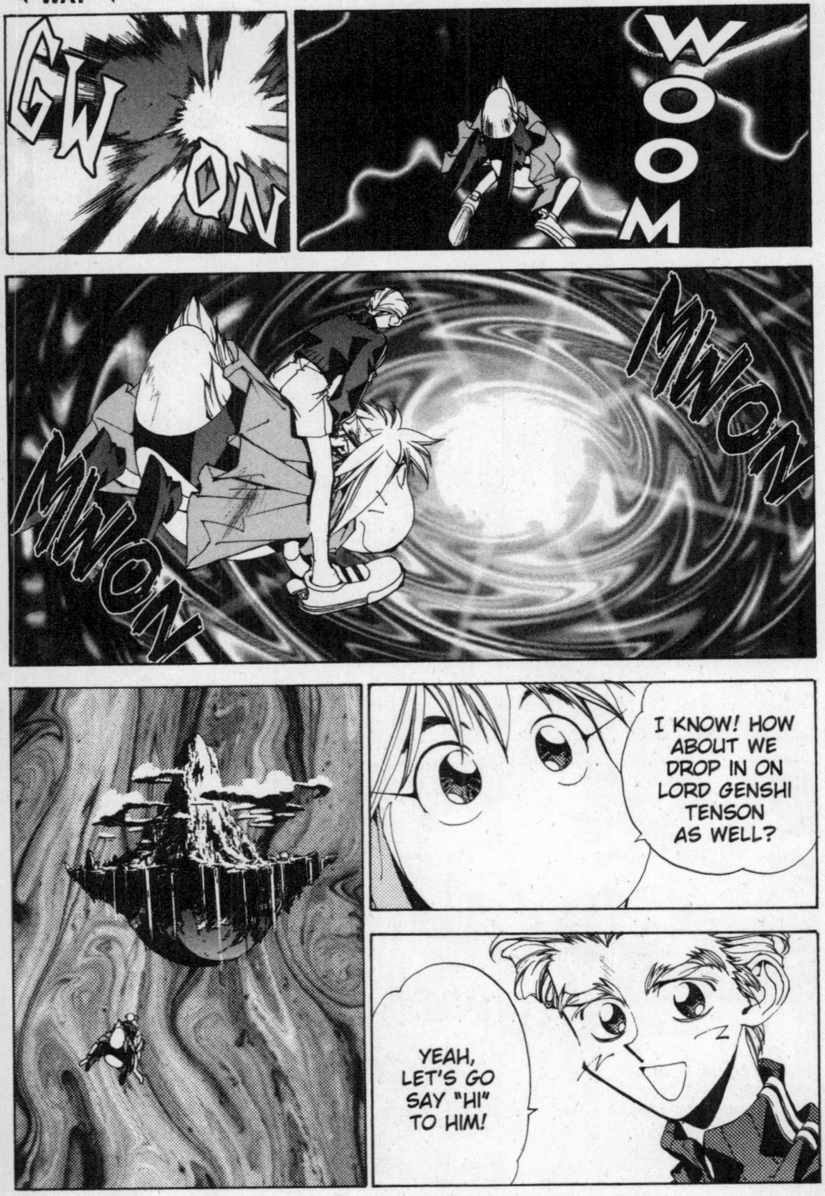
WOOOM
GWON
MWON
MWON
I KNOW! HOW ABOUT WE DROP IN ON LORD GENSHI TENSON AS WELL?
YEAH, LET'S GO SAY "HI" TO HIM!

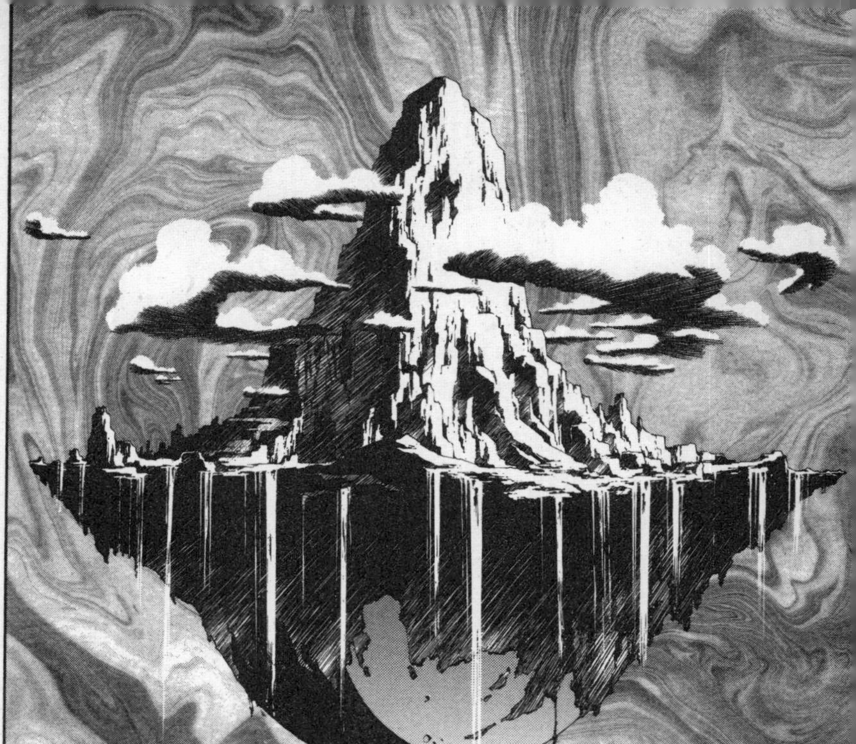

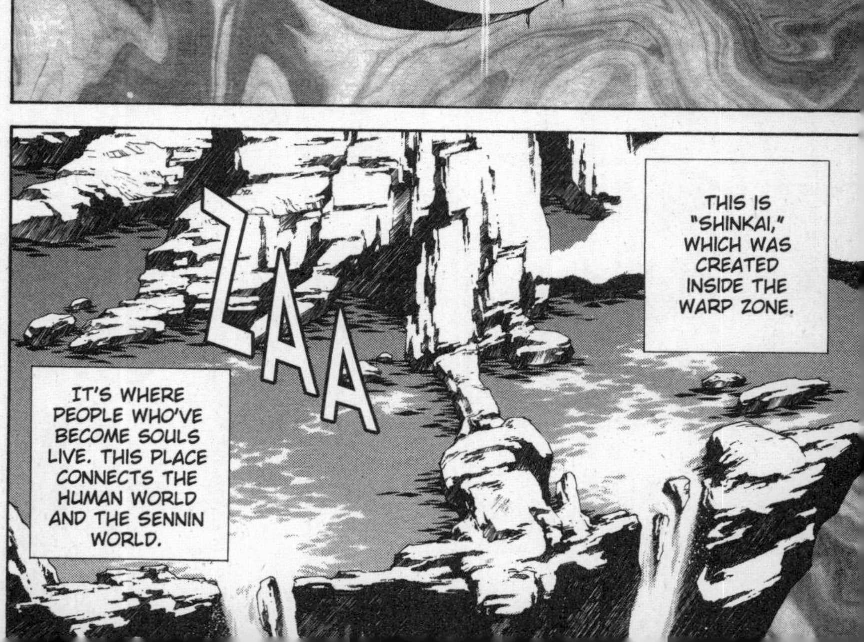
THIS IS "SHINKAI," WHICH WAS CREATED INSIDE THE WARP ZONE.
ZAA
IT'S WHERE PEOPLE WHO'VE BECOME SOULS LIVE. THIS PLACE CONNECTS THE HUMAN WORLD AND THE SENNIN WORLD.

READ THIS WAY

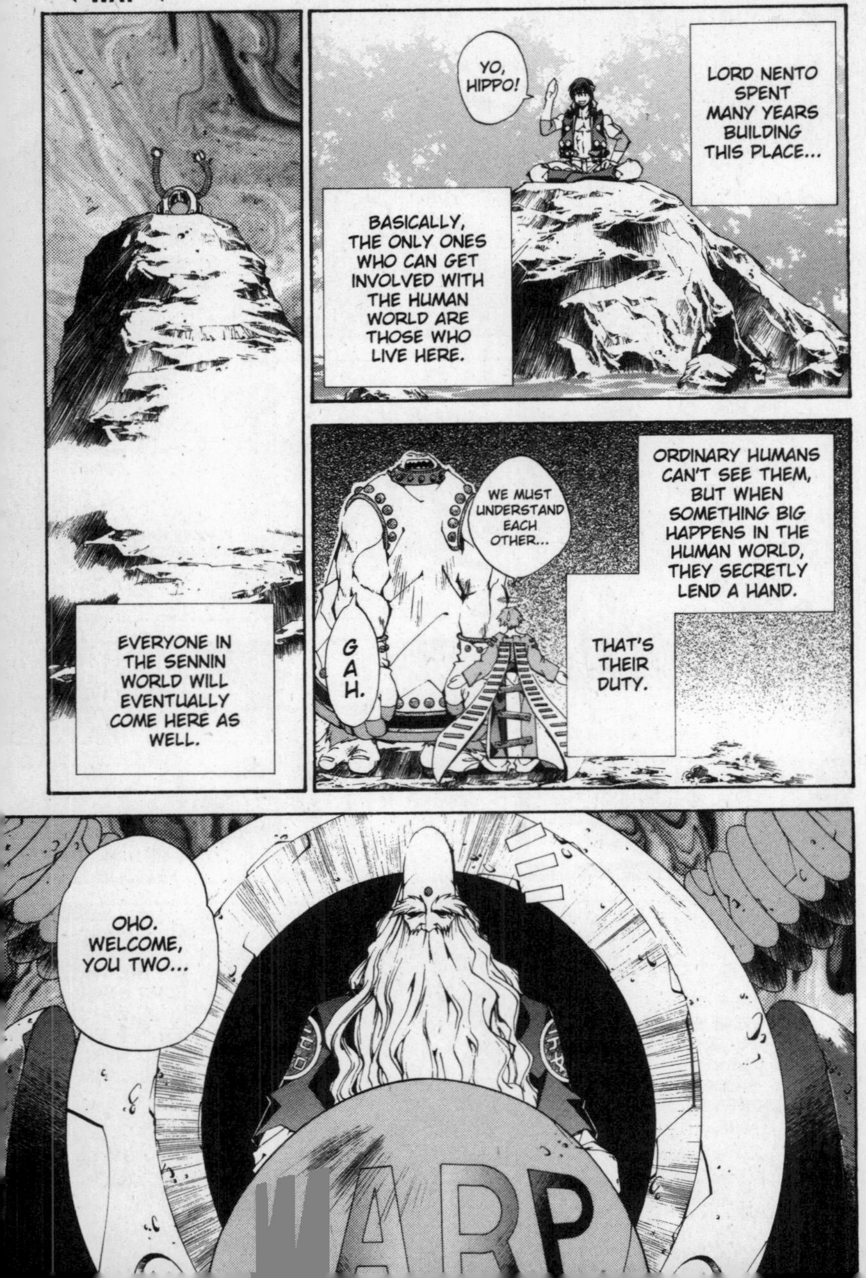

LORD NENTO SPENT MANY YEARS BUILDING THIS PLACE...
YO, HIPPO!
BASICALLY, THE ONLY ONES WHO CAN GET INVOLVED WITH THE HUMAN WORLD ARE THOSE WHO LIVE HERE.
ORDINARY HUMANS CAN'T SEE THEM, BUT WHEN SOMETHING BIG HAPPENS IN THE HUMAN WORLD, THEY SECRETLY LEND A HAND.
WE MUST UNDERSTAND EACH OTHER...
THAT'S THEIR DUTY.
GAH.
EVERYONE IN THE SENNIN WORLD WILL EVENTUALLY COME HERE AS WELL.
OHO. WELCOME, YOU TWO...

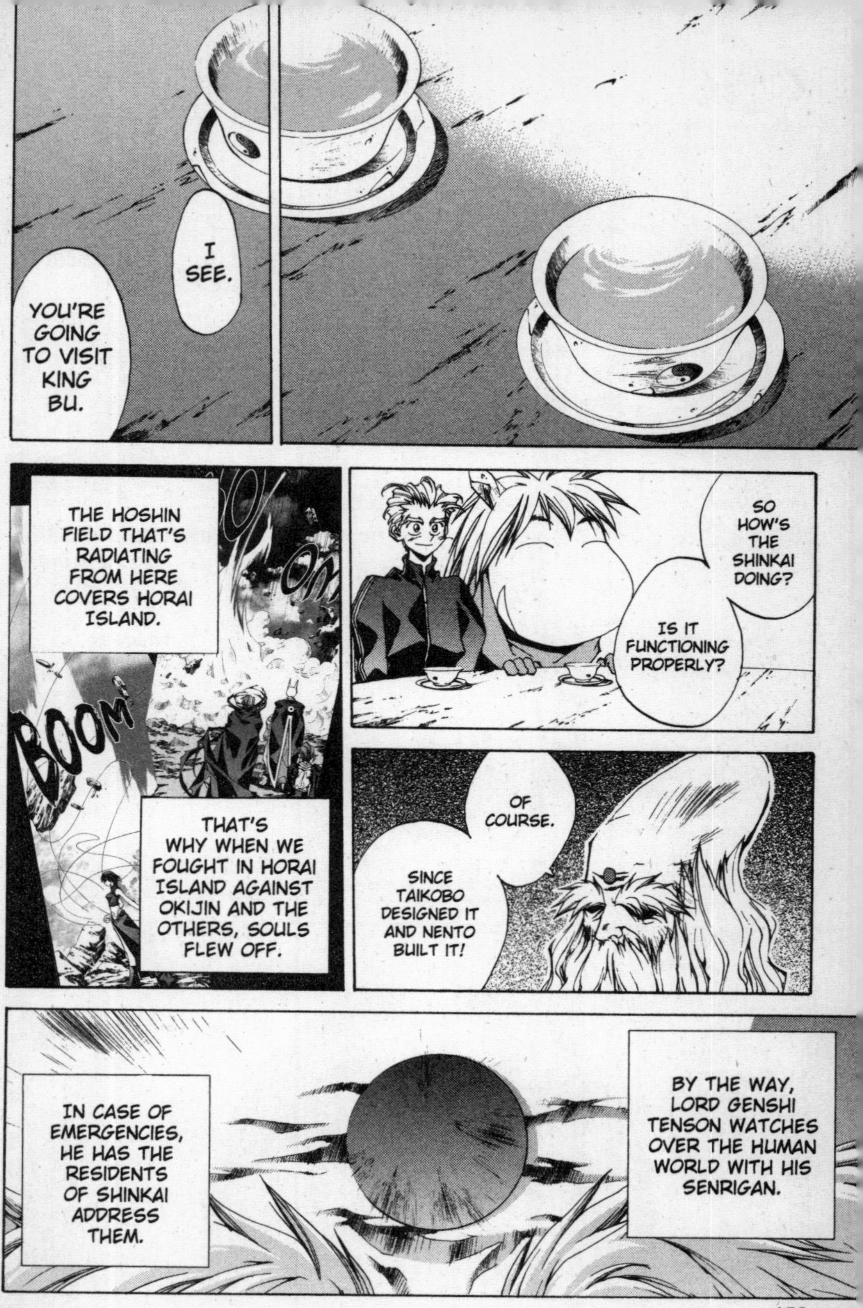
I SEE.
YOU'RE GOING TO VISIT KING BU.
SO HOW'S THE SHINKAI DOING?
IS IT FUNCTIONING PROPERLY?
OF COURSE.
SINCE TAIKOBO DESIGNED IT AND NENTO BUILT IT!
THE HOSHIN FIELD THAT'S RADIATING FROM HERE COVERS HORAI ISLAND.
BOOM
THAT'S WHY WHEN WE FOUGHT IN HORAI ISLAND AGAINST OKIJIN AND THE OTHERS, SOULS FLEW OFF.
BY THE WAY, LORD GENSHI TENSON WATCHES OVER THE HUMAN WORLD WITH HIS SENRIGAN.
IN CASE OF EMERGENCIES, HE HAS THE RESIDENTS OF SHINKAI ADDRESS THEM.

READ THIS WAY

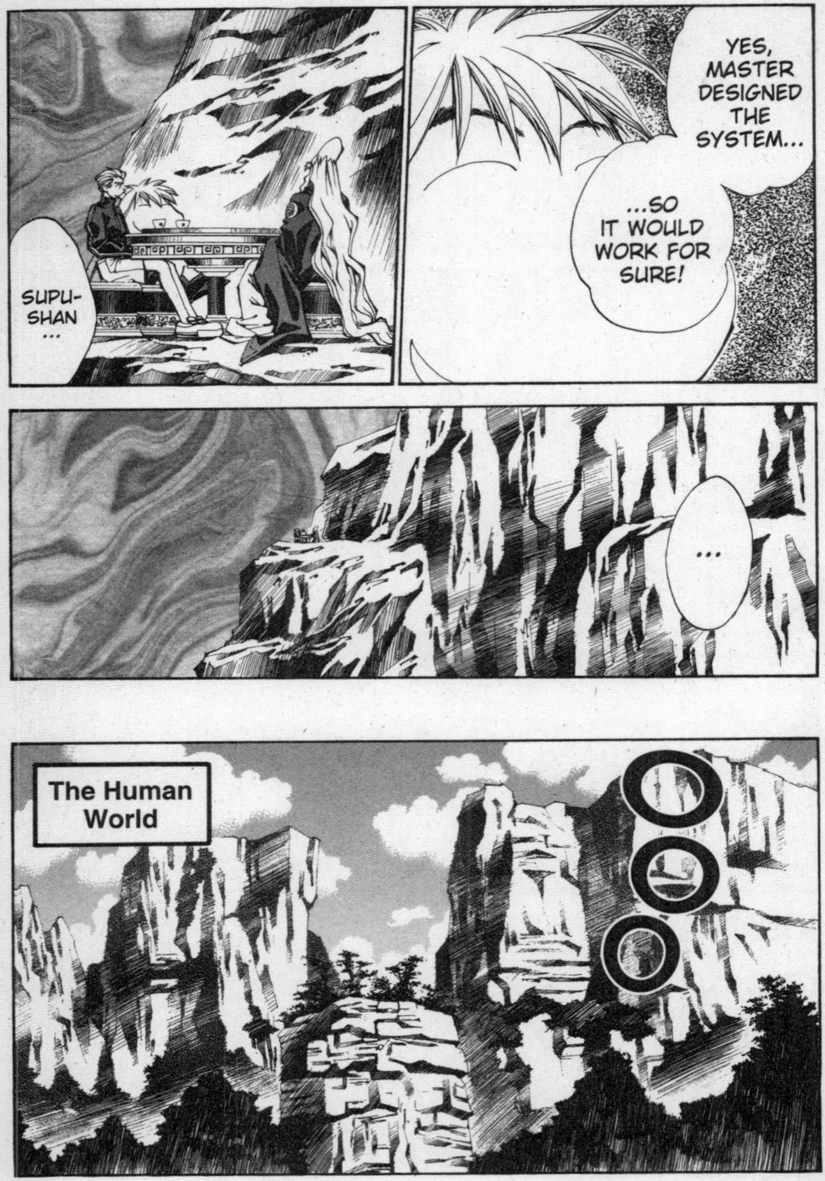
YES, MASTER DESIGNED THE SYSTEM...
...SO IT WOULD WORK FOR SURE!
SUPU-SHAN ...
...
The Human World

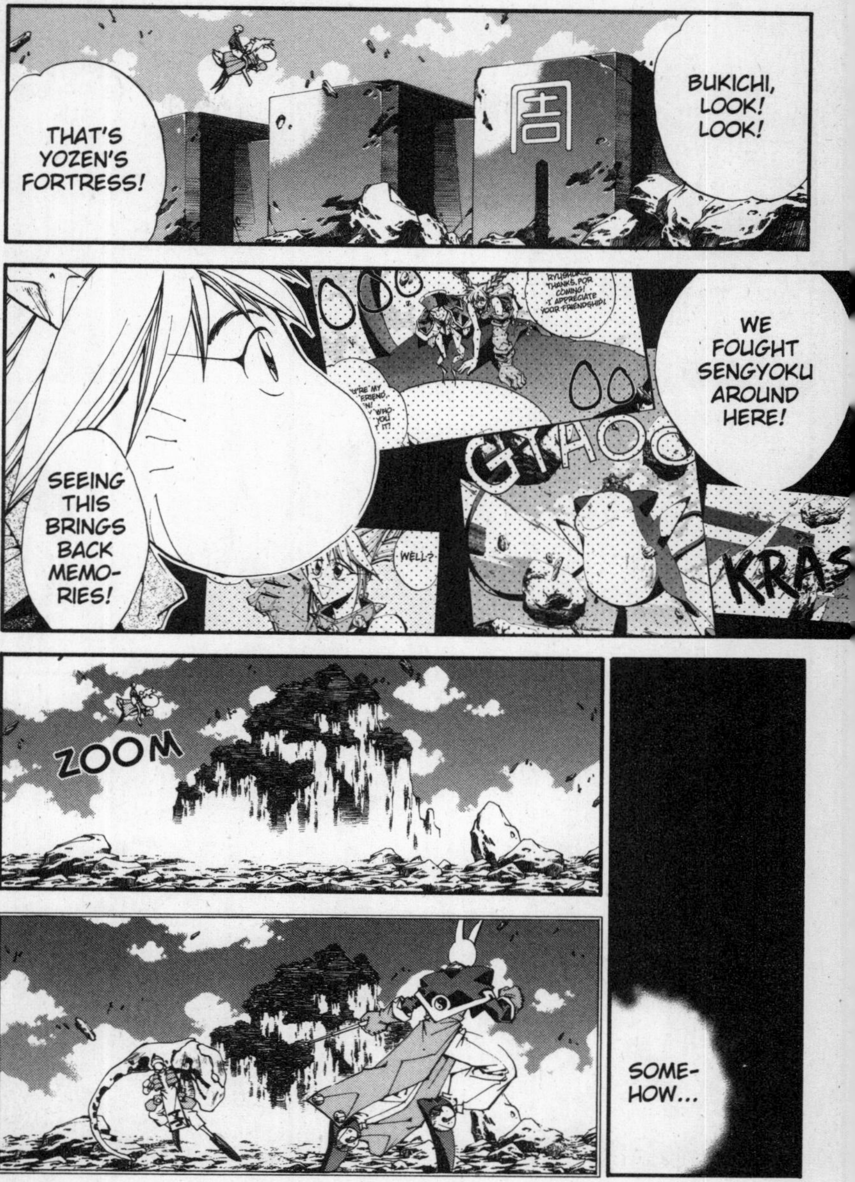
BUKICHI, LOOK! LOOK!
THAT'S YOZEN'S FORTRESS!
WE FOUGHT SENGYOKU AROUND HERE!
KRAS
GYAOO
THANKS, FOR COMING! I APPRECIATE YOUR FRIENDSHIP!
WELL?
SEEING THIS BRINGS BACK MEMO-RIES!
SOME-HOW...
ZOOM

READ THIS WAY

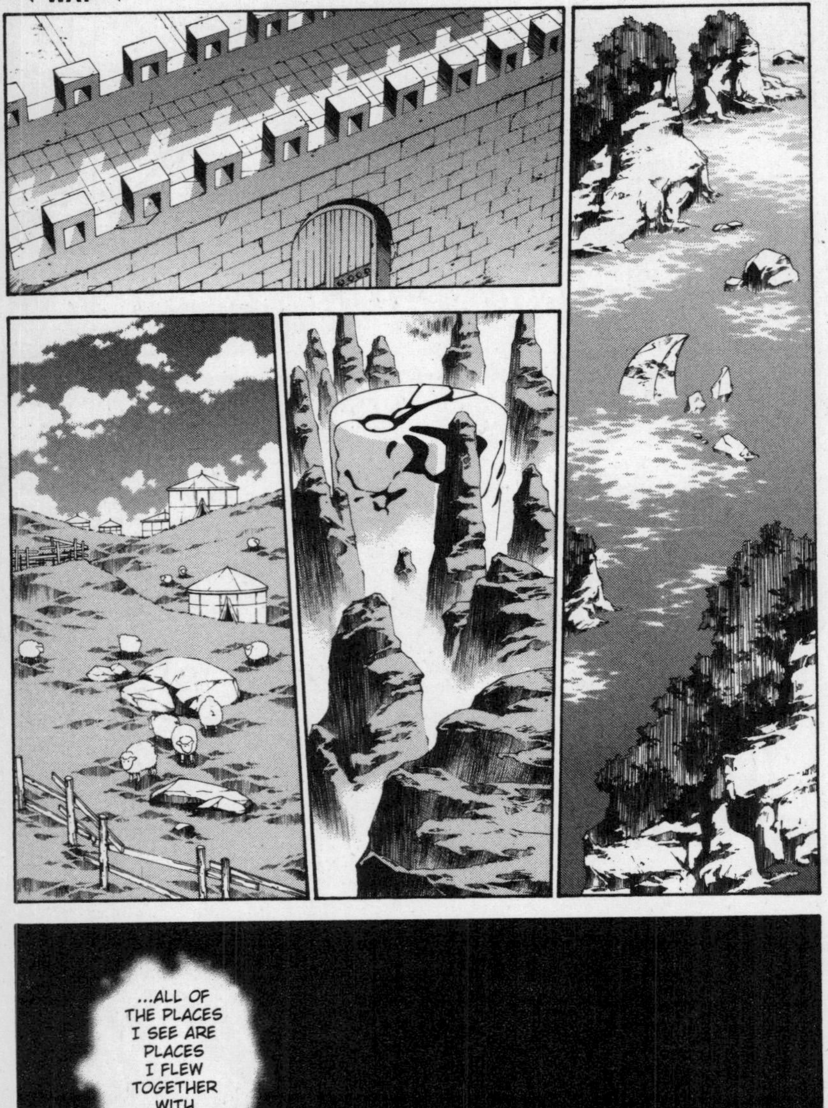
...ALL OF THE PLACES I SEE ARE PLACES I FLEW TOGETHER WITH MASTER...

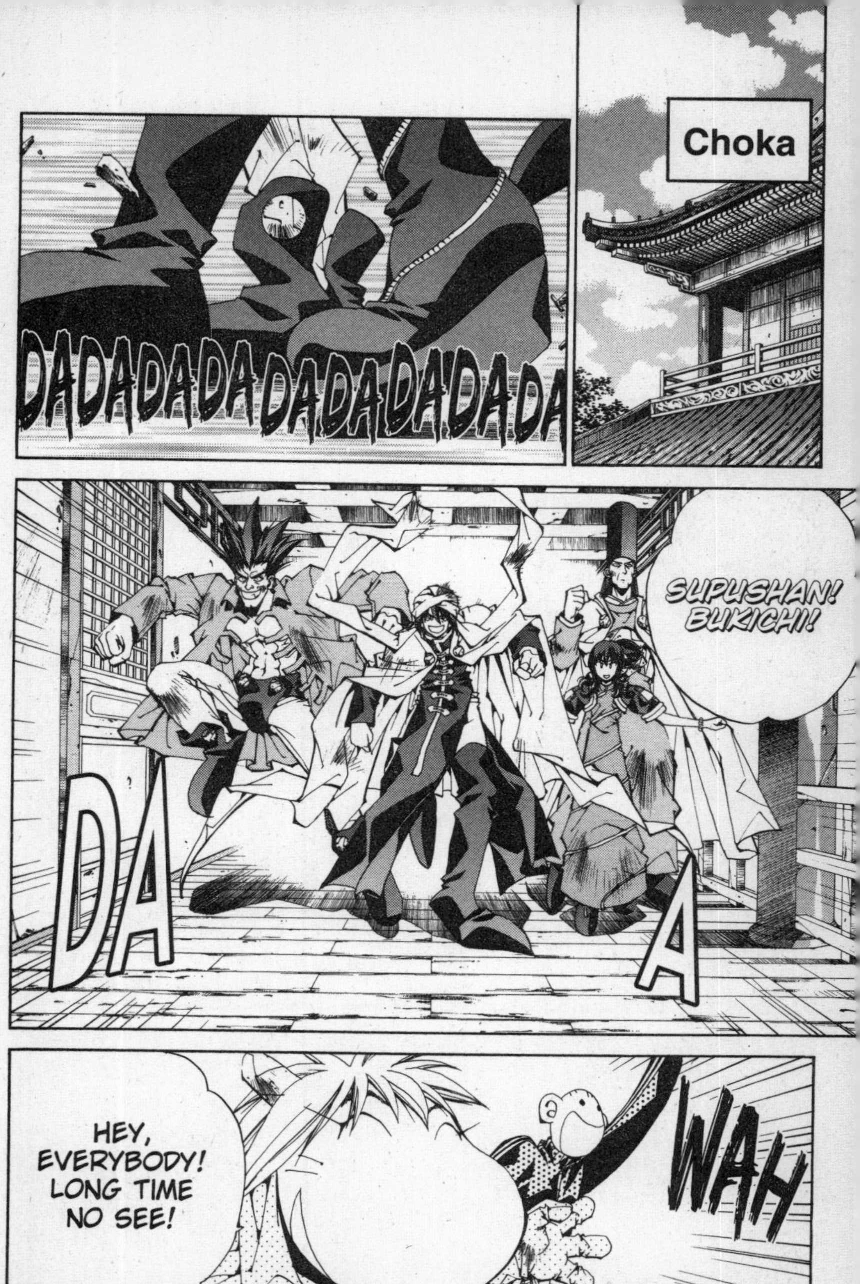
Choka
DADADADADADADADADA
SUPUSHAN! BUKICHI!
DA
A
WAH
HEY, EVERYBODY! LONG TIME NO SEE!

READ THIS WAY

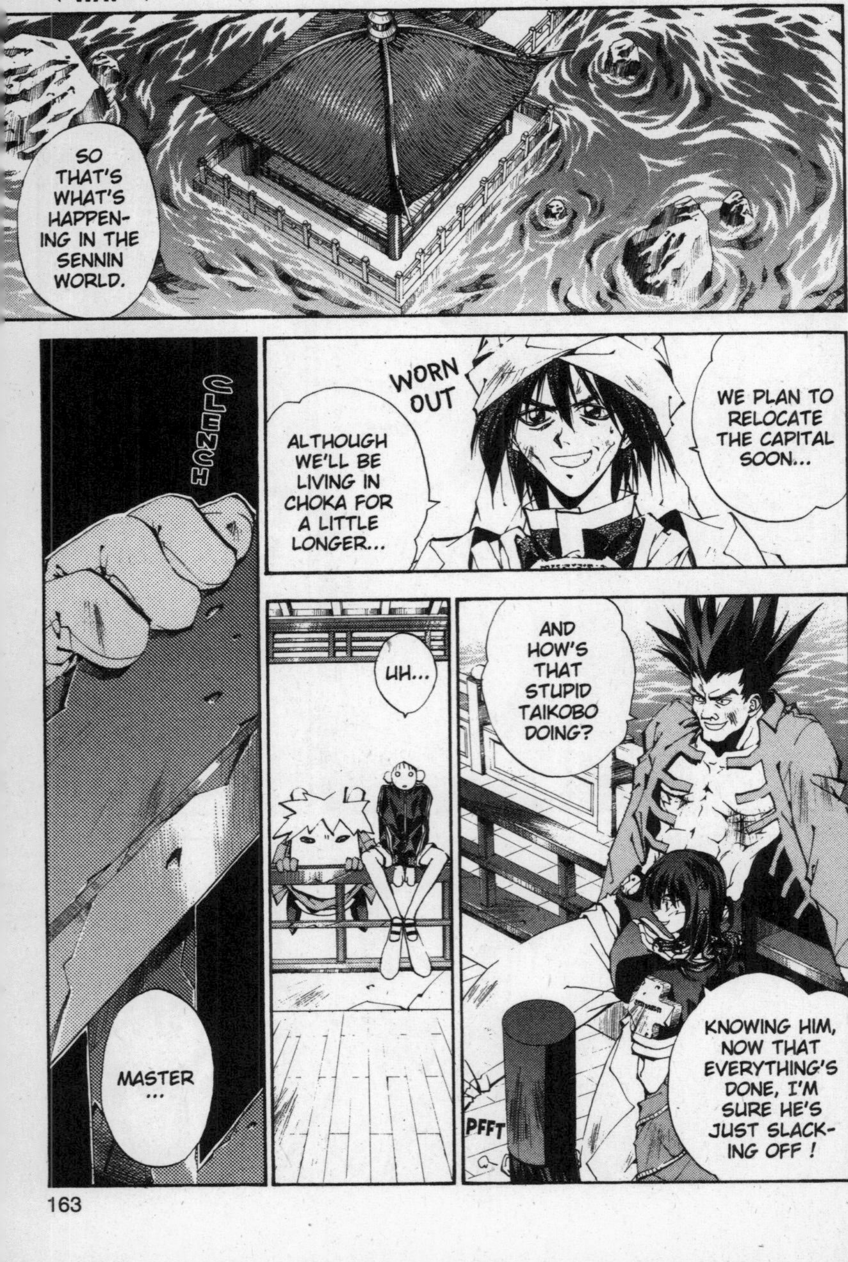
SO THAT'S WHAT'S HAPPENING IN THE SENNIN WORLD.
WE PLAN TO RELOCATE THE CAPITAL SOON...
WORN OUT
ALTHOUGH WE'LL BE LIVING IN CHOKA FOR A LITTLE LONGER...
AND HOW'S THAT STUPID TAIKOBO DOING?
KNOWING HIM, NOW THAT EVERYTHING'S DONE, I'M SURE HE'S JUST SLACKING OFF !
PFFT
UH...
CLENCH
MASTER ...

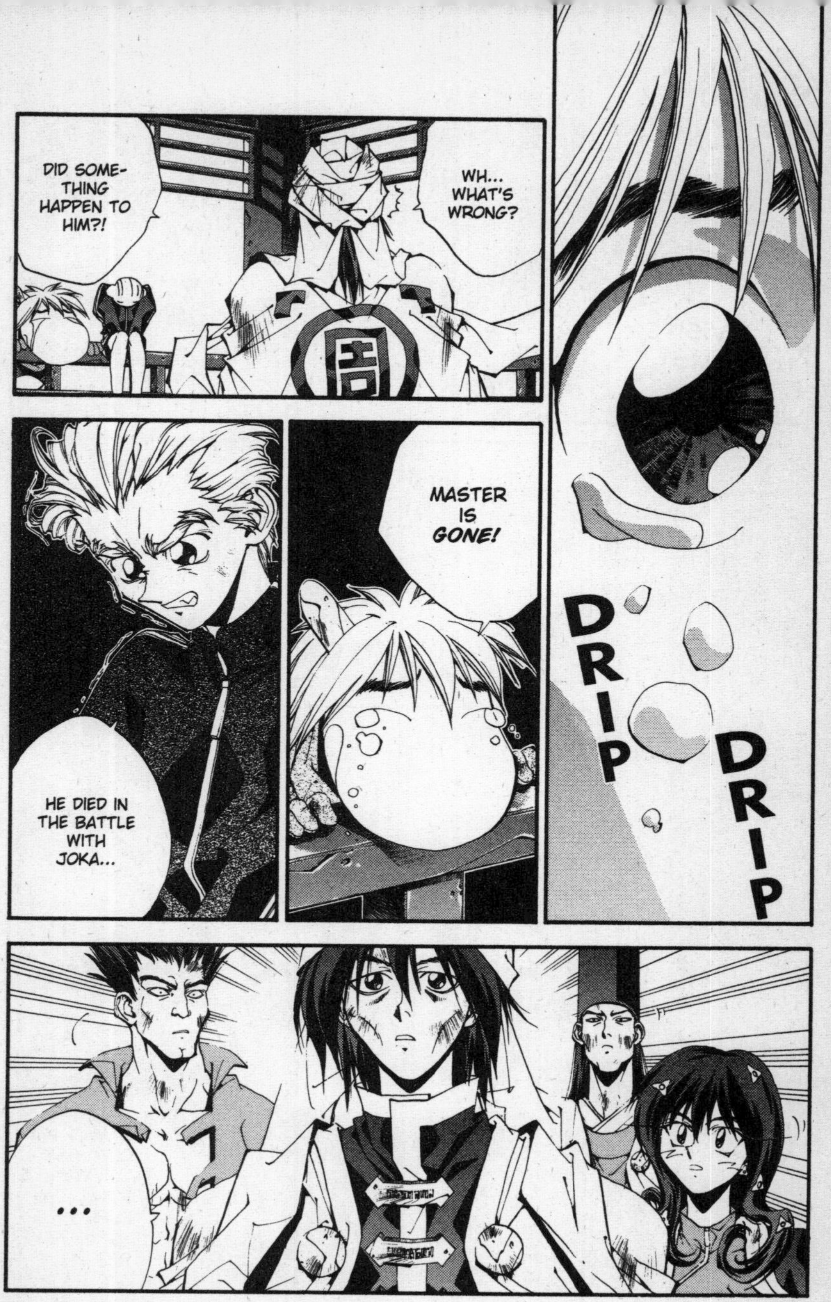
DRIP
DRIP
WH... WHAT'S WRONG?
DID SOME-THING HAPPEN TO HIM?!
MASTER IS *GONE!*
HE DIED IN THE BATTLE WITH JOKA...
...

READ THIS WAY

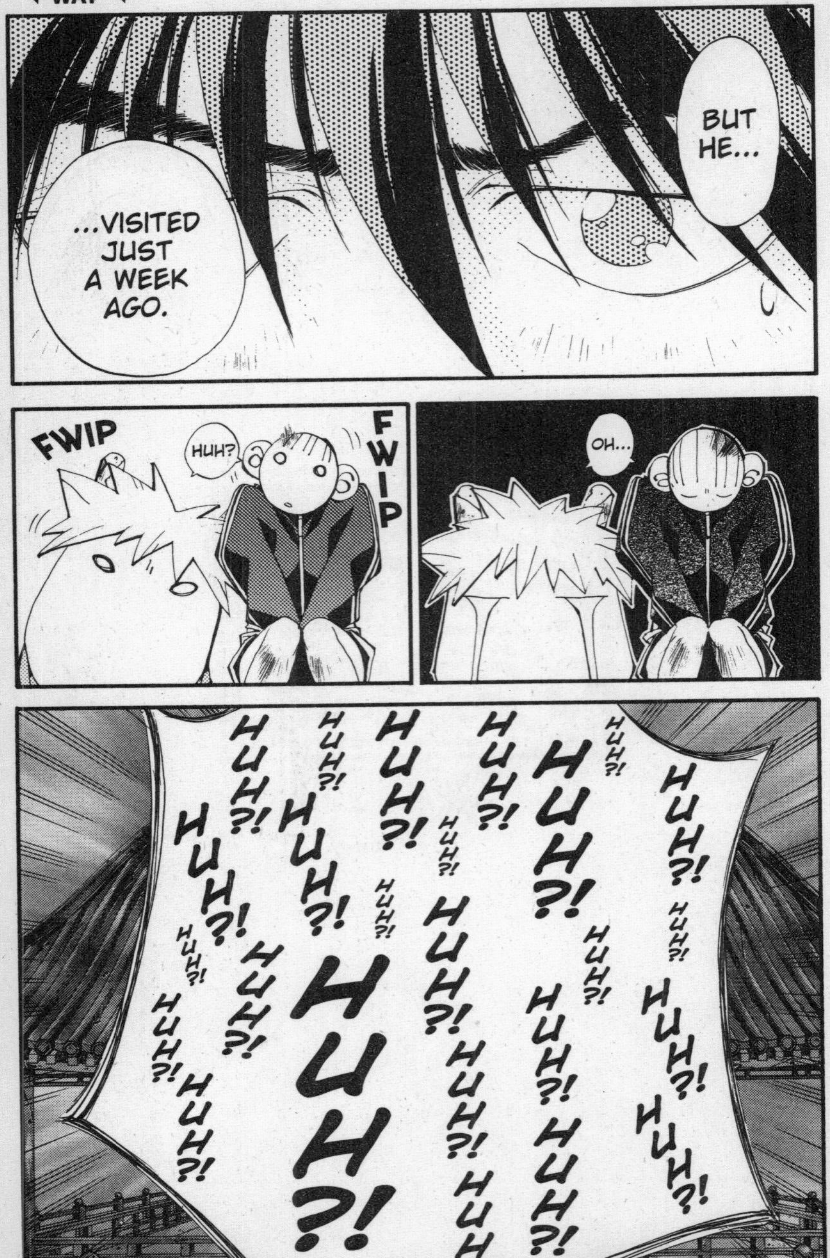

BUT HE...
...VISITED JUST A WEEK AGO.
OH...
FWIP
FWIP
HUH?
HUH?!
HUH?!
HUH?!
HUH?!
HUH?!
HUH?!
HUH?!
HUH?!

封神演義

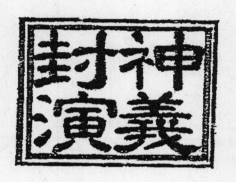

Chapter 204

PICKING UP THE PIECES, PART 2

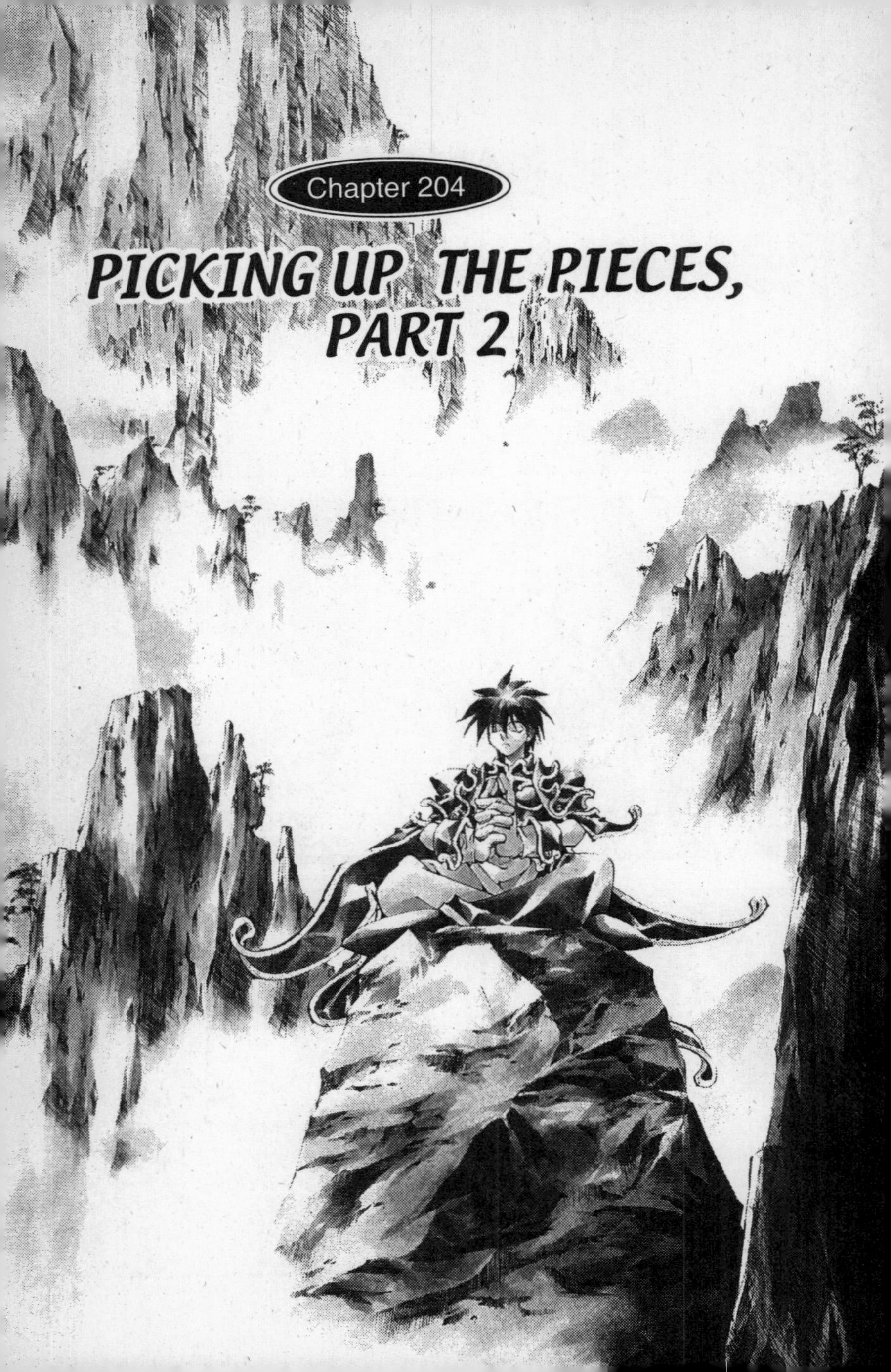

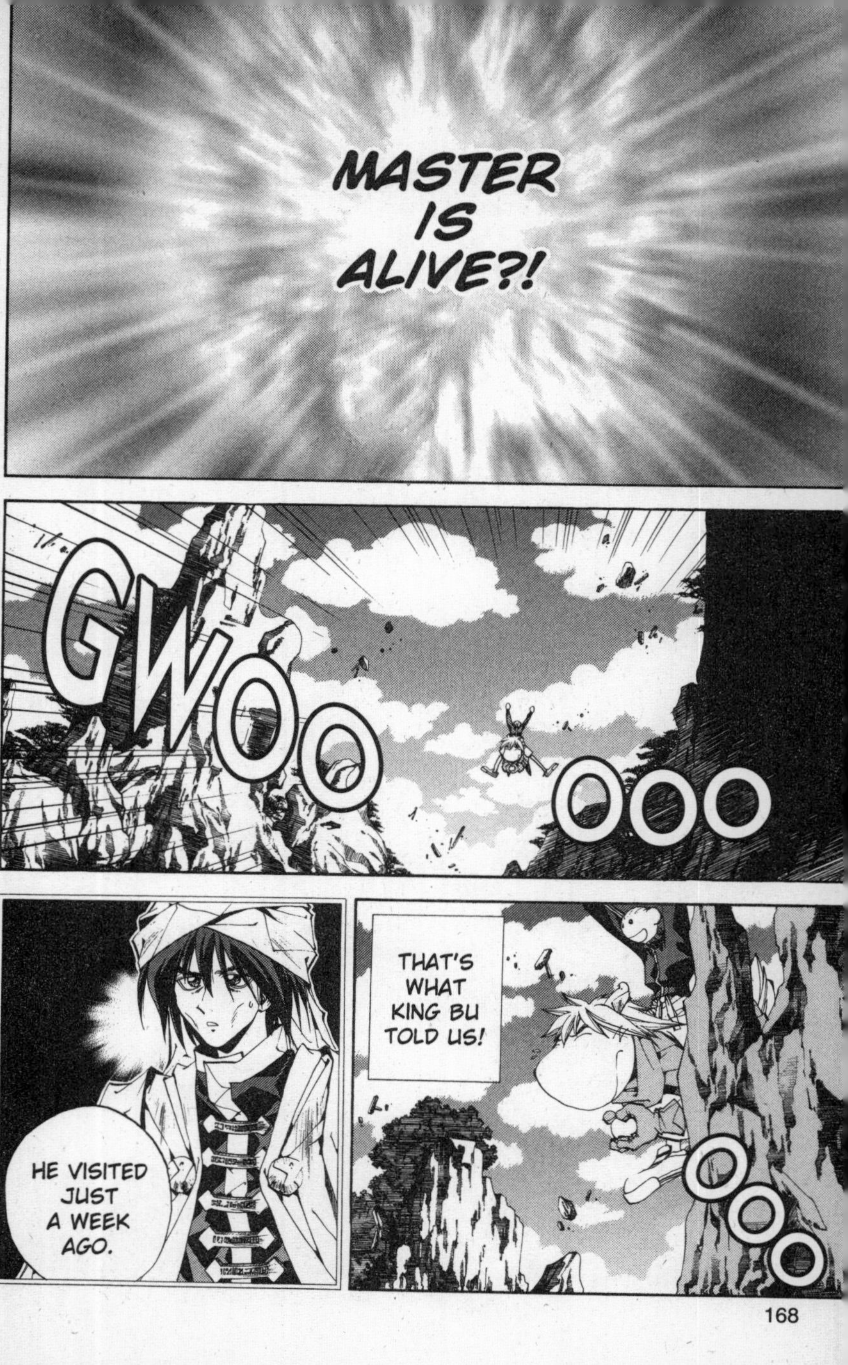
MASTER IS ALIVE?!
GWOO
OOO
THAT'S WHAT KING BU TOLD US!
OOO
HE VISITED JUST A WEEK AGO.

READ THIS WAY

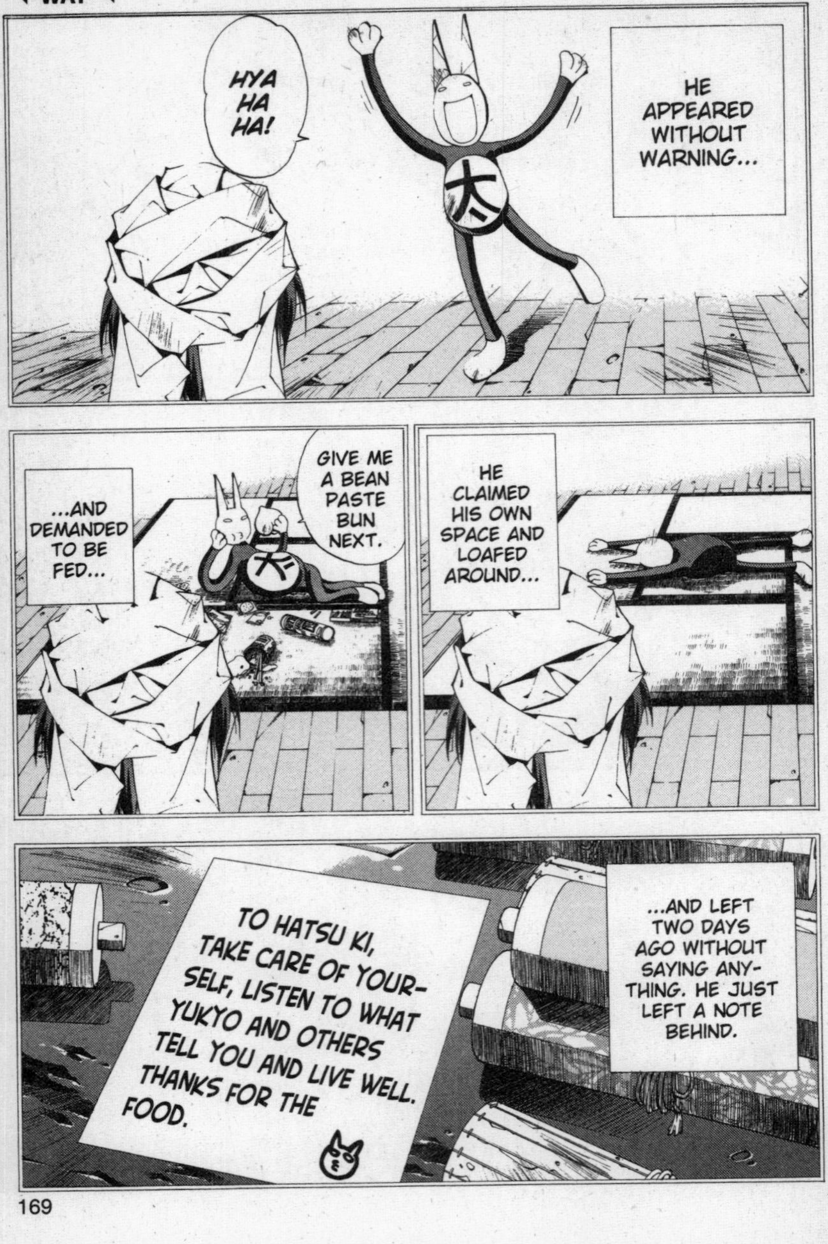
HE APPEARED WITHOUT WARNING...
HYA HA HA!
...AND DEMANDED TO BE FED...
GIVE ME A BEAN PASTE BUN NEXT.
HE CLAIMED HIS OWN SPACE AND LOAFED AROUND...
...AND LEFT TWO DAYS AGO WITHOUT SAYING ANY-THING. HE JUST LEFT A NOTE BEHIND.
TO HATSU KI, TAKE CARE OF YOUR-SELF, LISTEN TO WHAT YUKYO AND OTHERS TELL YOU AND LIVE WELL. THANKS FOR THE FOOD.

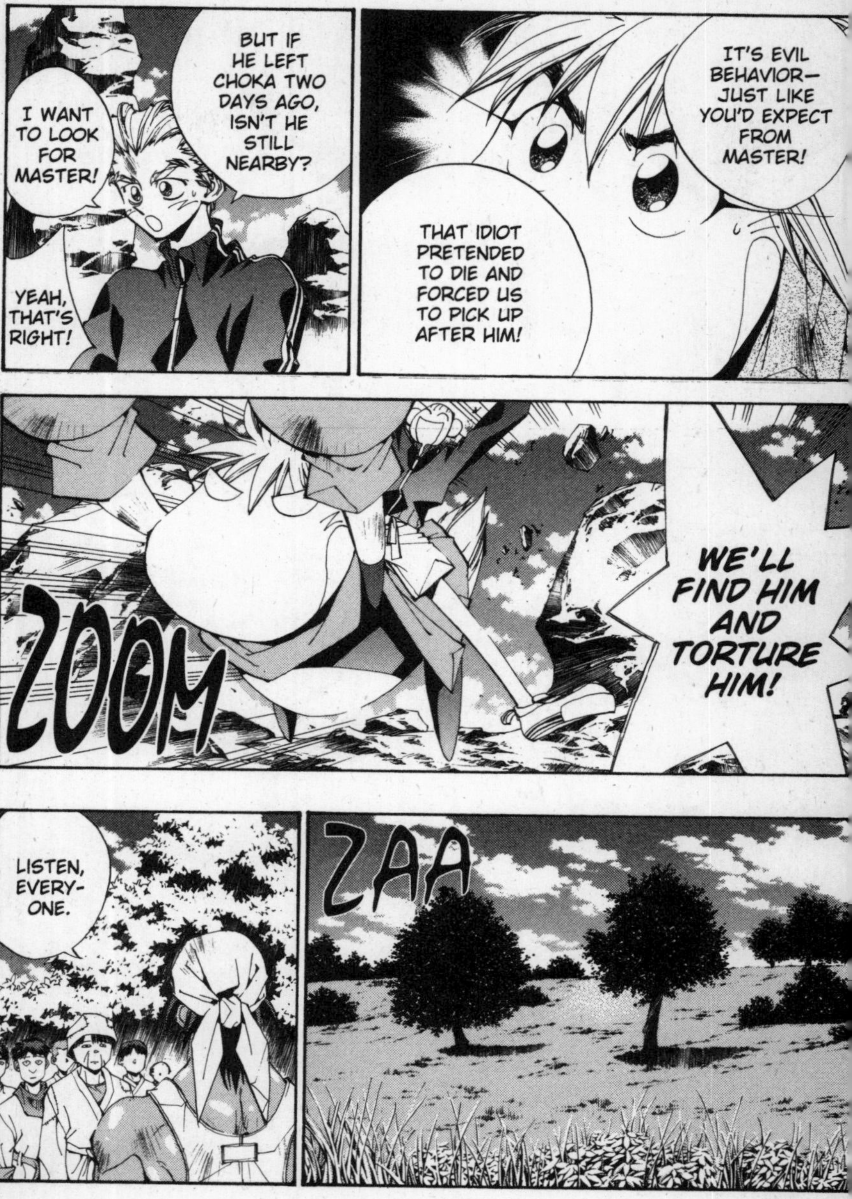
IT'S EVIL BEHAVIOR— JUST LIKE YOU'D EXPECT FROM MASTER!
THAT IDIOT PRETENDED TO DIE AND FORCED US TO PICK UP AFTER HIM!
BUT IF HE LEFT CHOKA TWO DAYS AGO, ISN'T HE STILL NEARBY?
I WANT TO LOOK FOR MASTER!
YEAH, THAT'S RIGHT!
WE'LL FIND HIM AND TORTURE HIM!
ZOOM
ZAA
LISTEN, EVERY-ONE.

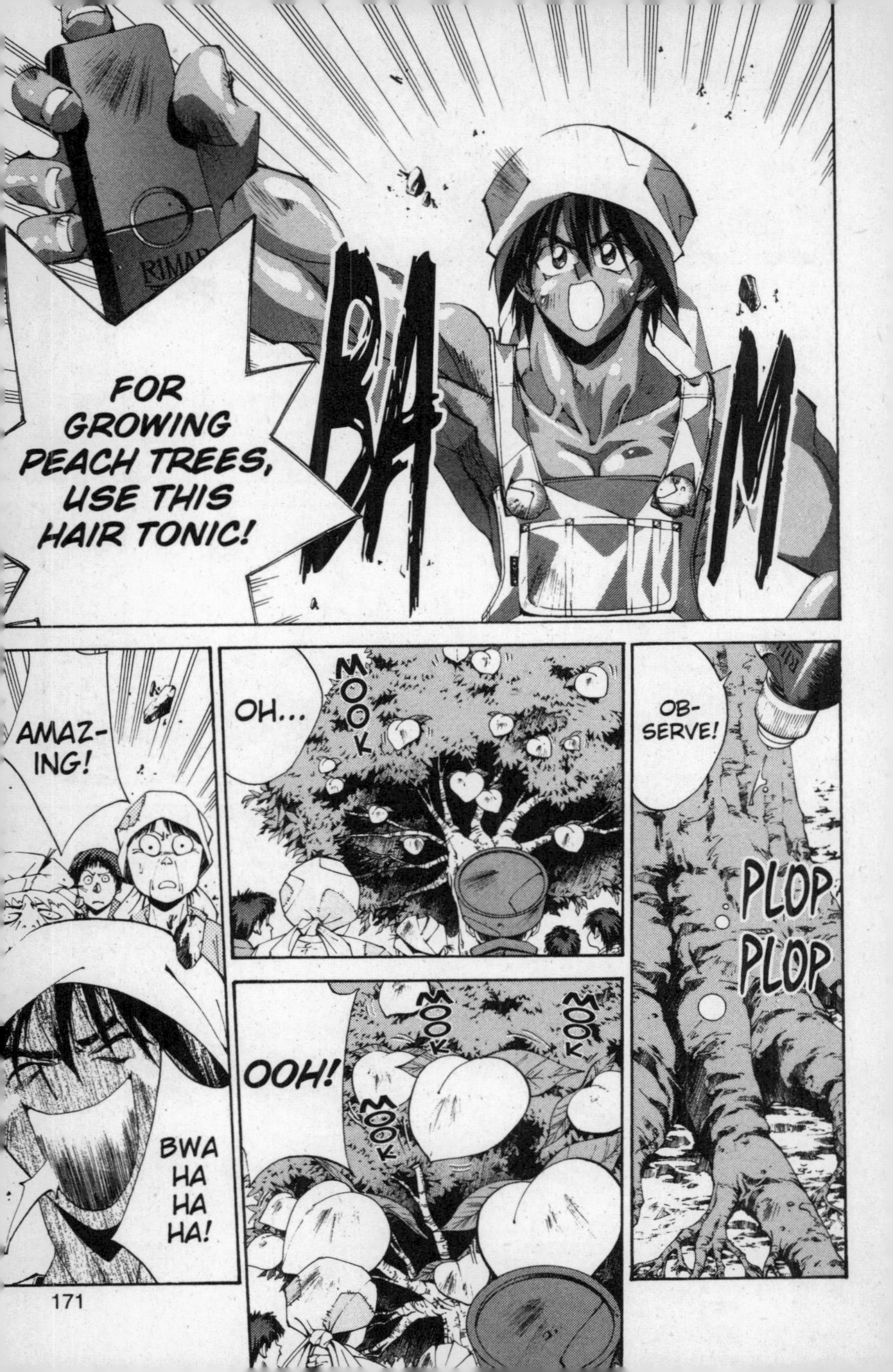
FOR GROWING PEACH TREES, USE THIS HAIR TONIC!
BAM
RIMAR
OB-SERVE!
PLOP PLOP
MOOK
OH...
AMAZ-ING!
MOOK
MOOK
OOH!
MOOK
BWA HA HA HA HA!

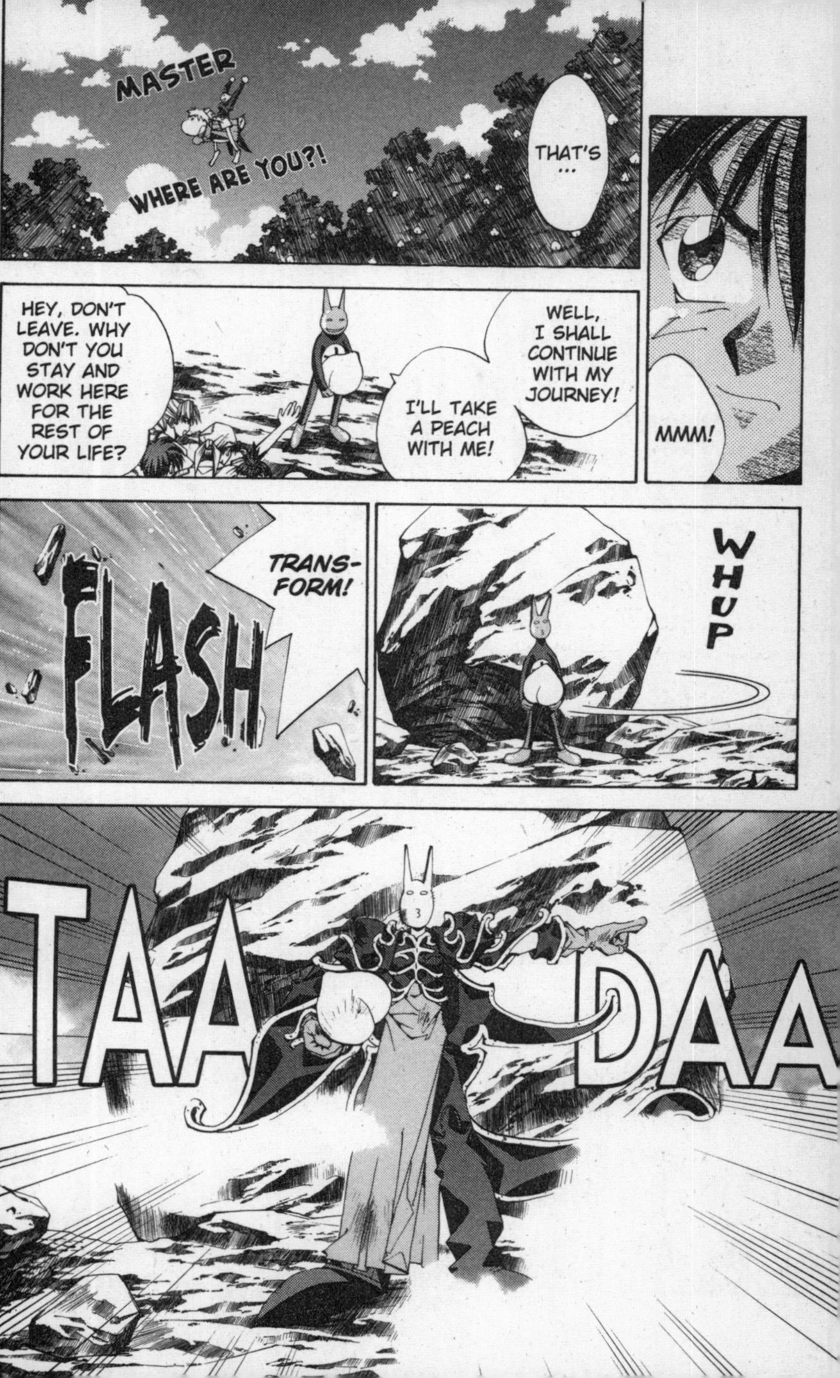
THAT'S ...
MASTER
WHERE ARE YOU?!
MMM!
WELL, I SHALL CONTINUE WITH MY JOURNEY!
I'LL TAKE A PEACH WITH ME!
HEY, DON'T LEAVE. WHY DON'T YOU STAY AND WORK HERE FOR THE REST OF YOUR LIFE?
WHUP
TRANS-FORM!
FLASH
TAA
DAA

READ THIS WAY

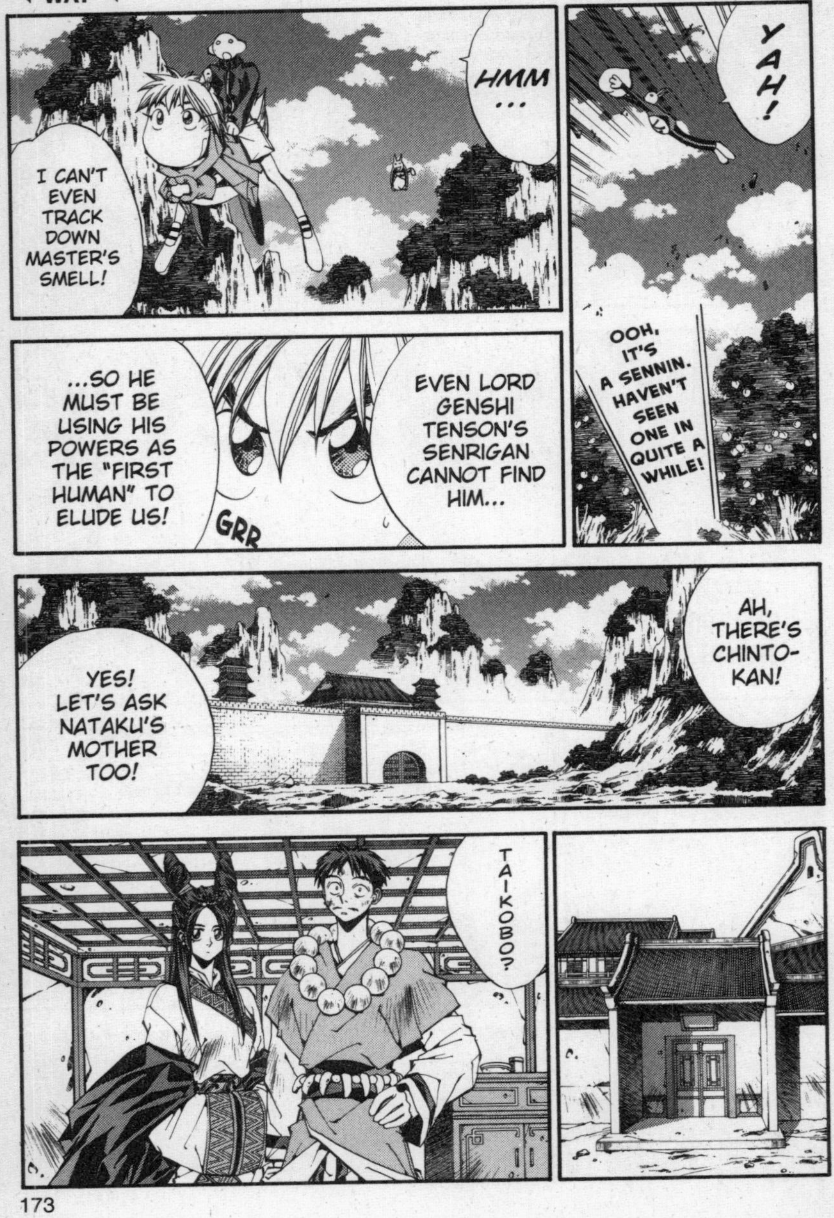
YAH!
OOH, IT'S A SENNIN. HAVEN'T SEEN ONE IN QUITE A WHILE!
HMM...
I CAN'T EVEN TRACK DOWN MASTER'S SMELL!
EVEN LORD GENSHI TENSON'S SENRIGAN CANNOT FIND HIM...
...SO HE MUST BE USING HIS POWERS AS THE "FIRST HUMAN" TO ELUDE US!
GRR
AH, THERE'S CHINTO-KAN!
YES! LET'S ASK NATAKU'S MOTHER TOO!
TAIKOBO?

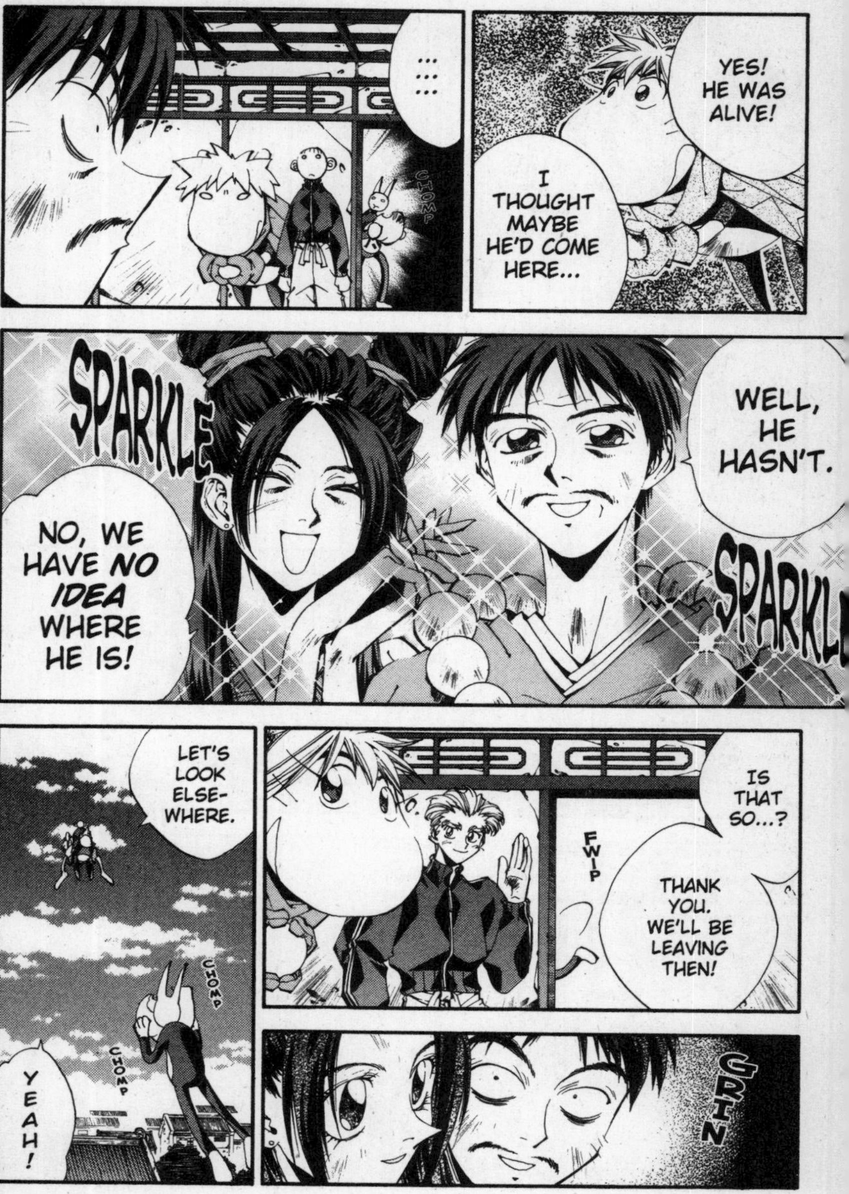
YES! HE WAS ALIVE!
I THOUGHT MAYBE HE'D COME HERE...
......
CHOMP
WELL, HE HASN'T.
SPARKLE
SPARKLE
NO, WE HAVE NO IDEA WHERE HE IS!
IS THAT SO...?
FWIP
THANK YOU. WE'LL BE LEAVING THEN!
GRIN
LET'S LOOK ELSE-WHERE.
CHOMP
CHOMP
YEAH!

READ THIS WAY

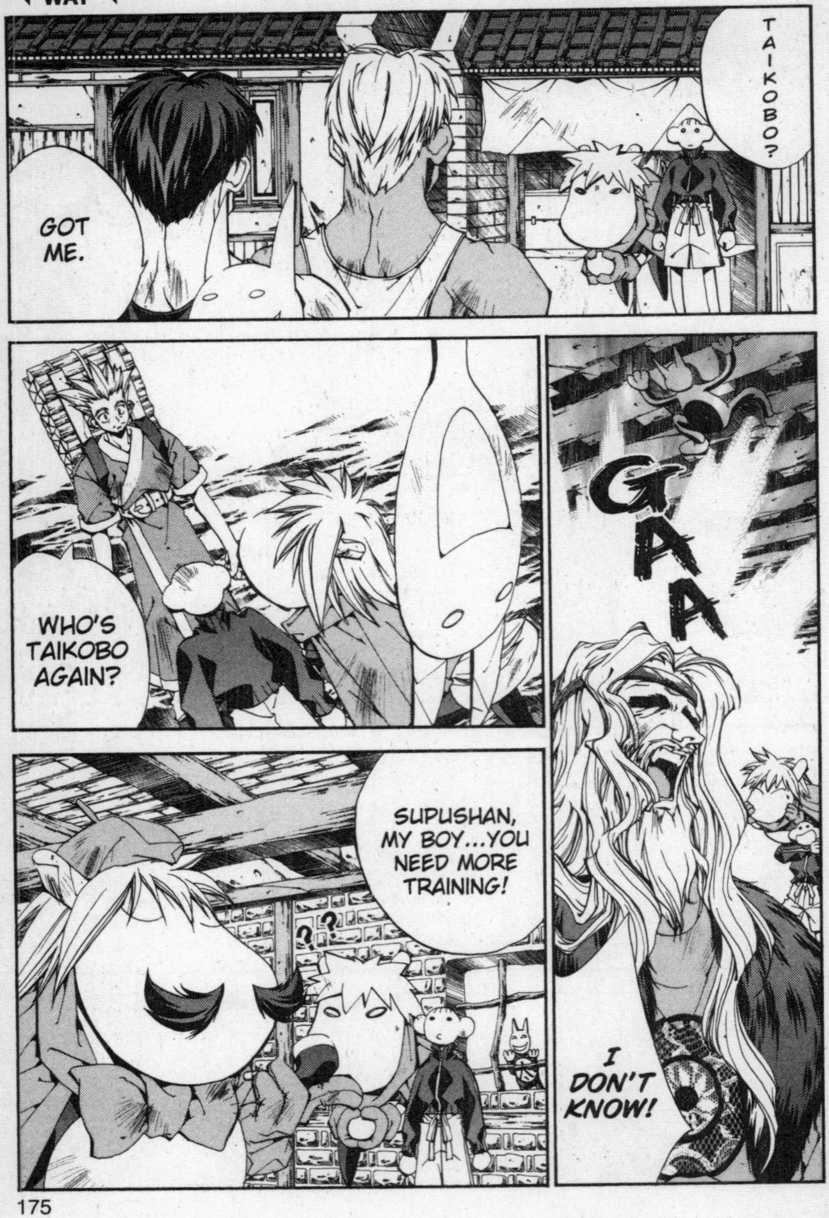
TAIKOBO?
GOT ME.
WHO'S TAIKOBO AGAIN?
GAA
I DON'T KNOW!
SUPUSHAN, MY BOY...YOU NEED MORE TRAINING!

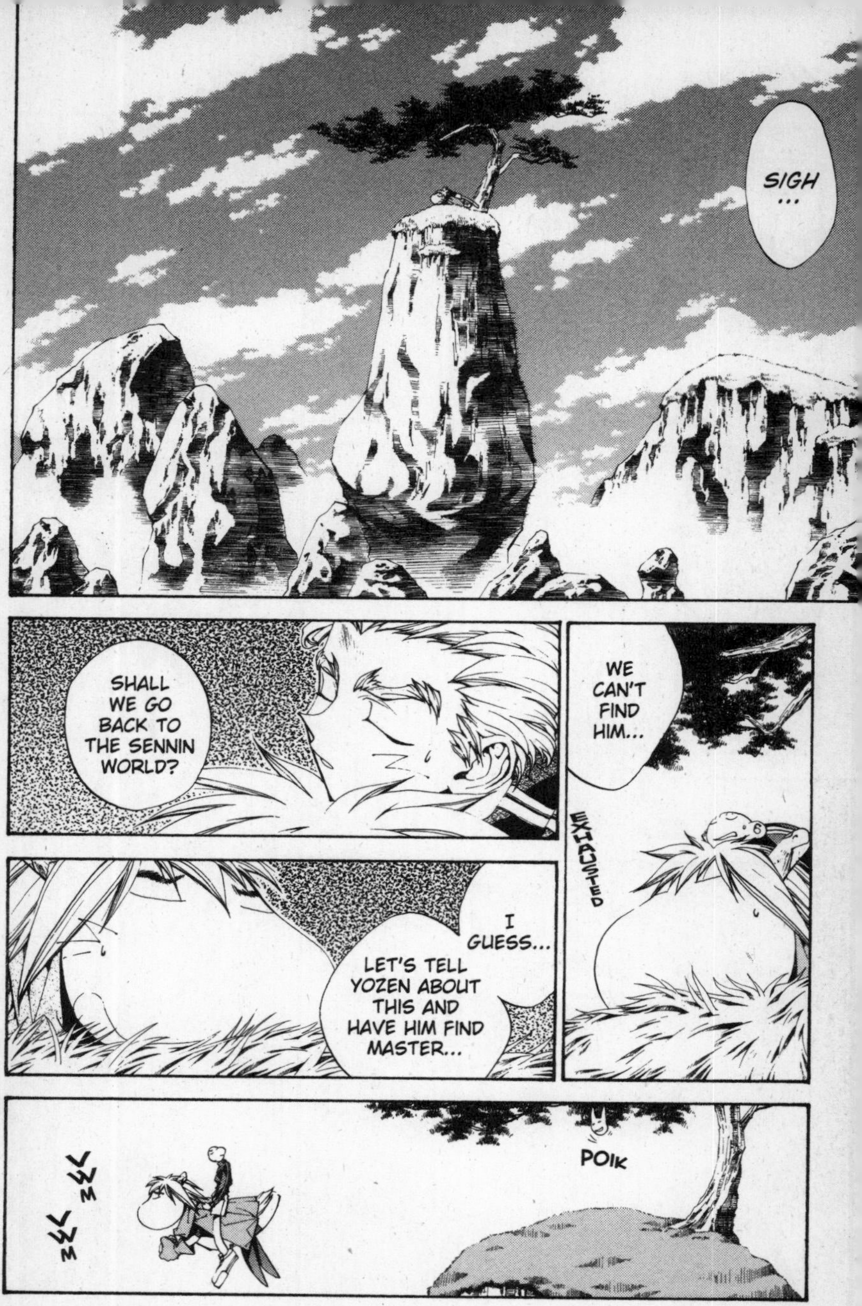
SIGH...
WE CAN'T FIND HIM...
EXHAUSTED
SHALL WE GO BACK TO THE SENNIN WORLD?
I GUESS...
LET'S TELL YOZEN ABOUT THIS AND HAVE HIM FIND MASTER...
POIK
VWM
VWM

READ THIS WAY

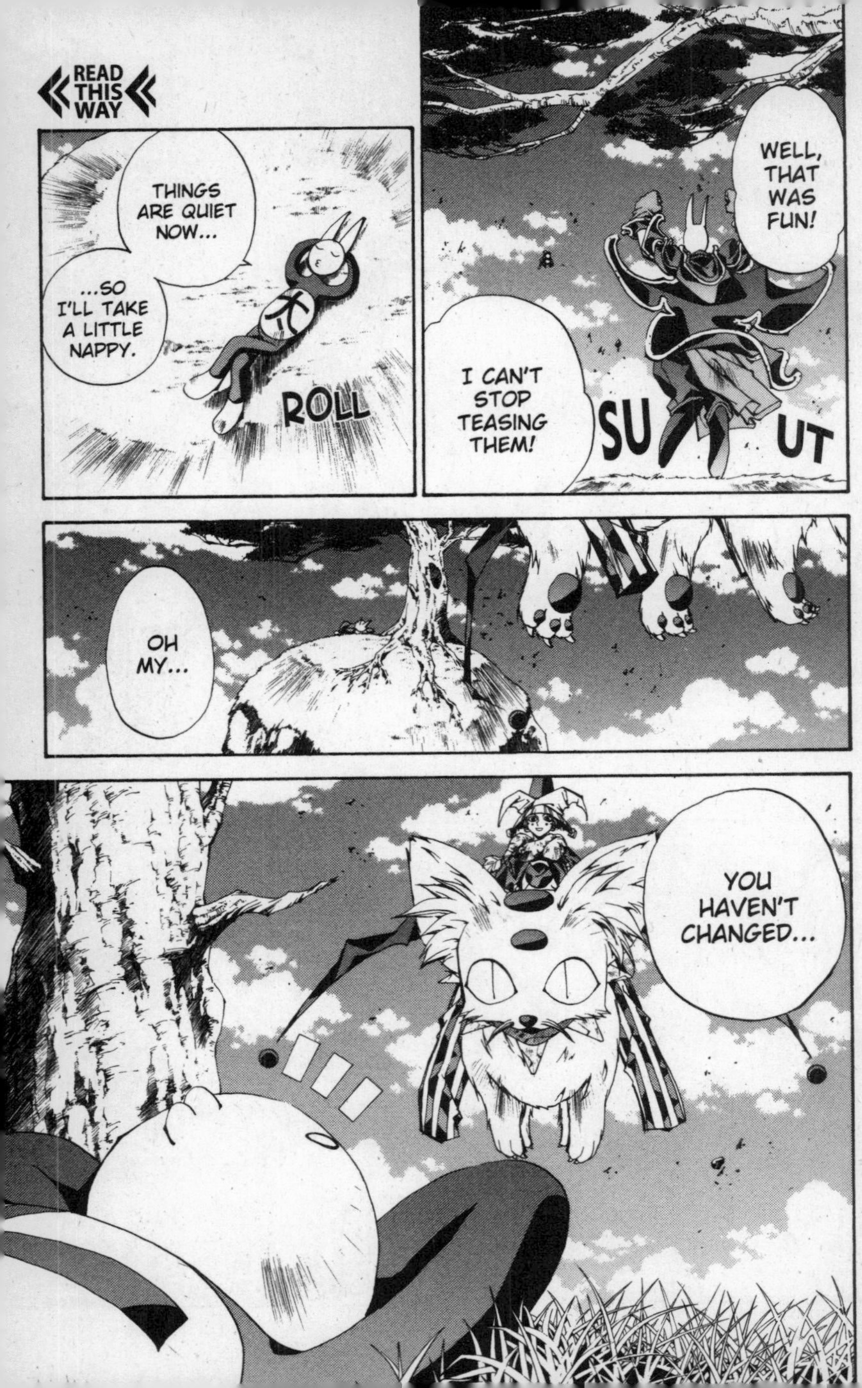
WELL, THAT WAS FUN!
I CAN'T STOP TEASING THEM!
SU UT
THINGS ARE QUIET NOW...
...SO I'LL TAKE A LITTLE NAPPY.
ROLL
OH MY...
YOU HAVEN'T CHANGED...

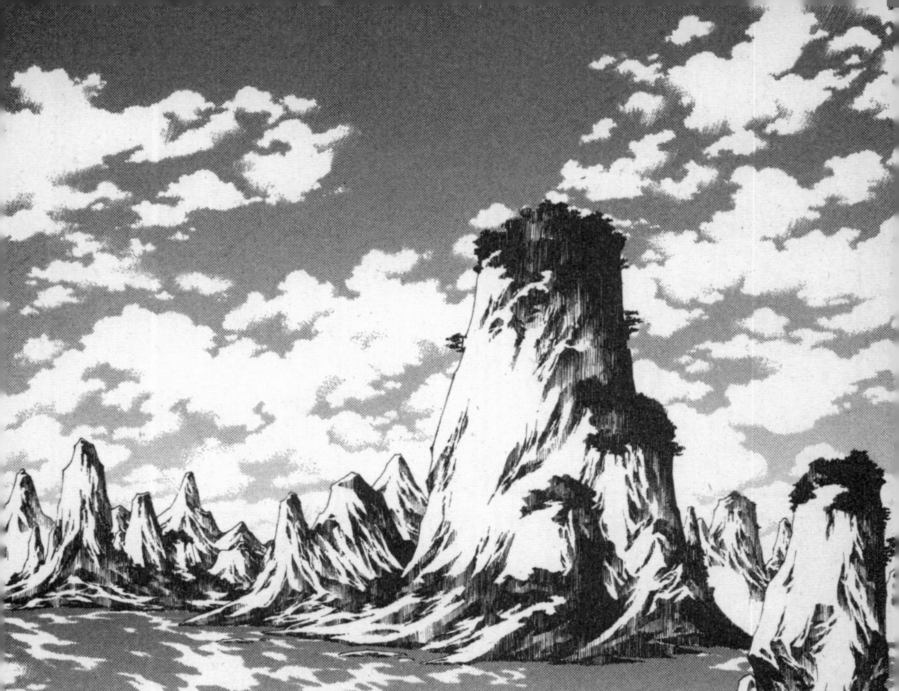

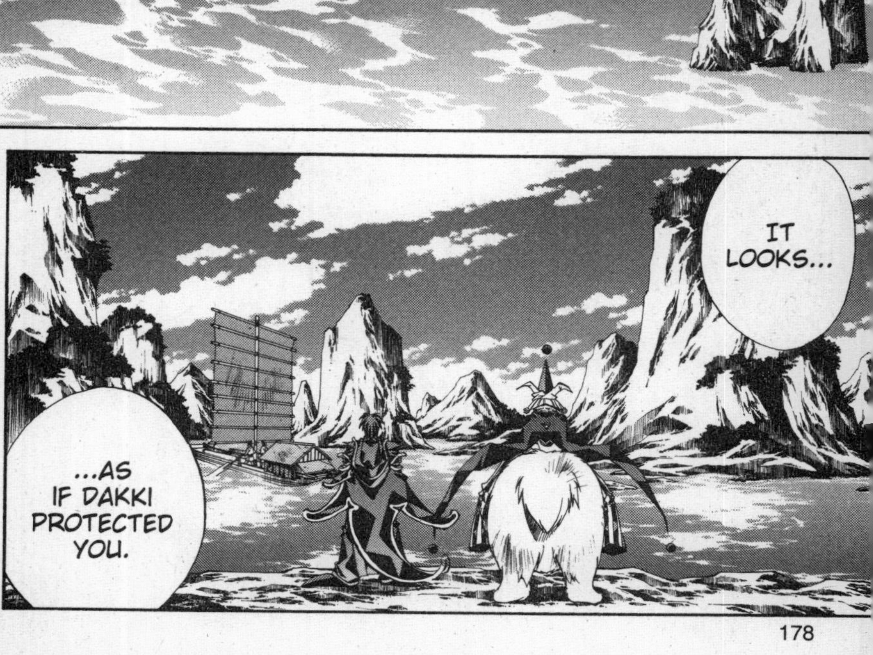
IT LOOKS...
...AS IF DAKKI PROTECTED YOU.

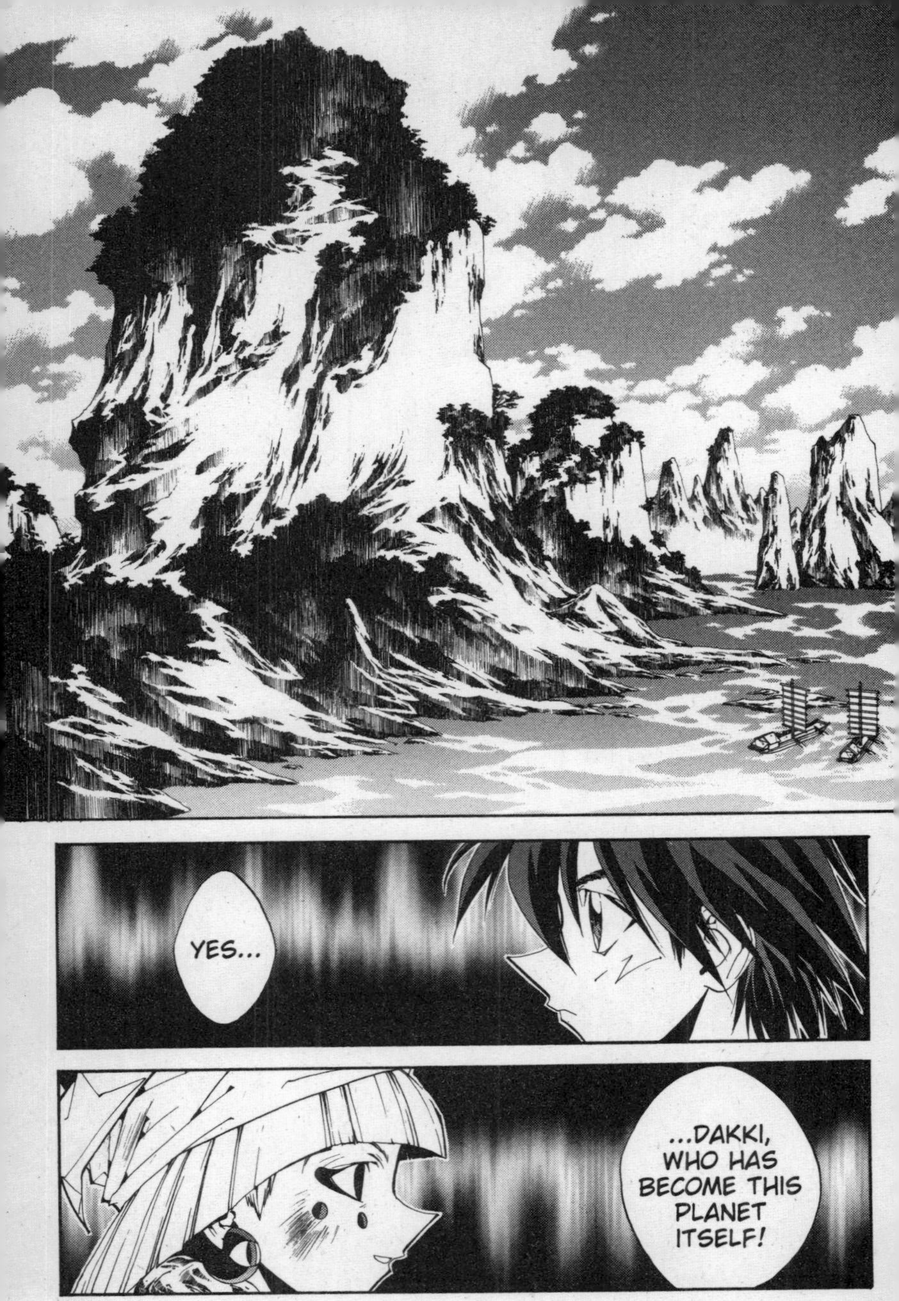
YES...
...DAKKI, WHO HAS BECOME THIS PLANET ITSELF!

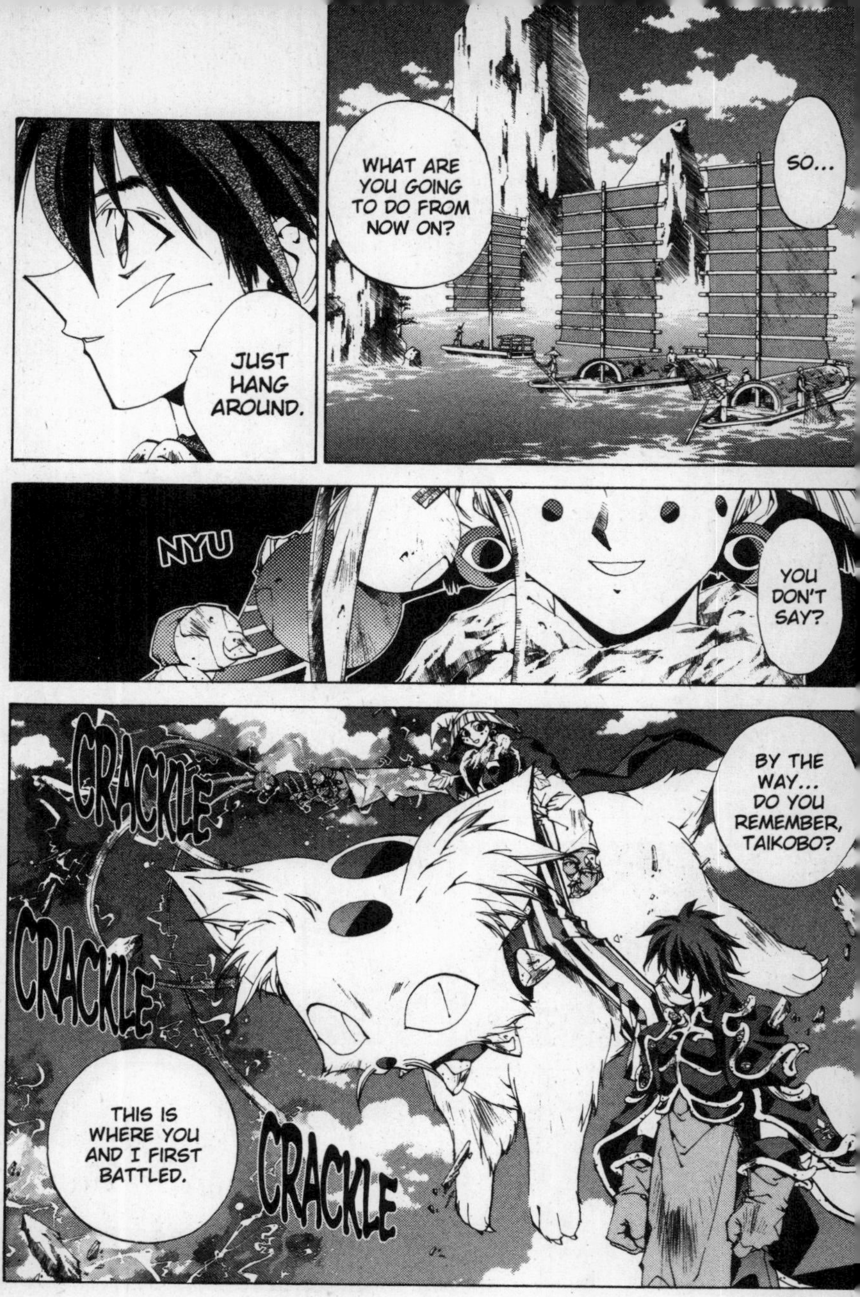
SO...
WHAT ARE YOU GOING TO DO FROM NOW ON?
JUST HANG AROUND.
YOU DON'T SAY?
NYU
BY THE WAY... DO YOU REMEMBER, TAIKOBO?
CRACKLE
CRACKLE
THIS IS WHERE YOU AND I FIRST BATTLED.
CRACKLE

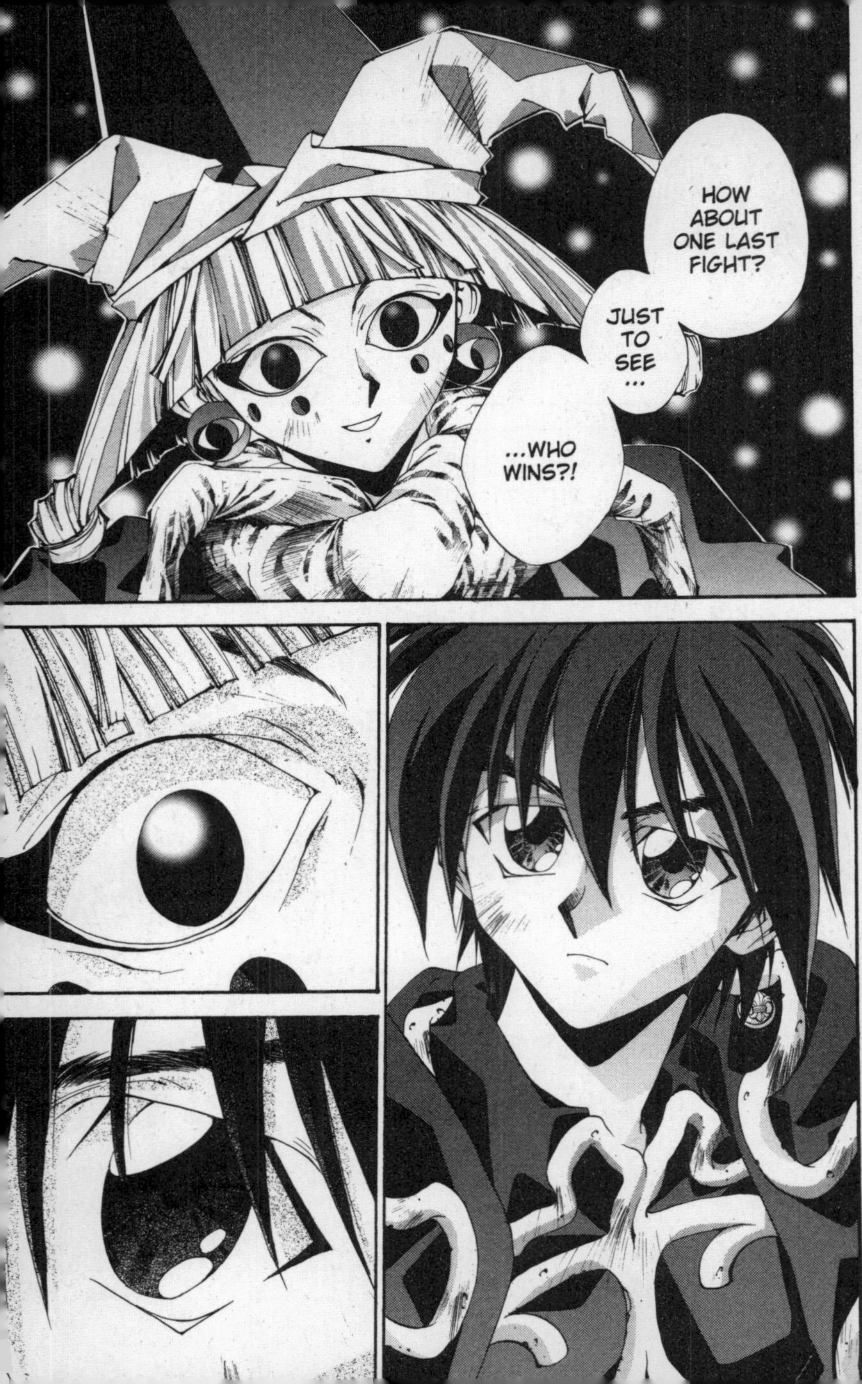
HOW ABOUT ONE LAST FIGHT?
JUST TO SEE ...
...WHO WINS?!

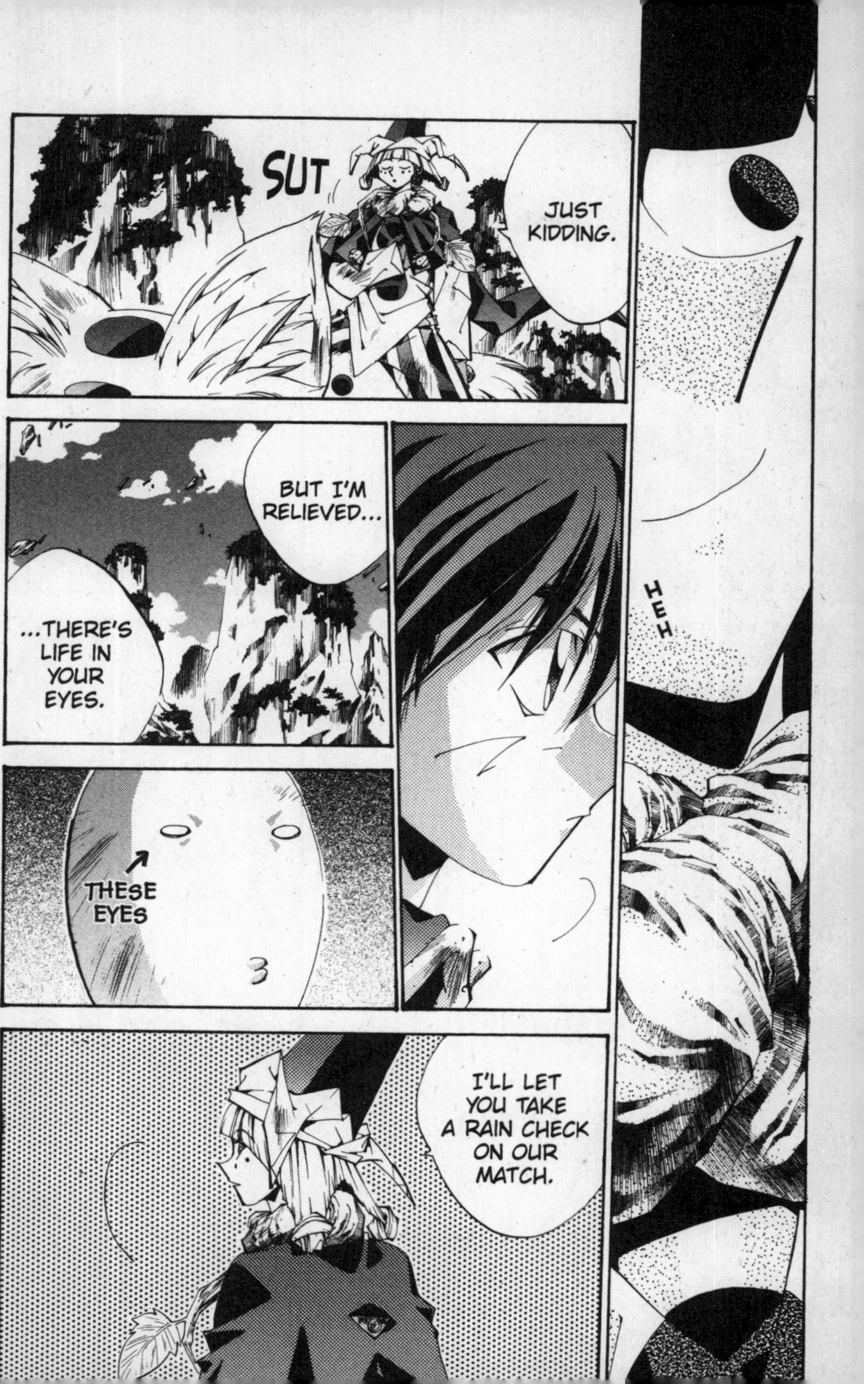
HEH
SUT
JUST KIDDING.
BUT I'M RELIEVED...
...THERE'S LIFE IN YOUR EYES.
THESE EYES
I'LL LET YOU TAKE A RAIN CHECK ON OUR MATCH.

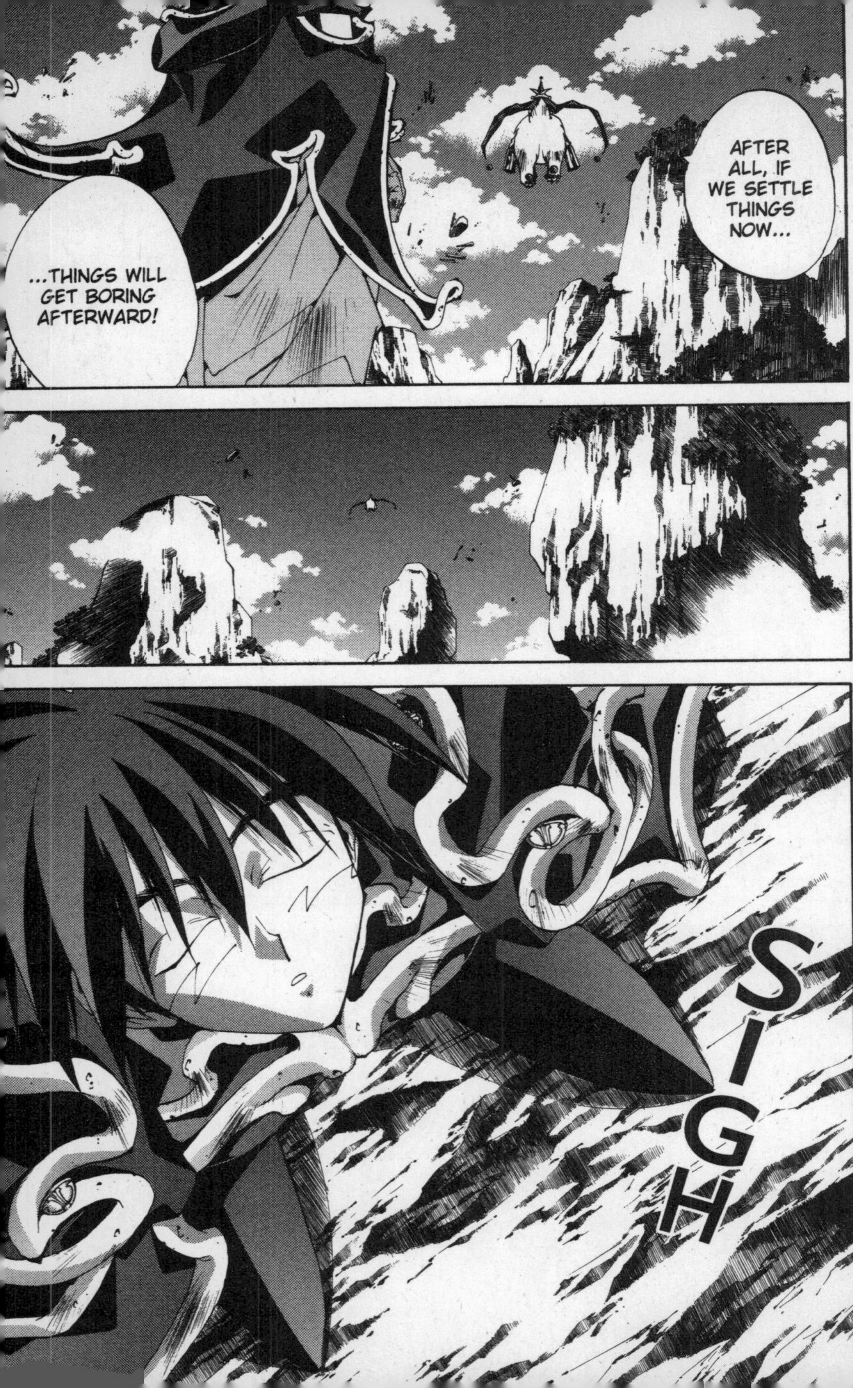
AFTER ALL, IF WE SETTLE THINGS NOW...
...THINGS WILL GET BORING AFTERWARD!
SIGH

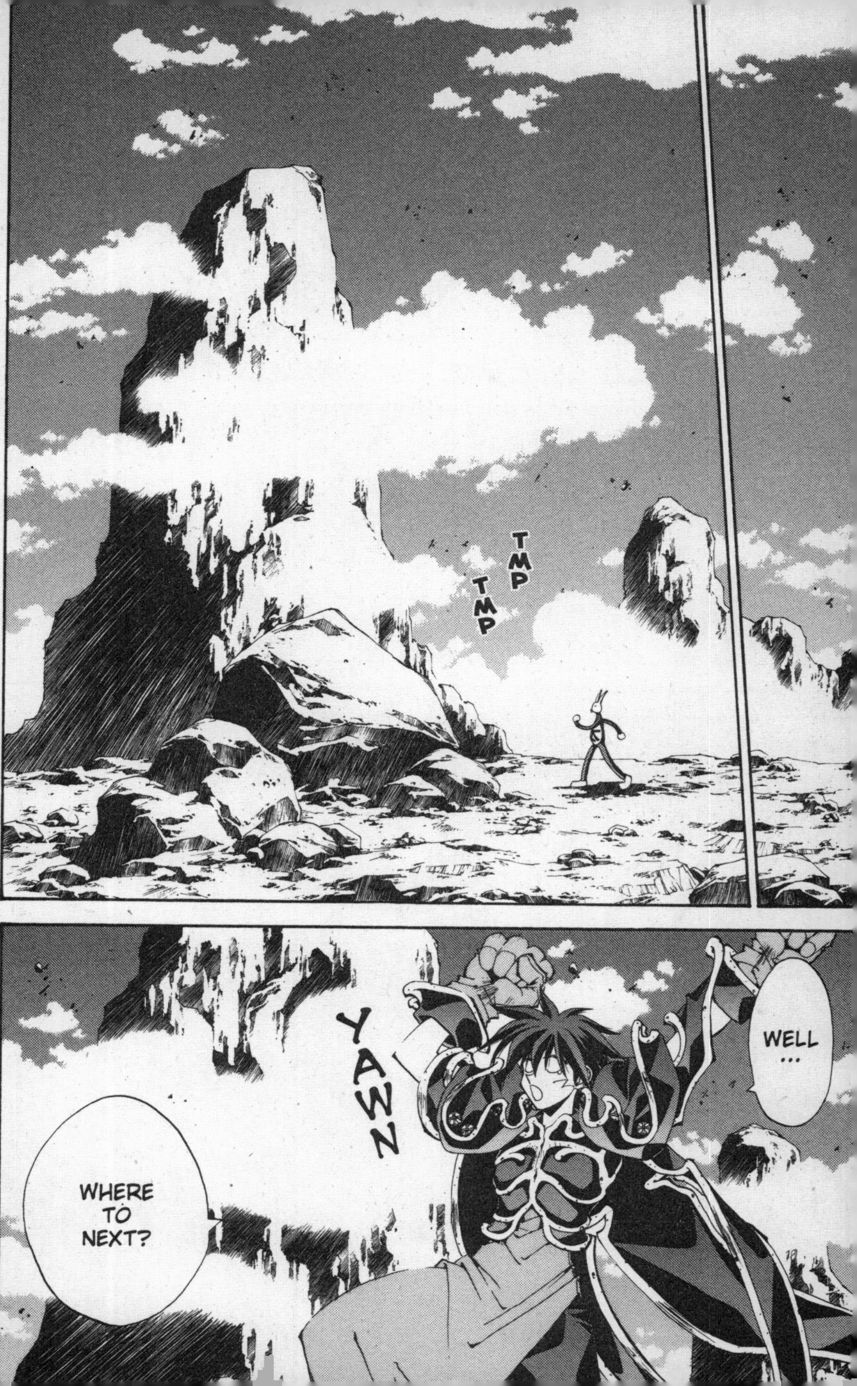
TMP
TMP
WELL ...
YAWN
WHERE TO NEXT?

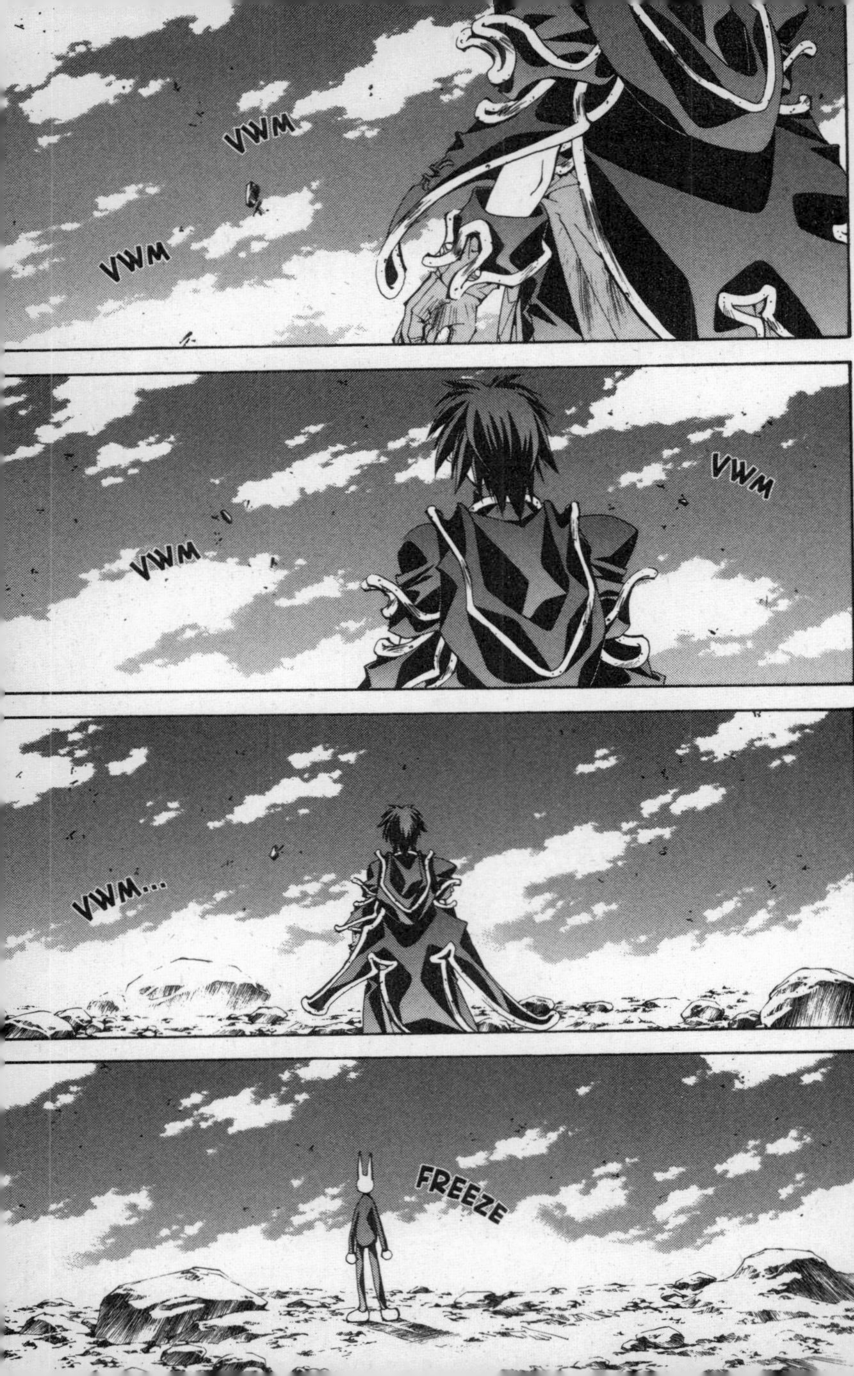
VWM
VWM
VWM
VWM
VWM...
FREEZE

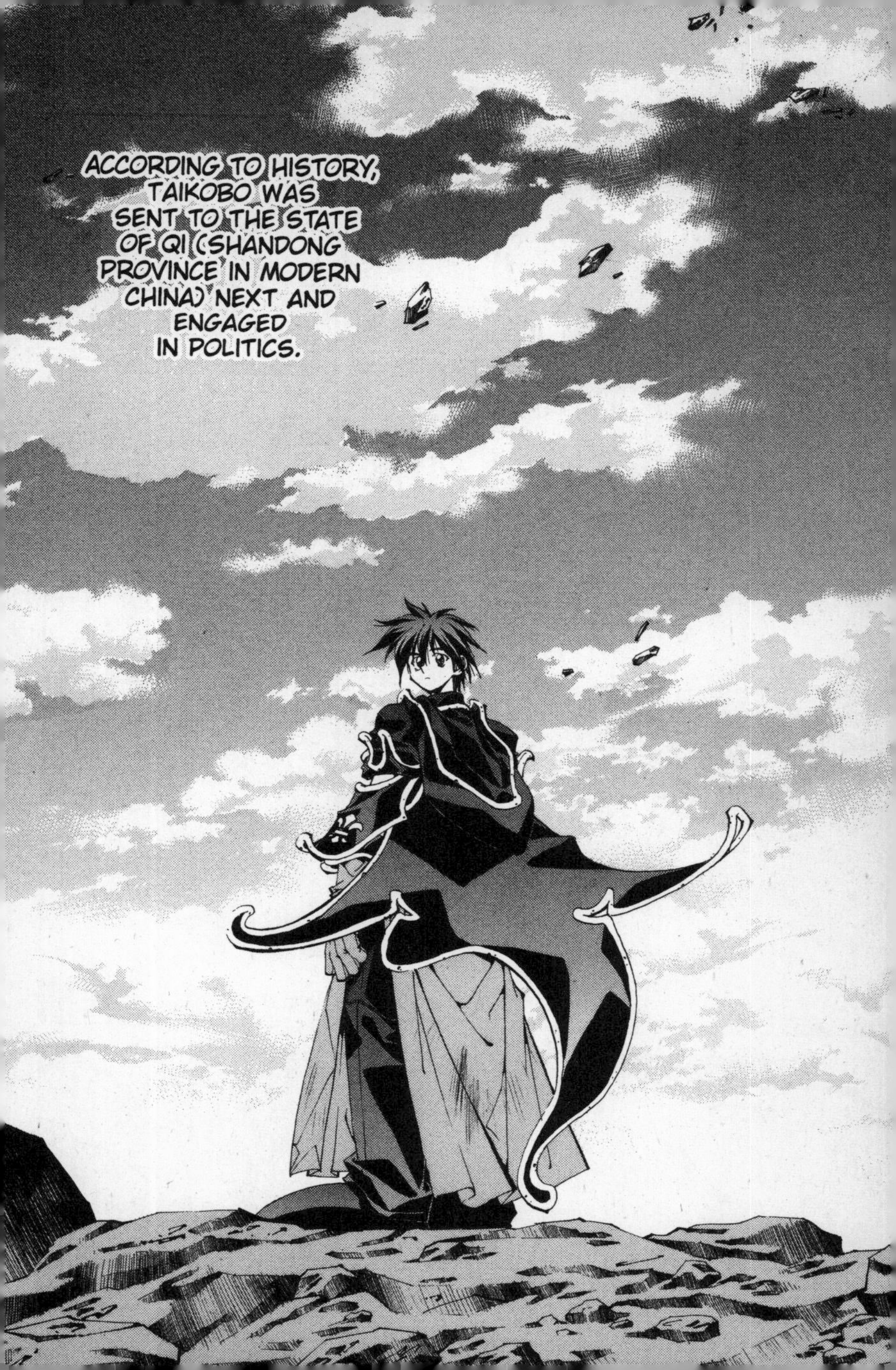
ACCORDING TO HISTORY, TAIKOBO WAS SENT TO THE STATE OF QI (SHANDONG PROVINCE IN MODERN CHINA) NEXT AND ENGAGED IN POLITICS.

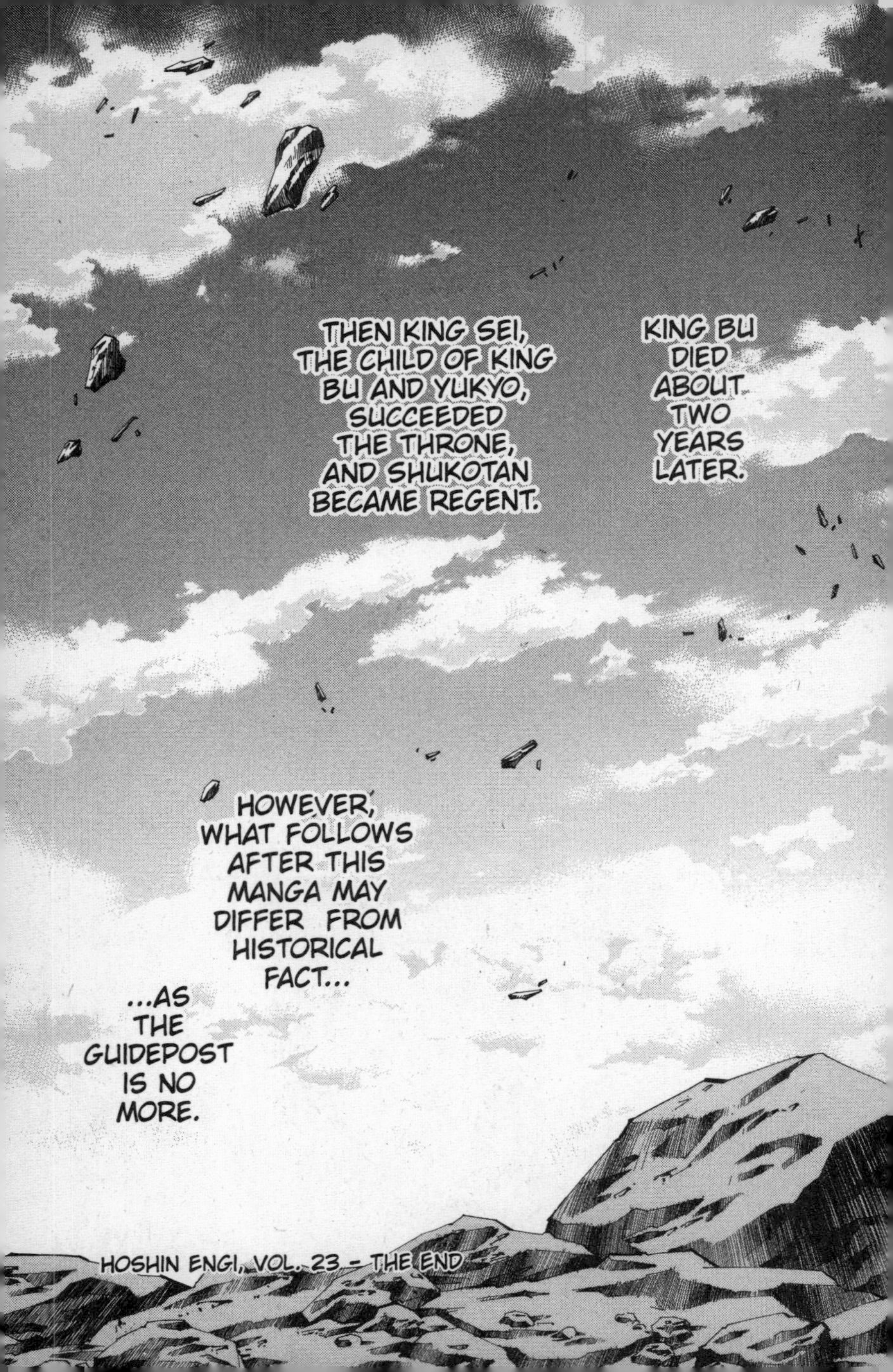
KING BU DIED ABOUT TWO YEARS LATER.
THEN KING SEI, THE CHILD OF KING BU AND YUKYO, SUCCEEDED THE THRONE, AND SHUKOTAN BECAME REGENT.
HOWEVER, WHAT FOLLOWS AFTER THIS MANGA MAY DIFFER FROM HISTORICAL FACT...
...AS THE GUIDEPOST IS NO MORE.
HOSHIN ENGI, VOL. 23 - THE END

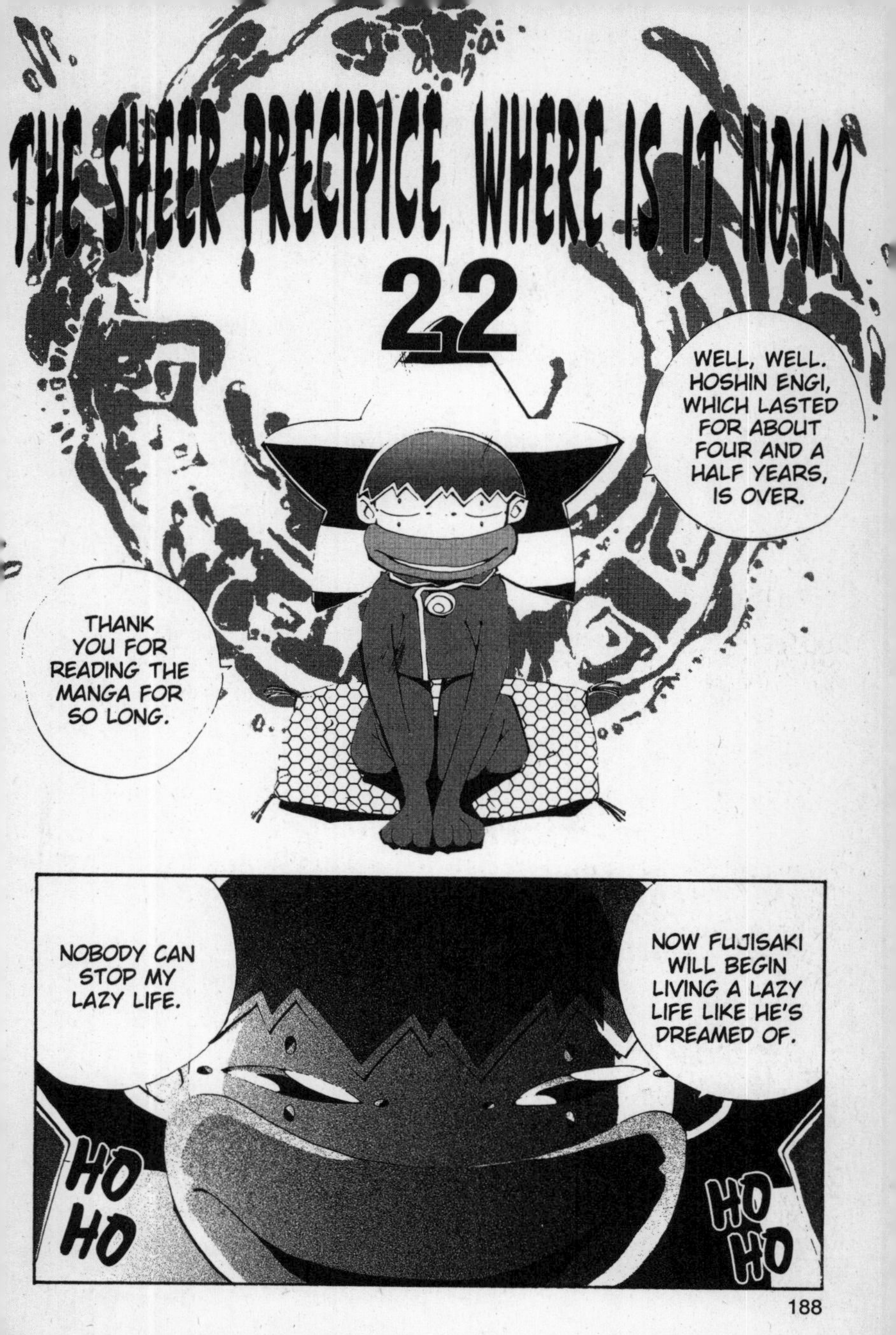
THE SHEER PRECIPICE, WHERE IS IT NOW? 22
WELL, WELL. HOSHIN ENGI, WHICH LASTED FOR ABOUT FOUR AND A HALF YEARS, IS OVER.
THANK YOU FOR READING THE MANGA FOR SO LONG.
NOW FUJISAKI WILL BEGIN LIVING A LAZY LIFE LIKE HE'S DREAMED OF.
HO HO
NOBODY CAN STOP MY LAZY LIFE.
HO HO

READ THIS WAY

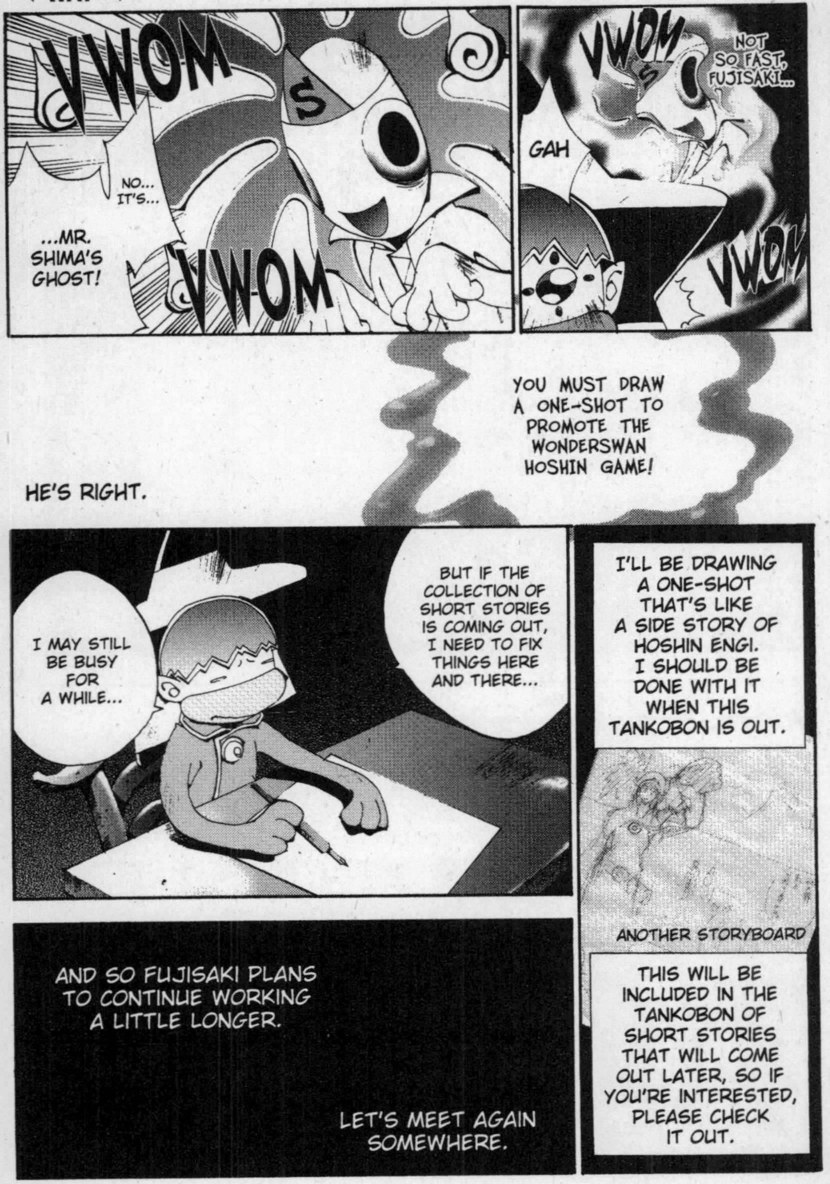

NOT SO FAST, FUJISAKI...
VWOM
GAH
VWOM
VWOM
NO... IT'S...
...MR. SHIMA'S GHOST!
VWOM
YOU MUST DRAW A ONE-SHOT TO PROMOTE THE WONDERSWAN HOSHIN GAME!
HE'S RIGHT.
I'LL BE DRAWING A ONE-SHOT THAT'S LIKE A SIDE STORY OF HOSHIN ENGI. I SHOULD BE DONE WITH IT WHEN THIS TANKOBON IS OUT.
ANOTHER STORYBOARD
THIS WILL BE INCLUDED IN THE TANKOBON OF SHORT STORIES THAT WILL COME OUT LATER, SO IF YOU'RE INTERESTED, PLEASE CHECK IT OUT.
BUT IF THE COLLECTION OF SHORT STORIES IS COMING OUT, I NEED TO FIX THINGS HERE AND THERE...
I MAY STILL BE BUSY FOR A WHILE...
AND SO FUJISAKI PLANS TO CONTINUE WORKING A LITTLE LONGER.
LET'S MEET AGAIN SOMEWHERE.

Hoshin Engi: The Rank File!

You'll find as you read *Hoshin Engi* that there are titles and ranks that you are probably unfamiliar with. While it may seem confusing, there is an order to the madness that is pulled from ancient Chinese mythology, Japanese culture, other manga and, of course, the incredible mind of *Hoshin Engi* creator Ryu Fujisaki.

Where we think it will help, we give you a hint in the margin on the page the name appears. But in addition, here's a quick primer on the titles you'll find in *Hoshin Engi* and what they mean:

Japanese	Title	Job Description
武成王	Buseio	Chief commanding officer
宰相	Saisho	Premier
太師	Taishi	The king's advisor/tutor
大金剛	Dai Kongo	Great vassals
軍師	Gunshi	Military tactician
大諸侯	Daishoko	Great feudal lord
東伯侯	Tohakuko	Lord of the east region
西伯侯	Seihakuko	Lord of the west region
北伯侯	Hokuhakuko	Lord of the north region
南伯侯	Nanhakuko	Lord of the south region

Hoshin Engi: The Immortal File

Also, you'll probably find the hierarchy of the Sennin, Sendo and Doshi somewhat complicated. Here, we spell it out the easiest way possible!

Japanese	Title	Description
道士	Doshi	Someone training to become Sennin
仙道	Sendo	Used to describe both Sennin and Doshi
仙人	Sennin	Those who have mastered the way. Once you "go Sennin" you are forever changed.
妖孼	Yogetsu	A Yosei who can transform into a human
妖怪仙人	Yokai Sennin	A Sennin whose original form is not human
妖精	Yosei	An animal or object exposed to moonlight and sunlight for more than 1,000 years

Hoshin Engi: The Magical File

Paope (宝貝) are powerful magical items used by Sennin and Doshi. Sometimes they look like regular objects, like a veil or hat. These are just a few of the magical items, both paope and otherwise, that you'll encounter in *Hoshin Engi!*

Japanese	Magic	Description
打神鞭	Dashinben	Known as the God-Striking Whip, Taikobo's paope manipulates the air and wind.
霊獣	Reiju	A magical flying beast that Sennin and Doshi use for transportation and support. Taikobo's reiju is his pal Supu.
五光石	Gokoseki	A rock that changes the face of whomever it strikes into a "weirdly erotic-looking" face.
莫邪の宝剣	Bakuya no Hoken	Tenka's weapon, a light saber.
蒼巾力士	Sokin Rikishi	Kingo's version of the Kokin Rikishi.
通天砲	Tsutenho	Kingo Island's principal gun.
エナジードレイン	Energy Drain	Adults of the Supu clan have the power to drain away paope energy and render the paope useless.
怠惰スーツ	Lazy Suit	An environmentally controlled protection suit that allows Taijo Rokun to sleep undisturbed for years.
山河社稷図	Sanga Shashokuzu	Psychokinetic worms that devour the space itself around an enemy, leaving them in a limitless void that destroys them psychologically.
四宝剣	Shihoken	A philosophical paope that changes the "probability of existence" of an object and destroys it.
万仙陣	Bansenjin	A paope energy net. Paope attacks within this net work against souls that make them.
飛焔剣	Hienken	Nento's sword.

Read Any Good Books Lately?

Hoshin Engi is based on *Fengshen Yanji* (*The Creation of the Gods*, written in the 1500s by Xu Zhonglin), one of China's four classic fantastical novels of adventure, magic and mystery. The other three are *Saiyuki* (*Journey to the West* by Cheng'en Wu, late 1500s), *Sangokushi Engi* (*Romance of the Three Kingdoms* by Guanzhong Luo) and *Shui Hu Zhuan* (*Outlaws of the Marsh* by Shi Nai'an, mid-1500s).

Want to read these books? You can! They're all still in print, more than 500 years later!

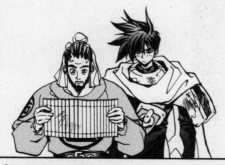

These books are North American in-print editions only.